# INSTITUTIONS AND ETHNIC POLITICS IN AFRICA

This book presents a theory to account for why and when politics revolves around one axis of social cleavage instead of another. It does so by examining the case of Zambia, where people identify themselves either as members of one of the country's six dozen tribes or as members of one of its four principal language groups. The book accounts for the conditions under which political competition in Zambia revolves around tribal differences and the conditions under which it revolves around language group differences. Drawing on a simple model of identity choice, it shows that the answer depends on whether the country is operating under single-party or multi-party rule. During periods of single-party rule, tribal identities serve as the axis of electoral mobilization and self-identification; during periods of multi-party rule, broader language group identities play this role. The book thus demonstrates how formal institutional rules determine the kinds of social cleavages that matter in politics.

Daniel N. Posner is Assistant Professor of Political Science at UCLA. His research focuses on ethnic politics, regime change, and the political economy of development in Africa. He has published articles in numerous journals, and he has received grants and fellowships from the Russell Sage Foundation, the Harry Frank Guggenheim Foundation, and the Harvard Academy for International and Area Studies. In 2001–2, he was a National Fellow at the Hoover Institution at Stanford University. He is currently a Carnegie Scholar of the Carnegie Corporation of New York.

POLITICAL ECONOMY OF INSTITUTIONS AND DECISIONS



***Other Books in the Series***

Alberto Alesina and Howard Rosenthal, *Partisan Politics, Divided Government, and the Economy*
Lee J. Alston, Thrainn Eggertsson, and Douglass C. North, eds., *Empirical Studies in Institutional Change*
Lee J. Alston and Joseph P. Ferrie, *Southern Paternalism and the Rise of the American Welfare State: Economics, Politics, and Institutions, 1865–1965*
James E. Alt and Kenneth Shepsle, eds., *Perspectives on Positive Political Economy*
Josephine T. Andrews, *When Majorities Fail: The Russian Parliament, 1990–1993*
Jeffrey S. Banks and Eric A. Hanushek, eds., *Modern Political Economy: Old Topics, New Directions*
Yoram Barzel, *Economic Analysis of Property Rights*, 2nd edition
Yoram Barzel, *A Theory of the State: Economic Rights, Legal Rights, and the Scope of the State*
Robert Bates, *Beyond the Miracle of the Market: The Political Economy of Agrarian Development in Kenya*, 2nd edition
Charles M. Cameron, *Veto Bargaining: Presidents and the Politics of Negative Power*
Kelly H. Chang, *Appointing Central Bankers: The Politics of Monetary Policy in the United States and the European Monetary Union*
Peter Cowhey and Mathew McCubbins, eds., *Structure and Policy in Japan and the United States: An Institutionalist Approach*
Gary W. Cox, *The Efficient Secret: The Cabinet and the Development of Political Parties in Victorian England*
Gary W. Cox, *Making Votes Count: Strategic Coordination in the World's Electoral Systems*

*Continued after the index*

# INSTITUTIONS AND ETHNIC POLITICS IN AFRICA

DANIEL N. POSNER
University of California, Los Angeles

CAMBRIDGE UNIVERSITY PRESS
Cambridge, New York, Melbourne, Madrid, Cape Town, Singapore,
São Paulo, Delhi, Dubai, Tokyo

Cambridge University Press
32 Avenue of the Americas, New York, NY 10013-2473, USA

www.cambridge.org
Information on this title: www.cambridge.org/9780521541794



First published 2005
Reprinted 2007

*A catalog record for this publication is available from the British Library*

*Library of Congress Cataloging in Publication data*

Posner, Daniel N.
Institutions and ethnic politics in Africa / Daniel N. Posner.
p. cm. – (Political economy of institutions and decisions)
Includes bibliographical references and index.
ISBN 0-521-83398-1 – ISBN 0-521-54179-4 (pbk.)
1. Politics, Practical – Zambia. 2. Zambia – Politics and government.
3. Zambia – Ethnic relations – Political aspects. I. Title. II. Series.
JQ2831.P67 2004
324'.089'0096894–dc22 2004045197

ISBN 978-0-521-83398-1 Hardback
ISBN 978-0-521-54179-4 Paperback

Transferred to digital printing 2010

*For Rebecca*

# *Contents*

# *Preface*

This is a book about ethnic conflict, but it is not about ethnic conflict in the usual sense. Most treatments of the subject focus on explaining variation in the occurrence or intensity of ethnic violence across time and space. They ask: why did tensions between Hutus and Tutsis in Rwanda erupt into full-blown genocide in 1994 (Prunier 1995; Gourevitch 1998)? Why have Hindu–Muslim riots taken place in some Indian towns but not in others (Varshney 2002; Wilkinson 2004)? Why, since the mid-1970s, has there been so much more ethnic violence in Sri Lanka than in Malaysia (Horowitz 1989)? This book, by contrast, seeks to explain not when or where communal conflict breaks out but why it breaks out along one line of ethnic division instead of another. It seeks to explain why politics comes to revolve around the particular axis of ethnic cleavage that it does.

I fell into this research topic by accident. When I first went to Zambia in 1993, I thought I was going to be studying how Zambia's recent transition to multi-party politics had affected the relations among the country's ethnic groups. I thought I was going to be studying whether the introduction of competitive multi-party elections had deepened ethnic divisions and made ethnicity a more salient part of the country's political affairs. Given this motivating question, I began my research by conducting a series of open-ended interviews in one of Lusaka's poor residential compounds to probe how people from different ethnic communities were getting along in the new multi-party era. Again and again, I was told that ethnic politics was rife. I was also told that one group in particular – the Bembas – were dominating the country and that Zambian politics had been transformed into a conflict between Bemba power-holders and everyone else. Almost always, these charges of Bemba domination were substantiated with long lists of Bembas who had been appointed as cabinet ministers, diplomats, or senior civil servants, had emerged as business leaders, or were otherwise enjoying more than their fair share of the best jobs and government contracts.

Yet when I then met with the people whose names had been provided, many of them told me that they were not, in fact, Bemba. One identified himself as Bisa; another as Lunda; another as Chishinga; another as Mambwe. All of them were members of tribes that belonged to the broader Bemba language family, but they did not self-identify as Bembas.

At first I was confused. How could there be such a disconnect between the way people saw themselves and the way they were viewed by others? Eventually, I came to understand that Zambians saw their country's politics through multiple lenses. Some saw it through the lens of language group differences. Through this lens, all of the allegedly "Bemba" winners in the regime change were, in fact, Bembas, since they all were members of Bemba-speaking tribes. But other Zambians viewed the country's politics through the prism of tribal differences rather than language. Seen this way, all of the "Bembas" who were benefiting from the change in government were from other – and, in some cases, *under-represented* – ethnic communities. Whether or not Bembas were dominating the country depended entirely on the rule – linguistic or tribal – that one applied to code the people in the positions of power.

As soon as I recognized that this was what was going on, I realized that I had to acquire a better understanding of the conditions under which people came to understand the country's politics in terms of language differences versus tribal differences. My quest for an understanding of when and why conflict arises was transformed into a mission to comprehend why conflict was perceived to be taking place along the lines of one ethnic cleavage instead of another.

In the nearly ten years that I have worked on this project, I have benefited from the support of a number of institutions and from the insights, intellectual stimulation, friendship, and generosity of a great many individuals. My greatest debt of gratitude is to the hundreds of Zambians who served as survey respondents and focus group participants and to the many current and former politicians who patiently answered my endless questions. To the extent that this book "gets Zambian politics right," it is because of their generous tutoring in its intricacies.

My research in Zambia would have been impossible without the hard work of a team of tremendous research assistants: Misheck Banda, Richard Banda, Maureen Kashempa, Charlotte Lwanga, Hilary Mwale, Kris Mwanangombe, Robert Mwanza, Godfrey Sibeso, and Joseph

Tembo. I could not have completed this project without their help. My nineteen months of field research were immensely enriched by the good company and friendship of Philip and Julie Alderfer, Lisa Cliggett, Mike Hall, Melinda Ham, Jim and Michelle Polhemus, Lise Rakner, Jeffrey Ryen, David Simon, and Jeremy Weinstein. I want to especially thank Malcolm McPherson, Deborah Hoover, and Heather and Malinda McPherson, who invited me into their family and provided me with a home base in Lusaka that was truly a home away from home. At the Institute for African Studies (now the Institute for Economic and Social Research) at the University of Zambia, Ilse Mwanza and Chris Simuyemba were, as they have been for foreign researchers in Zambia for more than two decades, sources of administrative guidance, advice, and friendship. I would also like to thank Kumbutso Dzekedzeke, the census manager at the Central Statistical Office in Lusaka; Joel Sikazwe, director of the Electoral Commission of Zambia; and the staff of the Zambia Consolidated Copper Mines archives in Ndola for help that went well beyond the call of duty. I also thank Fred M'membe and Ngandi Mwananjidi for our numerous stimulating conversations. To all of these people I am immensely grateful.

This book began as a doctoral dissertation in the Department of Government at Harvard University. I owe a deep intellectual debt to my three dissertation advisors, Samuel Huntington, Robert Bates, and Jennifer Widner. Throughout my graduate training, and during the two years I subsequently spent as an Academy Scholar in the Harvard Academy for International and Area Studies, they were wonderful mentors. They were also terrific role models. Much of what I have learned about political science, about Africa, and about conducting myself as a scholar I have learned from their fine examples. I am also indebted to a group of remarkable friends and colleagues at Harvard, whose camaraderie and incisive comments contributed much to this project. In particular, I would like to single out Henry Hale, Devesh Kapur, Michael Kevane, Pauline Jones Luong, Shaun Malarney, Michael Montasano, Maria Victoria Murillo, Mark Nagel, Karissa Price, Richard Snyder, Edward Steinfeld, Ashutosh Varshney, and Steven Wilkinson.

The Department of Political Science at UCLA and the Hoover Institution at Stanford University, where I was National Fellow in 2001–2, provided extremely supportive environments in which to complete the project. At UCLA, I benefited from the hard work of research assistants Timothy Ayieko, Maria Dahlin, Johan Lanner, Luciana Noguiera, and David Yaminishi. At the Hoover Institution, Larry Diamond and Joy

Taylor provided much appreciated help and support. I received useful feedback on various pieces of the project at meetings of the Laboratory in Comparative Ethnic Processes and the American Political Science Association, and at workshops at Stanford University, Princeton University, the University of Chicago, New York University, UCLA, and the Santa Fe Institute. In addition to the helpful criticisms offered by participants in these workshops and seminars, I received valuable comments and suggestions from Joel Barkan, Carles Boix, Michael Bratton, Kanchan Chandra, Alberto Diaz-Cayeros, Pierre Englebert, James Fearon, Karen Ferree, Judy Geist, Jeffrey Herbst, Macartan Humphreys, Nahomi Ichino, Nelson Kasfir, David Laitin, Drew Linzer, Beatriz Magaloni, Shaheen Mozaffar, Benjamin Reilly, Robert Rotberg, James Scarritt, Kenneth Scheve, David Simon, Smita Singh, Richard Sklar, Paul Sniderman, Michael Thies, Matthew Turner, Nicolas van de Walle, Ashutosh Varshney, Leonard Wantchekon, Lisa Wedeen, Steven Wilkinson, Elisabeth Wood, and anonymous reviewers of the manuscript. Their comments strengthened the book immeasurably.

Intellectual support may be a necessary condition for writing, but it is not sufficient for research involving field work and large amounts of data collection. Financial support is also necessary. I am therefore particularly grateful to the institutions that provided financial support for the project at various stages. The International Predissertation Fellowship Program of the Social Science Research Council funded my initial trip to Zambia. A Dissertation Improvement Grant from the National Science Foundation made possible a nine-month follow-up trip the next year. The Harvard Academy for International and Area Studies provided two extremely valuable years of support at the dissertation stage of the project and underwrote a third field research trip. At UCLA, the Academic Senate provided support for the project throughout its transformation from a dissertation into a book. The Hoover Institution at Stanford provided a year of support during which I completely rewrote the manuscript. A Faculty Career Development Award at UCLA also provided useful resources at a key stage. I also owe thanks to the UCLA International Institute and the James S. Coleman African Studies Center at UCLA, particularly its former director, Edmond Keller, for their support of this project.

Lewis Bateman, the senior editor for political science and history at Cambridge University Press, patiently shepherded this book through production and was a source of advice and unstinting encouragement throughout the process. I am very thankful for his support.

Finally, I thank my parents, Robert and Rita Posner, who never in a million years would have guessed that their son would write a book about African politics. They taught me how to read and ask questions, and kindled in me a desire to try to understand the world outside of Tenafly, New Jersey. They did not read a single page of the manuscript or offer much in the way of comments or suggestions. But their fingerprints are everywhere on its pages. Most of all, I thank my wife, Rebecca. She joined me late in the process of writing this book but provided the love and support – the home – I needed to finally get it finished. This book is for her.

INSTITUTIONS AND ETHNIC POLITICS IN AFRICA

# 1

## Introduction

### Institutions and Ethnic Politics

Nearly all multi-ethnic political systems contain more than one dimension of ethnic cleavage. Israel is divided by religion, but its citizens are also divided by their places of origin and their degrees of secularism. South Africa is divided by race, but also by language differences and by tribe.[1] India is divided by language (which serves as the basis for its federalism), but also by religion and caste. Switzerland is divided by religion and by language. Nigeria is divided by religion, region, and tribe. Even subnational units are frequently ethnically multi-dimensional: cities like New York, Los Angeles, and Miami all contain prominent racial cleavages, but also cleavages based on their residents' countries of origin, languages of communication, and lengths of residence in the United States.

Given these multiple bases of ethnic division, when does politics revolve around one of them rather than another? Journalists and scholars who write about the politics of ethnically divided societies tend to take the axis of ethnic cleavage that serves as the basis for political competition and conflict as a given. They write eloquently about hostilities between Hindus and Muslims in India but never pause to ask why that country's conflict takes place along religious lines rather than among Hindi-speakers, Bengali-speakers, and Marathi-speakers. They discuss the competition among Hausas, Yorubas, and Igbos in Nigeria but never stop to question why the political rivalries in that nation rage among these broad ethno-regional communities rather than between Christians and Muslims.

[1] "Tribe" is a loaded word. Here, and throughout the book, I use the term to refer to an ethnic community that is (or was historically) organized under the authority of a traditional chief. Membership in a tribe is determined by the answer to the question: are you (or were your parents) subjects of Chief X? For an extended discussion of how "tribes" were created during the colonial era, and why "tribe" and "language" cannot be used interchangeably, see Chapters 2 and 3.

They probe the conflict between blacks and Latinos in Miami but never think to inquire why the city's tensions revolve around racial differences rather than divisions among Haitians, Cubans, Dominicans, and other Caribbean immigrants, or between immigrants and non-immigrants. In country after country and city after city, they provide detailed accounts of how and why politicians "play the ethnic card." Yet they almost never bother to ask why politicians play the particular ethnic card that they do.

Why, given multiple potentially mobilizable bases of ethnic division, does political competition and conflict come to be organized along the lines of one ethnic cleavage rather than another? Why do politicians emphasize (and why do people respond positively to appeals couched in terms of) race rather than language, religion rather than tribe, caste rather than state? Under what conditions does the dimension of ethnic cleavage that is salient change? When does politics shift from being about religious differences to being about language differences, from being about country of origin to being about race? These are the questions that this book seeks to answer. It seeks to account for *when* and *why*, given multiple axes of ethnic division in a society, one cleavage becomes the basis of political competition and conflict rather than another. It builds its explanation by distinguishing between two distinct, but often conflated, processes: identity construction (the process through which the repertoire of political identities in society that might be mobilized is constructed) and identity choice (the process through which political actors decide to emphasize one identity from this set of potentially mobilizable social categories rather than another). I argue that the cleavage that emerges as salient is the aggregation of all actors' individual decisions about the identity that will serve them best, and that these decisions are constrained, first, by the option set from which the actors are choosing, and, second, by the formal institutional rules that govern political competition, which make some identities more advantageous than others.

## THE ARGUMENT

Political institutions are the formal rules, regulations, and policies that structure social and political interactions.[2] This book shows how they

[2] This definition is significantly narrower than, for example, North (1990: 3), who defines institutions as "the rules of the game in a society, or, more formally . . . the humanly devised constraints that shape human interaction." North's definition, like that of others (e.g., Bates 1988; World Bank 2002), would include such social

help to determine which ethnic cleavage becomes politically salient in two stages, and via two distinct causal mechanisms. First, they shape the repertoires of potentially mobilizable ethnic identities that individuals possess. That is, they determine why some of the myriad objectively identifiable bases of cultural difference in society come to be viewed as at least potentially politically salient, and why others do not. Second, they shape peoples' incentives for selecting one of these potentially salient ethnic identities rather than another, and then coordinate these choices across individuals so as to produce a society-level outcome. To borrow the metaphor of a card game, political institutions explain, first, why players' hands contain the cards they do and, then, why the players play one of these cards rather than another. They also explain why one player or set of players ultimately wins the game.

The part of the argument about how political institutions shape individuals' identity choices – about why players play the cards that they do – is built from three simple, well-established propositions: people want resources from the state. They believe that having someone from their ethnic group in a position of political power will facilitate their access to those resources. And they understand that the best way to get someone from their ethnic group into a position of political power is to build or join a political coalition with fellow group members. Taken together, these propositions suggest that ethnic politics can be viewed in terms of the politics of coalition-building and that ethnic identity choice can be seen in terms of the quest to gain membership in the coalition that will be most politically and economically useful. The idea that ethnic politics can be interpreted as a kind of coalition-building was first articulated by Robert Bates, who described ethnic groups as "coalitions which have been formed as a part of rational efforts to secure benefits created by the forces of modernization" (1983: 152). This book builds on Bates's insight by extending this argument beyond the question of why ethnicity is politically useful and applying it to the question of why individuals choose to emphasize the particular ethnic identities they do.

phenomena as markets, traditional lineage structures, and even norms of behavior. In the more restricted definition used here, institutions are the formal, codified rules, regulations, or policies to which the existence of these structures, and norms might be traced, not the structures and norms themselves. Markets, lineage structures, and behavioral norms are (or may be) *products* of institutions, but, by the definition employed here, they are not institutions themselves. How the formal rules gave rise to these social phenomena is left as something to be explained rather than simply assumed.

Ethnic coalition-building is straightforward in a world where individuals have only a single ethnic identity. In such a context, political actors turn to ethnicity because of the mobilizational advantages it brings (Bates 1983; Hardin 1995; Hechter 2001; Chandra 2004) or because of the ability it affords them to limit access to the spoils that successful mobilization provides (Fearon 1999; Caselli and Coleman 2001). However, matters become more complicated when we recognize that individuals possess multiple ethnic identities, each of which might serve as a basis for coalition formation. Given multiple ethnic group memberships, the question is: which coalition should a political actor interested in gaining access to state resources seek to mobilize or join? The one with their fellow tribe members? The one with their fellow language-speakers? The one with their co-religionists? Which will be the most advantageous identity to select?

To the extent that access to resources is determined through a process of electoral competition, the most useful identity to mobilize will be, as Riker (1962) showed, the one that puts the person in a winning coalition (or, if more than one coalition is winning, then the one that is *minimum* winning – the one that contains the fewest members with whom the spoils of power will have to be shared). Individuals will consider each of the identity groups in which they can claim membership (and which others will recognize as meaningful) and embrace the one that defines the most usefully sized group. They will consider each of the principles of group division that divide the political community (religion, language, race, clan, etc.), compare the size of their own group with that of the other groups that each of these cleavages defines, and then select the identity that puts them in a minimum winning coalition. Thus, a Sinhalese Christian from Sri Lanka would begin by comparing the size of her religious group (Christians) with the sizes of the other religious groups in the country (Buddhists, Muslims, and Hindus) and the size of her language group (Sinhalese) with the sizes of the other language groups (Tamil and English). Then, she would select the ethnic affiliation that puts her in the most advantageous group and attempt to build or join a coalition with fellow members of that group. In this particular case, she would choose her language group, since Sinhalese-speakers are a majority vis-à-vis other language groups in Sri Lanka, whereas Christians are a minority vis-à-vis other religions. Her identity choice – that is, her choice about which identity to use to identify herself politically – is constrained by the options in her repertoire (her Christian religion; her Sinhalese language group membership), both of which are commonsensically part of who she understands herself to be due to history, government policy, and childhood socialization. But she is free to choose between these two identity options to select the one that will be most advantageous given the situation in which she finds herself.

Why, then, do political institutions matter? First, they matter because the usefulness of any coalition will depend on the boundaries of the arena in which political competition is taking place, and these boundaries are products of institutional rules.[3] As the formal rules governing political competition change, the boundaries of the political arena will often expand or contract, and this will cause memberships in ethnic groups of different sizes to become more or less useful as bases for political coalition-building. For example, our Sinhalese Christian found it advantageous to emphasize her language group identity because she was engaged in a competition for political power at the national level and, at that level, being Sinhalese was more useful than being Christian. If she had been competing for a share of power in her town (say, in the context of a mayoral race) or in her region (say, in the context of an election to a provincial council), her choice might have been quite different. The particular ethnic coalition in which it will make sense for her to seek membership, and thus the particular identity she will invoke to try to do so, will depend on the boundaries of the arena in which she is competing. To the extent that these boundaries are defined by institutional rules – in this example, rules devolving power to municipalities or sub-national units – those rules will be central to our explanation of her identity choices.

The second reason institutions matter is because, in addition to shaping the strategic choices that individuals make, they also coordinate these choices. People's decisions about which identity will serve them best are influenced by a great many contextual factors, including who their interacting partners are, the events or issues of the moment, and the physical location in which they find themselves at the time they are making their choice. What makes the choice-shaping effects of political institutions different from these more fleeting and individualized sorts of contexts is that

[3] Institutions may also affect ethnic identity choices more directly by providing for the preferential treatment of members of certain groups (Weiner and Katzenstein 1981; Horowitz 1985), prohibiting appeals made in terms of certain kinds of identities (Brass 1991), or facilitating political representation by small groups and thereby creating incentives for mobilization along such lines, as, for example, in proportional representation (PR) electoral systems (Reilly and Reynolds 1997). The emphasis here on how political institutions affect identity choices by defining the arena of political competition is a somewhat different argument from these more familiar ones.

political institutions affect everyone in society that is subject to them. They define a uniform context in which coalition-building calculations are made. Moreover, everyone knows that this is the case, so individuals are able to choose the strategies that are best for them in light of what they can infer about the best strategies for others. Institutions provide common knowledge (Chwe 2001) about the incentives faced by everyone in society. This gives them the power not just to shape how individuals identify themselves but also to coordinate these identity choices so as to affect which ethnic cleavage becomes politically salient in society more generally.

But before political actors even face the choice about which ethnic identity to mobilize, political institutions will have already affected their decisions in another, less proximate, way by shaping the universe of possible ethnic identities from which they are choosing. To suggest that individuals can choose their ethnic affiliations strategically is not to suggest that the range of options from which they are choosing is infinite. The identities they seize upon must be ones that both they and other members of society view as commonsensical units of social division and political self-identification. While appeals to race or language might resonate in most societies, appeals to "hazel-eyed people" or "left-handed people" will be unlikely to lead to energetic political mobilization, since neither eye color nor left-handedness is understood as a meaningful principle of groupness – at least not in any society of which I am aware. Ethnic mobilization requires coordination, and this requires that the identity around which the mobilization is to take place be understood by would-be mobilizers as at least potentially politically salient.

The kinds of identities that are understood to be potentially politically salient will vary from society to society. For example, the distinction between religious and non-religious people might resonate in Holland (where it has served as a basis for the Dutch party system) but not in Iran or Afghanistan, since nobody in these countries sees themselves, or others, in terms of these categories. Only those identities that are part of society members' shared understandings of how the social landscape of the polity might conceivably be divided up can serve as viable bases for political coalition-building. Thus, before we inquire into why political actors embrace or seek to mobilize the ethnic identities they do, we must first account for why some identities are understood to be meaningful candidates for mobilization and others are not. We need to explain why, when people think about politics and reflect on who they are, they conjure up the range of identities they do.

This is where the second part of the argument about the role of political institutions comes in. In addition to shaping players' choices about which cards to play, political institutions also help to determine the cards that they hold in their hands. They affect the process of subconscious socialization and conscious investment that determines the contents of individuals' identity choice sets. Most instrumentalist accounts of ethnic identity choice simply take people's identity repertoires as given and begin their analysis by stipulating that the individuals in question have the particular identities that they do. In contrast, I seek to account for these identity repertoires. I do this by showing that the ethnic identities that people use to define who they are can often be traced to specific state policies, regulations, and administrative structures: that is, to institutions. Further, I demonstrate that the numbers, sizes, and distributions of the groups that these identities define can also be shown to be products of administrative structures and policies. As we shall see, the relative sizes and physical locations of groups are important, since these factors determine whether or not they will serve as useful bases of self-identification and political mobilization.

This book thus treats the question of why political conflict in a given community comes to revolve around the particular dimension of ethnic division that it does as the outcome of two separate but equally important processes: the process by which the menu of people's identity options is generated and the process by which the choices from this menu are made. It separates the process of *identity construction* from the process of *identity choice*. The former operates over the long term and, as I shall show, involves a mix of subconscious social learning and conscious investments by individuals in particular group memberships. The latter is a short-term process that is immediately sensitive to alterations in the rules of the political game and is viewed here as an outcome of strategic choice. The process of identity construction operates in keeping with the "sociological institutionalist" tradition; the process of identity choice operates in keeping with a "rational choice institutionalist" perspective (Hall and Taylor 1996). Although the two are different, both mechanisms are products of the formal institutional environment in which political and social life is carried out. The complementary roles that each of these processes play in shaping ethnic cleavage outcomes are depicted in Figure 1.1.

To demonstrate how political institutions shape ethnic cleavage outcomes in both of these ways, this book draws on empirical materials from Zambia. In Zambia, political actors identify themselves as members

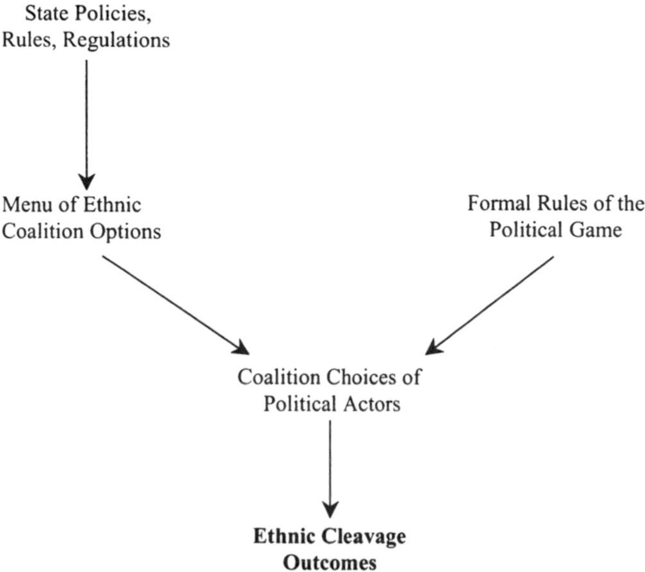


Figure 1.1. The Institutional Origins of Ethnic Cleavage Outcomes

of (and can build political coalitions around) ethnic groups defined either in terms of tribal affiliation or language group membership. The tribal cleavage divides the country into roughly seventy small groups, whereas the linguistic cleavage partitions it into four broad regional coalitions. To explain Zambians' ethnic identity choices, the first task, accomplished in Part I of the book, is to account for why tribe and language, but not other bases of social identity, have come to serve as the key components of Zambians' identity repertoires and thus as the central bases of potential ethnic political cleavage in the country. The second task, accomplished in Parts II and III, is to account for why one of these axes of ethnic division emerges as the basis for political competition and conflict rather than the other. As it turns out, the salient cleavage in Zambia changes over time. The specific question that I address is therefore: when (and why) does political competition in Zambia revolve around tribal divisions and when (and why) does it revolve around language group distinctions? My answer is that the relative political salience of the linguistic and tribal cleavages depends on the nature of the country's formal political institutions – in particular, on whether the country is operating under a multi-party or one-party political system. I show that, during periods of multi-party rule, language group cleavages serve as the central axis of coalition-building and political conflict in Zambia, whereas, during periods of one-party rule, tribal cleavages play this role.

The analysis I present is not meant to provide an all-encompassing theory of how institutions shape ethnic cleavages. The particular institutional rules that I emphasize (party system type) are only one of a larger set of formal institutional arrangements that might affect people's ethnic identity choices. Moreover, even if we restrict our focus to the specific rules that I treat here – that is, even if we try to generalize about the effects of shifting from a one-party to a multi-party political system in a context of single-member plurality electoral rules – the specific tribal and linguistic cleavage outcomes that I show this change to generate in Zambia are not generalizable in themselves. The kinds of ethnic cleavages that will become salient in one-party and multi-party elections in other countries and political arenas will depend on the contents of the identity option set from which political actors in those places are choosing. This will become clear in Chapter 9, where I apply the model to other African cases. In Zambia, it just happens that, for reasons I will explain at length, language and tribal identities are the only two options in the option set.

My purpose, instead, is to develop and apply a simple, general model that illustrates the power of formal institutional rules to determine the kinds of identities that individuals will embrace and, through these identity choices, the social cleavages that will emerge as politically salient. The "discovery" – and, over the last forty years, gradual acceptance – that ethnic identities are situational and strategic constitutes probably the most important general insight that has yet been made in the study of ethnicity and ethnic politics. From the standpoint of heightening awareness of the complexity of ethnic identifications, this insight has been extraordinarily useful. Descriptive inferences about the nature of ethnic identities are made much more carefully today than in the past. Research techniques designed to measure ethnic loyalties and their political and social consequences are becoming increasingly nuanced and sophisticated (Banton and Mansur 1992; Laitin 1986, 1998; Wilkinson 1999). But from the standpoint of theory building, the discovery that ethnic identities are fluid and situation bound has been paralyzing. The recognition that ethnic identities may shift from situation to situation has made students of ethnicity hesitant to propose general hypotheses about people's identity choices that apply to more than a unique context or a single individual. As a consequence, the literature on ethnic politics is almost entirely devoid of generalizations about the conditions under which one ethnic identity or cleavage will be likely to emerge as politically salient rather than another. The principal purpose of this book is to develop and document the empirical basis for an argument that can begin to fill this gap.

## ETHNICITY AND ETHNIC CLEAVAGES

To even pose the question that this study seeks to answer, let alone answer it in the way that I propose, is to embrace a conceptualization of ethnicity and ethnic cleavages that differs in important ways from how these subjects have traditionally been treated in the literature. Before proceeding with the discussion in the chapters that follow, it will be useful first to explain and justify in greater detail the perspective that this book adopts.

### *Ethnicity*

As I have noted, a first way in which the treatment of ethnicity in this book differs from that in most studies is in the outcome it seeks to explain. Whereas most studies of ethnic conflict seek to explain when and where conflict occurs, this study seeks to explain why it is carried out in the name of one set of identities rather than another. A second way in which this book differs from many studies of ethnic conflict is that it focuses its attention not just on ethnic violence but also on the logic and dynamics of ethnic political competition more generally. Headline-grabbing events in Rwanda, Bosnia, Nigeria, and India notwithstanding, communal riots, civil war, and other forms of violent ethnic conflict are the exception rather than the rule in multi-ethnic societies. Even in stereotypically violent places like Africa, ethnic divisions only rarely generate inter-group violence: Fearon and Laitin (1996) estimate that there has only been one instance of ethnic violence in Africa for every two thousand cases that would have been predicted on the basis of ethnic differences alone. Thus, whereas trying to understand the roots of communal violence may be a worthy goal, limiting our theory-building efforts to accounting for ethnic bloodshed risks leaving us without the appropriate tools for understanding ethnicity's contribution to voting patterns, policy choices, government formation, and other important yet non-violent political outcomes. A goal of this book is to introduce a way of thinking about ethnic politics that provides new leverage on issues of these sorts. Of course, an implication of such an approach is that, to the extent that the dynamics of ethnic violence are different from the dynamics of non-violent ethnic politics, the account presented here may be applicable only to explaining the latter.

Apart from the way this book defines its dependent variable, it also differs from many treatments of ethnic conflict in the way it conceptualizes ethnicity itself. Following the lead of constructivist scholars such as Mitchell (1956), Epstein (1958), and Barth (1969), this book adopts a conceptualization of ethnic identity as fluid and situation bound. I assume that, rather than being hard wired with a single ethnic identity, individuals possess repertoires of identities whose relevance wax and wane with changes in context. Eric Hobsbawm (1996: 87) captures this idea well when he writes that "whether a Mr. Patel in London will think of himself primarily as an Indian, a British citizen, a Hindu, a Gujarati speaker, an ex-colonist from Kenya, a member of a specific caste or kin-group, or in some other capacity depends on whether he faces an immigration officer, a Pakistani, a Sikh or Moslem, a Bengali-speaker and so on." Hobsbawm's point is that Mr. Patel *is* all of these things. But the circumstances in which he finds himself will determine which of the identities in his repertoire – Indian, British, Hindu, and so forth – will become relevant for how he understands who he is.

Following such scholars as Cohen (1969, 1974), Patterson (1975), Young (1976), Kasfir (1979), Bates (1983), and Brass (1991), I assume further that ethnic identities are not just situational but instrumental. My argument turns on the assumption that the context in which a person finds herself does more than simply provide a perceptual frame that subconsciously shapes the person's way of thinking about who she is and how she relates to her environment. I suggest that it also affects the conscious choices she makes about which identity will serve her best. This book thus views the link between a person's environment and her identity not as the outcome of some passive psychological process (although sometimes it may be) but as the product of a deliberate decision designed to maximize payoffs. These payoffs need not be material. Sometimes they will involve non-material ends such as prestige, social acceptance, or protection against shunning, as, for example, when an upper caste Indian identifies herself as a Brahmin rather than more broadly as Hindu, or when a Thai villager identifies himself as Lue (a high-status group) to distinguish himself from the lower-status hill people among whom he lives, or when an Arab-American wears an American flag on his lapel in the aftermath of the terrorist attacks of September 11, 2001, to make his national loyalties clear.[4] My contention is that, irrespective of the specific

[4] The Lue example is from Moerman (1974). For similar discussions, see Nagata (1974) and Horowitz (1985).

nature of the payoffs, the identity that is chosen is selected because of the rewards to which it provides access.

This much is fairly well accepted.[5] Where I enter somewhat more controversial waters is in my contention that the connection between the identity the person chooses and the payoff she receives lies in nothing more than the size of the group that the identity defines. Indeed, the argument this book presents is built on the claim that ethnic groups are mobilized or joined not because of the depth of attachment that people feel toward them but because of the usefulness of the political coalitions that they define – a usefulness determined exclusively by their sizes relative to those of other coalitions. Conceptualizing ethnicity in this way strips it of its affect. Ethnic labels cease being sources of pride or markers of stigma and become simply conveyors of information about which coalition a person belongs to. Ethnic groups are transformed (conceptually at least) from organic entities with symbols, traditions, and histories into merely the units from which political coalitions are built. Ethnicity becomes simply an admission card for membership to a coalition of a particular size and a source of information about the political coalitions to which others belong.

Some readers will find this approach dubious. They will point to the incompatibility between the thinness of ethnic loyalties that such a perspective assumes and the depth of attachment that ethnicity often entails. They will dispute the implication that ethnic identities can be adopted and discarded like articles of clothing. They will point to the difficulties that members of disadvantaged groups face when (as the logic of the instrumentalist argument implies they will) they try to "pass" as members of more advantaged groups. And, while conceding that identities certainly do change, they will emphasize that identities change within strict limits and certainly not through the kind of overtly strategic coalition-building calculations that I assume. These are important critiques, and I have several responses.

First, when I strip ethnicity of its affect I am not denying that ethnic identities are sometimes sources of extremely strong feelings. Like ethnicity itself, the applicability of the strict instrumentalist approach I adopt is situational. In many contexts (e.g., during times of civil war where a person's life can be threatened on account of ethnic group membership, or in a non-political setting where a person's choice of ethnic identity will

[5] For a recent review of the instrumentalist/constructivist perspective and the cumulative research findings it has generated, see Chandra (2001).

have no bearing on access to political or economic resources), viewing ethnic identity change as a product of strategic calculations about coalition size will be counter-productive and lead to misinterpretations of the motivations for social behavior. I am not claiming that suicide bombers are motivated by a desire to build minimum winning coalitions. Nor do I want to suggest that emotions such as fear, hatred, or resentment do not trump rational calculations in motivating ethnic behavior in some contexts (Horowitz 2001; Petersen 2002; Varshney 2003). Of course ethnicity can be a source of great passion. But it can also be a tool deployed by coolly calculating political actors. My rationale for adopting a purely instrumental view of ethnicity in this study is simply that, while not appropriate for every explanation, it is appropriate for the expressly political context that this book treats. Moreover, the assumption that ethnicity is situational and strategic can be treated as a working hypothesis, to be tested along with the model that employs this conceptualization. If the model is not able to account for the behavior that it purports to explain, then we can conclude that the assumption on which it is based is probably flawed. Skeptics will be surprised, however, at how much the spare understanding that this book employs is able to explain.

Second, even if we allow that one of the things that makes ethnic group memberships different from non–ethnic group memberships is the depth of feeling that people attach to them, leaving affect aside can still be justified – indeed, may even be necessary – for answering the question of why people choose the ethnic identities they do. The problem is that *all* of the identities in a person's repertoire are sources of affect, to at least some degree. This is what distinguishes an identity in a person's repertoire (which answers the question "who am I?") from the myriad physical and cultural traits that might identify the person objectively, but which have no bearing on how the person sees herself subjectively.[6] Skin color, height, hair type, place of birth, dialect, religion, gender, clothing, and marriage practices are all attributes that might describe an individual. But, for historical and sociological reasons, often having to do with state policies, only a subset of these attributes is likely to shape how individuals see themselves vis-à-vis others, and how others see them.[7] Those attributes that do are what I call "identities," and part of what separates them from

[6] For an elaboration of this distinction, and a theory for why some attributes (cultural differences) come to have meaning (become politically salient), see Posner (2004).

[7] For a fascinating study of how certain objective attributes become meaningful to people as identity categories in Creole Louisiana, see Dominguez (1986).

the objective cultural traits that are not part of how the person views herself is that they are deeply felt – or, at any rate, are more deeply felt than those that do not provide candidate answers to the "who am I?" question. The emotional bond is what makes the trait an identity. But precisely because this is the case, "depth of feeling" is not likely to be an adequate explanation for why one ethnic identity becomes politically salient rather than another. Conceptualizing ethnicity as I do – as something stripped of its affect – is simply a way of focusing attention on what I claim is doing the work in accounting for changes in the salience of different identities over time and across contexts.

Moreover, reducing ethnic groups to units distinguishable only by their sizes and distributions is far from new. Studies that trace the likelihood of ethnic violence to the shares of different groups in the social arena (e.g., Spilerman 1976) or that locate the character of democratic politics in the numbers and sizes of ethnic groups that are competing for power (e.g., Dahl 1971; Collier 2001) are adopting a view of ethnicity that is identical to the one that I employ here. The voluminous literature that attempts to explain political, social, and economic outcomes in terms of a political system's degree of ethnic fractionalization also implicitly embraces a conceptualization of ethnic groups as nothing more than units of a particular size. The difference between my treatment and these others is simply that I am being explicit about the fact that I am doing this.

Finally, when I assert that individuals are able to change their identities strategically in response to situational incentives, I am not claiming that people can choose any identity they want. Their choices are limited to the identities that are in their repertoire. Take the case of an Igbo-speaking Ikwerre Christian from Nigeria. Depending on the context in which he finds himself, and the usefulness, given that context, of each affiliation, this person could unproblematically claim membership in the community of fellow Igbo-speakers, fellow Ikwerres, or fellow Christians, for he is all of these things. But he could not easily claim membership in the community of Hausa-speakers, Tivs, or Muslims – that is, in other Nigerian linguistic, tribal, or religious communities – no matter what the payoffs for identifying himself in such terms might be.[8] In Waters's (1990) terms, the former are "ethnic options" for him, but the latter are not. Similarly, a

[8] Of course, he could *claim* membership in these groups, but such claims would almost certainly be rejected by members of the groups into which he was seeking entry, particularly if, by admitting him, they would be forced to share the resources that the group controls.

Chinese Buddhist from Malaysia could easily "switch her ethnicity" from Chinese to Buddhist, since these are both in her repertoire: she *is* both of these things. But she would find it extremely difficult, and perhaps impossible, to "switch her ethnicity" from Chinese to Malay or from Buddhist to Muslim. We would never refer to the first kind of identity change as "passing" – a term that implies an attempt to pass oneself off as something one is not. But that is exactly how we would characterize her attempt to shift her identity in the second way.

Identity changes within a person's repertoire are natural; changes outside the repertoire are not. In response to instrumentalist assumptions about the flexibility of ethnic identities, most primordialists take a position summarized by the biblical refrain: can the Ethiopian change his skin or the leopard his spots? My response is that while the Ethiopian cannot change his skin, he *can* choose to define himself in terms of a component of his identity repertoire other than skin color – for example, as a Christian, an Oromo, or a Southerner. When instrumentalists insist that ethnic identities are fluid, they almost always have examples of this sort of within-repertoire identity change in mind. When their critics retort that ethnic identities are not nearly so plastic as the instrumentalists claim, they are almost always thinking of the impossibility (or extreme difficulty) of identity changes outside of a person's repertoire (e.g., the Ethiopian trying to adopt an identity as "Muslim," "Tigre," or "Northerner"). The two perspectives do not necessarily contradict one another. They just locate their supporting or disconfirming examples in different types of identity change.

## *Ethnic Cleavages*

The outcome this book seeks to account for is the dimension of ethnic cleavage that becomes the axis of political competition and conflict. The concept of an ethnic cleavage is thus central to the analysis. But what, exactly, is an ethnic cleavage? And what is the relationship between ethnic cleavages, ethnic groups, and identity repertoires?

A useful way to answer these questions, and also to clarify the terminology I will employ throughout the book, is to build on a distinction made by Harvey Sacks (1992) between "identity categories" and "category sets."[9] Identity categories are the group labels that people use to define

[9] Chandra and Boulet (2003) make a similar distinction, although they also add a third component, *attributes*, which refers to the observable characteristics – skin

who they are. They include classifications like "Swedish," "Muslim," "Tutsi," "Northerner," and "Spanish-speaker." Category sets, by contrast, are the broad axes of social division into which these categories can be sorted. They include religion, race, tribe, nationality, region, and language. Sacks calls them "'which'-type sets" because they lend themselves to the question "which, for some set, are you?" – for example, which region do you come from? to which tribe do you belong? which religion do you practice? – and he underscores that "none" and "both" are not permissible answers to such questions. In other words, if region, tribe, and religion are bases of ethnic division in a given society, then everyone in that society should have a regional ancestry, a tribal membership, and a religious affiliation, and nobody should have more than one of each.

To illustrate, and to introduce a notation that I will employ again in Chapter 5, take the example of a hypothetical community in Los Angeles whose population can be sorted on the basis of language, race, and religion into nine distinct groups (with obviously overlapping memberships): English-speakers, Spanish-speakers, Korean-speakers, blacks, Latinos, Asians, whites, Catholics, and Protestants. In this example, language, race, and religion are the category sets and English-speaker, Spanish-speaker, and so on are the identity categories. Together, these nine identity categories constitute the complete universe of social units into which community members might sort themselves or be sorted by others. Each individual community member, however, can only assign herself (or be assigned) to one of these categories for each set; that is, one language category, one racial category, and one religious category. The community's ethnic cleavage structure can be depicted as (L, R, F), where L = language, R = race, and F = religion (faith), and

$L = \{l_1, l_2, l_3\}$, where $l_1$ = English-speaking; $l_2$ = Spanish-speaking; and $l_3$ = Korean-speaking
$R = \{r_1, r_2, r_3, r_4\}$, where $r_1$ = black; $r_2$ = Latino; $r_3$ = Asian; and $r_4$ = white
$F = \{f_1, f_2\}$, where $f_1$ = Catholic and $f_2$ = Protestant

The difference between ethnic cleavages, ethnic groups, and identity repertoires can now be stated clearly. *Ethnic cleavages* are what Sacks calls category sets. In this example they are language, race, and religion

color, education, surname, dietary practices, dress, etc. – that allow people to sort others, and gain entry themselves, into ethnic categories.

(L, R, and F). Throughout the book I will refer to each category set as a different dimension of ethnic cleavage. *Ethnic groups* are the identity categories that each set contains (in this example, $l_1, l_2, l_3, r_1, r_2, r_3, r_4, f_1$, and $f_2$). Together, the number of cleavage dimensions that the community contains and the number and relative sizes of the groups on each cleavage dimension define its *ethnic cleavage structure*. Finally, *identity repertoires* are the inventory of ethnic group memberships that individuals possess – one from each cleavage dimension. In our example, we can depict them as $(l_i, r_j, f_k)$, where $i$ is a number from 1 to 3, $j$ is a number from 1 to 4, and $k$ is either 1 or 2. Thus, Jose, a Spanish-speaking Latino Catholic, has an identity repertoire $(l_2, r_2, f_1)$, and Janet, an English-speaking black Protestant, has an identity repertoire $(l_1, r_1, f_2)$. Note that individuals have as many identities in their repertoires as the cleavage structure has cleavage dimensions.

In addition to helping define our terms more precisely, Sacks's terminology also helps to clarify the goals and argument of this book. Restated in Sacks's vocabulary, the objectives of this study can be expressed as follows: first, the book develops an argument to account for the contents of actors' identity repertoires by explaining which category sets (or cleavages) come to be viewed as commonsensical alternatives for dividing up the political landscape. Here the outcome to be explained is the country's ethnic cleavage structure: why it contains the number of ethnic cleavages it does and why the groups on each cleavage dimension have the relative sizes they do. Then the book presents an explanation for which of the multiple dimensions of ethnic cleavage that the cleavage structure contains will emerge as the axis of political competition and conflict. It does this by comparing the relative benefits that actors will receive by identifying themselves in each of the identity categories (or group memberships) they have in their identity repertoires. I argue that these benefits are a function of the sizes of these groups relative to the other groups that are located within the same category set. Thus Jose, with identity repertoire $(l_2, r_2, f_1)$, would compare the size of his language group $(l_2)$ with the sizes of the other language groups ($l_1$ and $l_3$), the size of his racial group $(r_2)$ with the sizes of the other racial groups ($r_1$, $r_3$, and $r_4$), and the size of his religious group $(f_1)$ with the size of the only other religious group in the community $(f_2)$ and choose the one that puts him in the most advantageous ethnic coalition vis-à-vis the others. This is precisely the exercise to which I am referring when I say that actors will compare the size of their ethnic group with that of all the others located on each cleavage dimension.

## WHY ZAMBIA?

The question this book addresses is a general one. To develop and test a theory to answer it, I might, in principle, draw on empirical materials from any country or political system that contains more than one dimension of ethnic cleavage. Why Zambia?

Zambia is a fortuitous case for studying the association between political institutions and ethnic cleavages for several reasons. First, the Zambian case provides variation on the institutions that structure political competition. From independence in 1964 through 1972, Zambia operated under a multi-party political system. Between 1973 and 1991, it became a one-party state. Then, following a political transition in late 1991, the country returned to multi-party rule. Zambia thus has gone through three distinct institutional periods (or republics). This variation in regime type allows us to test the theoretical expectations that the book develops by checking whether the shifts from multi-party to one-party rule (and back) generated the predicted changes in patterns of ethnic coalition-building. An additional advantage stems from the fact that the two multi-party eras were separated by twenty years and corresponded with periods of dramatically different economic well-being. As I stress in Chapter 6, this pattern of variation makes it possible to control for a key competing explanation for the observed changes in our dependent variable.

A second advantageous feature of the Zambian case lies in its ethnic cleavage structure. As I have noted (and shall elaborate further), Zambia's ethnic cleavage structure contains two dimensions of cleavage, and each defines a very different ethnic landscape. The language cleavage divides the country into four large regional groups, while the tribal cleavage divides it into roughly seventy small and highly localized groups. The large differences in the linguistic and tribal cleavage landscapes guarantee that the strategic dynamics of coalition-building will be very different on each cleavage dimension. The fact that Zambian ethnic cleavage structure has just two potentially mobilizable axes of cleavage also simplifies the analysis considerably. These facts, combined with Zambia's single-member plurality electoral system, which gives power to the greatest vote winners even if they fail to achieve a majority, turn out to be quite important for generating clear theoretical expectations about how changes in institutional structures affect people's incentives for building or joining political coalitions constructed along one cleavage line rather than the other.

Finally, the Zambian case is highly advantageous for reasons of data availability. Studies of politics in developing nations are frequently hampered by the unavailability or unreliability of basic social and economic data (Kapur, Lewis, and Webb 1997: 726–29). Treatments of ethnic politics in developing countries face even greater obstacles, since the potentially inflammatory nature of accurate information about ethnic demographics means that ethnic demographic data are rarely collected, let alone made public. Yet having such data is essential for investigating and documenting the patterns of ethnic voting and coalition-building that are at the heart of most theories of ethnic politics. A final reason why Zambia is such a good place to study the issues that this book addresses is because the country's 1990 census included an item on the questionnaire about respondents' tribal affiliations.[10] Although this information was dropped in all official publications of the census results, it remained as part of the complete census data set, and I was able to gain access to it through the Zambian Central Statistical Office. A number of the analyses that I undertake in this study to document the effects of political institutions on ethnic cleavage outcomes would have been impossible without this unique data source.

## THE PLAN OF THE BOOK

The book is organized in four parts. Part I, comprising Chapters 2 and 3, accounts for why Zambian political actors have the coalition-building options that they do. It shows how a series of policies and regulations implemented by the colonial state and its missionary and mining company allies led to a situation where, when Zambians today think about who they are and who their potential ethnic coalition partners might be, they think of themselves either as members of one of the country's seventy-odd tribes or as members of one of the country's four broad language groups, and why, for each of these bases of ethnic cleavage, the landscape of social divisions has come to look as it does.

Having established the nature of Zambia's ethnic cleavage structure in Part I, Part II then addresses the central question of the book: why and when do tribal and linguistic differences emerge as the basis of political coalition-building? Chapter 4 builds a foundation for the analysis by showing how and why ethnicity matters in Zambian politics and

[10] The census asked respondents "What is your Zambian tribe?" Enumerators coded the respondent's exact answer according to one of the sixty-one different options in the census code book. If the respondent's answer did not match any of the available options, the response was coded as "other."

illustrating how political actors exploit and manipulate the country's ethnic multi-dimensionality. Chapter 5 then presents a simple model to explain why political actors make the ethnic identity choices they do and how the shift from one-party to multi-party political institutions creates incentives for them to alter these choices. The model thus shows how institutional change is responsible for the pattern of variation we observe in the relative salience of tribe and language across Zambia's three republics.

Part III of the book employs a broad variety of qualitative and quantitative data to test a series of observable implications of this model. Drawing on secondary source materials, interviews, original survey and focus group data, and a combination of electoral returns, ethnic demographic data, and information I collected on the tribal backgrounds of more than 2,200 parliamentary candidates, I ask: do politicians "push the ethnic buttons" that the model expects they will? Do they choose the constituencies in which they run and invest in ethnic civic associations in the way that the model would predict? Do voters behave in keeping with the model's expectations? Do they support candidates from their own tribes in one-party elections and candidates associated with their language groups in multi-party contests? After Chapter 6 rules out alternative explanations, Chapter 7 focuses on the model's implications for the behavior of political elites, and Chapter 8 focuses on its implications for non-elite behavior, principally voting patterns.

Part IV takes the argument of the book beyond Zambia to test its explanatory power in other contexts. Chapter 9 explicitly tests the model's performance in an additional African country: Kenya. Chapter 10 then shows how the arguments developed in Chapter 5 can account for why political actors choose the identities they do and why particular social cleavages emerge as axes of political competition and conflict in a number of settings outside of Africa. The chapter concludes by underscoring the need to treat the ethnic cleavages that organize politics as outcomes to be explained rather than simply as the unquestioned "social facts" out of which analyses and explanation are built.

PART I

# Introduction to Part I

## Accounting for the Ethnic Cleavage Structure

This book develops and tests an argument to account for why and when one ethnic cleavage in an ethnically multi-dimensional society emerges as the axis of political competition and conflict instead of another. It builds its explanation around an account of the relative benefits that individuals receive from building or joining political coalitions constructed around different ethnic identities. I argue that the most beneficial identity will be the one that puts the person in a minimum winning coalition, and I show that, if everyone in society makes identity choices with this goal in mind, then a predictable ethnic cleavage will emerge as the basis of conflict in the political system.

The particular identities that individuals will find it most advantageous to choose will depend on the nature of the political system's ethnic cleavage structure. Understanding what the cleavage structure looks like is therefore a prerequisite for understanding the choices that political actors will make. To explain their choices, we will need to know two things about that structure. First, we will need to know the number of cleavage dimensions it contains. This will tell us the number of identities in people's repertoires and thus what the range of options is from which they are choosing. Second, we will need to know the number and relative sizes of the groups located on each cleavage dimension. This will help us (and the political actors) determine which identity it will be most useful to embrace.

One way of proceeding would be to take the ethnic cleavage structure as given. We could assume that both actors' identity repertoires and the relative sizes of the ethnic groups in society are determined exogenously and focus our attention on establishing actors' coalition-building incentives in light of these predetermined social facts. In short, we could assume that players' hands contain certain cards and focus our energies on explaining which cards they play. This is the approach taken in most accounts of ethnic identity choice. But given the central importance that the ethnic cleavage structure plays in the explanation, a comprehensive answer to the question of why particular identities are chosen, and thus why a certain ethnic cleavage emerges as politically salient, requires that we account for the origins of that structure. It requires accounting for why players' hands contain the cards that they do. Doing this is the aim of Part I.

Taken together, Chapters 2 and 3 show why, when Zambians think about who they are, and thus about the kinds of ethnic cleavages that might conceivably be used as bases for political coalition-building, they think in terms of either tribe or language. The chapters do this by delving into Zambia's colonial history to identify the colonial-era policies, rules, and regulations that caused tribal and linguistic divisions to become the two central ways that Zambians think about their nation's ethnic landscape. I show how the administrative structures and policies of the colonial state and its missionary and mining company allies created both schemes of social categorization and, even more importantly, incentives for people to embrace and invest in these schemes such that, by the end of the colonial era, identities built around tribal membership and language group lineage had come to be understood by all Zambians as the two commonsensical ways of thinking about who was, and was not, a member of their ethnic groups. The chapters also show how these administrative structures and policies caused the country's linguistic landscape to have four large groups and its tribal landscape to be composed of a much larger number of smaller groups. The chapters thus provide an explanation for both why tribe and language came to be viewed as natural potential building blocks for political coalitions in the post-colonial era and why the coalitions built from these identities came to have the sizes – and thus the political attractiveness or unattractiveness – that they do.

Explaining why tribe and language are part of Zambians' identity repertoires is part of the task. But fully accounting for the menu of coalition-building options from which Zambian political actors can choose also entails explaining why other objectively identifiable bases of social difference have *not* become part of their inventories of commonsensical social classifications. Thus, at the end of Chapter 3, I provide a brief discussion of why two other potential bases of social division – urban/rural identities and class distinctions – have not emerged as competitors to language and tribe as bases for national-scale political coalition-building. In developing this account, I show that the same colonial-era policies and administrative structures that made tribal and linguistic distinctions natural ways for Zambians to see themselves and categorize their fellow citizens also prevented urban/rural or class-based distinctions from playing similar identity-defining roles.

In tracing the origins of contemporary Zambian ethnic identities to the institutions of colonial rule, I am following an extremely well-trodden path.[1] In fact, the notion that the colonial state created or heightened the importance of ethnic identities in post-colonial Africa is so accepted these days that to argue *otherwise* would probably be controversial. Nonetheless, my argument departs from standard accounts in significant ways. The first, and most obvious, way is in my assertion that the institutions of colonialism generated not just ethnicity but *ethnicities*. I show that the colonial experience in Zambia (then Northern Rhodesia) led to the creation not simply of "tribalism" (e.g., Vail 1989) but to the emergence of two distinct dimensions of ethnic identity: tribe and language. I underscore this point by devoting separate chapters to tracing the development of each identity to different sets of colonial-era policies, rules, and regulations.

A second major difference between my account and others involves my assertion that colonialism was responsible not just for the formation of ethnic groups or the creation of ethnic identities but also for shaping their numbers, relative sizes, and spatial distributions. Thus while one of the goals of Chapters 2 and 3 is to explain why contemporary Zambians see themselves as members of tribes and language groups, another is to account for why, when they think of themselves in each way, they see themselves as members of groups of particular sizes surrounded by a certain number of other groups with particular sizes relative to their own. In short, my goal is to trace the effects of colonial rule in two dimensions: on maps of group distributions as well as on categories of identity. Given the argument I advance in this book about why political actors make the coalition-building choices that they do, accounting for the sizes and physical locations of the ethnic groups in the political system is obviously critical. To have accounted for the range of identity choices open to Zambian political actors but not for the corresponding cleavage structures that each choice implies would have been to provide the material with which to ask the right question (i.e., which identity is chosen at

[1] A representative sampling of studies in this tradition would include Apthorpe (1968), Gulliver (1969), Lemarchand (1970), Ekeh (1975), Kasfir (1976), Young (1976), Laitin (1986), Vail (1989), Bayart (1993), Young (1994), Mamdani (1996), and Werbner and Ranger (1996).

which times?) without the information needed to answer it (i.e., what is it about each identity that makes it an attractive basis for coalition-building?).

The final difference between the approach presented here and most others lies in the mechanism through which I claim that colonial-era policies and administrative structures led to the emergence of particular ethnic identities. Whereas most accounts of the colonial origins of ethnicity imply that the simple act of administrative categorization was enough to cause people to begin thinking of themselves in new ways, the account here emphasizes the incentives that colonial institutions created for people actively to embrace and identify themselves in terms of particular group memberships. In short, whereas most accounts tell a story about passive socialization, I tell a story about active, strategic investment. The key issue that distinguishes my approach from others in this respect is the question of how the administrative categorization implemented by the colonial regime from above shaped identities on the ground. For most authors, this is a non-issue: the simple act of classifying people as members of particular groups is assumed to have been enough to make the new identities take root in the minds of the people who were so classified (e.g., Bayart 1993; Young 1994). By formalizing such distinctions on official maps, including them on government forms, teaching about them in schools, and making them the basis of the colony's administrative apparatus, these authors argue, the colonial state unilaterally altered the way people understood themselves and their compatriots. Ottaway (1999), for example, describes how the Zulus of South Africa were transformed from "the members of a small, obscure clan" to a large self-conscious ethnic community by the end of the colonial era by the simple act of being formally classified as a group. She writes that "the multiplication of the Zulus from a few hundred to seven million in the space of less than two centuries was not the result of a Malthusian nightmare of uncontrolled population growth but of a political process of ethnic reclassification and identity building" (301–302).

Such claims are not entirely without basis. The notion that social identities can be fostered in subjects simply by assigning them to groups finds support in the social psychology literature (Tajfel et al. 1971; Horowitz 1985; Brown 1986) and probably does account for some of the identity formation that took place in colonial societies. But the problem with such top-down, classification-focused explanations is that they portray Africans as acquiescent sponges, passively soaking up the social categories codified in the policies and bureaucratic structures of the colonial government. As Vail (1989: 4) puts it, such accounts depict Africans as "little more than either collaborating dupes or naïve and gullible people, beguiled by clever colonial administrators and untrustworthy anthropologists." In so doing, these accounts ignore the other, equally important, side of the story of identity formation in colonial societies: the story of how the policies of the colonial state generated incentives for people actively to invest in and cultivate the social distinctions that the state defined.

As I demonstrate, the reason that tribal and linguistic identities came to be internalized by Zambians is not simply because they were employed as units of administrative categorization by the colonial government. These identities "took" because a wide range of formal institutions – including land tenure regulations, labor policies, civil service hiring practices, local government structures, and even the organization of the judicial system – created incentives for Africans to invest in their identifications as tribespeople and language-speakers. Rather than passive objects of colonial classification and boundary drawing, Africans were active participants in the process of identity development. Thus, while embracing the argument that the process of African identity formation must be seen as an outcome of the rationalizing tendencies of the colonial state (Young 1994; Scott 1998), I go beyond most treatments in this vein by emphasizing the equally rational responses of the state's African subjects.

In elaborating on these themes, I institute a division of labor between the two chapters. Both chapters provide accounts of how colonial-era rules and policies caused the landscapes of tribal and linguistic groups to look as they do, and both chapters show how the ethnic identities that have emerged were products of conscious investments made for the purposes of gaining access to scarce resources. But Chapter 2, which focuses on the emergence of tribal identities in colonial Northern Rhodesia, puts much more emphasis on the latter point, whereas Chapter 3, which focuses on the emergence of linguistic identities, puts much more emphasis on the former.

# 2

## *Accounting for Zambia's Ethnic Cleavage Structure I*

### *The Emergence of Tribal Identities in Colonial Northern Rhodesia*

In this chapter, I explain why, when contemporary Zambians think about who they are, and about who is and is not a member of their ethnic group, one of the ways they do so is as members of one of the country's six dozen tribes. I begin by showing how the institutions of Northern Rhodesian colonial rule created incentives for rural Africans to invest in their identities as tribe members. Then I account for the perpetuation (and reinforcement) of these identities among urban migrants. I conclude by explaining how the landscape of tribal divisions came to have its present contours.

#### THE ORIGINS OF TRIBAL IDENTITIES IN RURAL ZAMBIA

The British South Africa Company (BSA Co.) took over the administration of the territory that later became Zambia in 1894. The company sought to administer the territory with two goals in mind. First, it sought to extract labor from the local population to sustain its mining efforts and satisfy the demands of its white settler population for African workers. Second, it sought to minimize its costs. Taxation was embraced from the beginning as the key vehicle for achieving both of these goals. It not only generated revenue but, because taxes were payable in cash only, it also induced large numbers of African men to take up wage employment for Europeans.[1] First imposed in the northeastern part of the territory in 1900 and in the northwestern part in 1904, taxation quickly became "the heart and

[1] Although taxation produced abundant migrant labor for the company's mines and the settlers' farms, it never did generate enough revenue to meet the BSA Co.'s administrative expenses. The company ran large budget deficits during every year of its administration. Gann (1958: 12); Slinn (in Bostock and Harvey 1972: 26).

soul of Company government in Northern Rhodesia, and the constant preoccupation of district officials" (Coombe 1968: 12).

The company's problem was that taxation was itself a labor intensive activity, requiring far more staff than the company had at its disposal. At the turn of the century, the BSA Co. had fewer than fifty administrators in a territory of more than 290,000 square miles, far too few to administer the tax on their own (Johnston 1897: 152; Gann 1958: 101).[2] In addition, collecting the tax required detailed information about the distribution of the African population – information that the company did not possess. Although early missionary and travelers' accounts had provided some data about the peoples that were scattered about the territory (e.g., Johnston 1897; Chapman 1909; Moubray 1912), this information was piecemeal and uneven. Only in a handful of areas where mission stations were located or where particularly powerful chiefs held sway had the boundaries of local groups been mapped and the number of African inhabitants counted and made known to BSA Co. administrators. As late as 1934, the director of surveys for Northern Rhodesia could write that "the layman or tourist passing through the Territory . . . would in the course of a few days traverse the lands of so many tribes whose names bear no relation to each other that in the absence of a map he would be bound to be confused and . . . go away with only the haziest notion of the country of any of the particular tribes in which he will be interested" (Thomson 1934: 3). The BSA Co. possessed no such maps at the time it sought to begin collecting taxes, and its sense of the numbers and locations of the would-be taxpayers in much of the country were as hazy as the survey director's hypothetical tourist.

The solution adopted, in Northern Rhodesia as throughout Africa, was to enlist the help of indigenous chiefs. It was assumed that these local rulers knew the locations of the taxable males in the areas under their control and already possessed a machinery for extracting tribute that could be employed for the collection of taxes. The company thus sought to strike a bargain with local rulers whereby the rulers would use their authority and local administrative capacity to extract revenues from their subjects and, in return, the company would protect them from their rivals and guarantee their status as local leaders.

[2] By 1935, the number of administrators had risen to just 134; by 1960, when the colonial administration was at its largest, the number of colonial officers was still just 274 – fewer than one administrator per 100 square miles (Fields 1985).

Several difficulties presented themselves in the implementation of these arrangements, however. First, contrary to European assumptions about the tribal nature of African society, not all areas of the territory had chiefs that were capable of organizing or enforcing the collection of the tax.[3] A few tribes, such as the Lozi, Bemba, Ngoni, and Lunda, were organized around highly centralized chieftainships and possessed developed bureaucracies that were well-suited for tax collection. The districts in which these groups were located were among the first to comply with the tax (Gann 1958: 81).[4] At the other extreme, however, were groups such as the Tonga, an acephalous community of cattle herders whose members "recognized no common name and had no feeling that they belonged to a common polity" (Colson 1969: 29). For chiefs to be employed as BSA Co. agents in Tonga areas, they first had to be created. Most of the tribes in the territory, comprising perhaps two-thirds of the total population, fell between these two poles: chiefs were part of these groups' traditional social organization, but the tribes' bureaucratic institutions were undeveloped and weak. In such cases, tribal institutions had to be made stronger if chiefs were to be able to extract resources from their subjects.

To promote efficient tax collection among such tribes, the BSA Co. implemented a series of administrative actions to bolster the authority of existing chiefs and to create new chiefs where they did not exist but would be administratively useful. The basis for these actions was the Administration of Natives Proclamation of 1916, which gave the BSA

[3] In addition, of course, not all chiefs were willing to serve as tax collectors for the BSA Co., and, even where they were, not all of their subjects were willing to accept the imposition of the tax (Gann 1958: 83; Meebelo 1971: ch. 3). The company responded to this resistance by replacing recalcitrant chiefs with more compliant ones, publicly flogging tax evaders and burning their huts, and increasing the taxes of troublesome tribes as a form of collective punishment (Meebelo 1971; Roberts 1976: 179; Rotberg 1965: 45). By the second decade of the 1900s, these tactics had achieved their desired effect, and the tax was collected without difficulty nearly everywhere in Northern Rhodesia.

[4] The Lozi were a special case. The dependability of their tax compliance stemmed from the fact that, unlike the chiefs of other tribes, the Lozi king (Litunga) was permitted to keep 10 percent of the tax revenue that was collected in his territory. This unique arrangement was a legacy of the 1890 Lochner agreement between the Litunga and the BSA Co. which granted the company mineral rights throughout Northwestern Rhodesia in exchange for the promise of protection from the Ndebele, an annual £2,000 subsidy, and development and technical aid for the Lozi area (Roberts 1976: 160). Although most of these promises were not kept, the notion that the Lozi were to be accorded special status was reflected in many other areas of colonial administration.

Co. the power to appoint or dismiss chiefs as it saw fit and provided for the fining or imprisonment of subjects who failed to carry out their chief's orders. Backed by the implicit threat of European force if its dictates were disobeyed, the proclamation had the effect of standardizing the role and power of the chief among the tribes of the territory, boosting the authority of all chiefs to at least the point where they were able to collect the tax effectively. The impact of this policy was, of course, far greater in those areas where chiefs had previously been weak or non-existent than in areas where chiefs were already powerful local actors. But the large number of areas in the former category meant that the BSA Co.'s interventions had a transformative effect on the territory's local authority structures. The ostensibly "traditional" tribal institutions visible in many Zambian rural communities today have their origins in the BSA Co.'s authority-building efforts during this early period.

A second difficulty with employing chiefs as agents of tax administration was that the territories that the chiefs controlled were not clearly defined. Chiefdoms were "galaxy-like" (Tambiah 1976), with power radiating from the chief's palace and diminishing toward its edges, rather than territorial, like the more familiar and administratively convenient European nation-states with which company administrators were naturally more familiar. Most of the early maps prepared for the BSA Co. reflected the ambiguous boundaries of tribal communities by indicating the names of tribes in the general areas where they were located but leaving dividing lines between tribes unmarked; the names of tribes that covered larger areas were simply printed in a larger font.[5] For lines of accountability for tax collection to be established, and to insure that villagers located on the fringes of chiefdoms would not slip through the taxation net, the BSA Co. recognized that it was critically important that the boundaries of tribal authority be formalized and rendered territorial. It would be nearly impossible for district officers to monitor the tax

[5] See, for example, the maps reproduced in Stone (1979) as figures 9 and 10 and the map reproduced in Prins (1980: 36–37). In the few cases where the missionaries and district officers that drew these early maps did try to indicate boundaries between tribal units, the precision they conveyed was entirely artificial. (See, e.g., the map of the southern part of Northern Rhodesia prepared by the Native Department, Kalomo, Northwestern Rhodesia, January 1905 [London: Public Record Office]). Such maps reflected little more than the subjective judgments of their European makers about where allegiances to one chief ended and another began, not true patterns of authority on the ground.

collection efforts of the chiefs under their supervision if the areas from which each chief was responsible for collecting taxes was not clearly defined.

Drawing on powers conferred in the 1916 proclamation, the company therefore acted to rationalize tribal boundaries. It parceled up the territory into tribal areas, recorded the boundaries between these areas on official maps, and then imposed and enforced these boundaries on the ground. By threatening, violence against anyone who refused to recognize the lines of authority that these new demarcations entailed, the company forced the round peg of existing authority patterns into the square hole of territory-based administration. Over time, what began as little more than administrative wishful thinking was transformed into a new reality on the ground.

The decision to use chiefs as agents of rural tax collection, and the policies employed to solve the various problems that arose as a consequence of this decision, had important implications for the structure of African society and for the nature of post-colonial identities. Together, these policies transformed chiefs from embodiments of customary authority into agents of European administration, and tribes from communities with fluid boundaries and varying degrees of internal cohesion into entities that, while not entirely fixed or uniform, were far more territory bound and standardized in their social and political organization than in the past. Although rural life in most parts of the territory had been at least loosely organized along tribal lines before the introduction of European administration, village, lineage, and clan loyalties served as important parallel bases of social and political organization. Under the BSA Co., a more rigid form of expressly tribal organization was imposed as the norm. This standardization and tribalization of rural administration was a momentous first step in the construction of the tribal dimension of Zambia's post-colonial ethnic cleavage structure. For it was only by organizing local administrative activities around tribal units that incentives could emerge for Africans to invest in their tribal identities rather than simply to accept them or allow them to wither away.

These transformations in the nature of African society were taken several steps further when the British Colonial Office took over responsibility for the territory from the BSA Co. in 1924. Following a practice that had already been established in Nigeria and Tanganyika, the colonial government introduced a system of Indirect Rule in Northern Rhodesia in 1929. Like the BSA Co., the colonial administration adopted the tribe as its unit of rural administrative organization. The principal innovation in the new system, however, was the replacement of chiefs by local governmental structures called Native Authorities. Although run by chiefs, Native Authorities were far more than the individual traditional rulers tapped to act as the agents of European administration under company rule. Equipped with their own courts, schools, treasuries, and, by the end of the colonial era, staffs of clerks, court assessors, police and, in some cases, even health, veterinary, fish, and education officers, these new administrative units were miniature rural bureaucracies in their own right (Chipungu 1992b: 75). This is not to suggest that Native Authorities did not have significant limitations on their powers. Important policy decisions continued to be made by colonial officials in the territorial and district capitals, and many chiefs lacked the education or administrative skills to run their Native Authorities effectively. In practice, Rotberg (1965: 50) notes, "district commissioners were reluctant to transfer any important governmental functions to the Native Authorities for fear that they would perform the required tasks inefficiently and incompetently." Harry Franklin (1974: 143), a long-serving colonial officer in Northern Rhodesia, concurs that devolving administrative power to chiefs "made more work than it saved and it never worked well except eventually in a few areas which had progressive chiefs and councilors." Even so, the new legal powers that the Native Authorities commanded, combined with the valuable resources and services over which they presided, guaranteed the chiefs that ran them and the tribes around which they were built central positions in the local political economy.

As with the BSA Co., this devolution of administrative responsibility was born in part from a calculation that giving power to local actors would keep administrative costs down. But the decision to introduce Indirect Rule to Northern Rhodesia was also a product of the genuine belief by colonial officials that African societies were naturally communitarian and that the most appropriate way to organize rural administration was in tribal units (Bates 1984: 244–45; Crehan 1997: 206). To develop the institutions of Indirect Rule, it was assumed, would be to "preserve and maintain all that is good in native custom and tribal organization . . . [and] make the natives more contented."[6] Yet, rather than preserve and maintain customary modes of authority, Indirect Rule accelerated the process that had begun under the BSA Co. of

[6] J. Moffat Thomson, secretary for Native Affairs, in a speech to the Legislative Council, 18 March 1929, quoted in Meebelo (1971: 187).

undermining traditional norms. Writing generally about the institution of Indirect Rule in British Africa, Lord Hailey (1950, pt. IV: 36) remarked that

> it might even be felt that the use now made of [traditional institutions] is tending to undercut the foundation on which their value to the Administration originally rested [i.e., the customary authority of the chief]. Even though they may continue to make some appeal as recalling established custom, the community is constantly being made aware that the sanction on which the institution rests is no longer tradition or religion but the authority of the Government. Custom ceases in short to be recognized as custom when it is stamped with the Government seal.

Indeed, by the mid-1940s, some chiefs in Northern Rhodesia were "maintained in their present position only by virtue of the powers conferred on them by the Native Authority Ordinance and by the support given to them by the Government" (Hailey 1950, pt. II: 142).

Paradoxically, while the substitution of government sanction for custom as the rationale for obeying chiefs may have altered the basis of their authority, it did not diminish, and in some cases it may in fact have strengthened, the chiefs' ability to command allegiance and respect. It did this by transforming the nature of the chiefs' relationships with their subjects. Powerful chiefs had always been able to command the allegiance of their followers by providing them with protection from outside threats and serving as arbiters of internal disputes. While the former function was rendered obsolete by the imposition of colonial authority across the territory, the latter was still served, and in many ways enhanced, by the chief's role as the head of the Native Authority's courts. What was new in the institution of Indirect Rule was the vesting in chiefs of control, through their positions as heads of Native Authorities, over valuable resources (like medicines, agricultural expertise, treasury funds, and land) and unprecedented judicial powers (like the ability to prosecute or to waive a host of administrative fines and regulations) that had previously been outside their scope of authority. The chief's control over these resources gave his subjects a new, if different, set of reasons for investing in their relationship with both him and the tribe that he presided over. The decline of the customary basis of chiefly authority therefore did not imply a decline in the importance of the chief or of the tribe in rural life, just a shift in its foundations.

Take the case of the Native Treasuries, which were established by ordinance in 1936 and funded by allowing Native Authorities to keep a portion of the taxes collected from their tribe members.[7] Although the treasuries took several years to evolve into solvent financial institutions, and although some treasuries never had sufficient funds to do much more than pay the salaries of their Native Authority staff, the system as a whole flourished. By 1954 the total annual expenditures of Northern Rhodesia's Native Treasuries exceeded £350,000 and their surplus funds were more than £530,000.[8] These were significant sums of money, and they allowed many treasuries to provide valuable projects and public services. In 1943, for example, funds from the treasury of the Plateau Tonga Native Authority paid for the maintenance of wells, the construction of new schools and court buildings, the upkeep of roads, the building of dams, and the creation of rural buying stations for produce (Carey Jones 1944: 46–47). In other Native Authorities, treasury funds provided for dispensaries, dip tanks, famine relief, rural postal services, and even the showing of free films (ibid.; Chipungu 1992b: 80).

By controlling the Native Treasuries, chiefs controlled where such services were sited. This allowed them to transform what were originally public goods into quasi-private goods, usable by all but much more valuable to those who lived closer to where the new services or infrastructure were physically located. The patronage powers that chiefs derived from their control over the siting of such projects gave their subjects incentives to cultivate close relationships with them. And because the power of the chief was reflected in the wealth, reputation, and cultural vitality of the tribe, it also created an impetus for subjects to make investments in the tribe itself. Such investments were made through the traditions subjects learned, the customs they observed, and, most importantly, the way they identified themselves to outsiders.

Further reasons for subjects to strengthen their associations with their chief and tribe derived from the fact that, in addition to providing services of the sort just described, the Native Treasuries also provided loans to individual tribe members. Even the smallest Native Treasuries offered such loans, and the larger treasuries allocated substantial sums for this purpose. In 1960, for example, the Plateau Tonga Native Treasury had nearly £10,000 outstanding in "advances and loans" to individuals.[9] Since

[7] Ordinances nos. 9, 10, and 25 of 1936. Additional, though less important, sources of revenue included court fines, license and permit fees, levies on livestock slaughtered, market fees, and dipping charges.

[8] *Report of the Comptroller and Auditor General of the Public Accounts of Northern Rhodesia*, 1955.

[9] That such loans were rarely repaid only added to their value (Chipungu 1992b: 83).

Native Authorities processed loan applications, and since chiefs ran the Native Authorities, chiefs were in a position to reward those subjects that had cultivated their association with the tribe. Loan-seeking subjects knew that to secure access to financial capital it was necessary for them to make social and cultural, and sometimes also economic, investments in the tribal community.

Another valuable commodity controlled by the Native Authorities was land. Although most chiefs already controlled access to land prior to the imposition of European rule, this power was formalized when the Colonial Office took over the administration of the territory. The reason the colonial regime did this, Bates explains, "was that a system of communal rights empowered locally based confederates: it gave control over the allocation of the key resource in an agrarian economy to those who would govern on behalf of the colonial powers – the tribal chiefs" (1984: 245). Since the system of Indirect Rule rested on the power of the chiefs, it was critical for the system's success that chiefs retain as much authority as possible. Defending the authority of chiefs over the distribution of land was embraced by the colonial government as the key means of doing this. Bates (1984: 246) quotes C. K. Meek's 1949 treatise *Land Law and Custom in the Colonies*: "if 'indirect rule' is to continue to be a cardinal principle of British policy, it would appear to be essential that the local Native Authorities should remain the ultimate 'owners' of as much land as possible."[10] The result of the formalization of communal land rights was the creation of a system in which loyalty to the chief and membership in a tribe became prerequisites for gaining access to land. In colonial Northern Rhodesia, "men and women . . . were recognized as having a legal claim [to land] only in the territory of the group to which they belonged by birth" (Colson 1968: 204). Preserving that claim required investing in one's credentials as a tribe member in good standing. This meant abiding by customary rules, participating in the social life of the community, and otherwise investing in one's identity as a tribe member.

In addition to land and local development funds, Native Authorities also controlled the local system of civil and criminal justice: the Native Courts. More often a fee-levying nuisance than a resource to which Africans worried about securing access, the Native Courts nonetheless played an important role in fortifying the local authority of the chief and reinforcing the importance of the tribe as a focus of identity. Initially established in 1929, the Native Courts emerged as important local institutions

[10] See also Firmin-Sellers (1996: 32).

when their powers were expanded and more clearly specified in 1936. Empowered after that date with applying "native law and custom" (Chanock 1985) to most civil and criminal matters, the Native Courts touched the lives, at one time or another, of almost all rural Africans. In the mid-1940s, Native Courts heard an average of one case each year for every twenty-eight people in Northern Rhodesia.[11] To interpret this ratio, we must remember that rural Africans tend to live in large, tightly knit family units comprised of several nuclear families and upwards of twenty members. Reframed to reflect the number of cases heard by the Native Courts *per family unit*, we approach – and in some districts even exceed – an average of one court case per family per year. By this calculation, it is clear that the Native Courts were a central feature of rural life. On a roughly annual basis, they reminded people in a (nearly) personal way of both the authority of the chief, who presided over the court proceedings and had the power to imprison, cane, or fine people found guilty of crimes, and the centrality of the tribe, in the name of whose traditions and customs the court's judgments were rendered.

In addition to hearing civil and criminal cases, the Native Courts were also responsible for enforcing dozens of local regulations and assessing an ever-growing assortment of levies and fees. While some of the regulations that the Native Courts were responsible for enforcing (involving such things as the provision of marriage licenses or the granting of permits to travel to town or to relocate to other Native Authority areas) were highly demanded, many others (involving such things as the licensing of dogs, guns, or bicycles or the levying of fees on fish caught or livestock slaughtered) were deeply resented (Chipungu 1992a: 55–61). The inability of colonial officials to oversee the everyday workings of the Native Authorities allowed chiefs a great deal of latitude in how they ran this aspect of the local administrative system. They could provide licenses and permits expeditiously, or they could drag their feet in the hopes of

[11] In some districts, this ratio was as low as 1 to 11; in others, it was as high as 1 to 67. These ratios were calculated by comparing district-level population figures from 1946 with figures provided in Hailey (1950, pt. II) on the number of cases heard by the courts of each Native Authority in single years ranging from 1942 to 1948. In districts containing more than one Native Authority, the figures for cases heard were added together to produce district-level totals. The analysis excludes districts in Barotseland, whose court system was run independently from the rest of Northern Rhodesia and for which Hailey does not provide data on court cases heard. In addition, three of the remaining twenty-five districts were omitted from the analysis because they contained Native Authorities for which Hailey fails to provide court case data.

extracting bribes from those who needed such documents immediately (Franklin 1974). They could be strict in their enforcement of unpopular regulations and their assessment of fees, or they could turn a blind eye to statutory violations and unpaid levies (Chipungu 1992a: 55–61). As with the patronage powers that derived from the chiefs' control over other valued resources such as land and soft loans, the discretion chiefs possessed over the application of legal sanctions gave subjects important reasons to invest in their association with the chiefs.

### *A Test of the Argument*

As the basis of identification with one's chief came to rest ever more centrally on his position as the senior executive of the Native Authority, a gulf began to emerge between those tribes whose chiefs were appointed heads of Native Authorities and those whose chiefs were not. Indirect Rule was designed to be a comprehensive and efficient system of rural administration built on pre-existing tribal units. The problem was that the number of units – seventy-three, according to the authoritative count of the day (Thomson 1934) – was recognized to be too large for viable administration (Chipungu 1992a: 52). Over the years, a series of consolidations and reorganizations by the colonial government shrank the number of Native Authorities to just thirty-nine by 1948. Some of these thirty-nine Native Authorities were "hyphenated" combinations of two or more named groups (e.g., the Mukulu-Unga Native Authority). Others were one of a pair of Native Authorities affiliated with a single tribe (e.g., the Plateau Tonga and Gwembe Tonga Native Authorities or the Chewa and Southern Chewa Native Authorities).[12] In all, the thirty-nine Native Authorities carried the names (and were run by the chiefs) of just slightly more than half of the tribes that had been officially identified by the government. Although these tended to be the larger tribes, this still meant that a large number of people – roughly a sixth of the total population – lived in (and, for purposes of local government, were ruled by) Native Authorities whose chiefs were from tribes other than their own.

If my argument about the incentives that the Native Authority system generated for investing in one's tribal identity are right, then we should find tribal identifications becoming stronger among the members of tribes

[12] The Lozi also had their own complex system of independent local administration, with five separate sub-units, but these were not technically part of the larger system of Indirect Rule.

Table 2.1. *Effects of Native Authority Designations on Tribal Identities, 1930/33–1962*

| | Change in share of national population during Indirect Rule[a] (in %) | Percentage of tribes with increasing population shares during Indirect Rule |
|---|---|---|
| Tribes with Native Authorities[b] | +6.7 | 58 (22 of 38) |
| Tribes without Native Authorities | −28.5 | 23 (8 of 35) |

[a] Only tribes included in both the 1930/33 and the 1962 counts are included in the analysis.

[b] Tribes in this category are those that had their own (or were part of a hyphenated) Native Authority after the reorganization of Native Authorities in 1948.

that were given their own Native Authorities and weaker among the members of tribes that were not. Over time, people who were members of tribes that were not granted Native Authorities, or whose Native Authorities had been consolidated or done away with over the years, should have altered their tribal identifications to match the tribe that was associated with the Native Authority under whose jurisdiction they lived. The decline of the customary and the rise of the administrative basis of chiefly authority should have provided less and less reason for such people to maintain their linkages with their "original" tribe and more and more reason for them to begin investing in their relationship with the entity that mattered: the tribe whose chief controlled their Native Authority.

Evidence for this trend of identity consolidation is presented in Table 2.1, which compares the change over the course of Indirect Rule in the shares of the population of tribes that did and did not have their own Native Authorities. Figures for the start of Indirect Rule are the average of the figures for 1930 and 1933, as reported in the Northern Rhodesian *Annual Report on Native Affairs* for these years. I take the average of the two figures to guard against the potential unreliability of either single tally. Population shares for the end of Indirect Rule are from the *Annual Report on African Affairs* for 1962, as reprinted in Brelsford (1965). If my argument about the Native Authorities' creating incentives for investments in tribal identities is correct, we would expect to find an increase in the share of the population of tribes that had their own Native Authorities (as people from tribes without Native Authorities came to identify and invest in their relationships with tribes that had them) and a decrease in the share of the population of tribes that did not have their own Native Authorities (as members of such tribes came to identify with tribes that did). This is the trend that Table 2.1 reveals.

Over the course of the period of Indirect Rule, the percentage of the population identified as members of tribes that had their own Native Authorities (or shared hyphenated ones) rose by 6.7 percent. The significance of this seemingly minor change becomes apparent when we compare it to the 28.5 percent decline over the same period in the percentage of the population identified with tribes that did not have their own Native Authorities. In addition, tribes that had their own Native Authorities already comprised 81 percent of Northern Rhodesia's total population at the beginning of Indirect Rule, so there was an upper limit on the extent to which their share might possibly increase of roughly 25 percent. Moreover, whereas 58 percent of the tribes that had their own Native Authorities experienced an increase in their sizes between the beginning and the end of Indirect Rule, only 23 percent of tribes without Native Authorities experienced any growth (which is to say that 77 percent contracted). There was, of course, significant variation among the tribes within these two categories (Appendix A provides a tribe-by-tribe breakdown). But the general trend is clear: tribes with Native Authorities grew in size; tribes without Native Authorities shrank.

Despite the clarity of the trend, these findings are vulnerable to the criticism that the data on which they are based were not a true census and reflects the tribal affiliations ascribed to people by the rural district officials who filled out the population census forms rather than the self-reported tribal identities of individual villagers. It is quite plausible that the way the colonial officers recorded the tribal affiliations of the African populations in their districts was shaped by the system of Indirect Rule that these officers were themselves responsible for administering. If this is the case, then the changes reported in Table 2.1 might reflect the effects of changes in that system on the perceptions of district officers rather than on the identities of African villagers.

One way of assessing the weight of this objection is to compare the 1930/33 figures with self-reported tribal identities recorded in Zambia's 1990 census – the only nationally comprehensive source of information about tribal self-identifications ever collected in Zambia. The fact that the 1990 census was administered nearly thirty years after the end of Indirect Rule means that it almost certainly captures identity changes that took place after that period in addition to during it. It would require heroic assumptions about path dependence to believe that the identities reported

Table 2.2. *Effects of Native Authority Designations on Tribal Identities, 1930/33–1990*

| | Change in share of national population during Indirect Rule[a] (in %) | Percentage of tribes with increasing population shares during Indirect Rule |
|---|---|---|
| Tribes with Native Authorities | +10.9 | 39 (14 of 36) |
| Tribes without Native Authorities | −56.9 | 16 (3 of 19) |

[a] Figures for 1990 are from the *Republic of Zambia Census of Population and Housing* (1990). Only tribes included in both the 1930/33 and the 1990 counts are included in the analysis.

in 1990 were wholly the outcome of institutional arrangements that were in effect between 1929 and the early 1960s. Despite this clear limitation, however, the census data have the virtue of doing something that the 1962 data do not do: directly measuring our dependent variable. On balance, therefore, the 1990 data constitute a source that is in some ways superior and in some ways inferior to the source on which the results reported in Table 2.1 are based. By comparing the results derived from each data source, we can, in some measure, use the strengths of one to offset the weaknesses of the other. Table 2.2 reports the results of the 1930/33–1990 comparison (Appendix A breaks down the results in greater detail).

As in Table 2.1, Table 2.2 reveals a sharp disparity between tribes with and without Native Authorities. Here, however, the results are even starker. Tribes that had Native Authorities during the colonial era recorded a 10.9 percent increase in their share of the national population between 1930/33 and 1990, whereas tribes that did not have Native Authorities recorded a 56.9 percent decline in their share. The fact that only 39 percent of the tribes in the first category saw their share of the national population increase during this period confirms that the possession of a Native Authority during the colonial era is not the only factor that accounts for the strengthening of tribal identifications over time. Still, the fact that fully 84 percent of the tribes that did not have Native Authorities saw their share of the national population decrease between 1930/33 and 1990 – often by very large margins – strongly suggests that the possession of a Native Authority under Indirect Rule was a prerequisite for a tribe's avoiding a slide into irrelevance. By 1990, those tribes that did not have Native Authorities under colonialism comprised just 7 percent of the

Zambian population, down from 16 percent in 1930/33. These findings suggest that the 1962 tribal census figures probably do reflect more than simply the best guesses of district officials.

Additional evidence of the identity- and outlook-shaping effects of the Native Authorities comes from survey data I collected in six case study districts in 1995.[13] To gauge the degree of social distance among members of different tribes, I asked respondents to identify the tribal backgrounds of their three closest friends. All but two of the 679 Zambian friends that were mentioned (fully 99.7 percent of total responses) were members of tribes that had possessed their own Native Authorities during the colonial era. Because the survey that generated this data was not administered nationally, these findings may be biased to some degree by the relatively narrow composition of the local pool of potential friends in each case study district. Though the findings can therefore only be suggestive, they do point to an interesting conclusion: namely, that Native Authorities seem to have shaped not only the way people identify themselves but also the range of categories into which they sort their friends and acquaintances.

Taken together, Tables 2.1 and 2.2 and the results of my own survey data support the contention that Native Authorities were the engines that drove the formation of tribal identities in rural Northern Rhodesia. This finding, in turn, supports the larger claim that it was the institutions of colonial rule (specifically, the institutions that created and governed the operations of the Native Authorities) that generated the impetus for rural Africans to embrace and invest in their identifications with their tribal groups.

But what about Africans who did not live in rural areas and who were therefore outside the jurisdiction of the Native Authorities? From the beginning of the century, the need to pay taxes, coupled with opportunities for comparatively well-paid employment in the Northern Rhodesian copper mines or in the mines and on the farms of neighboring countries, led thousands of Africans to migrate away from their rural homes. By 1963, fully 20 percent of the African population in Northern Rhodesia was living in an urban area (Bates 1976: 49), and almost as many others were formally registered in rural areas but were living, either temporarily or on a semi-permanent basis, in town. How can we account for the

[13] The survey work was conducted via a random stratified quota-sampling procedure with forty-two respondents in each of the six case study districts. Further details of the survey and its administration are provided in Appendix B.

maintenance, much less the growth, of tribal identities among these segments of the population? Absent the ability to benefit from rural development projects, access to land and credit, or the leniency of Native Court officials, why would urban migrants have had any incentive to invest in their identities as tribe members?

## THE ORIGINS OF TRIBAL IDENTITIES IN URBAN ZAMBIA

From as early as the turn of the twentieth century, the mines and farms of Southern and Central Africa demanded large numbers of African laborers. In its capacity as the owner of both a large share of the region's mines and the railroad systems that served them, the BSA Co. controlled the key enterprises that stood to suffer if the demand for labor was not met.[14] In its capacity as the administrator of Northern Rhodesia, it also controlled the territory from which African labor was sought. The company thus took advantage of its administrative powers to put policies in place that would insure that an abundant supply of African laborers would be available for the region's industries.

As we have seen, the principal instrument used by the company for this purpose was taxation. By "consciously [setting] the rate of tax at a level that would successfully draw African males away from their homes to the usually distant centres of white agriculture and industry," the administration forced thousands of Northern Rhodesians out of their villages (Rotberg 1965: 41). "In theory," Gann (1958: 84) writes,

> the tax could be earned by working only a fortnight in Southern or a month in Northern Rhodesia for wages. These calculations, however, took no account of traveling time nor of the fact that the migrant could not save all his pay. Besides, it was impossible for every male to undertake an annual journey, for there was much work women could not do. Thus every tribesman had to bring back enough to pay for some of his fellows; and lengthy journeys away from the village . . . became essential in order to meet their heavy obligations.

As early as the second decade of the century, the flow of migrants from rural Northern Rhodesia to the mines and farms of Southern Rhodesia,

[14] In addition to its business concerns, the company also had an economic interest in making sure that the labor requirements of the European settler populations of the Northern and Southern Rhodesian territories were met. Particularly in years when the company's mining and railroad properties yielded weak profits, a significant portion of the BSA Co.'s revenues came from the sale of land to white farmers and from the royalties it received on small-scale mining ventures undertaken by European settlers (Gann 1958: 79).

South Africa, and Katanga was so great that native commissioners in Northern Rhodesia began to complain that their districts were becoming "denuded of their menfolk" (ibid.: 86). By 1938, absentee rates of working-age males equaled or exceeded 50 percent in seven of Northern Rhodesia's thirty-three rural districts and approached that level in six others.[15] Roberts (1976: 191) estimates that, by approximately that date, "more than half the able-bodied male population of Northern Rhodesia was working for wages away from home."[16]

For the first two and a half decades of the century, the vast majority of Northern Rhodesian labor migrants traveled outside the territory to find work. But by the end of the 1920s, Northern Rhodesia's own copper industry also began hiring large numbers of African laborers. Although the wages paid by the Northern Rhodesian companies were lower than those paid at the more distant mines, the promise of employment closer to home led many Northern Rhodesian men to migrate to the Copperbelt rather than to Southern Rhodesia, South Africa, or Katanga, as they had previously. By 1930, the African labor force in the Copperbelt – more than 80 percent of whom were migrants from Northern Rhodesia itself – swelled to nearly 32,000 (Berger 1974: 13–15). Just as the Northern Rhodesian copper mines were entering production, however, the world market for copper collapsed. Beginning in 1931, mines were shut down, construction projects were halted, and labor recruitment was suspended. By the end of 1932, African employment in the Copperbelt had fallen to 6,677, more than 75 percent off its peak of little more than a year before (ibid.: 20).

To the great relief of the colonial government and the mining companies, the majority of migrant laborers responded to the mine and business closures by returning to their villages. However, the several thousand men that remained in the towns in the hopes of finding work caused great

[15] *Report of the Commission Appointed to Enquire into the Financial and Economic Position of Northern Rhodesia*, 1938, cited in Hellen (1968: 96).

[16] Roberts's estimate is supported by figures from the 1935 Northern Rhodesian *Annual Report on Native Affairs*. Drawing on these figures, C. F. Spearpoint, the compound manager at the Roan Antelope Copper Mine (RACM), calculated that 40.1 percent of all taxable males in Northern Rhodesia were employed away from their villages: 6.4 percent in the Northern Rhodesian mines, 17 percent outside of Northern Rhodesia, and 16.7 percent in non-mining work within Northern Rhodesia (memorandum from Spearpoint to RACM General Manager F. A. Ayer, 16 November 1936, Zambia Consolidated Copper Mines [ZCCM] Archives, file WMA 139). If we figure that only 80 percent of all taxable men are actually "able-bodied," then we arrive at almost exactly Roberts's estimate.

apprehension within the European community.[17] The presence of such large numbers of unemployed Africans in the predominantly white towns was blamed for an increase in crime and "immorality," and created what the 1933 *Report of the Northern Rhodesian Government Unemployment Committee* termed, with characteristic British understatement, "a situation with most undesirable features."[18]

Production resumed at most of the Copperbelt mines by the mid-1930s, and African employment returned to pre-depression levels by the early 1940s. Yet the experience of the mine closures made a deep impression on the Northern Rhodesian government. It weakened the government's faith in the long-term viability of the copper industry, and it heightened its fear that a future collapse in copper prices would send an even larger number of unemployed and discontented Africans into the streets. To guard against this possibility, the government began to emphasize the maintenance of ties between urban migrants and their rural homes in the hope that that this would facilitate the rapid return of unemployed laborers to their villages in the event that the mines were to close down again. After the experience of the mine closures of the early 1930s, the government was willing to support the resumption of wide-scale labor recruitment to the towns only if such a safety valve were firmly in place.

The fears of African unemployment that served as the impetus for the government's new policy of fostering urban/rural ties were reinforced by a number of quite practical considerations. First, if urban workers maintained their linkages with their villages, they would preserve their access to traditional social support systems that could take care of them in times of sickness and re-absorb them upon retirement. Encouraging urban migrants to keep up their rural ties was therefore a cost-saving measure for the colonial administration: as long as the government could count on migrants' rural relatives to provide for their kin in times of need, expenditures on hospitals and other social services for the African ill or aged could be avoided – and, in effect, passed on to the rural sector.

A second rationale for encouraging African migrants to maintain their connections with their villages was the presumption that doing so lessened

[17] As many as four thousand unemployed migrant workers remained in Ndola district, a key Copperbelt mining area. Maramba compound in Livingstone reportedly had "thousands" of unemployed migrant laborers during this period. Gann (1964: 254).

[18] P. 10. A separate report, investigating the Copperbelt strike of 1935, also drew attention to the "many thousands" of unemployed Africans, "numbers" of whom were "living on their wits as gamblers, thieves and the like" (quoted in Ferguson 1990: 398).

the damage done to rural society by the absence of so many working-age men. The *Annual Report on Native Affairs* for 1930 described the effects of widespread male absenteeism from the rural areas as "prejudicial, if not dangerous, to the [rural] community" and blamed it for breaking up family life, reducing birthrates, undermining tribal control, and leading to insufficient cultivation and food shortages (Hellen 1968: 95). The large number of official reports and monographs written during this period that drew links between labor migration and the breakdown of rural life provide a measure of the colonial government's preoccupation with the effects of male absenteeism.[19] By implementing policies that would encourage men to return to their villages periodically, the government sought to stem some of what it took to be the more serious effects of labor migration on rural society.

Encouraging workers to maintain links with their relatives in the villages also had the desirable effect of circulating cash in the rural districts. An internal mining company memorandum noted that "Government is very anxious to get natives to visit their homes, partly so that money will circulate to the rural areas and partly to avoid breaking up village life."[20] By finding ways to induce African workers to send money to their rural kin, the government sought to promote rural development while investing only minimal sums of its own. As Berger notes, "most of the African Reserves in Northern Rhodesia were so poor, and the Administration's exchequer so depleted, that the best hope for any economic progress in [the rural] areas seemed to lie in the circulation of wages earned at the mines and elsewhere" (Berger 1974: 36). To the extent that some of the "recirculated" money took the form of gifts to chiefs, the movement of funds from the urban economy to the villages served the additional purpose of fortifying the system of Indirect Rule on which the government's rural administration was built.

A combination of cost-saving considerations, paternalism, and the fear of widespread African unemployment convinced the colonial authorities of the need to encourage migrants to preserve their links with their rural

[19] Among the many reports in this vein, the 1936 *Nyasaland Report on Emigrant Labour* had a particularly important impact in Northern Rhodesian policy-making circles (Berger 1974: 36). Other key reports that emphasized the deleterious effects of labor migration on rural life include the *Report of the Commission Appointed to Enquire into the Financial and Economic Position of Northern Rhodesia* (1938) and J. Merle Davis's classic study *Modern Industry and the African* (1933).

[20] Mufulira Copper Mines memorandum on native leave and travel allowances, 8 November 1944 (ZCCM Archives, file WMA 135).

villages. Because village life was deliberately structured along tribal lines, preserving connections with the village meant preserving connections with the tribe. Indeed, for the colonial authorities, the challenge of reinforcing links between urban migrants and their rural homes was explicitly seen as the challenge of preventing "detribalization" (Wilson 1941). The policies that the administration put in place to do this were thus explicitly devised as ways to preserve and promote tribal identities among urban migrants.

The most obvious means of preventing the detribalization of migrant laborers was to structure urban life as much as possible along tribal lines. One mining company official made this goal explicit when he described government policy as seeking to "bring about as close a parallel to village conditions in the Compound... as is possible."[21] The government and the mining companies endeavored to do this in several ways. Councils of Tribal Elders were established in the municipal and mining compounds in the 1930s. Comprised of representatives elected by the members of each tribe and charged with serving as a link between the municipal authorities and the African population, the Tribal Elders were explicitly designed to serve as surrogates in the urban context for the headman back in the village.[22] Many elders were, in fact, relatives of chiefs, and a large part of their authority stemmed from this connection (Epstein 1958: 49–50).

Working in parallel with the Tribal Elders and similarly intended to serve as a manifestation of tribal authority in the urban setting was the system of Native Urban Courts. Set up in each of the protectorate's nine major urban population centers, the courts were comprised of three to six judges, each nominated by the senior chiefs of the tribes that had the largest representation in the urban area under the court's jurisdiction. Tribal custom served as the basis of the court's decisions, and efforts were made to insure that cases were heard by judges from the same tribe as the defendant. When cases involved defendants from tribes other than those represented on the court, elders from other tribes were called in to assist as advisors on applicable custom. Like the Tribal Elders, the judges in the Native Urban Courts provided "an important link between the urban dwellers and the tribal chiefs, and they themselves [saw] it as one of the most important aspects of their task to uphold and reaffirm the norms and values of tribal society" (ibid.: 223). Their important influence in this regard can be surmised from the very large number of cases that they

[21] Spearpoint to Ayer, memorandum on native labor policy, 28 August 1933 (Zambia National Archives, file RC/1275).

[22] Ibid.

heard: in 1947 alone, the Native Urban Courts of Northern Rhodesia heard a total of 10,030 civil and criminal cases – a very high average of one case for every nineteen Africans living in the urban areas.[23]

The establishment of the Urban Courts and the system of Tribal Elders constituted deliberate attempts by the colonial government to re-create patterns of tribal social organization in the urban domain. Other aspects of urban life that encouraged the maintenance of tribal identities were products not of intentional social engineering but of unconscious racism or even paternalistic considerations for African welfare. In the mines, for example, tribes tended to be segregated into particular occupational niches. This segregation had several causes. In part, it was due to stereotypes held by individual African personnel managers about which tribes were most suitable for which tasks (Papstein 1989: 382–83; Luchembe 1992: 31). A 1958 report on the African labor force at the Roan Antelope Copper Mine (RACM) went so far as to assign quasi-scientific ratings of the aptitude of each tribe for certain kinds of jobs. Evidence that such ratings were taken seriously comes from tables provided in the report showing that tribes with high ratings (potential supervisors) were, in fact, over-represented in supervisory positions, whereas tribes with low ratings tended to predominate in low-skilled, labor-intensive jobs. Patterns of occupational segregation in the mines were also at least partly a result of differences in educational opportunities in the various districts from which laborers migrated. The preferences of the African laborers themselves certainly also played a role.[24] Irrespective of its cause, however, the effect of occupational segregation was to reinforce tribal divisions and to undermine tendencies toward social homogenization in the workplace.

Unlike the machine shop or the blasting face, the compounds where the miners lived were not tribally segregated. Still, the maintenance of tribal differences was encouraged by the mine management through its sponsorship of inter-tribal recreational activities. Particularly important were tribal dancing competitions, which were a central feature of urban

[23] Figures calculated from data in Hailey (1950, pt. II: 151). Recall that the average for rural Northern Rhodesia as a whole was one court case per twenty-eight people.

[24] "From experience, I have found that natives of certain tribes much prefer work which is of the task or piece-work nature ... [whereas] natives of other tribes much prefer a steady routine kind of employment ... It has always been the policy [at RACM] to fit a native into the particular work which, by our experiences, best suits him" (Spearpoint 1937: 14). Lest we read too much into Spearpoint's claim, a word of caution is in order: what Spearpoint takes for "innate" tribal preferences was probably nothing more than the phenomenon of new migrants requesting assignment to jobs that already contained concentrations of their fellow tribesmen.

life in the Copperbelt (Mitchell 1956). The songs that were sung during these events, which almost always involved joking criticisms of rival tribal groups and frequently invoked images of village life and traditional authority, had the effect of solidifying tribal identities and reaffirming links between the urban and rural domains.

As a further means promoting tribal connections, the government and the mining companies periodically invited chiefs and headmen to visit their tribesmen at the mines at company expense. The popularity of these visits – one mining company official counted more than 150 at one mine in a single month[25] – stemmed from the fact that they served several purposes. For the mining companies and the colonial government, they were a means of "keep[ing] up contact between the natives and village life, and thereby acting to a small extent as a brake on detribalization."[26] For the chiefs, they provided an opportunity to extract tribute from their wage-earning subjects and a chance to remind their tribesmen of the importance of maintaining their (especially financial) links with their village. Savvy chiefs timed their visits to coincide with pay day.[27]

All of these policies – the creation of the system of Tribal Elders, the setting up of the Native Urban Courts, the practice of occupational segregation on the mines, and the encouragement of inter-tribal recreational competition and chiefly visits – were efforts to import aspects of rural life into the urban environment. A different set of policies attempted directly to encourage migrant workers to maintain their linkages with their rural homes. For example, at the insistence of the government, the mining companies bore the cost of repatriating migrant workers to their villages once their term of service had expired. In 1931 alone, more than 7,500 such workers were repatriated to their villages by the mining companies.[28] The companies were also persuaded to undertake the logistical burden of arranging for workers' pensions to be paid in their local districts, providing

[25] Letter from the acting secretary of the NRCM to the senior provincial commissioner, Ndola, 27 November 1957 (ZCCM Archives, file 12.7.9B).

[26] Spearpoint to Ayer, memorandum on native labor policy, 28 August 1933 (Zambia National Archives, file RC/1275).

[27] Davis (1967: 73) reports that "in the visit of one Paramount [chief] the tribute is said to have totaled over £150." In an interview during his visit to RACM, Chief Mumena of the Kaonde expressed hope that his "people who have worked very long and have obtained their pensions [would] come back home. We shall receive them with both hands and give them land, which they can make use of without any trouble" (*The African Roan Antelope*, February 1955).

[28] *Report of the Board of Management of the Northern Rhodesia Native Labour Association*, 1931 (ZCCM Archives, file 11.2.2E).

facilities for laborers to remit portions of their income directly to their relatives in the village and organizing a voluntary deferred payment scheme whereby part of a worker's salary would be held until the end of his service and paid to him once he had returned to his village. Also at the government's urging, the mining companies set up elaborate paid leave policies to encourage Africans to return to their rural areas periodically during their employment tenure.[29] According to figures from the Northern Rhodesia Chamber of Mines (NRCM), more than 91,000 African laborers were provided with such paid leave benefits between 1941 and 1953.[30]

To this point, I have discussed the various institutions that the colonial government and the mining companies put in place to facilitate urban/rural ties as if the colonial administration had to force urban migrants to maintain links with their tribes and villages. To the extent that these administration- and company-sponsored institutions served their intended purpose, however, it was precisely because labor migrants had incentives of their own to maintain their connections with their rural kin. Most of the measures devised by the government to foster tribal linkages were easily circumvented. Repatriation at the end of one's contract could be (and sometimes was) avoided. Tribal Elders could be ignored. In fact, in 1953 the institution of Tribal Elders was scrapped when mining-compound residents voted overwhelmingly for its abolition in an industrywide referendum (Epstein 1958: ch. 4). Remittances to rural relatives could be withheld. The deferred payment scheme could be refused. Chiefs' visits and tribal dancing competitions could be boycotted. And leave could easily be taken in town rather than in the village. The existence of these policies thus may explain how migrants who were already predisposed to maintaining their links with their rurally based tribes were able to do so, but the policies do not explain why migrants sought to maintain these links in the first place. To explain why migrants had an interest in maintaining and cultivating their tribal identities, we need to shift our attention to the factors that created not simply opportunities but incentives for migrants to invest in preserving their attachments to their rural homes.

For Copperbelt labor migrants, the most significant feature of urban life was its inseparable connection to formal wage employment. When formal employment ceased, so too did a laborer's access to housing, social services, and, to some degree, even food. Until the mid-1940s, almost all

[29] Memorandum on paid leave policies, Northern Rhodesia Chamber of Mines, 27 November 1945 (ZCCM Archives, file WMA 136).

[30] ZCCM Archives, files WMA 135 and WMA 136.

African housing was "tied" – that is, tied to employment – and had to be vacated upon retirement or rented from the former employer at rates that were unmanageable once a worker's wages ceased.[31] The possibility of building one's own house in, or near, the town was undermined by municipal ordinances that made most land in the urban and peri-urban areas unavailable for residential housing. In the few areas where it was legal for Africans to build, municipalities imposed excessively stringent standards for construction, thereby raising home-building expenses beyond the means of most retirees (Bates 1976: 62 and 291, n 78). The option of retiring to a home built in one of the illegal "shantytowns" that emerged on the outskirts of most urban areas was blocked by the periodic destruction of such communities by the municipal authorities.

Problems of housing were compounded by the expense of purchasing food. Bates (ibid.: 62) points out that "regulations enforced by the government forbade the growing of most crops in the urban townships, and land in the areas immediately adjacent to the townships . . . could not be legally converted into gardens." Absent the ability to maintain their own gardens, Africans who did not have formal employment were forced to purchase their food at the market, a situation that quickly became unsustainable in the absence of a regular salary. Attempts to supplement one's income by engaging in commercial activities outside the formal sector were illegal. Although restrictions on urban cultivation seem to have been more strict in some towns than in others,[32] zoning laws and township ordinances regulating the construction of urban gardens had an important effect on the household budget calculations of a very large number of would-be urban retirees.

The nearly total absence of health facilities for Africans outside of formal employment, and a tax structure that assessed urban dwellers at a rate that was nearly double that of their rural counterparts, compounded the already strong disincentives for urban retirement. The recognized unfeasibility of this option is revealed starkly in the results of surveys carried

[31] Even when workers received pensions for long service, the pensions generally did not provide enough income to meet urban rents (Berger 1974: 207).

[32] For example, Davis (1967: 86) reports that residents in the Ndola Native township could "make £3 a month growing vegetables, poultry and eggs and selling them on the location or in town." Kay (1967: 96) writes that 3.5 square miles around Ndola were under cultivation by town-dwelling residents in 1947. By 1954, this area had increased to 11.5 square miles. In addition, memoranda by Spearpoint (at RACM) and Field (at Mufulira) suggest that garden plots were actually encouraged by the mining companies as a form of employment for and income subsidization by workers' wives (ZCCM Archives, file 10.17.10B).

out in the early 1950s that found that anywhere from 60 to 90 percent of adult males in the Copperbelt intended eventually to return to their rural homes (Bates 1976: 57; Ferguson 1990: 609). Remarkably, even among men who had been in town from before the age of fifteen, nearly 75 percent expressed a desire ultimately to return to the village (ibid.).

The practical impossibility of remaining in town at the end of formal employment generated powerful incentives for migrants to do what they could during their tenure in the urban area to facilitate their eventual return to the village. As Epstein (1958: 238–39) puts it, urban laborers were "compelled by circumstance to retain a foot in the rural camp." The principal purpose of this rural foot was to protect the migrant's access to the land on which he would retire and to safeguard the possessions that he had left in the village until he did so.

As we have seen, the colonial regime's interest in bolstering the local authority of the traditional chiefs led it to introduce a communal, rather than title-based, form of land tenure in the rural areas. This policy shaped the investment strategies of migrant laborers by causing them to shift their energies from accumulating financial capital (which under a private property system might be used to purchase land upon retirement) to cultivating relationships with the individuals and traditional institutions that possessed authority over land distribution. Because land could not be bought, migrants interested in maintaining access to land in the future invested in their associations with their tribes and with the chiefs who would serve as the arbiters of their future land claims. A symbiotic relationship emerged between urban migrants and rural chiefs in which "chiefs and elders [held] land against the money which the younger men earned away from home, and . . . the younger men wanted this land against their ultimate retirement from labour migration" (Gluckman 1958: vii).

In addition to controlling the distribution of land, chiefs also served as guardians of the belongings that the migrant left behind in the rural village. The most important of these "belongings" was the migrant's wife and children (Vail 1989: 15). When men traveled to the distant towns for work, they entrusted chiefs to exercise their legal and cultural authority to dissuade wives from "seeking divorces or leaving the rural areas illegally to move to industrial and urban areas" (ibid.).[33] Because the chief's ability to serve this function depended on his stature in the local

[33] The migrant's reliance on the chief to watch over his wife was reciprocated by wives' use of the chiefs to guarantee that they would not be permanently abandoned by their absent husbands. The Northern Rhodesian *Annual Report on Native Affairs* for 1935 noted that some Native Authorities had introduced a local ordinance that

community, migrants had a strong interest in protecting and even building up that stature. Thus, in addition to maintaining their links with traditional chiefs as individuals, migrants also had an interest in making sure that the institution of the chieftainship itself was preserved and protected.

Beyond the somewhat narrow (albeit central) aims of safeguarding access to land and insuring the welfare of their nuclear families, migrants also had an interest in investing over the years in the general vitality of the tribal community to which they planned to return. "When [migrant laborers] eventually retire to the village," van Velsen (1966: 160) explains,

> they do not fall back upon the security of a tribal social system which *happens* to have continued during their absence; the migrants themselves, during their absence, have been contributing actively and consciously to its continuance because they know that they may have to rely on it when they are no longer usefully employed in their urban habitat. . . . The labour migrant sees his contribution as a kind of insurance premium: "How can we expect our *abali* (kin, friends) to help us later when we are old, if we do not help them now?"

This insurance premium was paid in various forms of coinage: gifts were given to the chief; remittances were sent to relatives; respect was paid to Tribal Elders, Native Court members, and other individuals that served as the tribe's urban agents; and opportunities were seized to visit the village from time to time. Although the value of gifts given to chiefs and the degree of respect accorded to urban-based tribal figureheads is difficult to assess, available evidence confirms that significant investments were made by migrants in these other areas. According to data compiled by Wilson, as summarized by Bates (1976: 57–58), urban males in the mining town of Broken Hill visited home on the average once every 3.3 years and spent one-quarter of their time since leaving the village "back home" in the rural area. Wilson also found that a full 10.5 percent of the wages earned in Broken Hill were sent as gifts and remittances to the rural areas. A 1957 survey of the household budgets of 204 African employees at RACM echoes these earlier findings. The survey found that workers spent an average of 11.9 percent of their income on gifts to relatives and remittances to support wives or mothers at home or to pay for the upkeep of cattle.[34] The Seers Report of 1964 provides further evidence of investments by migrant laborers in rural ties, estimating that as many

declared lack of support by an absent husband for two and a half years as good grounds for divorce.

[34] "African Budgeting and Feeding Habits" (ZCCM Archives). Average calculated by the author.

as 75 percent of "wage-earning males in the urban areas" kept up "rural homes with some land under cultivation" (Macmillan 1993: 700).

The data suggest clearly that, to safeguard their futures, urban migrants invested in their relationships with their tribal communities. Mitchell summarizes the pattern succinctly when he writes that the African migrant laborer's "participation in the cash economy in the towns . . . leaves his obligations and duties to his rural kinsmen and his general involvement in the tribal social system unchanged" (quoted in Ferguson 1999: 89). In terms of their investments in their tribal identities, urban Africans acted identically to their rural counterparts.[35] The kinds of investments made by people in each domain may have been slightly different, but the underlying incentives for investing in one's tribal affiliation, as well as the role of the institutions of the colonial state in shaping these incentives, were identical in both cases. Tribal identities among members of the urban segment of the Northern Rhodesian African population were as much a product of colonial policy making as were tribal identities among rural dwellers living under the jurisdiction of the rural Native Authorities.

## THE SHAPE OF THE TRIBAL MAP IN ZAMBIA

The story of why the tribal groups we find in Zambia today came to have the sizes, and also the physical locations, that they do is straightforward. As we have seen, tribes were transformed by the colonial regime into units of territorially based administration. In rural parts of the country, the locations of tribal communities today are a direct product of the boundaries of these administrative units, and their relative sizes are a function of their scope at the beginning of the colonial era plus or minus the members they attracted from or lost to adjacent tribes during Indirect Rule. In urban parts of the country located along the rail line, tribal compositions were

[35] An important body of literature suggests that, while tribal identities were present in both urban and rural domains, the meanings attached to these identities differed in each environment. As Ferguson (1999: 88), following Mitchell (1956), emphasizes, "'tribalism' in town was not simply a persistence of rural tradition but entailed the creation of ethnic categories and stereotypes for use in urban life . . . Even where urban practices seemed to resemble rural traditions, they had wholly different significances and social logics under urban conditions." This may be so, but for our purposes it is immaterial, since what matters for the patterns of ethnic coalition-building I will trace in later chapters is not the meaning attached to one's tribal identity but the information the identity conveys about who is and is not a member of one's group. In this respect, urban and rural tribal identities were identical.

shaped by migration patterns from particular rural areas to particular towns (of which I will say more in Chapter 3), though in no case did a single tribe come to dominate any urban population center. Thus while rural areas in Zambia are a patchwork of relatively small, homogeneous tribal communities, urban areas are tribally heterogeneous. The average index of tribal fractionalization for Zambia's 10 urban districts is 0.88 – implying that if one were to choose two urban Zambians at random there would be an 88 percent probability that they would be from different tribes. By comparison, in the country's 47 rural districts, the average index of tribal fractionalization is 0.54 – a figure that would be far lower if the districts were smaller, since many of them contain more than one tribal group. In 1990, the average size of a Zambian tribe was roughly 1.8 percent of the national population.[36]

Far more ambiguous than the issue of how tribes are distributed around the country and how large they are relative to each other is the question of how many tribes there are in total. The exact answer to this question is not crucial to our analysis, since, as we shall see, what matters for determining the relative political usefulness of tribal and linguistic coalitions is the relative numbers of linguistic and tribal communities in the country, and almost any count of Zambia's tribes will yield a number many times larger than the number of principal languages of communication. Still, the apparent contradiction in the number of tribes I have said Zambia to possess at different points in my discussion presents a puzzle. Perceptive readers will notice that I have provided two separate answers to the question of how many tribes there are in Zambia. On the one hand, I have argued that people's identities tended to coalesce around those tribes that had been designated as Native Authorities, and since only thirty-nine tribes were so designated, this would suggest a tribal map with only thirty-nine units. Yet, in Chapter 1, I claimed that when Zambians think of themselves in tribal terms they see a social landscape with roughly seventy, not thirty-nine, actors. How can we account for this apparent contradiction? Why are people's imaginings of the number of tribes in the country so different from the number of units that actually serve as objects of tribal self-identification?

[36] Standard deviation = 3 percent; max = 17 percent (the Bemba); min = 0.1 percent. The Bemba figure is almost certainly an overestimate generated by the tendency of many Bemba-speaking respondents who were not Bemba by tribe to respond to the census questionnaire by volunteering their linguistic rather than their tribal identity. I will return to this issue, and the data inference problems it generates, in Chapter 4.

The answer is that perceptions and individual-level identities were shaped by different forces. As we have seen, individual-level identifications were shaped by the creation and consolidation of the Native Authorities. The reason Zambians identify themselves and others in tribal terms is because the institutions of BSA Co. and Colonial Office rule classified them in this manner and generated incentives for them to invest in these classifications. Perceptions of the number of units on the tribal map, in contrast, were shaped by books, educational materials, and the pronouncements of colonial officials that, again and again, invoked the number seventy-three when specifying the number of tribes in the territory (Ohannessian and Kashoki 1978: 9). In newspaper articles and editorial columns,[37] political speeches,[38] and popular usage,[39] Zambians invariably invoke the number seventy-three when describing the country's tribal composition.[40]

The idea that there are seventy-three tribes in Zambia can be traced to J. Moffat Thomson's 1934 *Memorandum on the Native Tribes and Tribal Areas of Northern Rhodesia*. Thomson's classification was influential because his *Memorandum* was the first territory-wide count of the tribes of Northern Rhodesia. Although more detailed studies that appeared after his investigation produced slightly different tallies (University College of Rhodesia and Nyasaland 1958; Brelsford 1965; Kay 1967), and although the number that Thomson arrived at was itself arbitrary and subjective, the *Memorandum*'s count of seventy-three tribes quickly became

[37] For example, *Daily Mail*, 2 October 1969, 6 November 1978, 4 December 1978, 27 June 1995; *Sunday Mail*, 27 June 1993, 18 October 1998, 11 March 2001; *Times of Zambia*, 18 March 1997, 21 July 1997, 27 July 1999, 10 September 1999, 24 September 1999; *Weekly Post*, 27 December 1991–2 January 1992; *The Post*, 24 April 1992, 21 May 1993, 7 December 1995; *Weekly Standard*, 30 August–5 September 1993; *The Monitor*, 11–24 September 1998.

[38] Defending the diversity of his government's appointments in a speech to the Southern Province MMD Party Conference in 1995, President Chiluba underscored that "the government had carefully considered all appointments to government or parastatal positions taking into account the 73 ethnic groupings in Zambia" (*Sunday Mail*, 27 June 1995). See also reports of a Chiluba speech in *Times of Zambia*, 7 August 1990, and of a speech by Defense Minister Ben Mwila in *Times of Zambia*, 29 May 1995.

[39] In dozens of interviews and focus groups conducted with school teachers, market sellers, villagers, and church members throughout urban and rural Zambia in 1995, the idea that Zambia has seventy-three tribes was a common – and totally unprompted – theme to emerge in the discussions.

[40] Similar canonical counts of tribes, with similar origins and similarly fuzzy relationships to on-the-ground realities, are found in other African countries. In Kenya, for example, the ubiquitously repeated number is forty-two.

the canonical number that everyone used to summarize the country's tribal makeup.

So hegemonic was Thomson's count that a tendency has emerged among scholars to invoke the fact that Northern Rhodesia has "seventy-three tribes" even if they then go on to provide lists or maps that enumerate a different number. In his *African Survey*, for example, Lord Hailey (1950 pt. II: 81–82) claims that "there are now some 73 tribes in the Protectorate," though a subsequent table lists only fifty-one. Even Thomson himself, after claiming in the text of his *Memorandum* that he had classified the population of the territory into seventy-three different tribes, provides an appendix at the end of the document that lists only seventy-one. Publications by the Zambia Central Statistical Office regularly refer to the country's seventy-three tribes, yet only sixty-one tribal categories were made available to enumerators in the national census. Clearly, the dubious accuracy of the "seventy-three tribes" figure does not detract from the ubiquity of its use. Absent the ability to count the number of tribes with which their fellow citizens actually identify themselves, there is no way for people to know that the figure that they were taught in school and hear repeated in everyday discussions is different from the number of actual identity groupings on the ground. The "myth" of seventy-three tribes therefore co-exists quite comfortably with a very different reality.[41]

[41] Kashoki (n.d.: 7) calls the idea that there are seventy-three tribes in Zambia "a pervasive and erroneous notion."

# 3

## *Accounting for Zambia's Ethnic Cleavage Structure II*

### *The Emergence of Language Group Identities in Colonial Northern Rhodesia*

Chapter 2 showed how the institutions of colonial rule – that is, the policies, rules, and regulations put in place by the Northern Rhodesian colonial administration and its mining company partners – created incentives for Africans to invest in their identities as tribesmen and tribeswomen. In this chapter, I show how a different set of colonial-era actions and policies caused Africans also to think about themselves and the territory's ethnic divisions in language group terms. In addition, just as Chapter 2 showed how colonial-era institutions were responsible for shaping the locations and relative sizes of tribal communities, this chapter accounts for the number, distribution, and dimensions of the groups that make up Zambia's contemporary linguistic landscape.

The chapter is divided into four parts. The first part shows how colonial-era institutions led to the consolidation of language use patterns from a situation where dozens of different vernaculars were in use to one where four major languages predominated. The second part explains how these institutions led Zambia's four broad linguistic communities to have the relative sizes that they do and to be physically located in the parts of the country that they are. Having accounted for the contours of the landscape of linguistic divisions, the third part of the chapter explains why Africans in Northern Rhodesia had incentives to embrace and define themselves in terms of their language communities, and thus why language matters for self-identification and group classification in Zambia today. The final part of the chapter shows how colonial-era policies and regulations help to explain why two other potential bases of social cleavage – class and urban–rural divisions – have not become alternatives to tribe and language as axes of coalition-building in contemporary politics.

## THE CONSOLIDATION OF LANGUAGES IN ZAMBIA

When the first Europeans reached the territory that comprises present-day Zambia, language use corresponded almost perfectly with tribal affiliation. With the exception of a handful of trading peoples that learned regional languages of commerce to facilitate their trading efforts, Africans tended to speak the single language or dialect of their local community, and each community had, more or less, its own language or dialect. Indeed, so close was the connection between community boundaries and patterns of language use that almost all of the earliest tribal maps were, in fact, language maps, with linguistic distinctions serving as proxies for more difficult-to-measure markers like cultural difference or traditional authority boundaries (Prins 1980: 33). At the beginning of the colonial era, Northern Rhodesia was a Babel of languages.

By the end of the colonial era, patterns of language use had consolidated considerably. As early as the late 1940s, Lord Hailey could report the emergence of a set of distinct regional languages in Northern Rhodesia (Hailey 1950). In the northern part of the protectorate, he noted, "Chiwemba is practically the *lingua franca* of the tribes on the [central] plateau" (ibid.: 138). In the east, the dialects of the various groups were "gradually being merged into Chichewa, which is becoming the *lingua franca* of the [area]" (ibid.: 131). In the west, Hailey reported "an increasing fusion of language ... Silozi is becoming the *lingua franca* of the [region] and most of the tribes longest resident [there] understand it" (ibid.: 92). Although Hailey was silent on the extent of linguistic consolidation in the southern part of the protectorate, other authors writing during this period noted the emergence of Citonga as the dominant medium of communication in that region (e.g., Colson 1962).

By the time of Zambian independence in 1964, Bemba (what Hailey called Chiwemba),[1] Nyanja (Chichewa),[2] Tonga (Citonga), and Lozi (Silozi) had achieved the status of first among equals insofar as language use was concerned. By 1990, the first year for which reliable information is available, fully 78.8 percent of the Zambian population used one of

[1] Technically, the prefix "chi" (or "ci," or "si") is used before the name of the tribe to indicate the language spoken by its members (e.g., Chibemba is the language of the Bemba tribe; Citonga is the language of the Tonga tribe). Deferring to common usage in Zambia, I drop the prefix when I refer to languages.

[2] In Zambia, Chichewa and Chinyanja are different labels for the same language. There is no Nyanja tribe, only a Nyanja language. Chewas (and also Ngonis, Nsengas, and Tumbukas) speak Nyanja – although very occasionally they will refer to the language they speak as Chewa.

these four languages as either their first or second language of communication.[3] When we consider that probably no more than a quarter of the population spoke these languages a century before, this figure points to a remarkably rapid consolidation of language use.[4]

The extent to which Bemba, Nyanja, Tonga, and Lozi emerged as dominant regional languages in Zambia is demonstrated in Figure 3.1, which compares the percentage of the national population that used one of seventeen major Zambian languages as their first or second language of communication in 1990 with the estimated percentage of the population that used each language at the beginning of the colonial era.[5] As the figure indicates, the shares of the population using Bemba, Nyanja, Tonga, and Lozi in the pre-colonial period (indicated by the white bars) were only slightly larger than the shares using other languages. By 1990, however, the shares of the population using these four languages (indicated by the black bars) far exceeded the shares that used any of the other languages in the country. Close to 40 percent of Zambians used Bemba as their first or second language of communication, just over 30 percent used Nyanja, about 12 percent used Tonga, and just under 10 percent used Lozi. After these four languages, frequencies of language use drop off considerably. The next most frequently used languages, Tumbuka and Lamba, were used by only 3.8 and 3 percent of Zambians, respectively.

Part of the reason that Bemba, Nyanja, Tonga, and Lozi are as dominant as they are is that people came to learn and use these languages

[3] The reports of the censuses of 1969 and 1980 provide tables with information on first languages of communication only. The figures presented here were calculated from the complete data set of the 1990 census. To guard against double counting, I calculated the percentages of Zambians speaking Bemba, Nyanja, Tonga, or Lozi as a second language from the population of people who did not already use one of these four languages as a first language of communication.

[4] I estimated the percentage of the population that used these four languages prior to the colonial era from the percentage of the Northern Rhodesian population belonging to each of these tribes in 1930, the earliest date for which reliable and comprehensive figures are available. I used 1930 figures rather than 1990 figures for tribal proportions because, as I showed in Chapter 2, the population shares of some of the larger Zambian tribes have increased significantly since the beginning of the colonial era. Using more recent figures would have greatly over-estimated the size of these tribes in the pre-colonial era, and thus the percentage of the population that spoke their languages. My source for the 1930 figures is the Northern Rhodesian *Annual Report on Native Affairs*, 1930.

[5] In their counts of second language use, the figures reported for contemporary language use do not control for people who speak one of the thirteen other languages as a first language. Estimates for language use in the pre-colonial era were calculated as described in note 4 above.

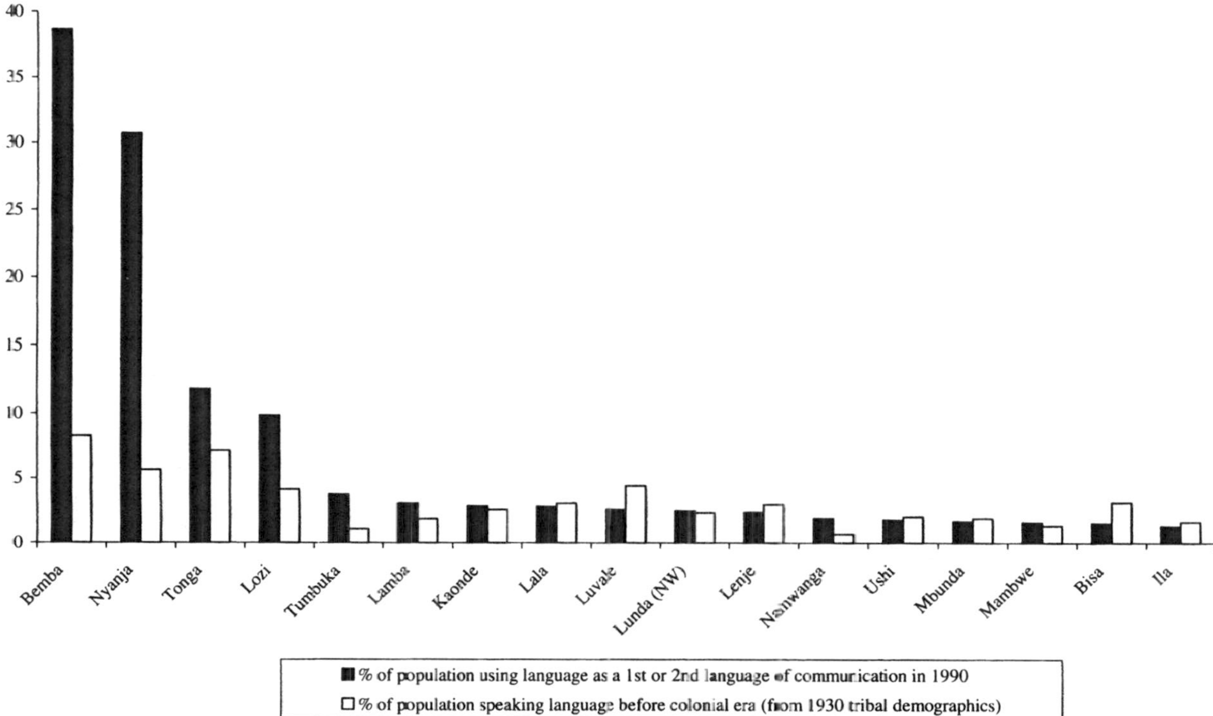


Figure 3.1. Language Use in Zambia/Northern Rhodesia

in lieu of the languages that were traditionally spoken by members of their tribes. Another important reason is that, over time, Zambians came to develop language repertoires that included more than one language of communication: usually one for home use (often their tribal language) and one or more others for commercial or social exchanges with members of other tribes (Laitin 1992). Bemba and Nyanja, and to a somewhat lesser degree Tonga and Lozi, emerged – along with English – as the key languages that came to play this second role. Figure 3.1 suggests that whereas a small part of the growth of these four languages came from stealing shares from other languages, much of it came from the acquisition of Bemba, Nyanja, Tonga, or Lozi as second languages of communication.[6] Indeed, 25 percent of the people who speak one of these four languages do so as their second language.

How can this dramatic consolidation of language use be explained? Some of it undoubtedly took place between the end of the colonial era and 1990. Yet to the extent that it did, this represents the continuation of a trend whose origins lie in the period before independence. Understanding how Zambia's linguistic map was transformed from one containing more than fifty languages to one containing just four major ones requires that we delve into colonial history. As I will show, three colonial-era forces in particular were responsible for the consolidation of language use in Zambia: missionary activity, colonial education policies, and labor migration.

## *Missionary Activity*

Between 1885 and 1945, nearly two dozen missionary societies set up shop in Northern Rhodesia, establishing between them more than a hundred mission stations around the country (Davis 1967; Snelson 1974; Henkel 1985).[7] Although formally set up as evangelical outposts, these mission stations had as important an impact on the territory's linguistic landscape as they did on its religious life. Language was central to the missionary enterprise for a simple reason: in order to teach the gospel, the Bible first had to be translated into the local language. And before the Bible could

[6] Some of it also comes from the nearly total disappearance of the several dozen other languages that were left out of Figure 3.1. Indeed, the seventeen languages included in the figure comprise only 54 percent of total languages in use in 1930.

[7] For similar accounts of the effects of missionary activity on linguistic standardization, see Gulliver (1969) on the Luhya of Western Kenya and Abernethy (1969) on the Igbo of Eastern Nigeria.

be translated, the local language itself had to be written down. Early missionaries in Northern Rhodesia therefore doubled as linguists. Many of them spent as much energy writing grammars, compiling dictionaries, and translating hymns, religious books, and readers into new written vernaculars as they did proselytizing (Johnston 1919; Doke 1945).

Because the transcription of an African language required an enormous investment, missionary societies sought to locate their stations, when they could, in areas where large numbers of people already spoke the same language. However, it was not always possible for missionary societies to choose the sites of their mission stations exactly as they pleased. More often than not, they simply set up shop wherever they could get a toehold away from stations already established on the ground, or where they thought they would be received reasonably well by the local chiefs. Thus many missionary societies found themselves in a position where, once they had reached the entirety of the population into whose language they had translated the key liturgical texts, they simply extended the use of that language to neighboring peoples who spoke different but structurally similar dialects. As Young (1976: 166) writes, "it was only natural to amortize [their investment] by maximizing the diffusion of the standardized language forms to neighboring groups, where possible." The local vernaculars into which the Bible was first translated and for which grammars and dictionaries were first written were thus "exported" from the domains where they were naturally spoken to adjacent areas, where they gradually replaced or came to co-exist with the languages that were previously in use.[8] The fact that the colonial administration encouraged missionary societies to concentrate their activities in separate areas of the protectorate reinforced this economy-of-scale logic and, with it, the process of regional language standardization.

The principal mechanism through which this "export" of vernaculars from one area to another came to affect language use on the ground was through mission-sponsored African education. By 1925, the year

[8] Although economies of scale initially led missionaries to favor using the same language in many settings, the logic of how missionaries in the field received funding from their home societies eventually generated incentives for embarking on translations of new languages. In addition to justifying funding for their work, translating new languages benefited individual missionaries by making them indispensable as experts on particular peoples. The general trend of missionary-led language consolidation therefore was offset to some degree by a counter-trend of (written) language proliferation (Robert Rotberg, personal communication). In some countries – Ghana, for example – missionary activity was actually associated with *increased* linguistic heterogeneity (Laitin 1994: 623). Also see Young and Turner (1985: 142).

Table 3.1. *Missionary Impact on Language Homogenization in Northern Rhodesia*

| Dependent variable is ratio of tribal and linguistic heterogeneity in the district | |
|---|---|
| Urban | 1.62** |
| | (0.527) |
| Log of educational commitment–weighted station decades | 0.758* |
| | (0.305) |
| Constant | 0.551 |
| | (0.435) |
| $R^2$ | 0.15 |

* Significant at the 0.05 level; ** significant at the 0.01 level; $N = 57$.

that the colonial government first entered the education field, missionaries were operating close to two thousand schools throughout Northern Rhodesia with combined enrollments of more than 89,000 pupils (Hall 1976: 83).[9] Even after that date, mission schools continued to play a central role in African education. According to enrollment figures in Snelson (1974: 296), it was not until 1940 that the number of African students in mission schools was exceeded by the number in government-run schools. Even at that time, mission schools had enrollments well in excess of 50,000 students. As "essentially . . . literacy centers, supplemented by training in whatever skills or interests the particular missionary possessed," the early missionary schools had an enormous effect on patterns of language use (Ragsdale 1986: 32). Over time, areas where mission stations proliferated tended to coincide with increasing linguistic homogeneity.

Evidence supporting this link is presented in Table 3.1, which reports the results of a statistical analysis of the relationship between missionary educational activities and the homogenization of language use in Zambia's fifty-seven administrative districts. The dependent variable is the ratio of tribal to linguistic heterogeneity in each district.[10] A perfect correspondence of tribal affiliation and language use (as I argue was the case at the

[9] Some caution is required in reading enrollment figures, as these numbers probably reflect students formally registered in schools rather than the (considerably smaller) number that actually attended school on a regular basis. Hall (1976) estimates that only two-thirds of the enrolled students actually attended.

[10] Heterogeneity ratios were calculated from 1990 census data on tribal affiliation and language usage by summing the squares of the percentages of every tribe (and language group) in the district that comprised more than 5 percent of the district's population and then subtracting the sum from one.

beginning of the colonial era) yields a value of one. Increasing linguistic homogenization is reflected in progressively larger values greater than one, since the denominator (linguistic fractionalization) decreases as the numerator (tribal fractionalization) remains constant. This ratio thus serves as an excellent indicator of the degree of linguistic homogenization that has taken place in the district since the beginning of the colonial era. Note that an advantage of defining the dependent variable in this manner is that it automatically controls for the tendency of missionary societies to locate their stations in districts that were already linguistically homogeneous.

Measuring the impact of missionary activities – the key independent variable – is somewhat more complicated. I began by identifying the present-day districts in which every mission station established in Northern Rhodesia between 1880 and 1960 was located.[11] After recording the number of stations in each district, I then weighted this value by the number of decades that each station was in operation, thereby producing a district-level count of "station-decades." Since education was the mechanism through which missionary activities affected language use, I then weighted each station's impact a second time by the educational commitment of the missionary society with which it was affiliated. Societies strongly committed to African education, like the Free Church of Scotland, the London Missionary Society, or the Universities Mission to Central Africa, received a score of five. Societies with very weak commitments to African education, like the Christian Missions in Many Lands or the South Africa General Mission, received a score of one.[12] These scores were then incorporated into the analysis to produce an "educational commitment–weighted station decades" value for each district. Finally, to smooth out the differences across districts, I took the log of this value for use in the regression analysis. Because language homogenization in urban areas has a logic of its own (to which I shall return), I also included a dummy variable to control for whether the district was urban.

The results of the analysis suggest, first, that urban location matters. For reasons I shall explore, urban settings generate a strong

[11] My key source for the presence and location of mission stations was Henkel (1985). When mission stations were located on or near district boundaries, I drew a circle with a radius of 50 kilometers around the station and assigned "credit" to each district in proportion to the share of the circle located in each. I thank Maria Dahlin for help in assembling this data set.

[12] The educational commitment of each missionary society was assessed by calculating the average number of schools per mission station and by consulting secondary sources on the activities and philosophies of the societies themselves. I am indebted to Robert Rotberg for his advice in this coding effort.

standardization of language use. The more important finding for our present purposes, however, is that, controlling for urban/rural location, districts that contained missionary societies that were committed to the education of Africans had significantly higher ratios of tribal to linguistic heterogeneity in 1990 (i.e., greater evidence of language homogenization) than other districts. Indeed, the estimated regression coefficients suggest that moving from a district with no mission stations to one with thirty years' worth of missionary activity by a society highly committed to African education increases the predicted degree of language standardization by a factor of four. The evidence thus supports the argument: missionary activity does seem to have led to the consolidation of language use.

## *Colonial Education Policies*

The homogenization of language use that was begun by the Christian missions was reinforced and expanded by the policies adopted by the colonial government when it took over primary responsibility for African education after 1925. The most important such policy was the decision taken by the Advisory Board on Native Education in July 1927 to simplify the administration's job by adopting just four languages – Bemba, Nyanja, Tonga, and Lozi – as languages of instruction in African schools.[13] The rationale for this decision was spelled out in a 1926 memorandum from the acting director of native education to the Northern Rhodesian chief secretary:

> Northern Rhodesia unfortunately suffers probably more than any other African protectorate from a diversity of dialects... What are we to do here and now? Our aim should be, I think, to select a limited number of the languages in use in the Territory and to adopt these as official mediums for vernacular teaching in elementary schools... [T]he principal vernacular dialects indicated are (1) Chila-Tonga [Tonga] and (2) Wemba [Bemba]. To these I would add (3) Sikololo [Lozi] for the Barotse District and (4) Chinyanja [Nyanja] for most of the East Luangwa District... no one would deny that there are many other languages in use in the Territory which may be worth preserving and which may survive whether they are adopted as educational mediums by the Government or not. I submit that it is not practicable for Government to support the production of literature in more than, say, four African languages.[14]

[13] "Extract from Minutes of the Ninth Meeting of the Advisory Board on Native Education," July 1927 (Zambia National Archives, file RC/1680).

[14] Letter from G. C. Latham to the chief secretary, Livingstone, 2 August 1926 (Zambia National Archives, file RC/1680).

Indeed, while the board recognized that some pupils initially would have to continue to receive their early primary education in languages other than Bemba, Nyanja, Tonga, and Lozi, it was assumed that eventually these four vernaculars would become, with English, the sole languages of instruction at all levels (Ohannessian and Kashoki 1978: 287).

To give effect to this new policy, the administration established an African Literature Committee – the first of its kind in Africa – to promote the publication of secular schoolbooks in each of these four languages. Between 1937 and 1959, the committee and its successor, the Joint Publications Bureau of Northern Rhodesia and Nyasaland, published or reprinted more than 1.7 million copies of 484 titles, more than 92 percent of which were in Bemba, Nyanja, Tonga, Lozi, or English.[15] The dominance of these languages among the books produced by the bureau is readily apparent in Figure 3.2, which shows the number of volumes published in each major Zambian language in the years 1949–59. Evidence that books in Bemba, Nyanja, Tonga, and Lozi were demanded as well as supplied comes from best-seller lists provided in the Publications Bureau's annual reports. These lists reveal that every single one of the best-selling books in these years was written in one of these four languages or in English.

The demand for vernacular language books was fueled by the growth of African education in the 1940s and 1950s. As Figure 3.3 demonstrates, both school enrollments and government expenditure on African education exploded at the end of the 1930s. Whereas only 25 percent of school-age children were estimated to have been attending school in 1924, the share attending school in 1945 reached 75 percent in some rural districts and exceeded that number in many of the major towns.[16] By 1958, the *Northern Rhodesian Annual Report* estimated that 60 percent of school-aged children were enrolled in schools territory-wide. Major efforts were also made to promote literacy among adults, particularly in

[15] Publications Bureau of Northern Rhodesia and Nyasaland, *Annual Report for 1959*. Although these figures also include a small number of books published for the Nyasaland market, the majority of these books were published in Nyanja and were therefore also usable in Northern Rhodesia. In addition to language texts, the books published by the bureau covered a variety of subjects, from tribal history and African folklore to child care and village sanitation.

[16] The 1924 estimate is from the report of the Phelps-Stokes Commission, cited in Gadsden (1992). Figures for 1945 are from Snelson (1974: 240). High rates of school attendance in the towns were an outcome of the government's decision, after the 1935 Copperbelt riots, to make education compulsory for children between twelve and sixteen years old in the mining towns. Doing so, it was felt, would "keep them out of trouble" (Greig 1985: 42).

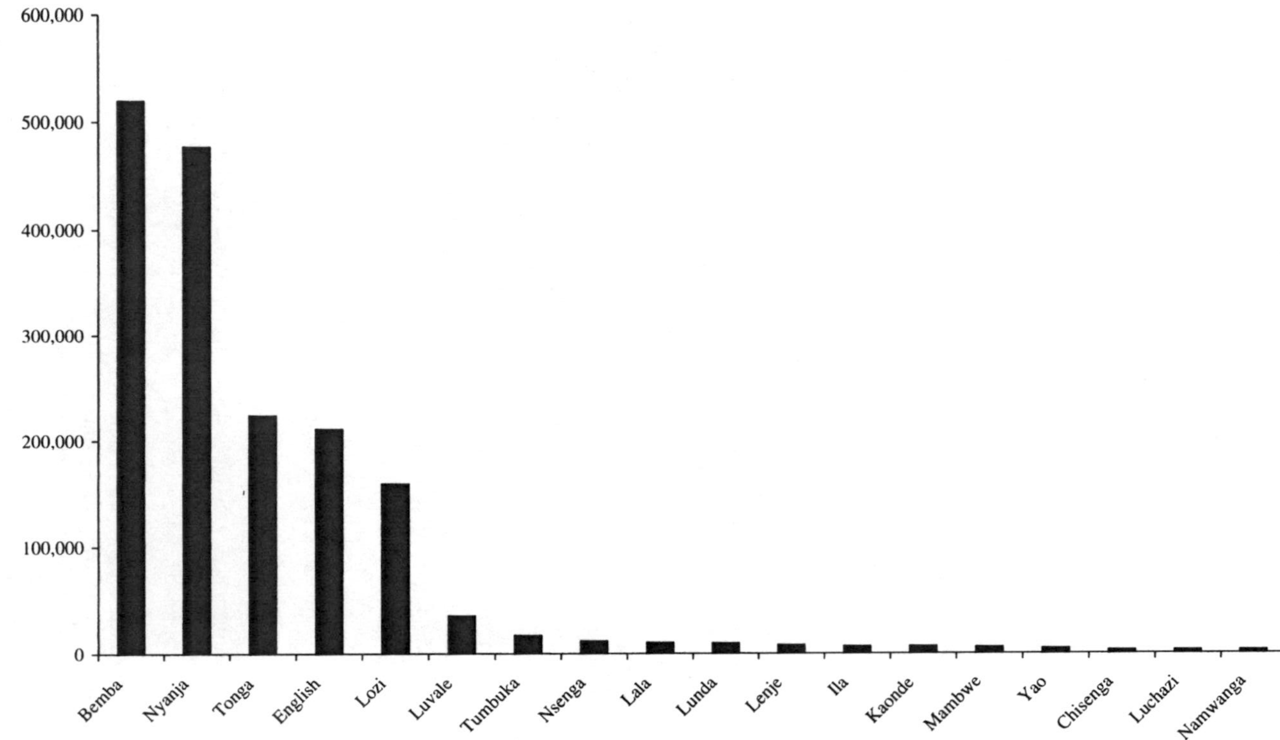


Figure 3.2. Books Published in Northern Rhodesia, by Language, 1949–59

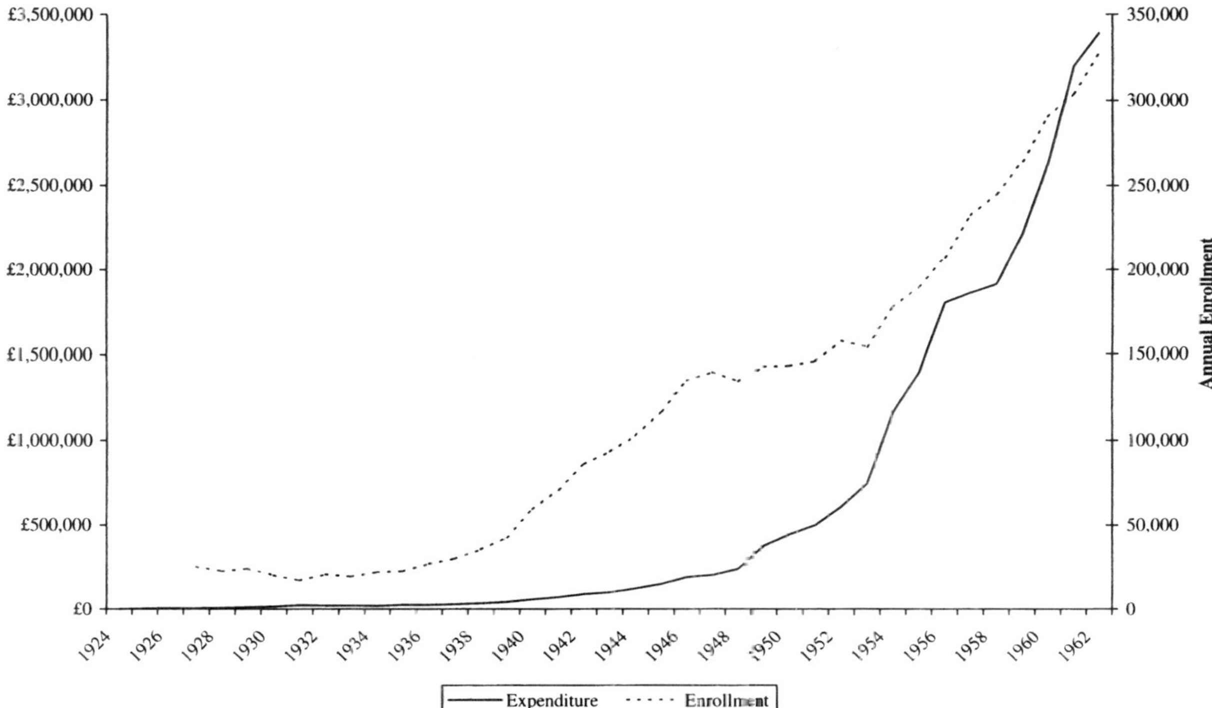


Figure 3.3. Expenditure on and Enrollment in Government-Aided Schools in Northern Rhodesia, 1924–62

the Copperbelt, where, by the late 1950s, more than 4,500 adult men and women attended educational classes each day (Hay 1947; Bromwich 1963). Although many areas of the country remained educational backwaters, the general trend was for greater and greater numbers of Africans to be exposed to formal education and for the quality of that education to improve gradually over time. The fact that the medium of instruction in these schools and literacy courses was either Bemba, Nyanja, Tonga, or Lozi meant that every newly literate student that did not already speak one of these languages as his or her native tongue became a member of one of these language groups.

The impact of formal education on language consolidation was reinforced by trends in the popular media. In 1936, the colonial government began publishing the African newspaper *Mutende* as a response to the Watch Tower Movement, an evangelical religious community whose authority-questioning literature was in wide circulation around the protectorate at the time. Published in Bemba, Nyanja, Tonga, Lozi, and English, *Mutende* reached a peak circulation of eighteen thousand during the war years (Hall 1976: 76). As with most African newspapers, however, the number of people that *Mutende* reached was many times its circulation. During the 1950s, the mining companies also began publishing monthly magazines for their workers. Although most of the stories in these magazines were initially in English, increasing numbers of articles appeared over the years in Bemba and, to a lesser degree, Nyanja.

Even more important than newspapers in bolstering the dominance of Bemba, Nyanja, Tonga, and Lozi in Northern Rhodesia was radio broadcasting. Thanks to the invention and rapid proliferation of the "saucepan special," an inexpensive battery-operated radio set developed specifically for the Northern Rhodesian African population, many thousands of Africans had access to radio in Northern Rhodesia by the 1950s.[17] Largely because it knew it had such a big audience of African listeners, the Northern Rhodesian Broadcasting Service was the first radio service in Africa to allocate significant air time – fully 72 percent in 1952 – to programming in African languages (Mytton 1978: 209). Bemba, Nyanja, Tonga, and Lozi were chosen, with English, as the languages of Northern Rhodesian broadcasting. Because radio broadcasts reached such a large population, the choice of these languages had a critical impact on patterns of language consolidation in the country – more, even, in all

[17] The "saucepan special" was invented by Northern Rhodesia's director of information, Harry Franklin. For a discussion of the radio's origins, see Franklin (1950).

likelihood, than the educational system, which directly touched fewer people. "Over time," Spitulnik (1992: 340) notes, "the selection and dominance of [these] four languages became mutually reinforcing." Africans learned Bemba, Nyanja, Tonga, and Lozi by listening to the radio and, having learned them, demanded more programming in these languages.

## *Labor Migration*

The third major force that contributed to the consolidation of language use in colonial Northern Rhodesia was labor migration. As we saw in Chapter 2, the colonial administration and its mining company partners enacted policies designed to attract thousands of African laborers to the territory's mining centers. The intra-territorial labor flows that resulted had a profound effect on the shape of the country's language map.

A key effect of the administration's policies was to bring an ever-increasing number of migrants from the hinterland to the industrial rail line that connected the mines of the Northern Rhodesian Copperbelt (and Katanga, just across the border in present-day Congo) with the ports of South Africa. Once the migrants were along the rail line, their patterns of language use changed. Since both productivity on the job and everyday interactions in the social sphere required that people be able to communicate with each other, a single language naturally emerged as a common medium of communication in each urban area.[18] And once such an urban lingua franca was established, new migrants who spoke other languages had incentives to learn that lingua franca too in order to participate in the activities of urban life (Epstein 1958). A strong tendency toward linguistic homogenization therefore emerged along Northern Rhodesia's rail line. And the policies that brought thousands of laborers there thus contributed significantly to the countrywide consolidation of language use.

This trend of urban linguistic homogenization is captured by the large and highly significant coefficient on the "urban" variable in Table 3.1, which picks up the wide gulf between the ratios of tribal and linguistic heterogeneity in urban and rural districts of the country. Whereas Zambia's ten urban districts have an average ratio of 2.23 (indicating that they are much more heterogeneous tribally than linguistically), its forty-seven rural districts have an average ratio of 1.5 (indicating that they are also more heterogeneous tribally than linguistically, but far less so than the urban

[18] I deal with the question of *which* language played this role in the next part of the chapter.

districts). Although some of the linguistic homogenization that these figures reflect undoubtedly took place after the colonial era, the data are still suggestive of the effect of labor migration on language consolidation. Since almost all urban residents during the colonial era started out as rural dwellers, the different ratios suggest that the act of moving from a rural to an urban environment affected the likelihood that a person would speak one of the country's principal lingua francas. The data are thus in keeping with the argument that the experience of migration contributed to the standardization of language use.

## THE SHAPE OF THE LINGUISTIC MAP IN ZAMBIA

Missionary activities and colonial education policies help to explain how the dozens of African languages spoken in the pre-colonial period gave way to four principal languages of communication by the time of independence in 1964. Labor migration helps to explain how this trend of language consolidation was carried over from the rural to the urban areas. But the causal mechanisms discussed thus far provide few clues as to why the populations that speak each of these languages came to be physically located in the areas of the country that they are. To be sure, the decision of the colonial administration in 1927 to adopt Bemba as the language of instruction in the northern part of the territory, Nyanja in the east, Tonga in the south, and Lozi in the west does account for the general spatial distribution of these language communities in the rural parts of the country. But it does not explain why different parts of the industrial rail line came to be dominated by the groups that they were. Nor do the variables I have described provide insight into why each language community came to have the size – and thus usefulness as a political coalition – that it does.

Underlying population densities in each region tell part of the story. But given that more than 40 percent of the Zambian population lives along the urban rail line, to fully account for the shape of Zambia's contemporary linguistic map we must look not just at the fact of labor migration but at its *pattern*. We must explain why certain language groups came to dominate certain urban centers.

The pattern to be explained is captured in Figure 3.4. Whereas Figure 3.1 told a story about the consolidation of language use, Figure 3.4 suggests a story about its spatial distribution. The map identifies districts in which, according to 1990 census data, more than 80 percent (dark shading) and 40 percent (light shading) of the population spoke Bemba,

Figure 3.4. Language Communities in Zambia

Nyanja, Tonga, or Lozi as their first or second language of communication in 1990. As the discussion thus far would lead us to expect, each language predominates in a particular region of the country: Bemba in the north, Nyanja in the east, Tonga in the south, and Lozi in the west.

The map also makes clear that, while Zambia's urban areas may share similarly homogeneous patterns of language use (hence the shading in the towns along the rail line), the particular languages that came to dominate each urban setting vary. Bemba emerged as the principal language of communication in the Copperbelt and in the mining town of Kabwe.[19] Nyanja served this purpose in Lusaka.[20] And Lozi came to play this role in

[19] According to 1990 census figures, 90.2 percent of Copperbelt residents (excluding Ndola Rural district) spoke Bemba as their first or second language of communication. In Kabwe, the figure is 77.1 percent.

[20] In 1990, 78 percent of Lusaka residents spoke Nyanja as their first or second language of communication.

Livingstone.[21] Thus, while the circumstances of urban life may have guaranteed the emergence of an urban lingua franca in every town, they did not guarantee that the same language would serve this purpose in each place. The language that emerged as dominant in each urban area was determined by patterns of migration: in keeping with Schelling's (1978) tipping model, the region of the country that supplied the largest percentage of the urban area's migrant population also supplied the language that the urban population came to speak. Accounting for patterns of migration from particular rural hinterlands to particular urban population centers is thus critical for explaining the shape of Zambia's language map. Doing so requires that we turn again to the policies of the colonial administration and the mining companies.

## *Linking Towns and Languages*

The direct link between government and mining company policies and the emergence of particular languages as dominant media of communication in specific urban areas is most evident in the cases of Kabwe and the Copperbelt, where conscious policies were put in place to encourage migration from Bemba-speaking rural areas to the mines that were located in these two places. In other parts of the protectorate, the government's concern was simply to stimulate migrant labor flows of sufficient magnitude to allow taxes to be paid in the rural areas. But in the Bemba-speaking northeast – that is, in roughly present-day Northern and Luapula Provinces – the government and the mining companies conspired not simply to encourage outward labor migration but to make certain that this migration would be channeled to the domestic copper mines. The dominance of the Bemba language in the mining towns was a direct outcome of these policies.

A number of factors having nothing to do with government policies ensured that migrants from the Bemba-speaking heartland would be easy to attract. A combination of poor soil, the presence of the tsetse fly in much of the area, and the great distance that agricultural products had to travel to the markets of the rail line ruled out cash cropping or animal husbandry as a means of earning money to pay one's taxes. The dearth

[21] The dominant position of the Lozi language has been undermined since independence by Tonga-speakers who have aggressively pushed the use of Tonga rather than Lozi on the grounds that, as the capital of a province whose people are overwhelmingly Tonga-speaking, Livingstone should rightly be a Tonga-speaking town. By 1990, only 44.4 percent of Livingstone residents said that they spoke Lozi as their first or second languages of communication.

of European settlers in the area also meant that local cash employment opportunities were limited. Thus, to an even greater degree than in most other regions of the protectorate, residents of the northeastern part of Northern Rhodesia had few alternatives to labor migration (Richards 1939; Moore and Vaughan 1994).

This may explain why Bemba-speakers were willing to come to the mines for work, but it does not explain why the government and mining companies went to such great lengths to bring them there. The reason they did had to do with the geography of the labor market in the southern African region. Of all the rural areas of Northern Rhodesia, the Bemba-speaking northeast was located farthest from the South African and Southern Rhodesian mines. Moreover, established labor migration routes from Bembaland ran from east to west (to Katanga, via the Northern Rhodesian Copperbelt) rather than from north to south (to Southern Rhodesia and South Africa), as they did in the other parts of the protectorate. At the time when the Northern Rhodesian mines began production in the late 1920s, the Bemba-speaking northeast thus constituted a labor reserve where the Copperbelt companies faced relatively little competition from their better-paying South African and Southern Rhodesian rivals.[22] By focusing the bulk of their labor-recruiting efforts on the northeast, and by protecting this region from competition by labor recruiters from the mining centers to the south, the Northern Rhodesian mining companies could – and did – keep the wages they paid at less than half the prevailing rates in the rest of Southern and Central Africa. In 1933, for example, wages at the Rand mines averaged three shillings per shift, while wages in the Northern Rhodesian mines averaged just one shilling per shift.[23]

Evidence from internal mining company documents confirms that wage calculations were the principal motivation for focusing labor-recruiting efforts on the northeastern part of the protectorate. A revealing moment

[22] The cessation of large-scale labor recruitment from Northern Rhodesia by the Union Miniere du Haut Katanga in the early 1930s removed the other potential rival for African labor from the northeast and freed up large numbers of Bemba-speaking men who might otherwise have followed traditional migration routes to Katanga. Because the Katanga mines paid very low wages – lower even than those paid by the Copperbelt companies – the Northern Rhodesian mines did not have to worry about matching the wages to which former Katanga workers were accustomed (Perrings 1979: 258).

[23] "Report of the [Northern Rhodesian Native Labour Association] Manager's Visit to Livingstone in Reference to Labour Matters," 20 September 1933 (ZCCM Archives, file WMA 139).

came in 1933 when the Union of South Africa withdrew its voluntary embargo on recruiting African labor from Northern Rhodesia. This alarmed the Copperbelt mining companies, who were concerned that the already steady flow of Northern Rhodesian migrants to the south might increase to the point where the protectorate's own labor supply would become insufficient to meet local needs. If this were to happen, the manager of the Northern Rhodesian Native Labour Association (NRNLA) worried, "our only means of meeting competition" from the South African mines would be to "increas[e] our wage scale...and the resultant extra costs to our mines would be £225,000 on a year...This extra cost would obviously result in a reduction of profits."[24] Anxious to avoid a situation of competitive recruiting with the Rand mines that might bid up African wages in the Northern Rhodesian mining areas, the Copperbelt companies told the Northern Rhodesian government that they would be "prepared to abandon all recruiting activities in the [western part of the protectorate] and leave that area open to the Rand recruiters provided that, in turn, they [the Rand recruiters] would not encroach on any other Northern Rhodesian districts."[25] The goal, the NRNLA manager made clear, was to ensure that the introduction of South African labor recruiting would "not materially diminish our labour resources in the Northern and Eastern areas."[26] Recognizing that its own revenues depended on the profitability of the Copperbelt mines, the government agreed to protect these areas by adopting the NRNLA's proposal to limit Rand recruiters to the western districts.

The mining companies' efforts to forge links between the Copperbelt and Kabwe and the Bemba-speaking northeast during the 1930s went far beyond the protection of this area from foreign labor-recruiting agents. When the NRNLA began recruiting labor for the Copperbelt and Kabwe-based mines in 1930, the largest share of recruits were intentionally drawn from Bemba-speaking areas.[27] When the mines came back on line in the mid-1930s after the depression, the first rural district officers instructed to lift their restrictions on issuing passes for migrants to travel to the Copperbelt were those in Kasama, Fort Rosebery, and Abercorn, three

[24] Ibid.

[25] Ibid.

[26] Ibid.

[27] In part, this was an outcome of stereotype-driven assumptions that the martial history of the Bemba tribe made Bembas good laborers. On the effects of such stereotypes on labor-recruiting policies and Copperbelt social relations, see Luchembe (1992: 30–49).

of the most populous Bemba-speaking districts.[28] And when, at the insistence of the colonial government, the mining companies agreed in 1939 to underwrite the construction of rest camps along labor migration routes to the Copperbelt and Kabwe, nine of the ten camps that were constructed were built along routes from the Bemba-speaking northeast.[29] This decision represented both a recognition of the nature of existing migrant flows and an investment in perpetuating them.

All of these efforts led, by the end of the 1930s, to the establishment of well-defined labor migration routes between Bembaland and the Northern Rhodesian mining centers. In 1937, fully 51 percent of the African workers employed at the Copperbelt's three largest mines were from the Bemba-speaking northeast (Pim report, cited in Berger 1974: 15). This is a remarkable figure when one considers that the northeast contained only between 20 and 25 percent of the protectorate's total population and that it was not the most proximate area from which labor might have been recruited. By 1961, the proportion of Copperbelt laborers from this area was over 60 percent (*Chamber of Mines Year Book*, cited in Harries-Jones 1965: 130).[30] This number was more than sufficient to tilt the linguistic balance in favor of Bemba as the urban lingua franca of the mining towns. Given that, by the time of independence, the mining areas contained nearly a quarter of Zambia's total population, the role of the colonial government and the mining companies in establishing Bemba as the principal language of communication in the mining towns had a profound effect on the shape of the contemporary Zambian linguistic – and also political – map.

The government's role in shaping the languages that came to dominate Livingstone and Lusaka, the territory's two other major urban population centers, was less direct than in Kabwe or the Copperbelt. Although the colonial administration did have a hand in encouraging the Lozi- and Nyanja-speaking migrants who came to dominate these towns to leave their rural homes in search of wage employment (it did this everywhere in the hopes of enabling rural Africans to meet their tax obligations), the administration did little specifically to encourage these migrants to settle in Livingstone or Lusaka. The fact that large numbers of Lozi- and

[28] Letter from NRNLA Manager A. Stephenson to RACM Manager F. Ayer, 4 August 1933 (ZCCM Archives, file WMA 139).

[29] ZCCM Archives, file WMA 135.

[30] This figure excludes alien laborers, who tended to return to their home countries after their period of employment and whose presence in the mining towns therefore did not permanently affect the language balance.

Nyanja-speaking migrants eventually settled in (and lent their languages to) these towns was, more than anything else, a product of the limited transportation infrastructure that was available at the time.

Livingstone became a Lozi-speaking town because, after the completion of the rail bridge connecting Northern and Southern Rhodesia in 1904, it served as the railroad terminus for trains heading south to the mines of South Africa and Southern Rhodesia. From before the turn of the century, the Lozi-speaking hinterland had served, with the administration's encouragement, as one of the major Northern Rhodesian labor reserves for these southern mines.[31] The construction of the Mulobezi-Livingstone railway, which covered half the distance from the center of Barotseland to the south-bound rail terminus at Livingstone, cemented the close link between Lozi migrants and the town by greatly reducing the cost of and time required to get to the Livingstone railhead (Philpott 1945: 50–54). Thus, when Livingstone-based industries like the Zambezi Sawmills began hiring larger numbers of workers in the 1930s and 1940s, the makeup of existing flows of south-bound migrant workers through Livingstone guaranteed that the most plentiful supply of laborers would be from Lozi-speaking areas. In addition, at least some Lozis were recruited directly to Livingstone by the Northern Rhodesian government. Intensive missionary education work undertaken in Barotseland at the behest of the Lozi paramount chief meant that Lozis were among the best-educated Africans during the first several decades of the century, and this made them especially sought after for the colonial civil service. During the brief period (1924–1935) that the colonial administration was situated in Livingstone, well-educated Lozis were recruited to work as government clerks and interpreters. By 1956, two-fifths of Livingstone's population was from Barotseland (McCulloch 1956). Although Lozi-speakers were never a majority, they were by far the largest group in the town, and the Lozi language became Livingstone's urban lingua franca.

Nyanja came to play this role in Lusaka for similar infrastructure-related reasons. Before the opening of the Northern Rhodesian copper mines, the colonial administration encouraged Nyanja-speaking migrants from the eastern part of Northern Rhodesia to forge links with the mines and farms of the south, particularly those in Southern Rhodesia. After the

[31] The close link between the Lozi-speaking western portion of the protectorate and the Rand mines was forged in 1940 when the Northern Rhodesian government began permitting the Witwatersrand Native Labour Association (WENELA) to recruit laborers from this area for the South African gold fields.

late 1920s, the government and mining companies also began recruiting men from this area to the Copperbelt. The nearly total absence of north–south roads directly linking eastern Northern Rhodesia with either Southern Rhodesia or the Copperbelt, however, meant that Nyanja-speaking migrants from the east had to travel along the Great East Road (completed in 1928) until it met the rail line in Lusaka before they could turn south or north toward their ultimate destinations. Until the late 1940s, Lusaka served as little more than a way station for these Nyanja-speaking migrants from the east. By the 1950s, however, both the colonial administration, which had moved to Lusaka in 1935, and the various businesses and industries that had located there began to demand significant numbers of African laborers. Since Nyanja-speakers from along the Great East Road comprised the majority of the available work force, they became the majority of settlers in the town. By 1959, they made up more than 40 percent of Lusaka's population (Bettison 1959). And because Nyanja-speakers made up the largest single language group, their language became the lingua franca of the town.

For all three of these urban areas, early patterns of labor migration – generated in one case by conscious policy and in the two others by infrastructure constraints – led to the entrenchment of migration links between each town or segment of the rail line and a different rural hinterland. In each case, the language of the rural hinterland became the lingua franca of the urban area. These linkages are evident in Figure 3.4, which depicts major roads and rail lines connecting the Bemba-speaking northeast with Kabwe and the Copperbelt, the Nyanja-speaking east with Lusaka, and the Lozi-speaking west with Livingstone.

Only the Tonga-speaking language area, which straddles the southern half of the line of rail, does not have its own urban enclave. In fact, the single major town located within the Tonga-speaking zone, Livingstone, is a Lozi-speaking rather than Tonga-speaking area. The reason for the absence of a Tonga-speaking urban enclave is that, in contrast to people living in the Bemba-, Nyanja-, or Lozi-speaking rural areas, Tonga-speakers had abundant opportunities for local employment, either on the many European farms located along the rail line or as cash croppers or cattle herders. The fact that Tongaland was bisected by the railway line meant that any crops or cattle that were raised there could be inexpensively transported to markets in the Copperbelt or in Southern Rhodesia. Tongas thus could meet their tax obligations either by hiring themselves out to local European farmers or by engaging in rural agricultural production. Migration to distant urban employment centers was unnecessary and, for the most part, avoided. According to data presented in Hellen (1968: 99), fully 62 percent of the taxable males from the Tonga-speaking Southern Province were at work locally in 1961. Comparable figures for the other major rural areas were just 20 percent for the combined Bemba-speaking populations of Northern and Luapula provinces, 21 percent for the Nyanja-speaking Eastern Province, and 25 percent for the Lozi-speaking Barotse Province.

Figure 3.4 also reveals another map-shaping effect of urban migration. In addition to affecting patterns of language use in the towns, the linking of each urban area with a specific rural hinterland also affected patterns of language use along the routes that the migrants traveled. Notice that the Bemba- and Nyanja-speaking zones extend like fingers from their linguistic epicenters toward their respective urban satellites.[32] Over time, the languages spoken in the rural hinterlands were diffused to the areas located between the migrants' homes and their urban destinations.

### *Northwestern Province: The Exception that Proves the Rule*

A final, quite obvious, point to note about the map provided in Figure 3.4 is that the entire northwestern portion of the country is unshaded, signifying that none of the four major languages of communication took hold in this area. Not only have Bemba, Nyanja, Tonga, and Lozi been unable to penetrate the northwest, but no single local language has managed to emerge as a dominant regional lingua franca for the area. Although the Lunda, Kaonde, and Luvale languages enjoy first-among-equals status in this part of the country, none of them has approached the positions of dominance that Bemba, Nyanja, Tonga, and Lozi have established in their respective rural regions. According to 1990 census figures, Lunda, Kaonde, and Luvale were spoken as a first or second language by 34.3, 28.1, and 23.9 percent of the population of Northwestern Province, respectively. By comparison, Bemba was spoken as a first or second language by 70 percent of the populations of Northern and Luapula Provinces, Nyanja was spoken as a first or second language by 86 percent of the population of Eastern Province, and Tonga was spoken as a first or second language by 79 percent of the population of Southern Province. From

[32] The absence of a similar bulge in the Lozi-speaking rural epicenter toward Livingstone is largely an artifact of the highly aggregated district-level data from which the map in Figure 3.4 was created. A map drawn from more fine-grained data would reflect the influence of Lozi-speaking migrants on patterns of language use in the area between Livingstone and the Lozi epicenter.

the standpoint of language use, the northwest constitutes the great exception to the trend of colonial policy–driven linguistic standardization in Northern Rhodesia. As I shall argue, however, it also constitutes the exception that proves the rule. For it is precisely the absence of the factors that explain the linguistic consolidation that took place in the rest of the country that explains the preservation of multiple languages of communication in Northwestern Zambia.

First, missionary societies, which played such a central role in consolidating patterns of language use elsewhere in the protectorate, could not play this role in the northwest for the simple reason that, because of population scarcity and transportation difficulties, very few missions were located there. Moreover, until 1931, the few missionary societies that did build stations in this area tended to be evangelical groups that were far less concerned with African education and language work than their counterparts from the mainline denominations that set up shop in other parts of the territory (Gadsden 1992: 104).[33] Indeed, while the average "educational commitment–weighted station decades" value for all rural Zambian districts is 33.5, the average for the six districts located in present-day Northwestern Province is just 8.2 – significantly lower than for any other rural province.

Second, colonial education policies, which had bolstered the positions of Bemba, Nyanja, Tonga, and Lozi by designating them as vernaculars of instruction in schools and making them priority languages for book publishing, made no special arrangements for the major northwestern languages and thus did nothing to stimulate their diffusion outside their tribally defined core areas. As Figure 3.2 revealed, only a small fraction of the books published by the government in the 1950s were in Lunda, Kaonde, or Luvale. Although radio broadcasts in Lunda and Luvale were begun in 1954 (Kaonde was added as a seventh language at independence ten years later), these two languages were allocated only half the air time of Tonga and Lozi and less than a third of the air time of Bemba and Nyanja (Mytton 1978: 210). The inclusion of these languages on the broadcasting roster, while no doubt contributing to their prestige (Spitulnik 1992: 341–42), thus probably had little effect on language standardization in the northwest.

[33] According to Doke (1945), the first grammars or dictionaries in Lunda, Kaonde, or Luvale did not appear until the 1920s. Bemba grammars and language handbooks, by contrast, dated from 1904; Nyanja sources from 1885; Tonga primers from 1906; and the first Lozi (Kololo) grammar from 1914.

Finally, although large numbers of men from northwestern Northern Rhodesia migrated to the Copperbelt (along with the Bemba-speaking northeast, the northwest had the largest percentage of males at work outside their villages of any region of the protectorate), Northwesterners never came close to equaling the number of Bemba-speaking migrants in even the most northwestern of the mining towns (Hellen 1968: 99). According to figures cited in Harries-Jones (1965: 130), migrants from the northwest constituted only 8 percent of the non-alien workforce in the Copperbelt mines in 1961. Of course, even if they had constituted a larger percentage, the variety of languages spoken by migrants from the northwest would have presented a significant obstacle to a northwestern linguistic takeover of the Copperbelt. Lunda, Kaonde, and Luvale therefore never challenged Bemba as the Copperbelt's lingua franca. Rather than recruit speakers of other languages to their own vernacular (as Bemba-speakers did in the mining towns, Lozi-speakers did in Livingstone, and Nyanja-speakers did in Lusaka), migrants from the northwest either adopted Bemba outright or expanded their linguistic repertoire to include Bemba as a supplementary language. Labor migration therefore did not have the same effect on the diffusion of the northwestern languages that it did for Bemba, Nyanja, or Lozi.

## FROM LANGUAGE USE TO LANGUAGE IDENTITY

Thus far I have shown why patterns of language use in Zambia have consolidated around Bemba, Nyanja, Tonga, and Lozi, and why the speakers of these languages have come to occupy the regions of the country that they have. I have yet to explain, however, why these languages became sources of self-identification among those who spoke them. Doing so is a prerequisite for understanding why language identities came to constitute such powerful axes of political mobilization after independence.

The principal forces that encouraged Northern Rhodesians to identify themselves in linguistic terms were migration and the competition for employment. When migrants came to work in the towns, they found themselves in a thoroughly unfamiliar environment. Quite naturally, they tended to congregate in groups of people similar to themselves. But because of the enormous diversity of tribes in the urban environment, understandings of "similarity" had a tendency to expand to include people from one's region (which meant language group) rather than simply one's tribe. "Urban residence," Young (1976: 42) explains, "places persons in juxtaposition and social interaction with culturally differentiated individuals . . . from far more diverse provenience than would be characteristic in the countryside. For both self and other, it is inconvenient to interpret social reality through too complex a mapping system." The process of simplifying one's "mapping system" involved substituting broad linguistic labels for more narrow tribal ones. This affected not only the way people divided up the highly heterogeneous world of "others" that confronted them in the urban environment but also the way they defined themselves in juxtaposition to the "others."

Describing the situation in the Northern Rhodesian Copperbelt during the 1950s, J. Clyde Mitchell, the preeminent student of urban ethnicity in Southern Africa noted that

> town-dwellers display their ethnic origin by the language they speak . . . this enables members of other tribal groups immediately to fit their neighbours and acquaintances into categories which determine the mode of behaviour towards them. For Africans in the Copperbelt, "tribe" [*sic*] is the primary category of social interaction, i.e., the first significant characteristic to which any African reacts in another. (1956: 32)

Although Mitchell employs the term "tribe," he makes it clear that the boundaries of the "tribal" groups he is describing were defined by both in-group members and out-group members in linguistic terms. "There is a tendency," he writes,

> for the Bemba and other tribes from the Northern Province to consider the Chewa, Nsenga, Kunda and other people from the Eastern Province, for example, as "Ngoni" [i.e., Nyanja-speaking] . . . In the same way, the Eastern Province tribes tend to lump together the Lungu, Tabwa, Eastern Lunda, Bemba and other Northern Province tribes in one category – the "Bemba." (1956: 30)

What was true in the Copperbelt was true in the other towns as well: the extreme heterogeneity of the Livingstone and Lusaka populations also undermined the usefulness of tribal designations as means of organizing and making sense of the urban environment. In these towns, as in the Copperbelt, broader linguistic criteria were used as the basis for social categorization. Thus, despite their centrality in the village setting, tribal identities and labels were eclipsed by linguistic designations in the urban areas. Social interactions and conflicts were viewed through a tribal lens in the village and through a linguistic lens in the towns, and migrants viewed their world through each of these different lenses as they passed back and forth between the urban and rural domains.

Prior to the era of widespread labor migration, when rural Africans' worldviews were constricted to the villages in which they lived, it might have been possible for villagers to view all social interactions in tribal terms. But the constant circulation of people between the urban and rural sectors meant that village life could not remain insulated from the perspective-broadening and identity-shaping influences of the towns. Thus, while tribal categories continued to organize social life in the village, over time linguistic categories came to be used by rural Africans to organize the broader world that lay outside of it. Thanks to the influence of migration, Africans' mental maps of the village-level and protectorate-wide social landscapes came to be built from different dimensions of ethnic identity. Local interactions and conflicts were seen in tribal terms, and national-scale interactions and conflicts were seen in linguistic terms.[34]

But linguistic identities were a product of more than simply a psychological need to simplify a complex social environment. As with tribal identities, there was also an important instrumental rationale in identifying oneself in language group terms. A striking illustration of this point is provided in Colson's account of rural Tongaland in the 1940s. Recalling what she saw at the time, Colson (1968: 204–5) writes that

> school boys recently returned home from the secondary school [in Lusaka] were ardent advocates of the development of local culture and the rights of the local [Tonga] language as against other African languages. They were angry that one of the languages of the territory, not their own, had been accepted as a school language in which examinations could be passed... [And] when they heard that [a language other than Tonga] was to be one of the languages of instruction in the territorial agricultural school to be built within their district, they argued passionately that this honor should be given to their own language because it was the language of the district.

Why was it so important for the schoolboys to protect the position of their Tonga language? Perhaps the passion of their reaction was a product of their exposure in Lusaka to an ethnically mixed environment, and to the deepening of linguistic identifications that such exposure generated. But a larger part of the explanation is almost certainly instrumental.

The expansion of the mining and administrative sectors in Northern Rhodesia during the 1940s brought a great demand for clerks and other literate civil service personnel in the towns. Coupled with the prestige that came from holding such positions, the salaries paid for these jobs, while low compared to what European employees earned, were as much as four

[34] The model presented in Chapter 5 provides a more formal, strategy-oriented explanation for the tendency for urban dwellers to ignore tribal distinctions and categorize themselves and others in language group terms.

times what one could earn as a peasant farmer. Berger (1974: 16) estimates that, "just after the Second World War, annual village income, including the estimated value of subsistence farming, was thought to be £4.16s per head, while the average income for a person in town was calculated at £16.17s." Prestige was also an economic asset: a man could use it to reduce the marriage payments he was required to make or to marry a "more desirable" woman from a wealthier family. This was an important consideration in a matrilineal society where a man's wife's family would provide for his children. The students' linguistic patriotism can thus be best interpreted as an attempt to preserve their access to high-paying civil service positions. This interpretation is supported by the fact that their central concern was that they would be forced to pass examinations in a language that was not their own, which, of course, would disadvantage them in the competition for civil service posts vis-à-vis job seekers from rival language communities. The students reacted as they did because the stakes – both in economic terms and in terms of social status – were so high.

Having devoted the time and energy to learning to read and write in a given vernacular – and colonial education policies guaranteed that this vernacular would be either Bemba, Nyanja, Tonga, or Lozi – educated Africans had strong incentives to protect the status of their language against the encroachments of others. And once certain languages had achieved special status in the civil service – which Bemba, Nyanja, Tonga, and Lozi did – people who had mastered literacy in them had strong incentives to identify themselves in terms of the languages in which they were proficient. By designating certain languages as civil service lingua francas, and by making literacy in these languages a prerequisite for consideration for civil service appointments, the colonial government created reasons for Africans to invest in their memberships in these privileged language groups by learning how to read and write in them and, once this was accomplished, to identify themselves publicly and proudly in those terms.

## THE WEAKNESS OF URBAN/RURAL AND CLASS IDENTITIES AS BASES FOR POLITICAL COALITION-BUILDING

Thus far, in the last chapter and this one, I have focused on showing how colonial-era policies and regulations caused tribal and linguistic identities to come to be viewed by political actors in post-independence Zambia as natural ways of thinking about the country's ethnic divisions. I suggest that this explains why these two identities have come to be viewed as potential building blocks for political coalitions in contemporary Zambian politics. In this final section, I seek to complete my account of the origins of Zambia's cleavage structure by explaining why two other identities – those built around urban/rural divisions and around class distinctions – failed to emerge as commonsensical bases of self-definition and group categorization. When Zambians think about the natural lines of political and social conflict in their country, they think in terms of tribe and language, but not in terms of urban/rural divisions or class. I show that the reason urban/rural identities have failed to emerge as a potential axes of political cleavage is because the policies and administrative structures of the colonial regime left no basis for their emergence as such. I show that colonial institutions played a somewhat less decisive, though still important, role in undermining the emergence of class identities as well.

Clearly, other identities, such as those based on gender, age, occupation, clan, lineage, or family position (among many others), also serve as bases of social differentiation in everyday life. But when Zambians turn their attention outward from the towns and villages in which they live to the domain of national political competition, these identities fail to provide blueprints for the country's wider social landscape. Despite their relevance at the family and local community levels, national-level political identity distinctions are simply not made in these terms. Part of the reason this is so is that the colonial state – the entity that grouped the disparate peoples of present-day Zambia into a common political unit and thereby made comparisons of the groups located within its boundaries thinkable – failed to employ these identities as categories of social organization.

### *Urban/Rural Divisions*

As we have seen, a variety of policies implemented by the Northern Rhodesian administration and the mining companies led to the migration of thousands of Africans from their rural villages to the urban rail line. Given the conflicting interests, concerns, and policy preferences that rise from living in each of these domains, we might have expected an urban/rural cleavage to have emerged between the residents of these two areas. We might have expected people's identities as townsmen/women and villagers to have solidified to the point where appeals to such identities would resonate and generate political mobilization. Yet this is not the case. The urban versus rural card has almost never been played in Zambian politics, and, when it has been, its mobilizational effect has been extremely weak. Take the case of the National Lima Party, which was formed prior to the 1996 general election as an explicitly farmer-oriented political organization. Although the party pitched its appeal at the roughly 70 percent of the population engaged in agricultural production, it managed to capture less than 7 percent of the vote. The party's very poor showing in the election, and its subsequent collapse, attests to the weakness of appeals couched in urban versus rural terms.

The unavailability of the urban/rural cleavage as an axis of political mobilization follows directly from the colonial-era policies that generated incentives for urban Africans to maintain close links with their rural kin. Thus far, I have focused on the consequences of these linkages for the perpetuation of tribal identities among urban migrants. Another important consequence was that households came to straddle the urban/rural divide. This, in turn, meant that the emergence of identities based on a person's urban or rural residence was unthinkable. For rural villagers to identify themselves as "rural" would be to exclude from their identity group the urban relatives on whose remittances they depended. For urban migrants to identify themselves as "urban" would be to erect a boundary between themselves and the sector on whose economic and social vitality they were counting on to support them in their retirement. The natural difference in interests between urban dwellers and rural dwellers highlighted by Bates (1981) and others, which might have driven a rift between town dwellers and villagers in the immediate post-independence era, was thus neutralized by the fact that, thanks to the colonial-era policies I have discussed, Zambians maintained one foot – either as individuals or through their extended families – in each of the camps.

This pattern of maintaining complementary interests in the urban and rural sectors, while perhaps a product of colonial-era institutions, has continued into the post-colonial era. Long after the lifting of the ban on permanent urban residence (and thus urban retirement) that forced Africans to maintain their linkages with their rural villages, urban-based Zambians still find it much cheaper to retire to the village, and thus they continue to maintain strong interests in the economic health of their former (and future) rural home areas. As Ferguson (1999: 110) writes:

> the precipitous decline of Zambia's urban economy in [the 1980s] has meant that retired or laid-off workers have found it much less desirable (often virtually impossible) to stay in town ... The continued relevance of rural retirement means that most mineworkers are obliged to consider some social nexus of relatives "back home" as an unavoidable part of their life's social context.

Ferguson reports that, of the fifty retiring mine workers he interviewed, "forty-seven were making active plans to return to a home village, while two were planning to start farming in rural areas surrounding the Copperbelt, and one was planning to join relatives in Lusaka" (ibid.: 40).

In the same way, village dwellers intent on benefiting from the lodging, jobs, capital, or market access made available by their urban-based kin have powerful reasons for viewing their own interests as bound up with those of the urban sector. Zambians have responded to the weakness of the country's economy by spreading their household members across urban and rural sectors so as to diversify their income streams (Ashbaugh 1996). In such a context, it is very difficult to code most Zambian families as either "urban" or "rural," let alone attribute homogeneously "urban" or "rural" interests (or identities) to their members. From the standpoint of political identity repertoires, such intra-family connections across towns and villages make it inconceivable for most Zambians to either view the country's political divisions in urban/rural terms or mobilize themselves for political action along urban/rural lines.[35]

## *Class Divisions*

What about class divisions? The salience of class in Africa, either as an objective social category or as a focus of subjective self-identification, is a subject of heated debate (Sklar 1979; Young 1986). The specific question here, however, is whether Zambians view their country's basic social divisions in class terms, and whether class distinctions might thus compete with tribal and linguistic distinctions when Zambians try to sort themselves into winning political coalitions. The answer is that, by and large, class identities are not sufficiently deeply felt for them to play this role. As with urban/rural identities, the reason they are not may be traced to policies and institutions that were put in place during the colonial era.

In the immediate post-independence era, the administrative regulations of the colonial state guaranteed that there would be very little class differentiation within the African population, at least outside the mining sector. Throughout the colonial era, Northern Rhodesia's economy was dominated by foreign capital and regulated by economic policies designed to block opportunities for wealth accumulation by indigenous Africans.

[35] A similar account can be provided for why gender has not been a viable axis of political mobilization: even more clearly than urban/rural distinctions, gender divides households.

Although a handful of African property owners and businessmen existed during this period, government policies insured that their numbers would be far too small for them to constitute (or for their members to see themselves as) a capital-holding class. Indeed, outside the mining sector, where the organization of production necessarily gave rise to class distinctions, measurable class stratification was almost nonexistent in the Zambian population at the end of the colonial era. Baylies and Szeftel (1982: 190) report that, on the eve of independence, only 6 percent of trading licenses were held by Africans, and these were overwhelmingly held by small traders. This figure almost certainly represents a high point, as the number of Africans with such licenses was undoubtedly lower during the earlier part of the colonial period. In the rural areas, objective differentiation among peasants was very modest and, at any rate, limited to a handful of wealthier agricultural districts (Momba 1985).

Since that time, however, a sharp gap has emerged – as it has in most African countries – between a small privileged elite that enjoys access to state resources and the vast majority of citizens that do not (Sklar 1979). The Africanization of the civil service, the expansion of the parastatal sector, and the economic reforms of the late 1960s and early 1970s all opened the door to capital accumulation and business ownership by those with ties to the state. This led, by the early 1970s, to the emergence of demonstrable differences in wealth and economic power across different segments of the population. In short, although the colonial experience left little basis for their formation, objective class differences did emerge in the post-independence era. But were such differences paralleled by the emergence of class consciousness? When Zambians think about their country's political and social conflicts, do they view them through a class lens? The answer to this question would need to be "yes" for class to serve as an alternative to tribe and language as a basis for political coalition-building.

The overwhelming answer given by scholars who have addressed this issue is "no." Class differences may be objectively identifiable in Zambia, but, except perhaps on the Copperbelt (Burawoy 1972; Gertzel 1975; Sklar 1975; Parpart 1983), they are peripheral to politics. Molteno (1974: 80) writes that "in Zambia, neither leaders nor followers have perceived class membership as a variable relevant to their political behavior." Scarritt (1983: 6) asserts that "extensive participation by the less privileged classes in conscious pursuit of their class interests has not occurred in Zambia to any significant extent." And Chikulo (1988: 48) argues that "although class formations have emerged [in Zambia], ... class *per se* has not become sufficiently important as a basis of cleavage and conflict in electoral politics." Survey evidence reported in Ollawa (1979) confirms the weakness of class identities in post-independence Zambia. Only 46 percent of respondents in his 1975–77 survey even identified the existence of a difference between the upper class and the working or lower class in Zambia, and fewer than half of these could identify what the basis of these class differences entailed.[36] Ollawa concludes that "despite the underprivileged position of the poverty-stricken masses vis-à-vis the members of the ruling class, the former do not on the average possess even the minimum degree of class sensitivity considered a prerequisite for the emergence of class consciousness" (380).

In post-independence Zambia, therefore, the dominant potentially mobilizable social cleavages have been limited to those built around tribal affiliation and language group membership. When Zambians think about who they are and who their potential ethnic coalition partners might be, they do so in terms of tribe and language. Political competition and conflict is seen through the lens of tribal affiliation and language group membership. These two bases of social identity constitute the complete menu of social identities that are available to Zambian political actors when they try to build and secure membership in winning political coalitions. I turn in the chapters that follow to the question of when and why they will find it most useful to choose one instead of the other.

[36] Ollawa's sample consisted of 1,491 respondents drawn from six towns: Lusaka, Luangwa, Mazabuka, Mongu, Kitwe, and Kasama.

PART II

# *Introduction to Part II*

## *Accounting for Ethnic Coalition-Building Choices*

As a consequence of the administrative policies of the Northern Rhodesian colonial state and its missionary and mining company partners, Zambians in the post-independence era came to view both their own ethnic identities and the country's larger social landscape in terms of two competing schemes of ethnic classification: one defined by affiliation with one of the country's six dozen tribes, and the other defined by membership in one of the country's four principal language groups. Each scheme of ethnic classification implies a very different landscape of political competition and conflict. It also provides people with a very different set of criteria for determining, in the course of that competition and conflict, who is and is not a member of their ethnic group.

The question is: given this ethnic multi-dimensionality, can we generalize about the conditions under which Zambians understand politics as a struggle among the country's tribes rather than as a conflict among its language groups? Can we construct an explanation to account for when one of these ethnic cleavages will become politically salient rather than the other? Part I furnished the background necessary to ask these questions. Part II provides the empirical and theoretical tools with which to answer them.

Chapter 4 provides the foundation for our explanation by showing why ethnicity matters in Zambia and how it is used politically. The chapter shows that ethnicity matters because of the widespread expectation that politicians will channel patronage resources to members of their own ethnic groups. It documents this claim with original data from surveys, focus groups, and elite interviews, as well as evidence from speeches, newspaper reports, and secondary sources. The chapter then shows how this expectation generates predictable patterns of ethnic appeal making by politicians and electoral support from voters. Whereas most studies of ethnic politics in Africa simply assume that ethnicity motivates political action and build their models of political and social conflict without accounting for why this might be the case, Chapter 4 carefully documents the expectations of ethnic favoritism that are at the heart of my explanation for Zambians' political behavior.

Having done this, Chapter 5 then presents an argument to account for why certain kinds of ethnic appeals and voting patterns tend to predominate in different institutional settings. The account begins with a simple model that builds on the empirical foundations laid in Chapter 4 to explain why political actors who possess multiple ethnic identities, and are thus faced with a decision about which one to mobilize, make the choices that they do. The chapter then relates this model to the question at hand by showing that the choices actors make will be sensitive to the boundaries of the arena in which political competition is taking place and that changes in political institutions (including the shift from multi-party to one-party rule) can alter the boundaries of the political arena and thereby change the choice outcome. The chapter then applies the model to the Zambian case to account for why tribal identities have tended to play a central role in the country's politics during periods of one-party rule whereas linguistic identities have tended to do so under periods of multi-party rule.

# 4

## *Ethnicity and Ethnic Politics in Zambia*

This chapter lays the foundation for the argument presented in Chapter 5 by accomplishing three tasks. In its first part, the chapter establishes the relevance of ethnicity in post-independence Zambia by showing that ethnic group memberships underlie people's perceptions of how patronage resources are distributed by those who enjoy access to them. I show that, in a context where all politicians promise to distribute jobs and development resources to the people whose votes they are seeking, voters use ethnicity as a cue to help them distinguish promises that are credible from promises that are not. I argue that it is the information that ethnicity is assumed to convey about likely patterns of patronage distribution – not atavism or tradition – that explains why it plays such an important role in Zambian political life.

The second part of the chapter shows how these expectations shape the strategies that politicians, parties, and individual voters employ to construct and secure membership in winning political coalitions. Specifically, I show that, because Zambians assume that having a member of their own ethnic group in a position of power will increase their access to patronage resources, they are inclined to join coalitions led by members of their own ethnic groups, to be sympathetic to electoral appeals couched in ethnic terms, and to be skeptical of promises made by leaders of groups other than their own. I show that, knowing this, politicians and parties appeal to voters' ethnic affiliations in predictable ways.

The third section of the chapter shows how the calculations that give rise to such coalition-building efforts are complicated by the fact that a person's ethnic background can be understood in more than one way. Depending on whether a person thinks of his ethnic background in tribal or linguistic terms, that person will identify himself with a very different set of in-group and out-group members, respond favorably to different kinds of ethnic appeals, and perceive as salient a very different axis of political competition and conflict. For coalition-building politicians and political parties, the ability to alter people's perceptions of the nature of the political playing field by invoking different dimensions of ethnic identity constitutes an extremely valuable political resource. For individual voters, the ability to claim membership in ethnic groups of different sizes is similarly advantageous. However, for the analyst of Zambian political affairs (and of ethnic politics more generally), the ability of politicians and voters to choose strategically the ethnic identity they will use to define themselves presents an empirical and theoretical challenge: namely, to identify the conditions under which one principle of group differentiation will emerge as the basis for ethnic coalition-building rather than another. Meeting that challenge is the objective of the chapter that follows.

It is important to underscore that the purpose of this chapter is *not* to show that ethnicity is the only factor motivating the behavior of Zambian politicians or voters. Not only is this not the case, but it need not be. Answering the question that this book poses does not depend on showing that ethnicity is the sole determinant of political action. It depends simply on being able to account for the relative salience of tribal and linguistic identities within the portion of people's political behavior that can be accounted for by ethnicity. Of course, ethnic motivations have to play at least some role in shaping people's behavior for this exercise to be meaningful – and the evidence presented here clearly shows that they do. But they need not be the only factor.[1]

## ETHNICITY IN ZAMBIA

In some respects, Zambia would appear to be an unlikely choice of country for a study about ethnic politics. High rates of inter-tribal marriage reveal many Zambians to be relatively unconcerned about ethnic attachments in their day-to-day social relations.[2] In surveys and focus groups, Zambians

[1] Of course, the fact that ethnic motivations are only part of the total explanation for political behavior has important implications for testing the arguments I advance, which I discuss in Part III of the book.

[2] Calculations from 1990 census figures suggest that roughly 46 percent of all married Zambians living in urban districts and 32 percent of those living in rural districts have spouses from different tribes. The rural figure is particularly striking when we recognize that many such areas are so homogeneous that simply *finding* a marriage partner from a different tribal group would be difficult (though, of course, many

claim to attach only minimal importance to ethnic group affiliations as motivations for their political behavior. Of the nearly 1,200 Zambians questioned in a 1996 University of Zambia/Michigan State University (UNZA/MSU) Democratic Governance Survey (Bratton 1996), fully 83.6 percent agreed that: "When it comes to politics, being a Zambian is more important than belonging to a particular tribe."[3] My own 1995 survey (N = 252) yielded very similar results.[4] When asked which they put first when it came to politics, being a Zambian or being "a member of their group," 83 percent of respondents said they put being a Zambian first. When asked which they thought was more important, to support a politician from their own group or to support the politician with the best abilities, even if he was from a different group, 85 percent said they thought it was better to support the politician with the best abilities. When asked whether they thought that "people can only rely on members of their own group," only 30 percent agreed. A focus group participant in Luanshya (LY T) spoke for many of her peers when, in response to the question about whether Zambians tend to support members of their own groups, she said: "The element of supporting members of your own tribe is there, but it is maybe one over a hundred or so" (i.e., 1/100 of the explanation). This remarkably "non-ethnic" political orientation is reflected in – and is in no small part a product of – the pronouncements of the country's public officials, newspaper editors, and civil society leaders, who regularly denounce "tribalism" as retrogressive and incompatible with national development.[5]

But public pronouncements (and survey responses) can be misleading. Zambians today may marry in large numbers across tribal lines, tell survey enumerators that they put their national identity before their ethnic

such couples may have met in urban areas and moved to rural districts by the time of the 1990 census).

3 These survey results, and all others reported here, exclude respondents who said they "were not sure."

4 Details of the survey and the accompanying focus group work, including information about the codes used in the citations, are provided in Appendix B.

5 Examples of such denouncements include: "A United Nation" [guest editorial by Vice President Mainza Chona], *Times of Zambia*, 24 October 1968; "The Dangers of Tribalism," *Daily Mail*, 2 October 1969; "Kapwepwe Raps Chimba: 'We Are All One Family,'" *Daily Mail*, 27 January 1971; "We Must Root Out Tribal Politics," *Daily Mail*, 15 November 1973; "Tribalism Out: Kaunda Warns of 'Zambian Chad,'" *Daily Mail*, 28 September 1983; "Chiluba Warns," *Sunday Mail*, 27 June 1993; "Is Zambia Going Tribal?" speech by MMD National Secretary Godfrey Miyanda, Pamodzi Hotel, 6 December 1993; "ZIMT Complains About Tribal Appointments," *The Post*, 18 July 1997.

affiliation, and loudly condemn manifestations of "tribalism" in the country's politics. Yet, below the surface, Zambia is still a place where ethnicity matters. Though disdained in public, ethnicity nonetheless serves as one of the principal lenses through which Zambians perceive their social and political environments. It undergirds expectations about how others will behave; it colors understandings about where social conflicts originate; and it shapes perceptions about who stands to gain – and to lose – from the current distribution of political power. It is "the topic of discussion at nearly all informal fora and gatherings" (*The Monitor*, 11–24 September 1998). Ethnicity may not play this role for every person or in every situation, but it does so much of the time and for a very large share of the population.

Indeed, for every Zambian who chooses a spouse from a different tribe, there are nearly two that marry within their groups. For every columnist who claims that "there is no such thing as tribalism in this country,"[6] there is another to pronounce such assertions as "naive" or as coming from someone who "definitely does not understand the problem."[7] And for every focus group participant who insists that "we should not support a person simply because he is a member of our group," there is another to argue that, although such a practice may be wrong, the attitudes that lead to it "are still there locked up in people's minds . . . It is not right that they do it that way but they are doing it" (LIV-M). The zeal with which Zambian political leaders, like political leaders across Africa, denounce tribalism reflects the existence of a strong social norm against open confessions of ethnic motivations, and this may explain why survey respondents are reluctant to admit to having their political behavior shaped by "tribal" considerations. When asked whether they would willingly support members of other ethnic groups Zambians may be engaging in what Kuran (1995) terms "preference falsification": they publicly espouse a view that they privately reject.[8]

[6] Carolyn Mwanza, *The Post*, 1 December 1995.

[7] Bill Mufana, responding to Mwanza, *The Post*, 24 January 1996.

[8] Some evidence that this may be the case is that focus group participants, when pushed by their peers, frequently conceded that ethnicity is, in fact, a more important component of their political calculations than they first admitted. Since the opinions of survey respondents could not be challenged in this manner, the survey results are probably more likely than the focus group discussions to have been colored by Zambia's strong anti-tribalist norms. Also, many focus group and survey respondents who insisted that ethnic considerations were not a part of their own political decision making were quick to describe members of other ethnic groups as "segregationist," "tribalistic," or otherwise ethnically motivated.

In many Zambian businesses, hiring decisions and promotion prospects are widely assumed to be linked to a person's ethnic group membership. "Someone gets into a company and then brings all their relatives," one focus group participant explained. "Jobs are *wako ni wako* [Nyanja for 'yours is yours' or, more loosely, 'your relatives first']" (LIV-W).[9] A focus group participant from Luanshya expressed exactly this sentiment when he insisted that "Zambians put their own groups first" in the workplace:

> If Mr. Zulu [a common Eastern Province name] were to be a manager and he asks where I come from and I tell him that I come from Eastern Province, he will treat me properly and possibly employ me. But for some others . . . he would just know they are not from Eastern Province and tell them "there is no vacancy". (LY-MS-W)

Another focus group participant (LY-MS-M) explained: "If the man at the top comes from a certain area of Zambia . . . you find that the people who come after him are all from the same area . . . It is just a matter of helping someone because he is from the area, do[ing] a favor for him." A newspaper column echoes this theme:

> There are organizations in this country, even foreign-owned for that matter, where almost every name, from the manager down to the office orderly, belongs to one region . . . In this country, professionally qualified youngsters never find jobs if they belong to the "wrong" tribes . . . [W]hen you enter certain . . . offices, you get the impression they are tribal establishments. (*The Post*, 24 January 1996)

Respondents told me that even securing a bank loan can be difficult if one belongs to the "wrong" ethnic group. According to one account, whereas loan officers tend not to be particularly stringent with applicants from their own groups, applicants from other groups sometimes find that the lending institution will "work to rule [i.e., follow guidelines to the letter] instead of using common sense and being flexible as they do when they deal with their favorite applica[nts]" (*The Post*, 7 December 1995).

[9] The pervasiveness of this perception is reflected in the existence of similar sayings in other languages. For example, the equivalent phrase in Lozi is *wahao ki wahao*. Another common saying with a similar meaning is *naiwe ulilepo* (Bemba for, roughly, "you should also enjoy while I am there"). Often it is expressed as an injunction: *Tumubikepo tulilepo!* ("Let us put him there and benefit from him!"). Among Tonga-speakers, the proverb *mesu aangu nulimbele* ("my eyes go before me") carries a similar meaning: that people who have already arrived in positions of power will "look out" for opportunities for me.

Such perceptions of ethnic group favoritism, widespread in the private sector, are even more prevalent when it comes to resources controlled directly by the government. From the President to the lowest-ranking civil servant, public officeholders are assumed to use their power to assist members of their own ethnic groups. They may not have many resources to distribute – in many contemporary African states, budgets are extremely thin. But it is widely assumed that they will use whatever resources they can control to build schools, clinics, and roads in their home areas and provide jobs for people from their ethnic group. They are also expected to channel donor aid or relief food to their regions and to be helpfully selective in their enforcement of bothersome regulations and taxes.

Survey evidence confirms that almost half of Zambians think that the President's region of the country gets more than its share of development resources. In the 1996 UNZA/MSU survey (Bratton 1996), 49 percent of respondents agreed that "the President's region of the country gets more government services than any other region." In my own survey, 44 percent of respondents said that they thought that "people from the President's region benefit more than people from other areas of the country." "The President is not giving attention to other areas," one focus group participant complained. "He wants his area to develop through fishing and agriculture to become the second money-spinner after the Copperbelt" (LY-MS-M). "Yes, look at [then President Chiluba's home province of] Luapula," a survey respondent protested. "It is not a farming area but already fertilizer has been sent there" (SR 17). Another survey respondent complained that "the best road contractors are assigned to [President] Chiluba's favorite provinces ... while the [inferior] roads department is given the assignment of mending the roads here and in other provinces of little importance to him" (SR 99). Another recalled:

> One time I was watching a program on TV which showed Chiluba's village. It was being electrified. [It had a] good road network. They are doing so because that is where he comes from. It shows that you have to elect someone from your place because development will be there. (MON-R-M)

A veteran politician concurred that "people have come to expect that when you become President, the people of your area will benefit a lot."[10] A market seller in Chipata summarized the feelings of many Zambians when he said, simply: "Where I come from, I'll develop. That's what is going on" (CPTA-MS-M).

[10] Interview with William Chipango, Livingstone, 16 December 1995.

First learned during the rule of Zambia's first leader, Kenneth Kaunda, the lesson that the President will favor his own ethnic group has become, for many Zambians, an axiom of politics. Not surprisingly, this perception is particularly strong among Zambians that are not members of the President's group. At the time of my field research, Frederick Chiluba, a Bemba-speaker, was President. Whereas only 23 percent of Bemba-speakers in my survey said they thought that "people from the President's region benefit more than people from other areas of the country," 52 percent of non-Bemba-speakers said they thought that this was the case. These perceptions persist despite the fact that there is little evidence that patterns of resource expenditure actually *are* biased in favor of the President's region. This was the conclusion drawn by Dresang (1974) and Bates (1976) about the 1960s and early 1970s, and, to judge from figures in the annual reports of provincial development expenditure during the 1990s, it remained true under President Chiluba. In fact, some evidence suggests that President Chiluba's home province of Luapula was actually *disadvantaged* vis-à-vis other provinces in securing financial assistance from the government for its development programs (*Times of Zambia*, 4 September 1996). The widely held perception that the President's part of the country *must be* benefiting from his rule is much more powerful than the facts on the ground.

Evidence that this is the case comes from the fact that some of the most vocal critics of presidential favoritism routinely mis-identify the province the President comes from. A Livingstone market seller told me that she knew President Chiluba's region of the country was benefiting more than her own "because we hear through our ears and radios [that] in Kasama they have done this and that; in Kasama they are re-surfacing the road; in Kasama they have taken relief food there; in Kasama they have gone to assist the less privileged... We hear that development is being taken up there – a lot of it" (LIV-MS-W). Apart from her exaggeration of Kasama's good fortunes, the problem with the market seller's "evidence" is that Chiluba is not, in fact, from Kasama. He is from Luapula Province, another Bemba-speaking area some 250 kilometers away. Several other respondents made similar mistakes, variously identifying the President's home area as Kasama, Northern Province, or the Copperbelt – all Bemba-speaking areas, but not his actual home.

In addition to being perceived to be channeling development funds to his home region, the President is also widely assumed to favor members of his own ethnic group when it comes to making governmental appointments. Again, there is often a misidentification of beneficiaries, since the recipients of the most sought-after jobs and appointments tend to be close relatives of the President (in-laws, cousins, and other extended family members) rather than members of his ethnic community more broadly. Even so, the social unit that is presumed to benefit is the tribe or language group. Indeed, whenever a new cabinet is announced or an old one is reshuffled, newspaper columns and letters to the editor focus in minute detail on the number of positions won by each ethnic group and readers scrutinize these accounts like box scores, trying to confirm their expectation that members of the President's ethnic community have been given the most important positions.[11] Although every Zambian cabinet since independence has been mixed in its ethnic makeup, all of them have been alleged by one group or another to favor people from the President's ethnic community. President Kaunda's early cabinets were criticized for being Bemba-dominated; later, they came to be viewed as biased toward Nyanja-speakers (Molteno 1974; Bratton 1980: 212–13).[12] President Chiluba's cabinets were criticized for being filled with his fellow Bembas (*Weekly Post*, 15–21 November 1991; *The Sun*, 25–31 October 1993; *The Monitor*, 11–24 September 1998). One focus group participant protested that "if you look at the ministers, you find that... one man is a Bemba, a second man is a Bemba, a third man is a Bemba ... It is very bad" (CPTA-R-M). "Look at the key ministerial posts," another commented. "They are not evenly distributed. They are all held by the Bembas" (MON-R-M). "And you find," a third noted, "that [when the cabinet is reshuffled] these people who have dominated... are not shaken... Some tribes are permanent" (CPTA-T). As with the distribution of development resources, the perception of Bemba domination is particularly strong among non-Bembas.

[11] For examples of such scorekeeping, see: "Tribalism in Zambia: Who Are Encouraging It?" *The Mirror*, March 1968; the speech made by an unnamed Luapula minister, 25 March 1971, quoted in Bates (1976: 330 n17); "Provincial Autonomy Could Solve the Tribal Question," *Weekly Post*, 24–30 April 1992; "Tribal Feuds Continue," *The Sun*, 25–31 October 1993; "Bembas Are the Worst Tribalists" (letter to the editor), *The Post*, 24 March 1995; "Tribalism in Zambia," *The Monitor*, 11–24 September 1998.

[12] Kaunda's parents were missionaries from present-day Malawi who settled, when Kaunda was quite young, in Chinsali, in the heart of Bemba-speaking Northern Zambia. Thus despite a Malawian heritage that would ordinarily have placed him in the Nyanja-speaking camp, Kaunda was for many years identified as a Bemba (a categorization supported by the fact that he spoke Bemba far better than Nyanja). But his association with the Bemba grouping was severed in 1971 following his perceived betrayal of Simon Kapwepwe, the undisputed spokesperson for Bemba interests, after which point Kaunda came to be associated with Nyanja-speakers and the Eastern Province.

Although I did not ask respondents directly whether they thought that members of the President's ethnic group were over-represented in the cabinet, I did ask whether they thought that people from their own areas had received a fair share of government appointments. On average, only 36 percent of respondents thought that they had. But while fully 61 percent of Bemba-speakers answered the question affirmatively, only 27 percent of non-Bembas did so. This suggests that members of the President's group feel far less aggrieved about their group's representation in the senior government bureaucracy than do members of other groups.

Critics concede that Bembas do not occupy every ministerial position. But they are quick to emphasize that the non-Bembas who enjoy front bench appointments tend to occupy junior positions or to be given "dormant" portfolios that "[do] not wield the necessary power to benefit . . . the people in [their] province" (*Sunday Mail*, 7 January 1996). As one Southern Province focus group participant explained, the "minor appointments" that go to people from his part of the country are simply "cosmetic":

> You find that [Southerners] are appointed . . . as deputies. But where do their seniors come from? I think we should look at that angle as well. Why are we not given the priority of running a full ministry? When are we going to have Mr. Hachikoma [a Tonga-speaker from Southern Province] as Minister of Agriculture instead of Deputy Minister or Permanent Secretary? These people that are given the priority of running full ministries come from the same area as the President. (LIV-MS-M)

A column in *The Monitor* titled "All Zambians are equal but . . ." argues similarly that "one can argue that there are some positions that have gone to minority tribes like Tongas and Lozis, but . . . when you come to the crunch, these ministers from so-called minor tribes are not even influential, they are only there as figureheads, while the real power lies elsewhere . . . in the North" (11–24 September 1998).

The handful of non-Bembas who do hold important government portfolios tend to be dismissed by members of their ethnic groups as "inauthentic" representatives of their interests. For example, General Godfrey Miyanda, a Nsenga whose roots are in Eastern Province but who spent most of his life outside of the region, was widely perceived by Easterners during his tenure as Vice President as someone with no allegiance to Eastern Province.[13] Similarly, former Foreign Minister Vernon Mwaanga,

[13] Interview with Deputy Minister for Eastern Province Hosea Soko, Chipata, 17 October 1995.

a Tonga who grew up on the Bemba-dominated Copperbelt, was viewed with suspicion as a spokesperson for Tonga interests. This was vividly illustrated in 1996 when he rose to address the meeting of a Tonga cultural group and was greeted with shouts that he was "not one of us" and the taunt that he should change his name from Mwaanga (a characteristically Tonga name) to Mwansa (a characteristically Bemba one) (*Zambia Today*, 18 February 1996).

The assumption that the President favors members of his own ethnic group extends beyond the cabinet to include the people that he selects as parastatal chiefs, diplomats, judges, and members of government commissions. In the Kaunda era, it was alleged that "to get a job in Zambia today, one has to be a Zulu, a Phiri, a Tembo or a Banda [all Eastern Province names]."[14] After Chiluba took power in 1991, being a Bemba-speaker came to be perceived as the passport to senior government employment. "Chiluba's relations are the ones given those appointments," one survey respondent complained. "If you are not from 'that' tribe [i.e., if you are not a Bemba] you won't be [selected]" (SR 120). A letter to *The Post* (20 January 1999) complained that most of Zambia's diplomats "are in those positions purely on tribal and family grounds and not on merit or qualifications. Otherwise how do you explain the fact that nearly all the diplomats at the Zambian embassy in Belgium and elsewhere are Bembas?" Another letter writer criticized the appointment of the new managing director of the state-run Zambia National Oil Company on the grounds that "his only qualification is that he comes from Luapula Province and is somewhat related by marriage to one of the cabinet ministers. The capable person for the job, [the former director's] long-serving deputy . . . happens to come from the wrong tribe" (*The Post*, 6 January 1999).[15]

An open letter in 1993 from the Eastern Province executive committee of the Movement for Multiparty Democracy (MMD) to the party's national executive committee echoed such sentiments when it demanded to

[14] Peter Chanshi, MP for Mwansabombwe, during parliamentary debate, 1 December 1977, quoted in Ollawa (1979: 388).

[15] The author goes on to charge that, at the Zambia Electric Supply Company, another state-run parastatal, "the Chiluba tribal train has run over the Lozis on the board of directors in preference for Bembas and party cadres. John Muyunda and the only accountant on the board, Eddie Hamakowa, [both non-Bembas] have been removed in preference for Bwalya from Luanshya, the minister's constituency, Bennet Chileshe, Juliet Mpundu and [Sylvia] Masebo's mother [all Bemba names]. A list of Bembas is also reliably understood to have been drawn up to replace non-Bembas on the board of the [Zambia National Commercial Bank]."

know why Easterners who had held senior positions in the major parastatal companies during the Kaunda administration had been replaced by Bembas during the months after Chiluba took power and why no Easterners had been posted as ambassadors ("Open Letter to the MMD National Executive Committee," *Weekly Post*, 2–8 July 1993). A similar open letter from the MMD Southern Province executive committee charged that the party's leaders were behaving "as if the people of Southern Province had no right to lead others." Referring to the favoritism of Bembas over Tongas in appointments to leadership positions in the party, the letter asked: "Must some people in Zambia continue to herd and milk cattle while other selfish and sectarian people like yourselves continue to drink the milk?" ("Open Letter to Mr. Michael Charles Chilufya Sata and Mr. Elias Marko Chisha Chipimo," *Weekly Post*, 21–27 May 1993). Both the fact that the letter was addressed to two senior Bemba-speaking party officials (a point underscored by the authors' inclusion of the addressees' multiple, and tellingly Bemba, names) and the fact that Tongas are famous for their cattle keeping, while Bembas are not, made it perfectly clear to any Zambian reader which groups were the hardworking "herders" and which were the selfish "drinkers." Addressing the provincial party conference a month later, the provincial party chairman was less metaphorical when he complained directly that, in contrast with people from Bemba-speaking areas of the country, "people from the Southern Province have been sidelined in appointments to government, parastatal, civil service or diplomatic service [posts]" (*Weekly Post*, 9–15 July 1993). Such feelings of marginalization were not limited to MMD politicians from the Eastern and Southern Provinces. When President Chiluba nominated a Bemba-speaking candidate as the replacement for the ailing (non-Bemba) speaker of the National Assembly in 1998, MPs from other parts of the country joined those from the South and East in vowing to block the nomination on the grounds that "there is no way that all the key positions in the executive and the legislature should go to the same provinces" (*The Post*, 26 March 1998).

The perception that the President favors his own group is paralleled by an expectation that the ministers, parastatal employees, and other public officeholders that he appoints will also favor their fellow ethnic group members. Colson (1996: 72) notes that people in the Tonga villages where she worked in the 1980s "frequently commented that it was pointless to apply for jobs in such and such ministries because they were controlled by members of other ethnic groups who looked after their own." The ubiquity of such sentiments, which were echoed in comments made by survey and focus group respondents, can be attributed to a combination of personal experiences, secondhand rumors, and a steady diet of newspaper reports and government inquiries into the domination of particular ministries and government-owned companies by particular ethnic groups.[16]

Of course, not all ministers and government officials provide special treatment for their fellow group members,[17] and those that do are often quite discreet about their behavior. But even those who try to be discreet are sometimes discovered. In 1995, a private letter from a senior Bemba minister to President Chiluba surfaced in which the minister asked the President to appoint a fellow Bemba to replace a non-Bemba who was currently serving as permanent secretary in his ministry. The letter read in part: "He was born in Kasama and is Bemba-speaking... this is the man for the job" (*The Post*, 24 March 1995). Other public officeholders, however, are quite open about the fact that they look out for their co-ethnics. Another minister, responding to allegations that he had favored an applicant from his home province in filling a senior position in his ministry, told a reporter bluntly: "If I don't employ my own tribesmen, who will?" (*Weekly Post*, 17–23 April 1992). A focus group respondent almost certainly had such behavior in mind when he observed that "at the local level, [people] are made to believe that someone who can bring development or jobs is someone from that area or that tribe. Why are they saying so? Because they have got the example from the top leadership" (LIV-MS-M). Indeed, for most Zambians, the expectation that people with access to patronage resources will channel them to members of their own ethnic group stems from what they observe government officials saying and doing.

But expecting a certain kind of behavior from others is not the same thing as engaging in it oneself – particularly if one thinks the behavior

[16] On allegations of Lozi favoritism in the senior ranks of the army in the late 1980s, see *Times of Zambia*, 9 February 1990. On Tonga domination of the Zambia Railways in the late 1970s, see *Report of the Commission of Inquiry into the Affairs of the Zambia Railways*, quoted in Szeftel (1982: 16). On Bemba domination at the Kapiri Glass Company in the 1980s, see *The Post*, 24 March 1995. Further examples of how "certain units of the Zambian bureaucracy [became] the preserve of certain ethno-regional groups" are presented in Dresang (1974) and Szeftel (1982).

[17] In a 1993 World Bank/Government of Zambia survey of 1,218 civil servants (Palmer 1993), 55 percent of respondents said that they thought that their "work mates would find it difficult not to favor friends and relatives." A similar share of respondents (58 percent) agreed that "civil servants are under pressure to find jobs for friends and relatives." If this is accurate, then roughly half of civil servants do not provide special treatment for their fellow group members.

is wrong. Of course, many Zambians do not think that ethnic favoritism is wrong. Many feel a strong sense of obligation toward people from their own group, and their acceptance of ethnic favoritism stems from an assumption about what they would do if they were in a government position that allowed them to help their fellow group members. Indeed, several survey and focus group respondents suggested that the practice of favoring members of their own ethnic group or people from their home region was a moral obligation. "You can not go and clean someone else's house when yours isn't swept yet," a focus group respondent insisted.

> You can't do that because it is not normal ... [The President] is a leader. But just like any other person he knows where he comes from. So he has to take development there before he takes it to other areas. (LIV-MS-M)

A survey respondent argued similarly that "there is no one who can put a bone in his own plate and real meat in another man's plate" (SR 107).

At the same time, other Zambians – in fact, a large number – do feel that ethnic favoritism is wrong. A market seller in Kasama spoke for many others when he said that "there should be no discrimination. Just like the Bible puts it: when God made man he said he had made him in his image, not 'in his tribe.' This idea of focusing attention on tribes should not be entertained" (KAS-MS-M). However, Zambians with such views have little choice but to behave in accordance with the expectation that ethnic favoritism will take place. Faced with the logic of a prisoner's dilemma, most decide that, despite their misgivings about the practice, supporting members of their own group is preferable to not doing so and being dominated by people from other groups that do.[18] "It is bad to support a [person] simply because he comes from your tribe," a teacher in Mongu explained, "but we have a situation in Zambia where if you don't support your own man, who else is going to support him?"

> Bembas are supporting Bembas, so even Lozis should support Lozis ... Chiluba is a Bemba [and] Western Province is not benefiting. This is why people are saying now that if we can have a Lozi man on top maybe he will do wonders for us ... So now we support people from our own tribe, which is again very bad. (MON-T)

[18] In my survey, 40 percent of respondents agreed that "if people do not support members of their own group then they will be dominated by members of other groups who do." Tellingly, this share was far larger than the percentage of respondents who, though their answers to questions about whether or not they thought people could only rely on members of their own group (30 percent said yes) or whether they put being a Zambian before being a member of their ethnic group (16 percent said they did), admitted to holding what might be characterized as "tribalistic" views.

In the context of the expectation that others will favor their own, people know that they will be penalized if they do not do so themselves, and they adopt patterns of behavior that they would not have otherwise. As van den Berghe (1971: 515–16) explains:

> Everyone expects everybody to be a "tribalist," and thus finds it easy to justify his own ethnic particularism on defensive or pre-emptive grounds, or ostensibly to re-establish the balance destroyed by the "tribalism" of others. In short order, favouritism becomes endemic, ubiquitous, and virtually inescapable. Universal expectations of "tribalism" lead to a systematic interpretation of others' behaviour as "tribalistic," which in turn produces pre-emptive "tribalism," and the latter further reinforces the expectations. Expected and actual behaviour feed on each other in the classic self-fulfilling prophecy.

It ceases to matter whether people champion tribalism or frown on it. They will behave in a "tribalist" way because they fear the consequences of not doing so. The fact that so many survey respondents told me that tribalism was wrong thus does not imply that it is absent either from their calculations or from their behavior. Despite their preference for a situation in which resources are not distributed along ethnic lines, they find themselves trapped in an equilibrium where ethnic favoritism is the rule, and where they lose out on access to resources if they ignore its implications for political behavior.

## THE POLITICAL USES OF ETHNICITY IN ZAMBIA

The widespread expectation that people in positions of power will favor members of their own ethnic groups with access to jobs, development funds, and other state resources has important implications for the way politics is conducted in Zambia. First, it makes voters inclined to support politicians from their own ethnic groups over others. And because politicians know that voters will do this, it creates incentives for politicians to couch their electoral appeals and frame their coalition-building strategies in ethnic terms. Ethnicity thus emerges as a feature of Zambian politics not, as many commentators on Africa assume, because of the passions it inspires or the traditions it embodies but because of the information it conveys about the expected behaviors of other political actors. For voters, ethnicity provides insight into how candidates will distribute patronage if they are elected. It helps them determine the utility they will derive from having one candidate win the election instead of another. For politicians, it provides information about how voters are likely to cast their ballots and thus which kinds of ethnic coalitions it will be most useful for them to try to mobilize. In devising their strategies to win seats and secure access to public resources, both politicians and voters thus find ethnicity to be a powerful tool.

But why must voters focus exclusively on patronage flows, and not on the policies that each candidate promises to implement? Generally speaking, the utility that a voter derives from a particular political representative should be a function of two things: the utility they derive from the policies the politician implements on their behalf, and the utility they derive from the patronage the politician channels to them. However, in developing countries like Zambia, the policy part of the utility function tends to drop out of voters' calculations. Voters know that the policy-implementing capacity of the state is weak, so they discount the impact of formal policies. In addition, voters have very low levels of information about what their political representatives actually do for them to formulate, lobby for, or push through policies that might benefit them. Monitoring policy outcomes (which are a product partly of the representative's effort and partly of factors outside of the representative's control) is much more difficult for voters than monitoring patronage outcomes, which are immediately visible to members of the representative's constituency. Voters therefore tend to focus their attention on – and to judge prospective political representatives based on their assessments of – the representative's likely performance in the area they can monitor: the representative's distribution of patronage.

Apart from the tendency it generates for voters to allocate their support along ethnic lines, the expectation that people in positions of power will favor members of their own ethnic group also has a second implication: it makes it very difficult, or impossible, for politicians to build multi-ethnic coalitions. If people believe that being in the same ethnic group as a power-holder is a necessary condition for gaining access to the spoils that the power-holder controls, then they will put little stock in the promises of leaders of other groups to help them if they are elected. This does not necessarily imply that political leaders will not *attempt* to build coalitions across group lines. Indeed, for politicians from minority ethnic groups, this may be one of the only viable strategies to pursue. But given expectations about how patronage resources are distributed, politicians' promises to share the spoils of power with members of other groups are not likely to be viewed as credible. And absent an ability to commit credibly to sharing the spoils of power with members of other groups, cross-ethnic coalitions will be very difficult, if not impossible to build. The implications of this point will become clear in the next chapter.

Ethnicity thus serves as a valuable resource for political coalition-building but imposes limits on the kinds of coalitions that can be built. I turn now to a discussion of how ethnic coalition-building works in practice.

### *Candidates and Ethnic Coalition-Building*

In its simplest form, ethnic coalition-building involves politicians emphasizing their ethnic affiliations to fellow group members as a way of signaling their commitment to distribute patronage to those group members and thus win their votes. Of course, not all politicians will be advantaged by such a strategy. Politicians running in constituencies where their ethnic group is a minority will find it disadvantageous to draw voters' attention to their ethnic backgrounds lest they frighten off the supporters from other groups whose cross-over votes they will need to get elected. In such circumstances, politicians try to depict themselves as "above tribe" and focus voters' attention on non-ethnic issues, such as their experience, their record of service to the community, or their qualifications for the job. The best strategy for politicians to play thus depends on the circumstances in which they find themselves: they do best by emphasizing their ethnic group affiliation when running in constituencies where they are members of the dominant group and by playing down their ethnic backgrounds when they are not.

In addition to emphasizing (or de-emphasizing) their own ethnic affiliations, politicians also attempt to improve their electoral prospects by drawing attention to the ethnic backgrounds of their rivals. For the same reason that depicting oneself in ethnic terms is sometimes disadvantageous, emphasizing the ethnic affiliation of one's opponent can often be a very useful political strategy. First, it increases the likelihood that the rival will be able to draw support only from members of his own group. If the rival comes from a small ethnic community, limiting his support to that group can be strategically useful. In addition, drawing attention to one's opponent's ethnic background can be an effective way to mobilize members of one's own group for defensive action. When the charge is made that another candidate is practicing tribalism on behalf of his group, the implicit message is that members of one's own group should do likewise lest they be dominated by the other group. Allegations that secret meetings are being held or that tribal campaigning is taking place in certain areas are interpreted by fellow group members as thinly veiled calls to arms. Szeftel (1978: 343) explains that

> in such cases, no one is named and it is possible to make the appeal in terms of [the candidate's] own commitment to unity and non-tribalism. But the generalized assertion that "some people" are "going around" to organize their followers has a clear meaning to members of the speaker's [ethnic group] and often constitutes an exhortation to them to mobilize against a threat.

Szeftel notes that, during Zambia's 1973 elections, he observed "numerous instances of this 'negative tribalism' in which a candidate would denounce tribalism and immediately elicit the response from his followers that their own interests were being challenged" (ibid.: 343–44). Indeed, ethnic finger-pointing of this sort is such a useful strategy that politics in Zambia tends to revolve at least as much around accusations that rival candidates are affiliated with particular groups or engaged in "tribal campaigning" as it does around the efforts of candidates to identify themselves positively with their own ethnic communities. As with explicit calls for support from fellow group members, the utility of such a strategy stems from the expectation that people in power will channel patronage to their co-ethnics. Here, the emphasis on the rival's "tribalistic" tendencies is simply a means of reminding one's supporters of this fact.

### *Political Parties and Ethnic Coalition-Building*

Just as individual candidates exploit ethnicity as a political tool, so too do the political parties under whose auspices they run. Almost every political party that has ever been formed in Zambia has the words "national," "united," "Zambian," or "African" in its name. In part, this simply reflects the origins of these parties during, or shortly after, the independence struggle, when the goal was to build a unified national front against the British colonial regime. But the choice of these words is also part of an effort to make the parties appear to be national in their orientations: that is, to be "above tribe." Despite such efforts, however, and notwithstanding the fact that many Zambian political parties have historically enjoyed significant support across ethnic lines, every major political party in Zambia since independence has been perceived, to at least some degree and by at least some citizens, to represent the interests of a particular ethnic group or region of the country. In the First Republic, the African National Congress (ANC) was widely seen as a Tonga party, the United

Party (UP) was viewed as a Lozi party, and the United Progressive Party (UPP) was perceived as a Bemba party (*Times of Zambia*, 15 August 1968; Molteno 1972, 1974; Bates 1976; Szeftel 1978; Gertzel et al. 1984; *Weekly Post*, 24–30 April 1992). The ruling United National Independence Party (UNIP) was also viewed in many circles as a Bemba-oriented party, despite the fact that it had support across most of the country and that, by then end of this period, its base had begun to shift from the Bemba-speaking northern provinces to the Nyanja-speaking East. By the Third Republic, UNIP had come to be regarded as an unambiguously Eastern Province party. Indeed, a focus group participant claimed in 1995 that "Eastern Province is UNIP . . . If you come [there], you find that the Ngonis, Nsengas, Tumbukas all [support] UNIP" (CPTA-R-M).[19] Also during the Third Republic, the National Party (NP) was widely viewed first as a Lozi and Tonga party (*Daily Mail*, 24 August 1993; *The Sun*, 25–13 October 1993; *Times of Zambia*, 29 December 1995), and later as a party for the tribes of Northwestern Province (*Sunday Mail*, 13 August 1995; *Times of Zambia*, 18 March 1997). The Agenda for Zambia (AZ) was seen unequivocally as a Lozi party (*Times of Zambia*, 13 November 1996). The United Party for National Development (UPND) was viewed as a Tonga party (*Times of Zambia*, 24 September 1999 and 17 February 2000; *The Monitor*, 24–30 November 2000; *The Post*, 12 June 2001). And the ruling MMD, though enjoying at least some support from every ethnic group, was widely regarded by many Zambians as a party for the Bembas (*Weekly Post*, 8–15 April 1993; *Financial Mail*, 16–23 November 1993; *Times of Zambia*, 29 April 1995 [letter to the editor]; *Sunday Mail*, 13 August 1995; *The Post*, 2 April 1998).[20] Even the Zambia Democratic Congress (ZDC), a party that defied easy

[19] Some of the strongest evidence for the association of UNIP with the Nyanja-speaking tribes of the Eastern Province came in an exercise in which I asked focus group participants to work together to indicate the positions of "the most important groups in the country" – a deliberately non-leading set of instructions – on blank maps of Zambia that I provided (see Appendix B). After indicating the locations of the "most important groups," I asked them to shade, using colored pencils, the locations of the strongholds of the country's major political parties. In every case, Eastern Province was identified as the UNIP zone, and it was often the first party–region pair to be so designated.

[20] Evidence that such ethnic characterizations are not limited to letter-to-the-editor writers or elite newspaper columnists comes from the fact that all of the just-named parties (save AZ and UPND, which were formed after the time of my field work) were identified in both numerous focus group discussions and on the maps drawn by focus group respondents as being linked with the regions and/or groups mentioned.

classification, was identified by at least some political observers as a Bemba-dominated organization.[21]

In the case of every one of these political parties, the identification of the party with a particular ethnic group was as much an outcome of the unprompted equation in people's minds of the party with the ethnic group of the party's president as it was a consequence of active self-definition by party organizers. Given what we have seen of Zambians' expectations about in-group favoritism and what has been written about the highly "personal" nature of African politics (Jackson and Rosberg 1984; Young and Turner 1985; Chabal and Daloz 1999), the association between the ethnic affiliation of the party leader and the presumed sympathies of the party should not be surprising. Zambians simply assume that if the party president is a member of a particular ethnic group then, in directing the functions and setting the agenda of the party, he will put the interests of that group first. Even when the president surrounds himself with deputies from other groups (as party presidents invariably do), the overwhelming tendency is for voters to ignore the vice presidents, secretaries general, and party chairpersons from other groups and to draw their inferences about the party's patronage orientation from the ethnic background of its top leader.

So strong is the assumption that the patronage orientation of a political party can be deduced from the ethnic background of its president that when party leaders change so do peoples' perceptions of the ethnic orientations of the parties. When the National Party was founded in 1993, for example, its interim chairperson was Dr. Inonge Mbikusita Lewanika, the daughter of the former Lozi Paramount Chief. Largely because she was a member of such a prominent Lozi family, the party was viewed by many Zambians as a Lozi party. When Lewanika was replaced later in the year by Baldwin Nkumbula, a Tonga-speaker and the son of the late ANC president Harry Mwaanga Nkumbula, the party came to be seen as a Tonga party. And when Nkumbula was unseated at a party conference two years later by Humphrey Mulemba, a Northwesterner from the Kaonde tribe, the party's presumed ethnic and regional orientation changed yet again. In a similar vein, UNIP, while generally viewed first

[21] After its formation in 1995, the party was labeled by many observers as a vehicle for the "Mbala Mafia," a group of Bemba-speaking Northern Province politicians, two of whose leaders, Dean Mung'omba and Derrick Chitala, had resigned from MMD to form the ZDC. This characterization was echoed in the comments of several focus group respondents and in the maps drawn by focus group participants, which overwhelmingly identified the ZDC as a Northern Province party.

and foremost as a Nyanja-speakers' party, was perceived to have close ties to Tonga-speakers during the brief presidency of Kebby Musokotwane, a Tonga-speaking Southerner, and briefly became identified with Lozi-speakers following the election in 1995 of Lozi Senior Chief Inyambo Yeta as party vice president.

What are the political implications of the tendency for parties to be associated with the ethnic groups of their leaders? From the standpoint of winning support from voters in the leader's home region, the identification of the party with its leader's ethnic group is a great advantage. In fact, as I show in Chapter 8, the home regions of party presidents have been, historically, the parts of the country where Zambian political parties have had their greatest electoral successes.[22] From the standpoint of capturing national power, however, the tendency for Zambians to associate parties with the ethnic groups of their presidents is a problem, since even the largest ethnic group in the country (Bemba-speakers) comprises less than 40 percent of the total population. This means that no ethnic group can constitute a majority coalition in and of itself, and no party without a Bemba-speaker as its leader can win a plurality nationally so long as everyone in the country votes along ethnic lines. To be nationally viable, Zambian political parties must win support across ethnic communities, and this means eschewing public identification with any single ethnic group.

Given such a constraint, parties tend to adopt a strategy of emphasizing non-ethnic issues and condemning tribalism in their public pronouncements and official campaign literature, while quietly playing the ethnic card in the region with whose people they are identified. The goal of this dual strategy is to construct a solid ethnic coalition in the party's home region while still preserving the ability to win pan-ethnic (or non-ethnic) support in the rest of the country. A particularly revealing glimpse of how such a strategy is carried out is provided by the National Party. From the party's inception, as a senior party organizer told me, its founders foresaw that their success would depend on their ability to combat the party's association in voters' minds with Lozi-speakers from Western Province. To avoid this fate, the party adopted an explicitly pan-ethnic name (the "National Party") and chose a unifying symbol (clasped hands).

[22] Once such regional success is documented, it tends to reinforce the association of the party with the region. As a focus group participant explained, "When we see a particular area has more votes for the National Party, we say 'aah, that's the home of the National Party.' Like Eastern Province. They have more votes for UNIP and automatically we feel that it is a . . . UNIP area" (LIV-W).

In addition, whenever they campaigned outside of Western Province party leaders took great care to emphasize the vices of tribalism and the need for national unity and national development. But to make sure that the party would retain its foothold among Lozi-speaking Westerners, party organizers made it a practice, when campaigning in that part of the country, of always referring to the party by its Lozi name as the "Sicaba Party." To non-Lozis, the subtle shift in the party's designation was imperceptible – "Sicaba" was, after all, the direct Lozi translation of "national," and much campaigning in Zambia is ordinarily conducted in local languages. But to the Lozi audiences whose support the National Party leaders coveted, "Sicaba Party" was an obvious reference to the Lozi nationalist party of the same name that had been active in the region in the early 1960s. By alluding to it, the NP campaigners made their party's "true" ethnic orientation clear. But doing so in this manner limited the audience that would understand this message to fellow Lozi-speakers.[23]

The United Progressive Party provides another example of a party that employed national appeals for one audience and ethnic appeals for another.[24] Founded by Simon Kapwepwe, the pre-eminent Bemba politician of the independence era, the UPP drew almost all of its most senior leaders from the Bemba-speaking Northern Province and the Copperbelt.[25] As a consequence of its close association with the Bemba elite, the party was widely assumed to be a party for Bembas only. Thus while the party's leaders did campaign (clandestinely) along ethnic lines in Bemba-speaking areas to shore up their natural base (Bratton 1980: 212–20; Gertzel and Szeftel 1984: 131–35), they recognized that their more important task was to win support among non-Bemba voters. To do this, they "sought to establish [the UPP] as a national political party . . . and avoided expressing its appeal for popular support in regional or factional terms" (Szeftel 1980: 86). The party's manifesto emphasized that one of its goals was "to stamp out all forms of . . . tribalism and sectionalism by establishing real unity

[23] Interview with NP Organizing Secretary Mwitumwa Imbula, Mongu, 15 November 1995.

[24] The *Daily Mail* summarized the party as having "three different faces: one for the people of the urban areas, one for the people of the rural areas, and another for the expatriate community being wooed to support [it]" (15 December 1971).

[25] The UPP's base in these areas is "indicated by the list of those detained by the government for UPP activities and by press reports of defections from UNIP . . . [T]he vast majority of those detained had Bemba names" (Szeftel 1980: 86). Molteno (1972: 7) concurs: "When [Kapwepwe] announced the eight members of his interim central committee, five were Bemba, three were from Eastern Province (but political non-entities) and the other six had no representation at all."

through discussion" (*Daily Mail*, 25 August 1971). In his public campaign speeches, Kapwepwe focused on explicitly non-ethnic issues such as the evils of corruption, the need for economic change, and the importance of national unity. When a dispute broke out over allegations that Bembas were being mistreated by the UNIP government, Kapwepwe went out of his way to state publicly that it was his "hope and prayer that all leaders will avoid the temptation of speaking for particular groups... We are going to fight as a nation and not as Bembas, Tongas, Ngonis or Lozis" (*Daily Mail*, 27 January 1971). In these ways, the party attempted to preserve its viability as a national, rather than simply a regional, political force.

In addition to trying to help their fortunes by shaping perceptions about their own ethnic orientations, political parties, like individual candidates, also employ the strategy of ascribing ethnic orientations to their rivals. By successfully cultivating the identification of a rival party with a particular ethnic group, a savvy party leader can improve his own party's prospects by undermining the rival party's ability to win support beyond a relatively narrow area. Such a strategy is particularly common for ruling parties, which, having succeeded in capturing power, have an incentive to portray upstart opposition groups in terms that will undermine their ability to compete with them at the national level.

Faced with threats from the ANC and the UP in the 1960s, the UNIP accused both parties of being more interested in helping their narrow ethnic constituencies in Western and Southern Provinces than in fostering the development of the country as a whole.[26] In so doing, the UNIP hoped to – and largely did – undercut these parties' support outside of their regional home bases. The same tactic was employed against the UPP in 1971. "The party was depicted [by UNIP leaders] as a manifestation of Bemba tribalism and its adherents [from other ethnic groups] were dismissed as people of no consequence who were permitting themselves to be used to provide UPP with a national image" (Szeftel 1978: 356). In addition to accusations of this sort, the UNIP government arrested the UPP's two most senior non-Bemba leaders, Henry Msoni and Zipope Mumba, in an effort to disrupt the party's ability to point to these men as evidence of the organization's multi-ethnic roots. Kapwepwe reacted to his colleagues' detention by calling it an attempt by the UNIP to try to "prove their theory that this is a tribal party" (*Times of Zambia*, 25 August 1971). Although part of the reason the UPP found it so difficult to escape its Bemba label was because of Kapwepwe's strong association with the

[26] Interview with William Chipango, Livingstone, 16 December 1995; Molteno (1974).

Bemba cause, the UNIP's steadfast campaign to brand the party as a Bemba instrument also played an important role in shaping peoples' perceptions of the UPP's ethnic orientation.

The MMD also adopted the practice of ethnic finger-pointing as a means of limiting the threats posed by opposition parties. When the upstart National Party was formed in 1993, and then when the UPND was created in 1998, the MMD's principal response was to brand them as vehicles for Lozi and Tonga interests (*The Monitor*, 19–25 November 1999; 25 February–2 March 2000; *Daily Mail*, 13 September 2000). The extraordinary level of resources that the MMD devoted to defeating the NP candidate in the Malole by-election of 1993 – a race viewed around the country as a test of the NP's claim to be a truly national political organization – attests to the importance that the MMD attached to containing the NP in its relatively narrow Lozi- and Tonga-speaking ethnic heartlands. The by-election pitted Emmanuel Kasonde, a former finance minister who had been sacked by President Chiluba following unsubstantiated allegations of financial impropriety (*Weekly Post*, 23–29 April 1993), against an unknown MMD challenger. The significance of the by-election stemmed from the fact that Kasonde was one of the most powerful and visible Bemba politicians in the country and the man widely credited with having delivered Northern Province to the MMD in 1991. To have allowed him to win the seat would have been to give the NP a foothold outside of the South and West and to eliminate the MMD's ability to brand the NP as a regional party.[27] The MMD, like the UNIP before it, was willing to risk reinforcing the opposition party's hegemony in its home region so long as it could be assured of limiting its rival's ability to attract supporters across the country as a whole.

### *Candidates as Bearers of Both Individual Identities and Party Labels*

I have argued that voters use a candidate's ethnicity as a guide to how that person is likely to distribute patronage if elected. I have also argued that voters make their decisions about which political parties to support based on a similar assessment of the match between each party's ethnic orientation and their own. The goal for voters is to support the candidate or party that is perceived to represent the interests of their own ethnic group. The problem, however, is that the candidates among whom the

[27] For a fuller account of this key by-election, see the discussions in Chapters 7 and 8.

voters must choose are competing simultaneously as individuals and as representatives of particular political parties. This means that they can be "coded" ethnically in two different (and sometimes contradictory) ways: one way suggested by the candidate's own cultural background, and another way suggested by the ethnic orientation of the party on whose ticket the candidate is running. Both provide clues about how the politician is likely to behave if elected, but these clues may point in different directions. For example, the candidate may be from one ethnic group but running on the ticket of a party associated with another group. In such a situation, the ethnic community that the candidate is likely to favor once in office is not obvious. Which ethnic cue – the individual one or the party one – should voters focus on in making their decisions? And which ethnic affiliation should the candidates themselves try to emphasize in making thier electoral appeals?

The answer (to the second question, at least) depends on the context. Sometimes, the ethnic loyalties that are imputed to a candidate by virtue of his party affiliation run counter to the candidate's interests, as, for example, when the party on whose ticket he is running is associated in voters' minds with a region or group other than that of the voters themselves. In such a situation, the candidate will either try to stress his party's national orientation or, if he himself is a member of the dominant local group in the constituency, attempt to draw a distinction between his party's perceived ethnic orientation and his own, and encourage voters to focus on the latter. At other times, however, the party's ethnic coattails may be quite beneficial. For example, when a candidate is running for a seat in the region of the country with which her party is popularly identified, the candidate will have a strong incentive to underscore her party affiliation and the ethnic orientation that it conveys. These strategic considerations are at the heart of the explanation for why different dimensions of ethnic identity emerge as salient in one-party and multi-party electoral contests, and I will return to them in the next chapter.

## THE POLITICAL CONSEQUENCES OF ETHNIC MULTI-DIMENSIONALITY

Thus far, as I have discussed the coalition-building strategies of Zambian political actors, I have treated ethnicity as an unambiguous, unidimensional concept. I have described political parties as avoiding overt ethnic appeals in their public campaigns and as carefully playing the ethnic card in regions dominated by people whose interests they are perceived to represent. I have described candidates as either playing up or seeking to hide from their ethnic group affiliations, depending, first, on whether or not they happen to be located in constituencies dominated by members of their own groups and, second, on whether or not the parties on whose tickets they are running are popularly viewed as representatives of local interests. And I have described how both parties and candidates brand their rivals with ethnic labels, sometimes to restrict the breadth of their rivals' potential support base and sometimes to mobilize members of their own groups against implied outside threats. In each case, the strategic decisions made by the political actors have been cast as a choice between actively drawing upon ethnic identity or actively hiding from it.

Entirely absent from this discussion has been the possibility that political actors, in choosing whether to embrace ethnic labels or ascribe them to their rivals, might also be faced with a decision about which dimension of ethnic identity to embrace or ascribe. Yet ethnic coalition-building in Zambia requires precisely such a decision. Recall that two different dimensions of ethnic identity are available to Zambian political actors: one stemming from tribal affiliation, and the other from language group membership. This means that the calculation surrounding how best to employ ethnicity as a coalition-building tool entails an additional decision about whether to stress tribal connections or language ties. It also implies that the process of ethnic coalition-building is considerably more complex than has been suggested thus far.

Although both tribal and linguistic identities are commonly referred to as "tribal" in everyday social discourse – Zambians, like most Africans, almost never use the terms "ethnic group" or "ethnicity" – each designation refers to membership in a very different-sized social unit. Tribal affiliations identify their bearers as members of one of roughly six dozen highly localized groupings, whereas language group affiliations classify most people as members of one of four much larger coalitions. Since the size of the group with which a person (or political party) is identified is so different depending on whether the group is defined in tribal or linguistic terms, the decision to describe oneself (or one's political opponents) in terms of one dimension of ethnic identity rather than the other has important consequences. To define oneself in linguistic terms is to identify oneself not simply as a member of a particular ethnic group, but as a member of a large and nationally powerful coalition. To define one's rivals in such terms is to identify them with a large, potentially threatening, and perhaps unfairly favored ethnic grouping. Conversely, to define one's own (or one's opponent's) ethnic identity in terms of tribal affiliation is to emphasize one's own (or one's opponent's) local roots and to assert boundaries between narrower ethnic units that might otherwise be lumped together as part of the same linguistic entity. In each case, the perceived landscape of in-group and out-group members – and thus political allies and political adversaries – is quite different.

The ability of Zambian political actors to alter perceptions of the size of their own or their opponent's ethnic coalition by emphasizing tribal versus linguistic differences constitutes a valuable strategic resource. It allows politicians and political parties to define themselves and their rivals as members of groups on the dimension of ethnicity that will yield them the greatest political leverage given the situation in which they find themselves. As the situation changes, so too can the dimension of identity that they find it most advantageous to embrace. In the context of a struggle over the distribution of national development resources, cabinet positions, civil service jobs, or parastatal posts, for example, a Zambian politician can define himself in linguistic terms to signal the large size and political importance of the coalition whose support he can claim to represent. In the context of a campaign for re-election in his rural constituency, that same politician can play down his linguistic identity in favor of his affiliation with the dominant local tribe in the area to better distinguish himself from rivals (who probably share his language group background) and to underscore his authenticity as a representative of the interests of the local community. More generally, by framing political conflicts in terms of one dimension of ethnic identity rather than another, politicians and political parties can shape perceptions about the fairness of the distribution of government resources to convince voters that they are disadvantaged and that mobilization for change should be a priority. And by defining themselves in terms of the right (in the sense of strategically optimal) dimension of ethnic identity, they can also convince voters that this mobilization should take place behind their banner.

In Zambia, as in many contexts where social identities are multidimensional, the dynamics of such ethnic self-definition and ascription are complicated by the fact that the tribal and linguistic collectivities with which people identify themselves nest inside one another. Tribal and language groups are organized in concentric circles, with all the members of each tribal group located entirely within a single language category and each language category containing several different tribal groups. Thus, every Lozi tribesperson is also a Lozi-speaker, but every Lozi-speaker is not a Lozi tribesperson. The coalition of Lozi-speakers contains a great many tribal groups – Kwangwa, Kwandi, Mashi, Mbunda, Subiya, to name just a few – who are not Lozis in the tribal sense. The same is true of the coalition of Bemba-speakers (which includes people who are, among other things, Aushi, Bisa, Kabende, Lala, Lunda, Mambwe, Namwanga, and Ng'umbo by tribe), Tonga-speakers (which includes people who are tribally Lenje, Soli, Ila, and Toka-Leya), and Nyanja-speakers (which includes people who are tribally Chewa, Nsenga, Ngoni, Chikunda, and Tumbuka).

Such nesting of tribes within language groups need not cause confusion in and of itself. The confusion stems from the fact that, because of the way in which patterns of language use developed historically, the name of each of the four major language groups in Zambia is the same as the name of the largest tribe in each language coalition. These, of course, are the tribes whose local dialects became the bases for each of the four major regional linguas franca.[28] To refer to someone simply as a "Lozi" (or a "Bemba" or a "Tonga" or a "Nyanja"), as is commonly done in Zambia, is therefore fundamentally ambiguous, since there is no way of knowing whether we are referring to the person's tribal identity or to the person's language group affiliation. This ambiguity has very important political implications, which I will explore in the next section.

Before doing so, however, it is necessary to add an additional wrinkle to our discussion of the Zambian ethnic landscape. To this point, I have described the country's politically relevant social cleavages as being built along either tribal or linguistic lines. As I argued in Chapters 2 and 3, the reason that tribal and linguistic cleavages constitute such important bases for political coalition-building is because the colonial government and the Northern Rhodesian mining companies made access to state and company resources during the pre-independence era contingent on identifying oneself as either a member of a tribe or a speaker of one of the country's four principal languages. When independence and the advent of electoral politics shifted the competition for state resources from the offices of the district governors and the headquarters of Native Authorities to the arena of mass politics, Zambians continued to view this competition in terms of a struggle among coalitions defined in tribal or linguistic terms.

One of the important changes that came with independence was the emergence of provinces as units of development administration. Provinces had first been demarcated in Northern Rhodesia in the early 1930s, and

[28] See Chapter 3.

by the mid-1940s, each of the protectorate's (then) six provinces had its own African-staffed administrative council (Hall 1976: 68; Stone 1979). But it was not until after independence that the scale of the resources allocated for rural development through these units became large enough for provincial administrations to become perceived as sources of patronage. When this happened, provinces became focal points for political competition and Zambians came to view the struggle for state resources partly in terms of a conflict among the country's provinces.[29] In the post-independence era, provincial divisions have thus come to play a similar role to tribal and linguistic divisions as a foundation for political coalition-building.

The reason that the emergence of provincial identities as an alternative to tribe or language has not thoroughly altered the dynamics of Zambian political competition is that, by and large, provincial identities and linguistic identities overlap. Leaving aside the provinces located along the rail line whose migrant populations are so mixed as to have only weak provincial identities, the boundaries of provinces are generally, both in Zambians' imaginations and in fact, the same as the boundaries of the country's main language groups. Southern Province is more or less the Tonga-speaking part of the country, Eastern Province is the country's Nyanja-speaking region, and Western Province is the home of Zambia's Lozi-speakers.[30] In each of these cases, the name of the province and the name of the language group are used interchangeably in popular discourse: Tonga-speakers are referred to as Southerners, Nyanja-speakers as Easterners, and Lozi-speakers as Westerners.

There are, however, two important exceptions to the otherwise close match between provincial and linguistic boundaries. The first is Northwestern Province, which is not associated with any of the country's four major language groups. For reasons explained in Chapter 3, no single regional lingua franca took root in Northwestern Province, as it did in the other rural areas of Northern Rhodesia. Provincial identities thus tend to

[29] At independence, Zambia had eight provinces: Barotse, Central, Eastern, Luapula, Northern, Northwestern, Southern, and Western. In 1969, Western Province was renamed Copperbelt Province and Barotse Province was renamed Western Province. In 1978, a ninth province, Lusaka Province, was carved out of the former Central Province.

[30] The Nkoyas of Western Province, who reject their classification as Lozi-speakers (van Binsbergen 1982), and the Tumbukas of Eastern Province, who at times have been identified, either by themselves or by others, as distinct from the region's Nyanja-speaking population, constitute two minor exceptions.

play an analogous role for people in Northwestern Province to linguistic identities in other parts of the country. Zambians often refer to "Northwesterners" as the fifth major ethnic group alongside the Bemba-speakers, Nyanja-speakers, Tonga-speakers, and Lozi-speakers. People from Northwestern Province also commonly identify themselves in such terms.

The second of the exceptions is the Bemba-speaking region, which spans both Northern and Luapula Provinces (and, in the eyes of many Zambians, also Copperbelt Province and the northeastern portions of Central Province). The fact that the Bemba-speaking coalition does not map onto a single province means that, unlike the coalitions defined by the three other major language groups, Bemba-speakers can be divided not only into tribal sub-groupings but also into provincial sub-units. This, in turn, means that what is meant by "Bemba" is even more ambiguous than what is meant by "Tonga," "Nyanja," or "Lozi." When people are described (or describe themselves) as "Bemba" do they mean that they are members of the Bemba tribe? That they speak the Bemba language? Or that they are from Northern Province (the home of the Bemba tribe and thus the more "Bemba" of the two Bemba-speaking provinces)? In a political context where Bembas are widely perceived to dominate the most important positions in the government and to receive the lion's share of development resources, this ambiguity is a source of tremendous misunderstanding and conflict. The central question of whether or not Bembas are, in fact, over-represented in senior government positions or advantaged in the allocation of development funds depends entirely on which dimension of Bemba identity one uses in the counting. To develop this point, and to illustrate the political implications of Zambia's ethnic multi-dimensionality, I turn now to the question: what is a Bemba?

### *What Is a Bemba?*

For non-Bemba-speakers, almost all people who speak the Bemba language – or, more precisely, all people who are members of tribes or who trace their roots to provinces that are considered Bemba-speaking – are viewed as "Bembas." Epstein (1978: 11) relates a telling anecdote from his field work in the Copperbelt about a young laborer from Mwinilunga (a Kaonde area of Northwestern Province) whom he met one Sunday afternoon when the laborer was on his way home from watching a tribal dancing competition in the Ndola municipal compound. The young man explained that "he had not stayed there very long ... because his friend had not appeared and there were only Bemba dancing *Kalela* [a well-known tribal dance] that day." Epstein writes:

> Since I knew that *Kalela* was not danced by Bemba, I asked whether they were not really Bena Ng'umbo [members of a different Bemba-speaking tribe] whom he had seen. He replied (in Bemba): "those of us who come from afar know only the Bemba. It is just the same way they call us from the far west Kalwena ... even though we are of many different tribes."

"From afar," most Zambians ignore the internal complexity of the Bemba category and lump anyone who comes from a Bemba-speaking area into the same group.[31] "Aushi, Lala, Ng'umbo," a Lusaka focus group participant explained, "these are all Bembas because they speak the same language" (LSK-T1).

Even Bemba-speakers themselves sometimes define their group in undifferentiated terms. "Most of the people in Luapula are not Bemba [by tribe], and yet I have had many experiences where I have met people there who call themselves Bemba" a Catholic missionary from Northern Province recounted:

> [When this happens] I say "but you are not a Bemba, you are a Lunda." And they say "but Father, it is the same thing." Most of the people in Luapula Province who say they are Bemba are not. They say they are Bemba because they speak Bemba. All these tribes – the Bisa, the Lunda, the Aushi – they go to the Copperbelt and present themselves as Bemba because they speak Bemba.[32]

A market seller in Luanshya, herself a Lungu and a lifelong Copperbelt resident, followed precisely this pattern when she characterized people from Northern Province, Luapula Province, and the Copperbelt as "all the same ... all behaving like one group" (LY-MS-W). A former MP, now retired to the Copperbelt, agreed similarly that people from Luapula and Northern provinces were "just the same people, except that the dialect is a little different. To me, I feel that [people from] Luapula and Northern [provinces] should be one."[33]

Sometimes such characterizations are born from little more than a subconscious effort to simplify an otherwise complex social landscape. Among urban dwellers in particular, this is a common means of coping

[31] As the young laborer noted, the same applies to members of other linguistic categories.

[32] Interview with Fr. Joseph Melvin Doucette, Malole Mission, 8 September 1995.

[33] Interview with Leonard Mpundu, Luanshya, 17 December 1995.

with social complexity (Mitchell 1956, 1969, 1974, 1987). But in some situations, defining the Bemba coalition in linguistic terms is part of a conscious strategy, either by Bemba-speakers or by outsiders, to identify the Bembas as the country's largest ethnic coalition. For non-Bemba-speakers, the purpose of such a characterization is often to expand the universe of officeholders that can be labeled as "Bemba," thereby underscoring the degree to which "Bembas" dominate the most important positions in the government and dramatizing the need to mobilize against "Bemba" hegemony. For members of the Bemba-speaking group, by contrast, defining "Bemba" in linguistic terms is used to justify precisely such dominance. Faced in 1971 with accusations that Bembas held too many of the country's top posts, Justin Chimba, a senior Bemba minister at the time, argued that "this country must realize that Bembas are a majority... [We] comprise 58 percent [*sic*] of the Zambian population and should not be taken lightly" (*Daily Mail*, 25 January 1971).[34] In a similar vein, Unia Mwila, another senior government official, concluded a speech to the UNIP National Council meeting of February 1968 by pointing out that, if Bembas were a majority on the Central Committee, "it [was] because Bemba-speaking people number two million!"[35] In both cases, the speakers sought to defend their group's privileged status by defining their coalition in the broadest possible terms and then claiming that the size of their group justified its share of senior positions.

A second rationale for Bemba-speakers to define their ethnic coalition in linguistic terms is to maximize the number of supporters in their coalition. When the emergence of the National Party in 1993 seemed to threaten the MMD's grip on power, President Chiluba attempted to play precisely this strategy. Fearful that Northern Province Bemba-speakers might follow their leader, Emmanuel Kasonde, into the opposition camp, Chiluba called the Northern Province parliamentary delegation to a special State House meeting at which he "quot[ed] historical tribal links between the people of Luapula and Northern Province" and stressed that "family ties [between his province and theirs] should not be broken" (*Weekly Post*, 6–12 August 1993). By invoking the common linguistic ties between Northern Province and Luapula (his own home area), Chiluba hoped to keep intact the Bemba-speaking alliance that comprised the core of his party's supporters.

[34] Chimba's estimate of the size of the Bemba-speaking coalition was significantly inflated. Bemba-speakers in Zambia comprise closer to 40 percent of the population.

[35] Wina (1985: 22). Again, Mwila's figures are highly inflated.

But while Bemba-speakers may find it advantageous to emphasize their linguistic identities in some situations, in other situations they are eager to draw distinctions between themselves and other fellow language group members. Especially when they are faced with allegations that "Bembas" are enjoying more than their fair share of the national cake, many Bemba-speakers are quick to point out that only certain provincially or tribally defined segments of the larger Bemba-speaking coalition are, in fact, benefiting from a preferential access to power and resources. A letter to the editor of *The Times* (29 April 1995) from the chairman of the Bemba Ilamfya Council, the Bemba tribe's leading cultural association, provides an excellent example of such within-coalition boundary drawing:

> It has been said and it is being said that the MMD government is dominated by Bembas. This is not correct. If they mean [that the government is dominated by members of the Bemba] tribe, it is not true . . . The only Bemba minister is Chitalu Sampa. All those you see in the MMD government today just speak Bemba [but] they have their [own] tribes . . . Even President Chiluba is not a Bemba by tribe, he is just a Bemba-speaker. So it is wrong to say that Bembas have dominated the MMD government.

In response to allegations of Bemba over-representation in the government, Bemba Paramount Chief Chitimukulu himself issued a public statement in which he "humbly ask[ed] whoever is the proponent of the anti-Bemba sentiments . . . to stop pointing fingers at the Bembas because Bembas . . . constitute [only one of] the 73 tribes" (*Weekly Standard*, 30 August–5 September 1993). The rationale for both the chief's request and the chairman's letter was made explicit in the latter, which lamented that the tendency of Zambians to conflate Bemba tribespeople with Bemba-speakers more generally had resulted in a situation in which those who were Bemba by tribe were put "at a disadvantage in as far as employment, promotion or appointments to high offices is concerned" (*The Times*, 29 April 1995).

The most vocal protests against the assumption that all Bemba-speakers are part of the same group, however, have come not from Bemba tribal leaders but from politicians identifying themselves in provincial terms. In the late 1960s, politicians from Luapula Province began to speak out against what they perceived to be the insufficient rewards that they were receiving for the contribution they had made to bringing the UNIP to power (Bates 1976: ch. 10; Szeftel 1978: ch. 6). Many of their demands were couched in terms of a comparison between the meager resources allotted to their province and the far more generous allocations enjoyed by their Bemba-speaking neighbors in Northern Province. In 1969, a group of MPs from Luapula wrote to the President to protest "the lack of development and rewards accorded their region." The authors of the letter

> referred to slights and insults accorded Luapulans by people from Northern Province... They noted that in the past they had regarded Northern Province as a "sister province" and had accepted its leadership in the interest of unity. However, these insults... had opened their eyes to the costs of their support for Northern Province and they were determined that henceforth they would represent their own interests and seek their fair share of the "benefits of independence" (Szeftel 1978: 334–35)[36]

Later the same year, Luapula politicians asserted the distinction between Northern Province Bembas and Luapula Bembas once again by publicly rejecting the government's nominee for a parliamentary by-election in Kawambwa East constituency in Luapula Province. The nominee, John Mwanakatwe, was a Bemba-speaking Mambwe-Lungu from Isoka district in Northern Province. At the time of his nomination for the Kawambwa East seat, he was the secretary general to the government. Previously he had been a minister of education and a minister of mines. Despite his very senior status in the government, Mwanakatwe was rejected on the grounds that, although he was a Bemba-speaker, he was a Northerner rather than a local Luapulan (*Times of Zambia*, 14 July 1969). To build support for their opposition to Mwanakatwe's nomination, Luapula MPs spearheaded "an outpouring of letters, petitions and telegrams in support of their demand that 'the political interests of the province [be] looked after by its own sons and daughters,' and that 'no outsider be imposed' on the Luapula people" (Bates 1976: 229). In addition, they "devised and disseminated a... story [contending] that Mwanakatwe had chastised the Luapula people for aspiring to assert themselves politically and... [had] called the Luapula people *batubula*, or 'dumb fishermen' who were 'ordained to be ruled by others'" (ibid.). Although the allegation about Mwanakatwe's *batubula* slur was widely

[36] The MPs wrote: "We are now more convinced that it is because of this attitude against us that our people have not had the benefit of political appointments on the scale enjoyed by those from the Northern Province or other provinces. In this regard we may mention the appointments to Party leadership on the regional level in the [Copperbelt] Province, politically appointed District Secretaries, District Governors, appointments to foreign missions, membership of the statutory bodies and Government Boards, not to mention appointments in the public service" (quoted in Szeftel 1978: 335).

reported in the Zambian press at the time, Bates (1976: 229) claims to have investigated the matter and "found little basis for it." He concludes: "The significance of the story therefore lies not in its veracity. Rather, it lies in the political designs that underlay it. The story was clearly aimed at demonstrating the hauteur and insensitivity of the Northern Province politicians and at severing the bonds of political loyalty between the Luapula constituency and the national-level politicians from the north" (230).

In 1970, five high-ranking Luapula politicians in the Copperbelt sent another letter to President Kaunda demanding that their province be given a greater share of government appointments. To make their point, the authors attached a list of senior government officials "to point out how few of the positions had gone to Luapulans."[37] Bates (1976: 219) cites a 1971 speech given by a Luapula MP at a district-level political meeting that emphasizes the same themes:

> Since independence, the government has done nothing in this province... Before independence we were united together with other provinces, but since then other provinces have wanted [the] lion's share and to eat on their friends' heads... In Northern Province, government has established a railway line... so we want government to establish mines in Luapula.

In all of these examples, politicians from Luapula sought to increase their access to political power and public resources by asserting the difference between themselves and their fellow Bemba-speakers in Northern Province. What outsiders may have perceived, and depicted, as a uniformly privileged "Bemba" block was, in fact, deeply divided by internal factions, each seeking greater access to the coalition's spoils.

In the 1990s, the tables were turned. With the reins of power in the hands of President Chiluba – a Luapulan – it was the Northerners who emphasized the distinction between the two provincial groupings in complaining about inadequate resource allocation. A focus group respondent in Northern Province protested that "whenever they talk of people being favored by the government they talk of Bembas. But... we [Northerners] are not involved... It is the ones from over there [in Luapula] that are benefiting" (KAS-R-M). Echoing this sentiment, a newspaper report in the days leading up to the MMD's 1995 party convention describes

[37] Petition addressed by "The Copperbelt Luapula Delegation to his Excellency the President of the Republic of Zambia, Dr. K. D. Kaunda, on the following points," quoted in Szeftel (1978: 336). The petitioners "demanded that the President 'minimize' the appointment of people from areas 'whose representations have already monopolised the country.'"

Northerners as feeling "abandoned" by their party. "They claim President Chiluba . . . has sacrificed Northern Province for Southern Province, Luapula Province and Eastern Province" (*The Post*, 18 December 1995). Yet at the very moment that a senior MMD member from Northern Province was complaining to the reporter that "since the late Simon Kapwepwe's vice-presidency, no one from Northern Province has held a senior position in the politics of this country" (ibid.), many, if not most, of the non-Bemba-speaking delegates were convinced that Northerners were controlling both their party and the government. The fact that one of the groups that felt itself to be so ill-treated could be perceived by another group as favored attests to the power of Zambia's complex ethnic landscape to breed grievances and misunderstandings.

Nowhere are the possibilities for conflicting interpretations of the same reality more evident than in the composition of the cabinet. As we have seen, the ethnic breakdown of the cabinet is one of the most visible and closely watched indicators of ethnic group favoritism in Zambia. As we have also seen, the allegation that "Bembas" are dominating the cabinet has been, since independence, a central theme of Zambian politics. Figure 4.1 displays the share of "Bembas" in the cabinet in every odd year between 1965 and 1999 using different bars to indicate the share in each year of Bemba tribespeople, members from Northern Province, and Bemba-speakers.[38] As the figure makes clear, the accuracy of the claim that Bembas are dominating the cabinet depends entirely on how one defines "Bemba."

Defined in terms of language, Bembas occupied an average of 35 percent of all cabinet positions between 1965 and 1999, with a low of 22 percent and a high of 44 percent. Defined in terms of tribe, however, Bemba cabinet representation during the same period was less than a third of that rate, averaging just 11 percent, and ranging between a low of zero and a high of 25 percent. Defined a third way, in terms of province of origin (as cabinet members from Northern Province), the Bemba share of cabinet

[38] The roster of cabinet members used for each year was as of the first parliamentary sitting of the year, as recorded in the official record of parliamentary debates. The sole exceptions are 1989, for which such records were not published, and 1991, where the list of ministers is as of the beginning of the Third Republic in November. The cabinet was defined as the president, the vice president or prime minister, all full ministers, the attorney general, the secretary general to the government and designated members of the Central Committee in the House. Deputy ministers and ministers of state were not included. Cabinet members holding more than one portfolio were counted only once.

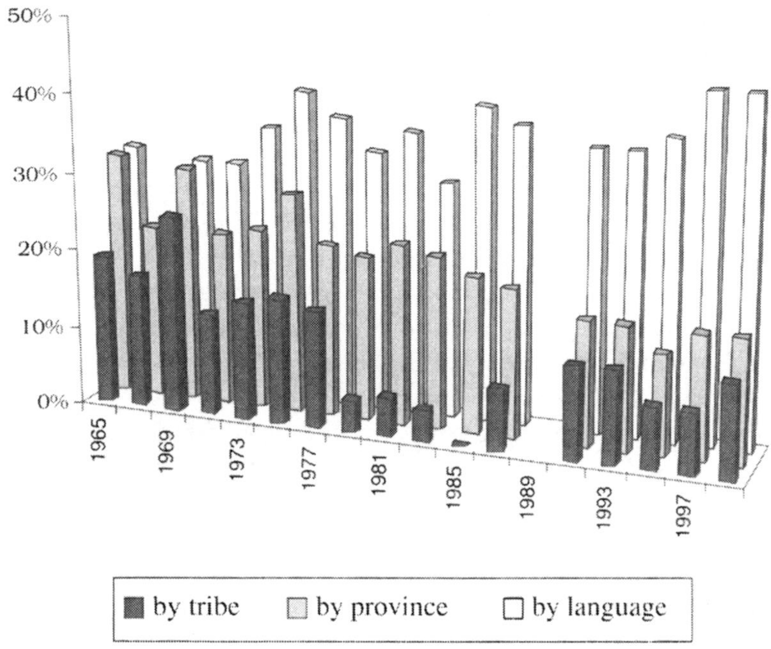


Figure 4.1. Share of Bembas in the Cabinet

seats averaged 21 percent, approximately the midpoint of the linguistic and tribal averages.[39] As these numbers make clear, and as Figure 4.1 graphically illustrates, the conclusion one draws about the dominance of Bembas in the government depends completely on which ethnic lens one employs in counting heads. When Bemba-speakers respond with disbelief and anger to allegations that they hold the lion's share of cabinet posts, it is often because the definition of "Bemba" that they are employing differs from the one being used by their accusers.

But whereas Figure 4.1 may help to explain why people can draw such different conclusions from looking at the same list of cabinet members, it does not provide very strong support for the conclusion that Bembas, irrespective of how they are defined, are actually over-represented in the cabinet. While the average share of Northerners in the cabinet does exceed the proportion of Northerners in the national population by a significant margin, the average proportions of cabinet ministers that are Bemba by tribe

39 If the "Bemba province" is defined as Luapula rather than Northern Province, the average between 1965 and 1999 drops to 12 percent, with a high of 24 percent in 1997 and 1999.

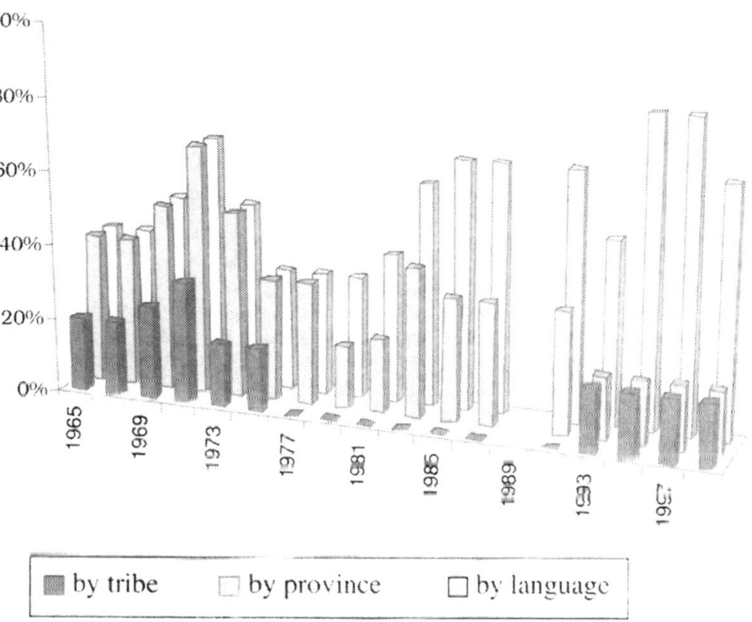


Figure 4.2. Share of Bembas in Top Six Cabinet Positions

are well below the percentages of Bemba tribespeople in the country as a whole, and the proportion of Bemba-speakers in the cabinet is fairly close to this group's share in the national population.[40] Part of the reason for this is that President Kaunda, whose cabinets comprise twelve of the seventeen in the sample, took great care to balance his cabinet appointments across ethnic groups. Where Kaunda was less evenhanded, however – and where Bemba dominance clearly does manifest itself – is in the composition of the top six cabinet positions. If we focus, as I do in Figure 4.2 (and as most Zambians do in practice) on the key positions of President, Vice President, and Ministers of Defense, Home Affairs, Foreign Affairs, and Finance, the source of the perception that "Bembas are running the country" becomes apparent.[41]

[40] According to 1990 census figures, people who identified themselves as Bemba by tribe constitute approximately 16 percent of the national population, residents of Northern Province make up roughly 12 percent, and Bemba-speakers comprise approximately 38 percent. The figure for Northern Province is misleadingly low, however, because it excludes people who have migrated from Northern Province to urban areas but who still consider themselves (and are considered by others) to be Northerners.

[41] These six positions were the ones to which focus group participants invariably referred when they made claims about Bemba domination. Their symbolic importance

In most years, the percentages of Bembas in the six top positions were significantly greater than in the cabinet as a whole, particularly when "Bemba" is defined in terms of province or language. Whereas an average of 35 percent of all cabinet ministers between 1965 and 1999 were Bemba-speakers, members of this group occupied an average of 55 percent of the top six posts. Similarly, whereas Northerners comprised 21 percent of all cabinet ministers during this thirty-year time frame, they accounted for 33 percent of the people in the six top positions. Interestingly, the decline in the share of Northerners after 1991 was paralleled by a dramatic rise in the share of senior ministers from President Chiluba's own Luapula Province. Over the period from 1991 to 1999, Luapulans occupied, on average, three of the top six cabinet positions. As in Figure 4.1, however, the clearest message conveyed by Figure 4.2 is the disparity in the shares of Bemba tribespeople, Northerners, and Bemba-speakers. Depending on whether one understood "Bemba" in tribal, provincial, or linguistic terms, one would reach quite different assessments of whether (or how much) Bembas were over-represented in the most powerful positions in the government.

## *An Observation in Need of a Theory*

The answer to the question "what is a Bemba?" is that it depends. It depends on who is being asked and what their interests are. Of course, people answer this very question (or one of its cousins: "what is a Lozi?" "what is a Nyanja?" or "what is a Tonga?") dozens of times every day without even knowing that they are doing so: one friend is implicitly thought of as a member of a different group because she speaks a different language; another is perceived as a kinsman because his village of birth is located in the same region of the country; a third is assumed not to be related because she does not share a particular funeral custom or pays allegiance to a different chief. In each of these cases, the person is accepted or rejected as a member of the ethnic group by virtue of a different set of standards for community membership: one linguistic, one regional, one tribal. In none of these cases, in all probability, is the decision to use one yardstick instead of another made strategically or as part of a larger plan to extract rewards or further material interests.

was confirmed by President Kaunda himself, who told me that, next to the presidency and the vice presidency, the portfolios for Defense, Home Affairs, Foreign Affairs, and Finance were the ones to which people paid the most attention (interview with Dr. Kenneth Kaunda, Lusaka, 17 January 1994).

However, in the realm of politics, questions of group membership are much more often answered through calculations of self-interest.[42] This is because ethnic identities are assumed to convey information about the likelihood that a person in a position of power will channel resources to another person – perhaps oneself, perhaps someone else – who does not directly enjoy access to those resources. The fact that people have more than one ethnic affiliation means simply that the information that ethnic identities convey about patronage commitments is ambiguous and sometimes misleading. But this ambiguity, while frustrating for the analyst of political or social affairs, is a valuable tool in the hands of a strategically minded politician or citizen who is trying to build or to secure membership in a winning political coalition. It allows people to present themselves, identify others, and make demands as members of groups of different sizes. And it allows them to tailor their choices in this regard to best serve their needs given the circumstances in which they find themselves. Whether they invoke or embrace tribal or linguistic (or even provincial) identity in their coalition-building or coalition-joining efforts will depend on their situation and the constraints and interests that follow from it.

Such a conclusion, while perhaps correct, is nonetheless not particularly satisfying. To summarize our discussion of the ways in which Zambian political actors take advantage of their country's ethnic multidimensionality by simply saying that they choose whatever identity will best serve their purposes is, frankly, not saying very much – or, at any rate, not saying anything particularly new. The real contribution, for both our understanding of Zambian politics and for the study of ethnic politics more generally, will come from articulating and providing theoretical support for a set of clear, generalizable propositions about the specific conditions under which one form of ethnic identity will be chosen rather than another. Doing precisely this is the objective of the next chapter.

[42] The self-interested use of ethnicity extends to business as well. A telling example is the case of two Scotsmen, both former senior members of the Scottish National Party, who, upon emigrating to Estonia, built and promoted a shopping development that they called "British House" (*The Economist*, 25 September 1999). Evidently they felt that identifying the shopping complex with Britain would generate stronger sales than identifying it with what, in their guises as Scottish National Party leaders, they surely had insisted was their "true" national homeland.

# 5

## *Explaining Changing Patterns of Ethnic Politics*

### *A Model of Political Institutions and Ethnic Cleavage Outcomes*

In 1984, Cherry Gertzel and her colleagues from the University of Zambia published a book, *The Dynamics of the One-Party State in Zambia*, whose purpose was to describe the origins and workings of the country's new single-party political system. Much of the book's analysis drew on a detailed study of the general election of 1973, the first contest held after the country suspended multi-party competition and moved to one-party rule. In the course of describing the campaign and interpreting the voting patterns that emerged in the 1973 race, the authors observed, almost in passing, that politicians seemed to be emphasizing, and voters seemed to be embracing, different kinds of ethnic identities than they had in 1968, the last election held under the old multi-party system. They noted that, whereas campaigning during the 1968 general election had revolved around the competition among broad, linguistically defined voting blocks, campaigning in 1973 seemed to revolve around the conflicts between local tribal groups. Whereas voters had overwhelmingly supported representatives of their language groups in the multi-party contest, they seemed to ignore language group distinctions and line up behind members of their tribes in the one-party race. It was not that ethnicity was more or less central in either election, for, as the authors made clear, it was highly salient in both. But the specific kinds of ethnic identities that served as bases of electoral competition and as motivations for political support were different.

The observation that the shift from the multi-party system to the one-party system had altered the political salience of linguistic and tribal identities was given little sustained attention by the contributors to the Gertzel et al. volume. Although the authors presented a number of anecdotes to suggest that the shift had taken place, they offered no systematic evidence to support the claim and articulated no clear mechanism to account for it. Despite this, their observation was a potentially important one. For if the change in institutional rules had led to a shift in the salient axis of ethnic cleavage, then it suggested the possibility of a general proposition about the conditions under which individuals with multiple ethnic identities might choose one identity instead of another. Clearly, something about the incentives generated by the one-party or multi-party nature of the country's political institutions had led to different kinds of ethnic identity choices. But what was the link? Why did Zambian politicians and voters focus on language group differences during multi-party elections and tribal differences during one-party contests? How was the institutional change causing the change in identity choices? This chapter suggests a mechanism. Chapters 7 and 8, which test a number of this mechanism's observable implications, provide additional empirical support for the connection between the party system type and the cleavage outcome.

I develop my account in four stages. First, I introduce a simple model of ethnic identity choice. This general model shows how, given a set of simple (and, in light of the discussion in Chapter 4, empirically justifiable) assumptions, we can predict the identities that individuals will choose and thus the cleavage dimension that will emerge as the axis of competition and conflict in the political system. Then I show how changing the boundaries of the arena in which political competition takes place can change the outcome that emerges. Next, I show how shifting from multi-party to one-party rule brings about a de facto alteration in the boundaries of the political arena and, with it, a change in both the choices individuals will make and, through those choices, the ethnic cleavage that will emerge as salient. I then apply the model to the Zambian case. The chapter concludes by revisiting some of the model's key assumptions to assess its portability to other settings.

## A SIMPLE MODEL OF ETHNIC IDENTITY CHOICE

Start with a political arena with a very simple ethnic cleavage structure (A, B), where A = $\{a_1, a_2, a_3, \ldots, a_n\}$ and B = $\{b_1, b_2, b_3, \ldots, b_m\}$ and where $a_1 > a_2 > a_3 > \ldots > a_n$ and $b_1 > b_2 > b_3 > \ldots > b_m$.[1] Recall from the notation introduced in Chapter 1 that A and B are the cleavages (e.g.,

[1] Although I define this as an *ethnic* cleavage structure, the logic extends to non-ethnic cleavages like class. Also, while the example contains only two cleavages, the logic of the model extends to cleavage structures with three or more cleavages.

|   | | B | | | | |
|---|---|---|---|---|---|---|
| | | $b_1$ | $b_2$ | $b_3$ | ... | $b_m$ |
| A | $a_1$ | | | | | |
| | $a_2$ | | | | | |
| | $a_3$ | | | | | |
| | $\vdots$ | | | | | |
| | $a_n$ | | | | | |

Figure 5.1. A Simple Ethnic Identity Matrix

race and language, religion and tribe, language and region) and $a_1$, $b_1$, $a_2$, $b_2, \ldots, a_n, b_m$ are the ethnic groups located on each cleavage dimension (e.g., black, white, English-speaker, Portuguese-speaker, Christian, Muslim). Every individual $i$ has an identity repertoire ($a_j$, $b_k$) that contains a single A identity and a single B identity. Each individual can thus be placed in one of the cells in the $n \times m$ ethnic identity matrix depicted in Figure 5.1.[2] If individuals can identify themselves in terms of only one identity at a time – that is, either as a column (an $a_j$) or as a row (a $b_k$) but not as both simultaneously – then which one will they choose?

First, assume that individuals will choose the ethnic identity that will maximize their access to resources. Second, assume that resources are made available through a distributive process in which a single power-holder shares resources only with, but equally among, members of his own ethnic group. Assume further that the power-holder is elected under plurality rules. Finally, assume that all individuals have perfect information about the sizes of all groups (i.e., they know the row and column totals of the matrix, though not necessarily the values in each cell).

These assumptions have a number of important implications. They imply that coalitions across group lines (i.e., across rows or across columns) will not be formed, since individuals will be willing to support only those leaders who will share resources with them, and only leaders from their own groups will do so. In addition, the condition that resources will be shared equally among group members means that sub-divisions of the group will not take place after power has been won. For the purposes of the model, ethnic groups are taken to be unitary blocks: uncombinable and internally undifferentiable. Instances where two or more groups might be combined under a single umbrella label – for example, Irish and Italians in New York as "European immigrants," Dinka and Nuer

[2] Note that some of the cells may be empty.

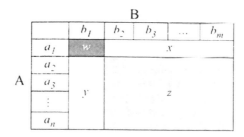

B

| A | | $b_1$ | $b_2$ | $b_3$ | … | $b_m$ |
|---|---|---|---|---|---|---|
| | $a_1$ | *w* | | *x* | | |
| | $a_2$ | | | | | |
| | $a_3$ | *y* | | *z* | | |
| | ⋮ | | | | | |
| | $a_n$ | | | | | |

Figure 5.2. Four Categories of Actors

in Sudan as "southerners," Episcopalians and Presbyterians in Ireland as "Protestants" – can be accommodated in the model not by allowing them to form a coalition but by adding another cleavage dimension (European immigrant/non-European immigrant, northerner/southerner, Protestant/Catholic). These assumptions are crucial to generating determinative outcomes; I will return at the end of the chapter to the implications of relaxing them.

Four different categories of actors can be identified, each with a different optimal strategy. I depict them in Figure 5.2 as *w*, *x*, *y*, and *z*.

Individuals located in the dark-shaded cell, *w*, are members of both the largest A group ($a_1$) and the largest B group ($b_1$). They will therefore be included in the winning coalition irrespective of whether power is held by the $a_1$s or the $b_1$s (the set-up of the matrix is such that, given plurality rules, power has to be held by one of them). They are the pivot. Their choice will determine which coalition wins. If they choose to identify themselves and to vote as $a_1$s, then $a_1$s will win power; if they choose to identify themselves and to vote as $b_1$s, then $b_1$s will hold power.

Individuals located in the unshaded cells, *x* and *y*, are the possible co-power-holders with *w*. They stand to be either part of the winning coalition or not, depending on what *w* chooses. Individuals located in the light-shaded cell, marked *z*, are members of neither $a_1$ nor $b_1$, so they will never be part of the winning coalition. In many situations they will outnumber *w*, *x*, and *y* combined. But because of their inherent internal divisions – the people in *z* are a collection of discrete and uncombinable communities grouped together only for analytical purposes – they will never be able to band together to wrest power from the $a_1$s or $b_1$s.

Which identity will individuals in each of these categories choose? Individuals in *w* stand to win either way. But because they seek to maximize the resources they will receive, they will prefer the identity that puts them in the *smaller* of the two possible winning coalitions, since this will require them to share the spoils of power with fewer other people. Their choice will therefore depend on the relative sizes of $x$ and $y$. When $x > y$, they will prefer to ally with $y$ by identifying themselves as $b_1$s. When $y > x$, they will prefer to build a coalition with $x$ by identifying themselves as $a_1$s. Only when $x > w + y$ or $y > w + x$ (i.e., when $x$ or $y$ are so large that they beat the minimum winning coalition of $w + y$ or $w + x$) will individuals in $w$ not necessarily choose the identity that defines them as members of the smaller winning ethnic group. In such a situation, whether the winning coalition is made up of $a_1$s or $b_1$s will be out of $w$'s control. Individuals in $w$ will be members of the winning group either way, but they will be powerless to impose one coalition over the other, so choosing membership in the smaller group is not necessarily advantageous.[3]

Individuals in $x$ and $y$ will always choose the identities $a_1$ and $b_1$, respectively, since these are the only identities that give them a possibility of being members of the winning coalition. However, since their ultimate ability to win power will depend on $w$'s choice rather than their own, they will devote most of their political energy to lobbying $w$. People in $y$ will insist that politics is really about cleavage B and that $b_1$s need to stick together against the $b_2$s, $b_3$s, and so on. People in $x$, meanwhile, will counter that the more important axis of political division is A and that the ethnic cleavage that really matters is the one that separates $a_1$s from the other $a_j$s.

Individuals in $z$ are in a lose–lose situation, since neither their A nor B identities will put them in the winning group. Their only viable strategy will be to try to change the game by pushing for the introduction of a new cleavage dimension.[4] Their plea will be that politics is not about either A or B but about some different cleavage, C. In theory, they should try to invoke a cleavage that defines them as members of a new minimum winning coalition. But they cannot choose – and expect people to mobilize in terms of – just any principle of social division. For the strategy to be

[3] Note that the rule that resources will be shared equally among members of the winning group means that members of $w$ can not be penalized by the other members of the winning group for not publicly defining themselves in the same way. Since individuals in $w$ are as much a part of $a_1$ as $x$ and as much a part of $b_1$ as $y$, they will be entitled to their share of the spoils of power irrespective of whether they publicly ally themselves with $x$ (in the situation where $x > w + y$) or $y$ (in the situation where $y > w + x$).

[4] Strictly speaking, this is not their only option: they could also try to join the winning coalition by acquiring the attributes that would allow them to pass as a member of $a_1$ or $b_1$. This is often quite difficult, however.

| | | B | | |
|---|---|---|---|---|
| | | $b_1$ | $b_2$ | $b_3$ |
| A | $a_1$ | $w$ | $x$ | |
| | $a_2$ | $y$ | $b_2-x_{b_2}$ | $b_3-x_{b_3}$ |
| | $a_3$ | | | |
| | $a_4$ | | | |
| | $a_5$ | | | |
| | $a_6$ | | | |

Figure 5.3. How a Sub-Coalition Within $z$ Might Affect $w$'s Choice

effective, the cleavage they propose must be an axis of social difference that others will recognize as at least potentially politically salient. Some bases of social division will fit this bill, but many others will not. This is why identifying the roster of potentially relevant cleavages in society is a prerequisite for employing the ethnic identity matrix.

Only in one special situation can people in $z$ affect $w$'s choice. This is when there exists within $z$ a sub-coalition of $a_j$s or $b_k$s that is greater than $w$ plus the smaller of $x$ and $y$ – that is, greater than the winning coalition that would otherwise form. This possibility is illustrated in Figure 5.3. Suppose that $x < y$. If this is the case, then the general rule should apply that $w$ will ally with $x$ and choose to identify itself as $a_1$. But if there exists within $z$ a sub-coalition $b_2 - x_{b_2} > w + x$ (where $x_{b_2}$ is the subset of $b_2$ that is in $x$), then $w$ will have no choice but to identify itself as $b_1$ and ally with $y$ (recall that since, by definition, $b_1$ is the largest B group, an alliance between $w$ and $y$ will beat any other $b_k$). Note that the existence of the sub-coalition $b_2 - x_{b_2} > w + x$ will not affect the fate of anyone in $z$: as soon as $w$ joins with $y$, everyone in $z$ will still be shut out of power. But the existence of the sub-coalition will have forced $w$ to make an identity choice that it otherwise would not have made. Situations of this sort frequently occur when the A and B cleavages are organized such that groups from one cleavage dimension nest inside groups from another (as, for instance, when the regions of a country each contain distinct sets of region-specific tribes, when a tribe is divided into clans, or when a linguistic community is divided into speakers of multiple dialects). Because ethnic cleavages in Africa are often nested, this special case turns out to be very important for understanding how ethnic coalition formation often works in this region.

The ethnic identity matrix helps to account for the choices of individuals. Yet the outcome this book seeks to explain is not just why individuals make the ethnic choices they do but also why particular ethnic cleavages

B

| | $b_1$ | $b_2$ | $b_3$ | ... | $b_m$ |
|---|---|---|---|---|---|
| A: $a_1$ | "ins" | | | | |
| $a_2$ | "outs" | | | | |
| $a_3$ | | | | | |
| ... | | | | | |
| $a_n$ | | | | | |

Figure 5.4. $w$ Chooses $x$; Politics Becomes About "A"

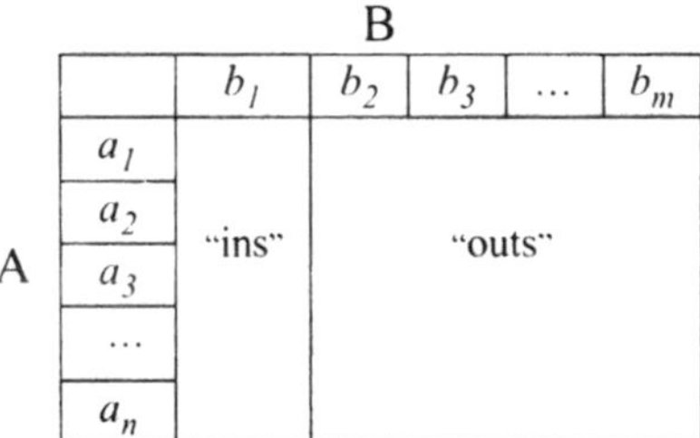

B
$b_1$
$b_2$
$b_3$
...
$b_m$
A
$a_1$
$a_2$
$a_3$
...
$a_n$
"ins"
"outs"


Figure 5.5. $w$ Chooses $y$; Politics Becomes About "B"

emerge as salient in the political system as a whole. How do the individual choices aggregate to determine the cleavage that becomes the axis of competition and conflict in the larger political system? The answer lies in the fact that, once $w$ chooses $x$ or $y$ as its coalition partner (and thus $a_1$ or $b_1$ as its identity), the social landscape is transformed. As soon as $w$ makes its choice (or as soon as other players figure out what choice $w$ will make), the distinctions among members of $a_1$, $a_2$, and $a_3$ or among members of $b_1$, $b_2$, and $b_3$ disappear and a new division emerges between those that are in power (the "ins") and those that are not (the "outs"). The particular dimension of cleavage that defines the difference between the "ins" and "outs" then becomes the axis of conflict in the political system. If $w$ chooses $x$ then politics comes to be about cleavage A – that is, about the struggle between $a_1$s and the other $a_j$s. If $w$ chooses $y$ then it becomes about cleavage B – that is, about the conflict between $b_1$s and the other $b_k$s. Note that the "outs" will still not be able to do anything to overturn the situation, since multi-ethnic coalitions are not feasible. But they will come to share the perception that political conflict is about what makes the "ins" different from everybody else. This is how individual-level choices determine which ethnic cleavage becomes politically salient. Figures 5.4 and 5.5 show the two possible outcomes.

| | | language | | | |
|---|---|---|---|---|---|
| | | English-speaking | Spanish-speaking | Korean-speaking | |
| race | Latino | 10 | 30 | 0 | 40 |
| | Asian | 15 | 0 | 20 | 35 |
| | Black | 15 | 0 | 0 | 15 |
| | White | 10 | 0 | 0 | 10 |
| | | 50 | 30 | 20 | |

Figure 5.6. An Ethnic Identity Matrix for a Hypothetical Los Angeles Community

### *An Illustration*

To show how this abstract model might be applied to a more concrete example, let us return to the hypothetical Los Angeles community described in Chapter 1. Recall that this community was divided by three different ethnic cleavages: language, race, and religion. The linguistic cleavage divided the community into English-speakers, Spanish-speakers, and Korean-speakers. The racial cleavage divided it into Latinos, Asians, blacks, and whites. And the religious cleavage partitioned it into Protestants and Catholics. Leaving the religious divisions aside to keep things simpler, we can represent the community's ethnic cleavage structure in the matrix depicted in Figure 5.6. As in the general set-up, I have shaded the $w$ and $z$ coalitions and ordered the groups on each cleavage dimension from largest to smallest. To make the incentives facing people clear, I have also provided the share of the population contained in each cell, as well as the totals for each row and column.

English-speaking Latinos are the pivot.[5] They will be in the winning coalition irrespective of whether it is formed on the basis of race or on the basis of language. The question is: which will they choose? Will they choose fellow Latinos as their coalition partners or fellow English-speakers? It is helpful to imagine one politician in the community urging them to mobilize as Latinos and another campaigning equally vigorously for them to mobilize as English-speakers. Indeed, we can imagine politicians standing at the end of each row and at the top of each column urging their fellow row- and column-members to mobilize in terms of the particular identity that they share: as Spanish-speakers, Asians, whites,

[5] Note that they are the pivot even though more English-speakers are black and Asian than are Latino and even though more Latinos are Spanish-speaking than English-speaking. What makes them the pivot is that they are members of both the most numerous racial and the most numerous linguistic communities.

and so on. Which politician will they follow? Which ethnic appeals will resonate, and which will go unheeded?

Traditional accounts of ethnic politics approach such questions by assuming that individuals will select the identity to which they have the deepest emotional commitment. The origin of this commitment is explained in a variety of ways: as a product of the inherently deeper attachment that people have to some kinds of identities than others – an argument frequently made about race (Mendelberg 2001); in terms of the hegemonic status that has been bestowed on a particular identity by history (Laitin 1986); or as an outcome of the work of some political entrepreneur who has succeeded in convincing people that one identity matters more than others (Cohen 1974; Bates 1983; Brass 1991). Irrespective of the explanation provided, all such approaches seek to account for the identity choice by providing a rationale for why one identity is more deeply felt than the other. The identity choice is then explained as a direct outcome of this greater depth of feeling.

This book takes an entirely different approach. Rather than assume that one identity is somehow innately stronger than another, I assume that all of the identities in a person's repertoire are equally important components of who they understand themselves to be. The decision of English-speaking Latinos to identify themselves in racial rather than linguistic terms (or vice versa) thus cannot be attributed to something inherent in racial or linguistic identities themselves. Instead, I argue that the choice is made purely instrumentally – for what the person gets for choosing one identity over the other, not for what it means for them to choose it. I argue that people will make their choice by weighing which identity will secure them access to the greatest share of political and economic resources and that this, in turn, will lead them to choose the identity that puts them in the group that, by virtue of its size vis-à-vis other groups, puts them in a minimum winning political coalition. As I stressed in Chapter 1, what is new in my account is neither the idea that people choose their ethnic identities instrumentally nor the idea that ethnic groups can be thought of as political coalitions mobilized to capture scarce resources. The innovation is to apply this logic to the question of when and why, given identity repertoires that contain multiple identities, individuals will choose to mobilize in terms of one identity rather than another.

If forming a minimum winning coalition is their goal, then English-speaking Latinos should ally with the smaller of the two groups in which they might claim membership. Since non-Latino English-speakers make up 40 percent of the population and non-English-speaking (i.e.,

Spanish-speaking) Latinos comprise just 30 percent, we should see English-speaking Latinos choosing their racial identity and building a coalition with their fellow Latinos. Asian, black, and white English-speakers will do their utmost to convince them to choose otherwise, but if all the pivot cares about is controlling the greatest share of resources that it can, then the lobbying of fellow English-speakers will go unheeded. And, once English-speaking Latinos have chosen to identify themselves in terms of their race, we should see the politics of the community polarized along racial lines. The elected representative will be a Latino, and whether the representative is English-speaking or Spanish-speaking will be immaterial to non-Latinos. In their eyes, all that will matter is that the representative is a Latino, played the race card to get elected, owes the position to the Latino vote, and can be expected to be beholden to Latino interests. Grievances about how resources are distributed within the community will thus be framed in terms of why Latinos are getting more than their fair share.

The critical point is that race emerges as the central axis of social identification and political division in this example not because racial identities are inherently or historically stronger than linguistic identities and not because politicians playing the race card are somehow more skillful than those attempting to mobilize the population along linguistic lines. Race emerges as politically salient because of the relative sizes of the community's racial and linguistic groups and, in this particular case, because the coalition of Latinos is smaller (and thus more useful from the perspective of the pivot) than the coalition of English-speakers. Group size, not depth of attachment, is what drives the individual-level choice and thus the society-level cleavage outcome.

## CHANGING BOUNDARIES, CHANGING OUTCOMES

The ethnic identity matrix helps to clarify why individuals make the identity choices that they do. It also helps make it clear how these choices are sensitive to changes in the boundaries of the political arena. To see why this is so, imagine that Los Angeles is redistricted and that our hypothetical community is divided into two separate electoral districts: "north" and "south." If racial and linguistic groups were evenly distributed across the original community, then this division would have no effect on people's ethnic coalition-building strategies. In both new districts, English-speaking Latinos would again be the pivot, and they would again seek to put themselves in a minimum winning coalition by allying with fellow

| race | | language | | | |
|---|---|---|---|---|---|
| | | Spanish-speaking | English-speaking | Korean-speaking | |
| | Latino | 54 | 16 | 0 | 70 |
| | Black | 0 | 20 | 0 | 20 |
| | White | 0 | 10 | 0 | 10 |
| | Asian | 0 | 0 | 0 | 0 |
| | | 54 | 46 | 0 | |

Figure 5.7. An Ethnic Identity Matrix for the "North" District

| race | | language | | | |
|---|---|---|---|---|---|
| | | English-speaking | Korean-speaking | Spanish-speaking | |
| | Asian | 30 | 40 | 0 | 70 |
| | Latino | 4 | 0 | 6 | 10 |
| | Black | 10 | 0 | 0 | 10 |
| | White | 10 | 0 | 0 | 10 |
| | | 54 | 40 | 6 | |

Figure 5.8. An Ethnic Identity Matrix for the "South" District

Latinos. But suppose that ethnic groups were not distributed evenly within the original community. Suppose that, due to patterns of residential segregation, the redistricting created a new district that was homogeneously Latino. With no other racial group in the new district (i.e., with $y = 0$), the only cleavage that would matter would be the one that divides English-speakers from Spanish-speakers. Language would thus become the axis of social division, and political coalition-building and conflict would take place along language group lines.

But suppose that the redistricting exercise did not divide the original community quite so neatly. Suppose that most of the Latino population from the original district wound up in the new "north" district and that all of the Asian population wound up in the new "south." The population distributions for each new community might look something like the matrices in Figures 5.7 and 5.8.

As these figures make clear, the partition of the original community leads to changes in the relative sizes of the linguistic and racial groups in each new political arena. Whereas Latinos outnumbered Asians in the pre-redistricting community, the opposite is the case in the post-redistricting "south." And whereas English-speakers were the predominant language community in the original district, they are outnumbered by Spanish-speakers in the new "north." These changes in the sizes of the groups bring corresponding changes in the coalition-building strategies that both politicians and voters will find it useful to employ. Strategies that made sense in the pre-redistricting setting will, for some groups, no longer be optimal in one or the other of the new contexts.

Take the case of the new "north" district. The shift in status between English-speakers and Spanish-speakers changes the pivot. Whereas English-speaking Latinos were the pivot in the original community, Spanish-speaking Latinos play this role in new one. English-speaking Latinos still do best by identifying themselves in racial terms, but this time whether or not they will share power will be out of their hands. Meanwhile, whereas Spanish-speaking Latinos did best in the pre-redistricting era by identifying themselves in racial terms and lobbying fellow Latinos to join them in a coalition along racial lines, they do best in the post-redistricting context by identifying themselves in linguistic terms and turning their backs on their English-speaking Latino brothers and sisters. Since English-speaking Latinos can be expected to respond to this situation by simply claiming that they speak Spanish too, much of the political action in the district will revolve around policing the border between the English- and Spanish-speaking components of the broader Latino community.

Individuals in the new "south" will experience similar changes in their optimal strategies. English-speaking Asians still do best by identifying themselves in linguistic terms. This time, however, they are the pivot and actually wind up in the winning coalition. Meanwhile English-speaking Latinos, who in the original community were best served by voting with their fellow Latinos, now do best by presenting themselves as English-speakers. For both of these groups, as for both the English- and Spanish-speaking Latinos in the new "north," changing the boundaries of the political arena either changes their incentives for identifying themselves in terms of a particular identity or, because of the altered behavior of others, changes the payoffs they will receive for having done so.[6] Horowitz (1985: 75) writes that "one of the most powerful influences on the scope and shape of 'we' and 'they' has been the scope and shape of political boundaries." This example, and the ethnic identity matrix heuristic on which it is based, shows why.

[6] In addition to altering the choices they make about which identities to emphasize, some people will have powerful incentives to try to change the contents of their identity repertoires. Korean-speaking Asians and Spanish-speaking Latinos, for example, will have incentives to invest in learning English.

Of course, I deliberately designed this illustration to show how changes in the boundaries of the political arena can alter the incentives for people to identify themselves in different ways. Lest readers think this illustration has no real-world parallels, consider the following examples.

Today, Telugu-speaking Andhra Pradesh is one of India's twenty-eight states. Before 1953, however, it was part of Tamil-speaking Madras. During the period when the two states were united, the principal axis of social conflict was linguistic and the central political divide was between Telugu-speakers, who demanded a separate state, and Tamil-speakers, who actively resisted these demands. Yet, after Andhra Pradesh was broken off from Madras in 1953, the language-based conflict was superseded in Andhra by a competition for control of the state between the Kamma and Reddi castes (both Telugu-speaking), and by a regional conflict between people living in the Telangana and Coastal regions of the state (Horowitz, 1985: 613–14). The altered boundaries of the arena of competition led to the emergence of a completely different set of salient cleavages.

The broader partition of India in 1947 offers another example. Before the partition, ethnic politics in the territory that was to become Pakistan revolved around the conflict between Hindus and Muslims. After Pakistan became an independent state, however, the paramount Hindu–Muslim cleavage was replaced by distinctions, varying from community to community, based on language, tribe, or region. Horowitz (1975: 135) writes that "hardly had the Indio-Pakistani subcontinent been partitioned along what were thought to be hard-and-fast Hindu–Muslim lines when, in 1948, Mohammed Ali Jinnah, who had done so much to foster subnational identities in undivided India, ironically found it necessary to warn against the 'curse of provincialism' in undivided Pakistan." The separation of Pakistan from India led to the replacement of one basis of ethnic division by another.

The experience of decolonization provides yet another illustration. In colony after colony, political conflict during the pre-independence era was between colonizers (British, French, Belgian, etc.) and colonized (Sri Lankans, Fijians, Ivoirians, Congolese, etc.), as the latter sought to wrest political control from the former. Since the political arena included both the non-white colony and the white metropole, the relevant axis of political cleavage during this period was race. But as soon as independence was won and the relevant arena of political competition shrank to the new nation itself, the once unified non-white community fractured into rival camps and the racial cleavage was superseded by cleavages based on language, religion, region, or tribe.

In all of these examples, changes in the boundaries of the political arena generated changes in the dimensions of ethnic identity that were mobilized. Although I do not provide them here, one could easily construct ethnic identity matrices for each case to show how the change in the boundaries of the political arena produced the changes in people's choices.

As in the Los Angeles example, these boundary changes all involved alterations in the physical boundaries of the political system. However, the physical boundaries of political units need not change for the boundaries of the *effective* political arena to be altered and for a shift to occur in individuals' incentives to emphasize one cleavage dimension rather than another. This can happen when a change in political institutions shifts the locus of political competition from one domain to another. Such a change can bring about a shift in the effective arena of political competition (and, with it, a shift in individuals' identity choices) even when the physical boundaries of the political system remain unaltered. The transitions in Zambia from multi-party to one-party rule (and back) did precisely this.

## MULTI-PARTY POLITICS, ONE-PARTY POLITICS, AND IDENTITY CHOICE

How are multi-party and one-party political systems different, and how do these differences generate different ethnic choice outcomes? Although multi-party and one-party political systems vary in a great many ways, the central institutional differences between the two can be reduced to two key issues. The first is whether multiple parties are legally permitted to compete for political power. In multi-party systems, where multiple parties are permitted, every parliamentary and presidential candidate runs on the ticket of a different party. In one-party systems, by contrast, political competition takes place under the auspices of a single ruling party and every candidate must run on the ticket of that party. The second key difference lies in whether or not the executive is chosen by the electorate. In one-party states, the norm is for the President to be chosen by the Central Committee of the ruling party and then ratified by voters through a simple up-or-down vote in the general election. In multi-party states, multiple presidential candidates compete for support in the election itself. Thus while presidential elections are held in both systems, only in multi-party contests do voters have a real choice among distinct alternatives. These seemingly minor differences turn out to have important effects. For our purposes, the most important effect is on the scope of the effective arena in which political competition takes place.

In one-party systems, where the outcome of the presidential election is determined in advance, the only electoral contest of consequence is the one over who will represent each parliamentary constituency. The parliamentary election thus becomes the central locus of competition in the political system. This has the effect of shrinking the effective arena of political conflict from the nation as a whole to the level of individual electoral constituencies. In multi-party elections, by contrast, when control over the executive *is* at issue, electoral competition takes place at two levels simultaneously: at the national level (for the presidency) and at the constituency level (for parliamentary representation). In practice, however, the effective arena of political competition for both the presidential and parliamentary contests is the national arena. This is because party labels transform parliamentary candidates into representatives of national coalitions, and this transforms the constituency-level conflicts in which they are engaged into contests for national power.

Party labels do not matter in one-party parliamentary elections because they do not vary across candidates: all candidates must, by law, run on the ticket of the ruling party. But in multi-party parliamentary elections, where each candidate runs on the ticket of a different party, voters will have two different sources of information to consider when they try to predict each candidate's future behavior: the candidate's personal attributes and the candidate's party affiliation. The relative importance that voters attach to these two sources of information will depend on the particular characteristics of the electoral system, including the degree of control that party leaders exercise over access to the party label, whether or not votes are pooled across parties, whether voters cast one vote or many, and the magnitude of electoral districts (Carey and Shugart 1995). It will also depend on whether or not presidential and parliamentary elections are held concurrently (Shugart and Carey 1992; Shugart 1995). In political systems with single-member plurality electoral rules, party endorsements, and concurrent presidential and parliamentary elections (such as in Zambia and most former British colonies), party labels will be much more important to voters than the personal attributes of the candidates (Carey and Shugart 1995). In such situations, voters will make their choices based not on the strengths and weaknesses of the candidates themselves but on the affinity the voters feel for the political parties the candidates each represent.[7] Voters in such a context will cast their parliamentary election ballots for individual candidates competing at the level of the constituency, but in deciding which candidate to support, they will look beyond the candidates and focus their attention on what their vote means for the battle among the political parties. And since political parties are competing for power at the national level, the effective arena of political competition becomes the nation as a whole.[8]

Thus even if the physical boundaries of a country's political system remain unchanged, altering its political institutions either to prohibit or to allow for competition among multiple political parties will change the boundaries of the effective arena of political competition. A shift from multi-party to one-party competition will shrink that arena from the nation as a whole to the level of the electoral constituency, and a shift from one-party to multi-party competition will expand it from the electoral constituency to the nation as a whole. These changes, in turn, affect the kinds of ethnic cleavages that will emerge as axes of political competition

[7] I provide evidence to substantiate the link between Zambia's electoral rules and voters' focus on candidates' party affiliations in Chapter 8. Perhaps the most famous example of a candidate's individual attributes being trumped by his party affiliation in an SMP system is Franklin D. Roosevelt, who never succeeded in carrying his home area, the traditionally Republican Duchess County, New York. Duchess County was a WASP bastion, and Roosevelt, though a WASP himself, was the Democratic candidate and was thus seen by the county's voters as representing the interests of the non-WASP coalition: Italians, Irish, and Jews (Key 1949: 38).

[8] Bates (1989: 92) provides a slightly different argument that leads to the same result. He argues that national issues, and the national frame, will be salient in multi-party elections because voters will view candidates as potential members of coalitions that might conceivably form the government and shape national policy. In single-party elections, however, voters know that each candidate will have only a negligible impact on national policy since, even if candidates are successful, they will be one of more than 100 Members of Parliament. This calculation, Bates argues, shifts voters' attention from national policy issues to patronage concerns, and from the question of "who has the best policy?" to the question of "which candidate will best deliver patronage to the constituency?" This, in turn, shifts the locus of political competition from "national rivalries between organized teams" to "individual rivalries at the constituency level." Thus, national issues and cleavages will animate multi-party politics and local-level rivalries will structure one-party politics. The problem with this argument is that, at least in the Zambian case (though I suspect in other developing country settings as well), it over-estimates the extent to which voters ever view candidates as shapers of national policy agendas and it under-estimates the role of patronage concerns in competitive party settings. The account that I provide reaches the same conclusion without making any assumptions about either the extent to which voters see candidates as policy-makers or the relative salience of patronage in one-party and multi-party regimes.

and conflict in each context. In one-party settings, political conflict will revolve around constituency-level ethnic cleavages. In multi-party elections, where the arena of political competition is the entire country, broader cleavages that define national-scale groups will become salient. In both settings, politicians will seek to build and voters will cast their votes so as to secure membership in minimum winning coalitions. But because the arenas of competition are different, the social material out of which these coalitions will be crafted will be different as well. In one-party settings, political competition and conflict will revolve around the ethnic groups that divide the constituency; in multi-party settings, it will revolve around the ethnic groups that divide the nation.

This logic, combined with the model of identity choice presented earlier, illustrates how institutional change can cause identity change. It also put us in a position to explain why tribal and linguistic identities each emerged in Zambia as bases for political coalition-building in the periods in which they did.

## APPLYING THE MODEL TO THE ZAMBIAN CASE

Recall from Chapters 2 and 3 that Zambians identify themselves ethnically as members either of one of the country's four language groups or of one of the country's roughly seventy tribes. Figure 5.9 provides an ethnic identity matrix for the country. As in the general example, the linguistic and tribal groups are ordered from largest to smallest. In addition, I have indicated the coalitions *w*, *x*, *y*, and *z*.

Bemba-speaking Bembas are the pivot; non-Bemba-speaking Bembas (an empty set) are *x*; and non-Bemba Bemba-speakers (e.g., members of the Bisa, Aushi, Kabende, and other Bemba-speaking tribes) are *y*. Since $y > x$, we would expect *w* to choose *x* and to transform national-level

<table>
<tr><td colspan="6">language</td></tr>
<tr><td rowspan="6">tribe</td><td></td><td>Bemba-speaking</td><td>Nyanja-speaking</td><td>Tonga-speaking</td><td>Lozi-speaking</td></tr>
<tr><td>Bemba</td><td>w</td><td colspan="3">x</td></tr>
<tr><td>Tonga</td><td rowspan="4">y</td><td rowspan="4" colspan="3">z</td></tr>
<tr><td>Chewa</td></tr>
<tr><td>...</td></tr>
<tr><td>$\text{tribe}_m$</td></tr>
</table>

Figure 5.9. An Ethnic Identity Matrix for Zambia

| | $Lang_{only}$ |
|---|---|
| $Tribe_1$ | $w$ |
| $Tribe_2$ | |
| $Tribe_3$ | |
| ... | $y$ |
| $Tribe_m$ | |

Figure 5.10. An Ethnic Identity Matrix for a Rural Constituency

conflict in Zambia into a struggle among the country's tribes. However, since the coalitions of Nyanja-speakers, Tonga-speakers, and Lozi-speakers are all larger than the coalition of Bemba tribespeople (i.e., for all $n > 1$, $Lang_n - x_{Lang_n} > w + x$), $w$ will be forced into a coalition with $y$.[9] Bemba-speaking Bembas will thus identify themselves in language group terms and unite with fellow Bemba-speakers to win power, and national-level political conflict in Zambia will revolve around language group differences.

A different outcome emerges when political competition is restricted to the constituency level. The spatial distribution of tribal and linguistic groups in Zambia guarantees that constituency-level ethnic landscapes (and identity matrices) will be quite different from the one depicted for the nation as a whole in Figure 5.9.[10] Rural constituencies, which comprise more than 80 percent of the total, are almost all homogeneous with respect to language and heterogeneous with respect to tribe (though a few are homogeneous with respect to both). Ethnic identity matrices for most rural constituencies thus look like the one provided in Figure 5.10. Urban constituencies, in contrast, contain migrants from multiple tribes, and, while one language group is usually dominant, one or more smaller language groups are usually also present. In terms of their ethnic composition, urban constituencies thus look more like the national political arena. An ethnic identity matrix for a typical urban constituency is provided in Figure 5.11.

In rural constituencies like the one depicted in Figure 5.10, the coalition-building outcome is clear: since $x = 0$, $y > x$ and the pivot will choose to build its coalition along tribal lines. Tribal divisions will thus

[9] Since $y > w + x$, $w$ would have no reason, in any case, to hold fast to its coalition with $x$.

[10] For a discussion of the origins of these spatial distributions, see Chapters 2 and 3.

| | $Lang_{dominant}$ | $Lang_2$ | $Lang_3$ |
|---|---|---|---|
| $Tribe_1$ | $w$ | $x$ | |
| $Tribe_2$ | | | |
| $Tribe_3$ | $y$ | $z$ | |
| ... | | | |
| $Tribe_m$ | | | |

Figure 5.11. An Ethnic Identity Matrix for an Urban Constituency

emerge as the axis of competition and conflict in rural constituencies. The particular tribal group that will play the role of pivot (and hold power) will vary from constituency to constituency, but political conflict will be played out in terms of the struggle between members of the dominant tribe and members of other tribes.

In urban constituencies, it will almost always be the case either that $y > w + x$ or that $Lang_n - x_{Lang_n} > w + x$. Thus, at the national level, the pivot will choose to identify itself in linguistic terms and to build a winning coalition by allying with fellow members of its language group. The only difference with the national-level outcome will be that the particular $w + y$ coalition will differ from urban location to urban location, depending on which language group happens to predominate in the town in which the constituency is located. The important point, however, is that the pivot will choose its linguistic, rather than its tribal, identity and that the linguistic cleavage will therefore emerge as the salient axis of political division.

The link between institutional change and changes in the kinds of ethnic cleavages that have emerged as politically salient during different periods of Zambia's post-independence history should now be clear. Since the locus of political conflict in multi-party elections is at the national level, and since national-level conflict in Zambia revolves around language group differences, we will observe political competition and coalition-building taking place along language group lines during periods when Zambia is under multi-party rule. We will observe politicians in such settings couching their appeals in language group terms and voters supporting candidates who, by virtue of their party affiliations, are perceived to represent the interests of their language groups. Of course, politicians who stand to lose from such an outcome – for instance, candidates who are running on the tickets of parties perceived to be affiliated with outsider language groups – can be expected to do what they can to combat the tendency for politics to be reduced to a struggle among language groups. To the extent that they try to break the hegemony of linguistic distinctions by emphasizing tribal differences, some non-linguistic ethnic campaigning may emerge. But every tribal appeal by such a politician will be met by a counter-claim that this person is simply trying to divert peoples' focus from the cleavage that matters: the one that divides the country along language group lines. So long as voters view the political process as a means of gaining control over resources controlled by the center, and so long as they view having a member of their own group in a position of political power at the center as the surest way to serve that end, the conflict between members of the dominant language group and others will emerge as the central axis of political competition. Political conflict in multi-party settings will be language group conflict.

During periods when the country is under one-party rule, a different axis of ethnic political conflict will emerge in most areas. In the one-party context, the locus of political conflict contracts to the electoral constituency and constituency-level cleavages will emerge as the central basis of political coalition-building. In rural areas this means that tribal divisions will emerge as salient, while in urban areas it means that political conflict will be organized (as it is in multi-party settings) along linguistic lines. Note that while the language cleavage will be salient in urban contexts in both one-party and multi-party elections, it will be salient for different reasons. In the multi-party context, language group differences matter because of the centrality of language group divisions in national affairs; in the one-party context, they matter because of the polyglot nature of urban electoral constituencies and because language communities always include members of multiple tribes.

As in the multi-party context, during one-party rule politicians who are disadvantaged by the salience of constituency-level ethnic cleavages – for example, members of non-dominant tribes running in rural constituencies or members of non-dominant language groups running in urban constituencies – can be expected to try to improve their lot by playing the other ethnic card. But this will not prevent either the candidate from the dominant group from winning or the struggle between members of the dominant group and others from emerging as the central axis of political conflict. The predominant outcome in rural areas will thus be politicians making appeals and voters casting their ballots along tribal lines, whereas in urban areas we will find them mobilizing along language group lines. Since the vast majority of electoral constituencies in Zambia are rural, however, we should find the general tendency in one-party settings to be for tribal campaigning and tribal voting to predominate.

## REVISITING THE ASSUMPTIONS OF THE MODEL

The model I have presented offers a simple account of identity and coalition-building choices that can explain why some ethnic cleavages become the axis of political competition rather than others. Yet, while powerful, the explanation rests on a number of important assumptions. How robust is the model to relaxing them? Are the assumptions reasonable for the Zambian case whose patterns of ethnic politics we seek to explain?

### *Single-Member Plurality Rules*

The first key assumption is that the winner of the political contest will be the single candidate who wins the plurality of the votes. Single-member plurality rules (along with the inability of politicians to form multi-ethnic coalitions) are necessary for there to be a unique equilibrium cleavage outcome. If more than one candidate can be selected in the constituency (i.e., if district magnitude is greater than one) then some voters will be able to allocate their support in terms of one dimension of identity to capture one of the available seats and other voters will be able to mobilize along the lines of a different identity dimension to capture one of the others. The identity choices of individual voters, and the cleavage outcome more generally, will cease to be predictable in advance. Note that the requirement that district magnitude be equal to one rules out proportional representation systems, which have multi-member districts.

The restriction to single-member plurality rule is clearly appropriate for Zambia, since these are the electoral rules that have been in operation in that country since independence. But it does limit the strict applicability of the model to some other cases.

### *Resources Shared Equally Among the Winners*

The model assumes that, once an ethnic group has won, resources will be shared equally with all group members. This would seem to be a critical assumption since, without it, it would be possible for a subset of the winning ethnic group (e.g., those who are not just members of the dominant language group or tribe but who come from the President's province or the MP's village) to keep most of the spoils of power for themselves. If this were the case, the columns and rows in the ethnic identity matrix could no longer be thought of as unified coalitions. Yet the results should still hold even if this were true. Even if a winning coalition member believes that she will receive less than a proportionate share of the benefits of power, this should not dissuade her from choosing as the model assumes she will *so long as she also believes that she will get zero if she is not in the winning row or column.* The likelihood that a fellow group member will give everyone in the winning coalition a fair share is less important than the likelihood that a non-group member would share resources with outsiders. And whereas a voter may believe that some members of her group will benefit more than she will if her group wins, she will almost certainly believe that she will still benefit more than if another group wins. As long as this is the case, it is not, strictly speaking, necessary that she assume that she will receive an equal share of the spoils of victory. It is necessary only that she believe that she will receive a greater amount than she would if the victor came from a group in which she could not claim membership.

### *Territoriality of the Potentially Salient Cleavages*

A third, unstated, assumption that is necessary for the model's predictions to hold is that the ethnic cleavages in question are based on identities that have a strong territorial component. Territoriality insures that the map of ethnic divisions at the national level is different from the map of ethnic cleavages in each individual constituency. To see why this is important, consider what would happen to the logic of the model if, instead of drawing upon territorially linked identities like language group affiliation or tribal loyalty, politicians sought to build coalitions along gender lines. Gender identity creates problems for the model because the groups that it defines are evenly distributed and thus produce identical constituency-level and national-level demographics: men and women each constitute roughly 50 percent of the population in each constituency and 50 percent of the population in the country as a whole. Politicians seeking to invoke gender cleavages would therefore face identical coalition-building incentives at both the national and constituency levels. Since the model's predictions rest on an expectation that political actors competing at the national level will face different coalition-building incentives from political actors competing at the constituency level, the fact that gender identities produce identical incentives in each arena undermines the model's usefulness. To be sure, gender identities constitute an extreme, even unique, identity type: most social identities are more like regional or tribal affiliation than like gender. But if we imagine a continuum of identity types, with gender at one end and regional identity at the other, the model will work best when the social cleavages that the political actors are choosing from are closer to the regional than to the gender end of the spectrum. The assumption of territoriality certainly holds in Zambia (and, for similar historical reasons, throughout Africa). But making the assumption clear is necessary to understand the contexts to which the model will, and will not, travel.

### *Perfect Information*

The model also assumes that, in choosing which contestant to support, voters have perfect information about the sizes of each tribal and language group in the political arena. If, as I assume is the case, individuals make their identity choices based on the size of the coalition to which their chosen identity gives them entry, knowing the sizes of the respective coalitions that they might choose (as well as the sizes of the coalitions against which they will be competing) is clearly important. But for practical purposes all that is necessary for such choices to be made is that people have a rough idea of the relative sizes of their groups vis-à-vis the other major groups in the political system.

The model also (implicitly) assumes that voters will have perfect information about the tribal background of each candidate and the language group affiliation of each party. It might seem unlikely that voters would be unable to identify contestants' tribal backgrounds – after all, most candidates are residents of the constituency in which they are running, so their family lineage is almost certainly known. However, the frequency of inter-tribal marriages in Zambia means that a significant number of candidates have parents who belong to different tribes, and this can make the candidate's own tribal affiliation ambiguous. In addition, in urban constituencies, where populations tend to be extremely heterogeneous and where the tendency in most social interactions is to identify people in terms of their broader regional or linguistic backgrounds, it is possible that at least some voters will be unable to put candidates into their correct tribal pigeonholes.

In multi-party elections, where the presumed language group orientations of political parties replace candidates' ethnic affiliations as the basis for predicting future patronage flows, even greater opportunities emerge for the misinterpretation of candidates' ethnic group loyalties. As we saw in Chapter 4, parties' language group affiliations are usually signaled by the language group memberships of their presidents. Sometimes, however, a president's language group affiliation is ambiguous. Take the case of President Kaunda, whose parents came from Nyanja-speaking Malawi but who grew up in Bemba-speaking Northern Province (and who, himself, spoke Bemba far better than Nyanja). Should he be coded as a Bemba-speaker or a Nyanja-speaker? A party's language group orientation may also be made unclear by the party's conscious effort to present itself in pan-ethnic terms.

To the extent that such efforts, or the other factors just described, cause some voters either to misconstrue the tribal backgrounds of candidates or to misinterpret the language group orientations of political parties, the model's expectations about voting behavior will not be borne out precisely. But while voters' uncertainty about candidates' and parties' ethnic affiliations may generate outcomes that deviate from the strict predictions of the model, the imperfect information voters possess about these and other issues paradoxically serves at the same time to strengthen the model's predictions in four ways.

First, it reinforces the importance of ethnic considerations in the voting calculus. In the absence of reliable information about either the policies that the competing candidates will pursue or the ability of each contestant to secure development resources for the constituency from the central government, voters will focus their attention on what little information they do have that will allow them to predict the candidates' future behavior: the candidates' ethnic affiliations. In fact, the less information that voters have about the contestants in the race, the more they will turn to ethnicity as a decision-making shorthand (Ferree 2003). Paraphrasing Downs's observation about the role of ideology (1957: 98), we might say that information about candidates' ethnic affiliations is useful to voters because it removes the necessity of relating the candidates' or parties' stand on every issue to their own. In the absence of other information that might allow them to forecast future behavior, it can be used as a predictor of the candidate's or party's stand on a variety of issues and behavior in a variety of situations.

For Downs, the tendency for voters to focus on ideology is a rational response to the high cost of being fully informed about politics. In developed countries, voters usually have a choice in this matter: should they choose to invest the time and energy to do so, it is possible for them to learn about the agendas, records, and policy positions of the parties and candidates competing in the race. In developing countries like Zambia, however, communication infrastructures are often so poorly developed and campaign organizations are often so weak that most voters, even if they want to, have little ability to obtain reliable information about what separates one candidate's or party's position on the issues from another's. In the 1973 campaign, for example, "many candidates remained unknown [because] there was an almost total lack of publicity concerning most aspects of the elections" (Chikulo 1979: 210). In the 1983 election, "party-organized election campaign meetings [did not do] much in the way of introducing the candidates, as attendance at most meetings [was] poor, largely because of the short notice given and the bad timing" (*Daily Mail*, 21 October 1983). Even when information about candidates and parties is available to voters, that information is often unbalanced in its coverage (usually focused on one candidate or party at the expense of others) and obtainable only in some parts of the country. In 1968, for example, while the UNIP spent considerable sums on campaign materials and was generally able to get its message out to most voters, the ANC had few funds for transport or publicity, received little coverage from the mass media, and was largely unable to contact voters outside of its Southern Province base (Molteno and Scott 1974: 179). With nine days to go before election day, "not a single [ANC] poster [had] been displayed" (*Times of Zambia*, 10 December 1968). Access to campaign resources and to the media was similarly skewed in favor of the ruling party during the 1996 election (Bratton and Posner 1998). In such a context of incomplete, uneven, or unreliable information about parties' and candidates' platforms and policy positions, voters' emphasis on ethnicity is a rational response.

Yet even if Zambian voters did have perfect information about candidates' and parties' platforms, our discussion in Chapter 4 suggests that such information probably would not have played a particularly central role in shaping many voters' decisions. As we saw, most Zambian voters make their choices based less on candidates' or parties' policy positions than on their perceptions of the likelihood that each candidate or party will deliver patronage to them. This likelihood, in turn, is a function of two factors: the ability of the candidate to secure development resources for the constituency from the central government, and the candidate's willingness to channel those resources to the constituents personally. In weighing these issues, problems of imperfect information also reinforce the salience of ethnic considerations. A schoolteacher in Chipata pointed out that, in weighing a candidate's ability to "deliver the goods,"

> the problem is that people do not know his capability in that position... You find that most of the people are ignorant about this... Sometimes they will not know how capable that person is, so you find most of the people just support [the candidate] for the reason that he comes from that area... There isn't much education or there is not much awareness [and this] makes people land into wrong choices. (CPTA-T)

A former parliamentary candidate agreed that voters "didn't know us. They didn't know what our qualifications were or what we could do for them. All that was abridged."[11]

To the extent that voters are unable to gauge the abilities of the various candidates to bargain successfully on their behalf to win development resources from the central government, they will be forced to make their choice based on other factors. In one-party elections, they will respond to the lack of reliable information about candidates' abilities by focusing on the likelihood that each candidate, if he *is* able to secure resources from the center, will distribute those resources to them personally rather than to other residents of the constituency. This will cause voters to focus their attention on the candidates' respective local tribal identities. In multi-party contests, before thinking about whether each candidate will be likely to channel the resources that he is able to secure from the center to them personally, voters must first focus their attention on the likelihood that the party on whose ticket each of the candidates is standing will allocate development resources to their region of the country rather than to other regions. This will encourage them to emphasize the presumed language group loyalties of the respective political parties. In each case, the inability of voters to ascertain reliably the abilities of the candidates forces them to look to other issues, and this reinforces their tendency to behave in ways that accord with the expectations of the model.

Imperfect information also encourages voters to behave in accordance with the expectations of the model in a third way by reducing the likelihood of strategic voting. If voters are in a position to gauge accurately the degree of support enjoyed by each candidate or party in the race, and if the candidate or party that is affiliated with their tribe or language group clearly has no chance of capturing power, then voters will have strong incentives to shift their support to second-choice alternatives. However, if a lack of information makes voters unable to predict whether or not their preferred candidate or party has a chance to capture power, then they will

[11] Interview with Hosea Soko, 17 October 1995.

be unlikely to vote in such a strategic manner. This effect is particularly important in multi-party elections, where a candidate's ability to deliver patronage depends not only on his getting elected in the constituency but also on his party being able to capture power at the national level. Even if voters are able to assess each candidate's prospects within the relatively narrow arena of their own constituency, they may not have enough information to judge the relative strength in the country as a whole of the parties with which each of the candidates is affiliated.[12] As one focus group respondent pointed out,

> the question of whether MMD or UNIP is strong [throughout the country] may be difficult to answer. This is because some of us are only in Mongu. We don't go to other places. Therefore you can't tell unless you listen on the radio, though sometimes [even then] you [still] can't understand. MMD is the ruling party so it is known to all. But opposition parties may be known in the area where you stay and when you go to other places you find that party is not popular or not there. (MON-MS-M)

In terms of being in a position to secure development resources through their MP from the state, Western Province residents would, in retrospect, have been better off had they not shifted their support from the ruling MMD to the NP, AZ, and UNIP in the by-elections held after 1991 and then again in the 1996 general elections. Eastern Province voters would probably also have been better off had they supported MMD candidates rather than UNIP candidates in 1991. But the lack of information about whether the local enthusiasm felt for these parties was shared by people in the rest of the country (many voters assumed, incorrectly, that it was) prevented Western and Eastern Province voters from strategically backing the winning horse.

A final way in which the lack of reliable information available to Zambian voters reinforces the importance of ethnic identities in the electoral process is by enhancing the ability of politicians to mobilize electoral support by exploiting rumors of ethnic group favoritism. As we saw in Chapter 4, one of the principal mobilizational tools used by non-Bemba-speaking politicians since independence has been the charge that Bembas enjoy more than their fair share of government jobs and development

[12] In one-party elections, where assessing the viability of a candidate from one's own tribe requires only knowing the relative sizes of the various tribes that populate the constituency, most voters will be able to predict whether or not a vote for a candidate from their tribe will be wasted, providing that people vote exclusively for their fellow tribespeople.

resources. But, as we also saw, analyses of the ethnic backgrounds of state officeholders and the regions of the country that have benefited from government spending reveal that such allegations, despite their wide acceptance as fact, are only weakly supported by the evidence. The reason that perceptions of governmental favoritism can be so out of line with reality is not only because non-Bemba politicians have an interest in promoting the misperception. A critical contributing element is the fact that the voters that the politicians hope to sway by making such allegations lack the information with which to corroborate the politicians' claims.

The incomplete information that prevents voters from double-checking claims about governmental favoritism also prevents them from disconfirming inflammatory allegations about slights made by rival group leaders or threats posed by other groups to their livelihood or security.[13] Recall, for example, that one of the key pieces of ammunition used by Luapula Province politicians in the 1969 Kawambwa East by-election campaign (described in Chapter 4) was the charge that outsider candidate John Mwanakatwe had referred to Luapulans as *batubula* (dumb fishermen). Had voters been able to confirm whether Mwanakatwe had ever, in fact, said this – and evidence suggests he probably did not (Bates 1976: 229) – the allegation might have been much less effective in generating ethnic polarization. Similarly, charges made during the 1973 election in Livingstone by Tonga- and Lozi-speaking politicians that members of the rival groups were mobilizing against them became a self-fulfilling prophecy precisely because the charges could not be disconfirmed (Baylies and Szeftel 1984: 37). In similar fashion, the claim by NP campaigners during the run-up to the 1993 Western Province by-elections that they possessed a letter written by President Chiluba to the Lozi Paramount Chief in which the President criticized the Lozi Royal Establishment for stirring up trouble between the Nkoyas and Lozis in Kaoma district would have been far less effective in turning Lozi-speaking voters against the MMD had it been possible to confirm that the letter was, in fact, a fabrication – which it ultimately turned out to be (*Daily Mail*, 10 November 1993). The success of all of these efforts depended on the fact that voters were unable to confirm the veracity of the allegations that were being made. Had reliable information

[13] For precisely this reason, improving the quality and quantity of such information is a key component of confidence-building measures aimed at conflict resolution. For a general discussion of the role of imperfect information in generating ethnic insecurity and ethnic conflict, see Posen (1993).

about the events or patterns of behavior on which these inflammatory allegations were based been available, these charges either would never have been made or would have had far less impact. In this way, as in the others described earlier, the imperfect information available to Zambian voters served to reinforce the model's expectations about ethnic voting.

PART III

# Introduction to Part III

## Testing the Argument

Chapter 5 presented a simple model of identity choice that helps us to account for why political competition in Zambia has tended to revolve around tribal differences in one-party settings and around language group differences in multi party settings. The chapters of Part III present a series of analyses that test several of the model's observable implications. Chapter 6 sets the stage for these analyses by addressing and ruling out competing explanations. Chapters 7 and 8 then turn to the implications of the model itself. Chapter 7 focuses on its implications for the behavior of political elites, and Chapter 8 focuses on its implications for mass voting.

It bears underscoring from the outset that the implications being tested are about the relative salience of tribal and linguistic identities in different institutional contexts, not about the salience of ethnicity per se. Some Zambian politicians run for Parliament for no other reason than because they want the attention that being a candidate brings. Others are motivated by a commitment to national service. Some voters make their electoral choices because they are swayed by a politician's credentials or record of performance. Others vote for a particular person or party because they are bribed. In the context of the extreme poverty in which elections are fought in Zambia, a bag of mealie meal, a bolt of cloth, or even a T-shirt (along with the implicit promise that more such gifts are on the way) may be enough to buy a voter's support. In short, many politicians and voters in Zambia are motivated by factors other than ethnicity. Yet this fact, while clearly important for some questions and issues, is not critical for the argument developed in this book. What matters from the standpoint of the argument is not whether every Zambian politician or voter is motivated by ethnicity, but whether those who *are* motivated by ethnicity are motivated by their tribal affiliations or by their language group memberships. Variation in the *kinds* of ethnic identities that motivate behavior in one-party and multi-party settings is more important than the share of the variance that ethnicity explains in either.

In trying to document these patterns of behavior and test them against the expectations of the model, my strategy is to make use of multiple tests and a diversity of data and methodologies. In doing so, I follow Robert Putnam's maxim that "the prudent social scientist, like the wise investor, must rely on diversification to magnify the strengths, and to offset the weaknesses, of any single instrument" (1993: 12). To document the kinds of appeals that politicians make in different institutional settings, I draw on newspaper accounts, secondary source materials, interviews with politicians, focus group discussions, and original survey data.[1] To test whether citizens voted and politicians chose the constituencies in which they would run in the way that the model would predict, I combine qualitative analyses of secondary sources, newspaper accounts, focus groups, and surveys with quantitative analyses of ethnic demographic data, election results from seven different general elections, and original data on the tribal backgrounds of each of the more than 2,200 parliamentary candidates that ran for election in Zambia between 1968 and 1999.[2] All told, I test more than a dozen different observable implications of the model. Taken individually, the results of each of these tests support the model's expectations. However, none of them alone provides as compelling a confirmation for the model's success as they do when taken together. Moreover, the diversity of the data and of the methods that these different tests employ protects my evaluation of the model's explanatory power from the imperfections of any individual data source or methodology.

[1] Details of the survey and focus group work are provided in Appendix B.
[2] Details of these data sources are provided in Appendices C and D.

# 6

## *Competing Explanations*

The motivation for the model presented in the last chapter was the observation that changes in regime type in Zambia seem to co-vary with changes in the relative political salience of linguistic and tribal identities in national elections. During multi-party contests, ethnic politics revolves around language group divisions, whereas during one-party elections it revolves around tribal differences. Given this pattern of co-variation, it is natural to assume that it is something about the multi-party or one-party nature of the electoral regime that is driving the salient cleavage outcome. However, it is at least possible that other factors that happen to co-vary with regime type could be responsible for the changes we see in the salience of tribal and linguistic identities. If so, these factors would offer competing explanations for the argument presented in Chapter 5. The first part of the present chapter explores this possibility.

The second part of the chapter takes up another potential problem: endogeneity. Even if we are able to rule out the possibility that something other than regime change has caused Zambian politicians and voters to shift their focus from one ethnic cleavage dimension to the other, we might still have the causal arrows backward. It is possible that changes in the salience of tribal and linguistic identities, driven by factors other than changes in regime type, are what caused the transitions from multi-party to one-party rule and back. This possibility needs to be ruled out for the argument advanced in the book to hold.

Finally, even if it can be established that changes in regime type were responsible for the shift in politically salient ethnic identities, and not the other way around, it is still possible that aspects of regime change other than the factors on which the model focuses could be doing the work in accounting for why one ethnic cleavage becomes politically salient rather than the other. In the model, the shift from multi-party to one-party rule (and vice versa) is a purely institutional change that involves just two factors: an alteration in the number of parties that are legally permitted to compete and a shift in whether the President is selected by the ruling party's Central Committee or by the voters. However, one-party and multi-party political systems typically differ in more than in just these two respects. The final part of the chapter addresses the possibility that aspects of the one-party and multi-party systems other than those captured in these two formal institutional rules might be responsible for causing the variation we seek to explain.

## COMPETING EXPLANATIONS

As I noted in Chapter 1, one of the major strengths of the Zambian case is that its political system shifted not just from multi-party to one-party rule but also from one-party rule back to multi-party politics. This back-and-forth shift in political institutions is advantageous because it makes it possible to double-check the effects of institutional change. If the shift from multi-party to one-party competition in 1973 was really responsible for the displacement of linguistic identities by tribal identities as axes of political conflict, then we should observe a shift back to pre-1973 patterns of ethnic political competition (in which language identities were most salient) after the transition back to multi-party politics in 1991. The fact that we do lends support to the argument that the book advances.

A second advantage of Zambia's back-and-forth pattern of regime change is that it allows us to rule out a large number of potential competing explanations for the outcomes we observe. For example, a key potential alternative explanation for the changes over time in the salience of tribal and linguistic identities is "modernization." The modernization explanation would suggest that tribal identities became more politically salient than linguistic identities in the mid-1970s because the conditions of an increasingly industrialized, urbanized, economically integrated, secular, rational, participatory, and communication-intensive society made that dimension of identity more socially or politically useful than the other. With the growth of communication in a common *lingua franca* (English), people might have found tribal distinctions to be more useful than language group distinctions as a way of categorizing in-group and out-group members, and this might account for the shift in the relative salience of tribal and linguistic identities in the 1970s and 1980s. As plausible as this line of reasoning might seem, however, it would be equally plausible to suppose that, under conditions of increasingly intense social interaction in a highly heterogeneous community, individuals might have found local tribal identities *less* helpful as labeling devices than more broadly encompassing linguistic affiliations. The work of Mitchell (1969, 1987), Epstein (1958, 1981, 1992) and others lends support to this possibility. Such a mechanism would lead us to expect not the increasing salience of tribal affiliations in the mid-1970s but their disappearance.

Apart from the contradictory outcomes that modernization could be argued to cause, the more important problem with this potential competing explanation is that modernization is a monotonic process that, presumably, generates monotonic effects. If the transition from linguistic identities to tribal identities as bases for political coalition-building in 1973 had not been followed in 1991 by a transition back to linguistic identities as the principal axis of political competition, or if the shift from tribe-based to language group–based coalition-building after 1991 had not been preceded by a shift in the opposite direction in 1973, we might reasonably entertain the possibility that modernization – or one of the group of economic and social transformations that it encompasses – had played a role in accounting for these changes. But the fact that the variation in the political salience of these competing dimensions of ethnic identity was neither uni-directional nor permanent, whereas the increasing modernization of Zambian society presumably was, allows us to rule out this possibility.

Another possibility is that the shift in cleavage salience was caused not by changes in the structure of the Zambian economy, or even by changes in the country's general level of development, but by shorter-term fluctuations in economic performance. The argument might go like this: in times of economic scarcity, people look for scapegoats and coping strategies. In the context of an ethnically divided society, the quest for both leads to a deepening of ethnic divisions (Olzak 1992; Hardin 1995; Woodward 1999; Jega 2000). If this is so, then it is at least conceivable that it might also lead to a heightening of the importance of some group identities over others. Indeed, some scholars make precisely this argument. Azarya and Chazan (1987) argue that economic decline leads to a process of "self-enclosure" in which narrower social ties become more important to individuals and localized cleavages take precedence over broader ones. Chazan (1982) suggests that the deterioration of the economy leads to "a retreat to . . . narrower bases of solidarity" as people turn toward their close kin for aid and social insurance. Empirical evidence seems to support this claim. In Zambia, as the economy declined during the 1980s, Colson (1996: 72) notes that "personal networks acquired new importance [in a context] where increasing numbers competed in a diminished resource pool." To the extent that these local personal networks were built along tribal lines, it is possible that the heightened salience of local tribal identities in Zambia during the 1970s and 1980s might have been a product of the country's conditions of increasing resource scarcity.

The salience of linguistic identities in the 1960s and 1990s, meanwhile, could plausibly be attributed to economic plenty. During economic boom times when government coffers are full, political entrepreneurs will do everything they can to extract resources from the government. One way they do this is by threatening to lead their ethnic groups into the opposition unless the government buys their loyalty by channeling resources to them (Bates 1976).[1] Since the leverage that blackmailing politicians can exert will depend on the size of the groups they are claiming to lead, politicians will have incentives to define their groups in the broadest possible terms. In the Zambian context, this means that they will present themselves in linguistic (or sometimes regional/provincial) terms. But blackmail of this sort will only be viable when the government's coffers are full. When the economy declines and the government's ability to buy off potential defectors disappears, so too will the incentives for political entrepreneurs to play this game. We would therefore expect to find language group appeals to be more prominent in periods of economic plenty than in periods of economic weakness.

Taken together, these two arguments would provide a powerful competing explanation for the variation I seek to explain if the health of the Zambian economy co-varied with one-party and multi-party rule. But, as Figure 6.1 makes clear, it does not.

At independence, and throughout the multi-party First Republic, Zambia enjoyed a booming economy bolstered by high world copper prices and relatively efficient mining and industrial management practices. The one-party Second Republic, by contrast, was a period of dramatic economic decline. Although it began in a context of economic plenty, the country's financial situation declined markedly in the mid-1970s when world copper prices plummeted and a combination of shortsighted macroeconomic policy making, a rising wage bill in state-owned enterprises, and an over-staffed and inefficient government bureaucracy sent the economy

[1] As Treisman (1999) shows, this logic extends not just to groups that threaten to defect from the ruling coalition but also to sub-units of the nation that threaten to secede from the state.

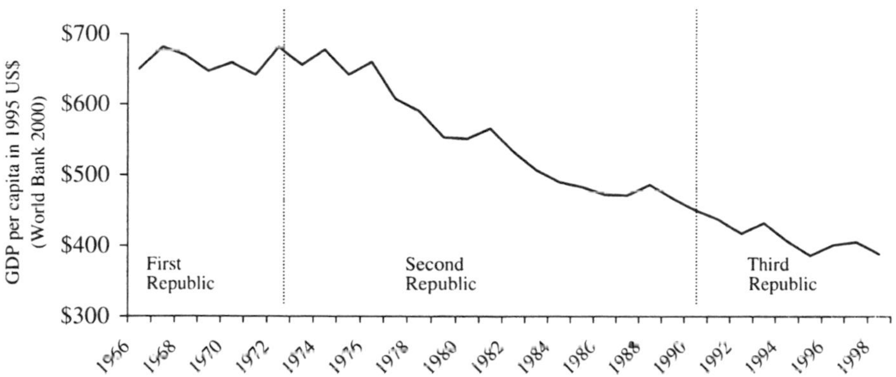


Figure 6.1. The Zambian Economy

into a tailspin. By the beginning of the Third Republic, in 1991, the Zambian economy was, on a per capita basis, only 60 percent as large as it had been when the Second Republic had begun in 1973. Despite the implementation of a series of aggressive economic reform programs in the 1990s, the Zambian economy remained weak throughout the first decade of the Third Republic.

The multi-party First and Third Republics thus had identical cleavage outcomes (language identities were most salient in both) but experienced very different conditions of economic health. Zambian political entrepreneurs evidently found it useful to play the language card (and voters responded positively to such appeals) both when state coffers were full and when they were empty. The state of the economy thus cannot account for the salience of linguistic identities in both periods. The one-party Second Republic, meanwhile, had a single cleavage outcome (tribe was the salient axis of political division throughout) but experienced varying economic conditions across its eighteen-year span. Zambians seem to have embraced narrow bases of ethnic solidarity even when the economy was healthy, or at any rate long before the economy had declined to the point where Azarya and Chazan tell us that "self-enclosure" should have begun. Given these patterns, we can rule out the health of the Zambian economy as a competing explanation for the outcome we seek to explain.

## AN ENDOGENEITY PROBLEM?

To support the argument that institutional change causes identity change, it is necessary to rule out the possibility of endogeneity. That is, it is necessary to establish that the shift from multi-party to one-party rule in 1973 and then from one-party back to multi-party rule in 1991 was the cause, rather than the outcome, of the shift in the ethnic cleavages that predominated in each context.

When President Kaunda announced in 1972 that he was going to introduce a new constitution that would ban opposition parties and bring about a one-party state, he was following a path that had already been taken by a number of other African rulers. In Zambia, as elsewhere, a principal official justification for scrapping inter-party competition was that such competition generated inter-ethnic violence. In a National Assembly speech, Vice President Mainza Chona made his case for the adoption of the new one-party system on precisely these grounds. "When we look round the entire country," he argued,

> we find that there has been peace in areas where there has been one party only. For example there was a lot of violence in the Eastern Province where both UNIP and ANC had substantial support [but] ... this violence ... completely died down when UNIP remained as the only party ... On the line of rail, political violence, riots and deaths have occurred mostly in Livingstone and Mufulira [where inter-party competition is strong] ... In places like the Southern Province and certain parts of Central Province [where inter-party competition is also strong] villagers have suffered a lot by being beaten up by political opponents, having their houses or their food stores burned ... and a lot of other criminal acts ... [By contrast,] in the Luapula, Northern and the Northwestern Provinces [where UNIP is dominant and inter-party competition is weak] we have had no violent incidents of a political nature at all except in Mwinilunga – the only district in the Northwestern Province where ANC was ... active. (*Parliamentary Debates*, 6 December 1972, cols. 54–59)

Chona's argument was clear: multi-party competition generated ethnic conflict, and this was why it had to be suspended in favor of single-party rule. More than two decades later, a former UNIP official agreed with the vice president's justification: "When we had multi-party politics, ANC and UNIP were fighting too much. This is why we decided to go to a one-party system. After that there was no fighting and the whole country was so quiet."[2]

To a large degree, the claim that a one-party state was necessary to end political violence in Zambia was, as it was in other African countries at the time, simply a convenient public rationale for the ruling party to ban its opponents. Yet there was truth to the contention that multi-party competition had exacerbated inter-group conflict. In the five

[2] Interview with Hudson Maimisa, Chipata, 16 October 1995.

years leading up to the elimination of multi-party politics, riots, arson, beatings, and other forms of violence had become regular features of political competition in several areas of the country. In August 1968, five people were killed in riots between UNIP and UP supporters in the Copperbelt town of Chililabombwe. In December 1969, a gun battle between UNIP and ANC supporters led to the hospitalization of members of both parties. In January 1972, UPP leader Simon Kapwepwe was beaten by a group of UNIP members after he left Parliament. Later that day, a UNIP minister was beaten in a retaliatory attack and a bomb was exploded in the UNIP regional office in Chingola. Twelve days later, a UNIP official was attacked and beaten by a crowd of UPP supporters in the Copperbelt. Summarizing the situation during this period, a former MP told me:

> There was a lot of violence. We did not accept one belonging to a different party. Sometimes property was destroyed. People were beaten. If you were a member of this party you had to drink in bars in one area. If you went to bars in another area where the other party was strong you got beaten.[3]

Thus, despite the fact that the UNIP government may have had ulterior motives for banning its opponents, it is not unreasonable to conclude that a desire to minimize violent conflicts may have also contributed to its decision to move from a multi-party to a one-party system. To the extent that this is the case, however, the direction of causality becomes murky: the ethnic outcome (or, more accurately, the anticipation of it) would appear to have caused the institutional change.

This apparent endogeneity problem disappears, however, when we recall that the dependent variable in this study is not the *depth* of ethnic conflict but the *dimension of ethnic identity that actors employ* to define themselves and identify their rivals. The argument that I present would be threatened by an endogeneity problem only if President Kaunda had decided to suspend multi-party political competition in 1973 (or to reinstate it in 1991) because of an expectation that doing so would affect the nature of the ethnic cleavages that would emerge as the basis for political coalition-building in the new institutional setting. There is no evidence that this was the case. The decision to declare the one-party state was based on an expectation that it would hamper UNIP's rivals, and perhaps also dampen the rising tide of ethnic violence in the country, not that it would affect the dimension of ethnic identity that would serve as the

[3] Interview with Leonard Mpundu, Luanshya, 17 December 1995.

central axis of political competition.[4] Nor is there any question that the return to multi-party politics in 1991 was motivated by anything other than a desire to respond to public outrage over the state of the economy and donor pressure to liberalize the political system (Bratton 1994). If institutional change went together with alterations in the political salience of tribal and linguistic identities, it is because the former caused the latter, not the other way around.

## CONTINUITIES AND DISCONTINUITIES IN THE NATURE OF POLITICAL COMPETITION ACROSS ZAMBIA'S THREE REPUBLICS

A final potential objection to the claim that the shift in the salience of tribal and linguistic identities was driven by institutional change is the possibility that aspects of Zambia's one-party and multi-party regimes other than their different formal institutional rules might account for the differences in the ethnic cleavages that became politically salient in each setting. The argument presented in Chapter 5 assumes that the only difference between Zambia's one-party and multi-party systems lies in the number of parties that were competing for power (one vs. many) and the manner in which the President was selected from among the many potential candidates for that job (by the party Central Committee vs. by the voters). Yet one-party and multi-party regimes also tend to differ in other ways. Compared with their one-party counterparts, multi-party regimes typically provide greater freedom for civil society groups and the press, greater opportunities for incumbent legislators to be displaced by challengers, and less governmental control over campaigning practices and electoral appeals. Indeed, it is precisely the presumed association

[4] Interview with Dr. Kenneth Kaunda, Lusaka, 17 January 1994. In April 1971, the government-owned *Daily Mail* published a map of Zambia displaying the locations and population shares of sixty different tribes. The accompanying text explained that "this map has been produced . . . with the one objective of helping to unite the people of Zambia into one powerful Nation. We believe that if the people of Zambia know the truth about themselves they will be more unified against diverse forces such as tribalism . . . [W]e hope the truth we have published will go a long way in proving that no one or two or three or even four tribes have a chance of succeeding in dominating others" (20 April 1971). The idea that an ethnic landscape with a large number of ethnic groups would generate less conflict thus seems to have been understood at the time Kaunda was contemplating the shift to one-party rule. But there is no evidence that Kaunda recognized that banning multiple parties from political competition would affect that landscape.

between these factors and regime type that explains the positive normative label that is usually attached to transitions from one-party to multi-party rule. Before assuming that the only relevant aspects of regime change are captured in the model, it will be important to rule out the independent effects of these other factors in the Zambian case. Doing so will also provide useful background information for the discussion of electoral campaigning that follows.

### Political Freedoms

For many countries, the suspension or resumption of multi-party political competition corresponds with a wholesale change in the character of political and social life. The suspension of multi-party rule in Czechoslovakia in 1948 or the move to multi-party competition in Taiwan in 1996, for example, brought dramatic transformations in the degree of political freedom enjoyed by the citizens of these countries. In Zambia, by contrast, the transition from multi-party to one-party politics in 1973 and then from one-party back to multi-party competition in 1991 brought comparatively little change in the nature of the country's political or social affairs.

Generally speaking, Zambians have enjoyed a relatively constant – and middling – level of political freedom throughout the post-independence period. With the exception of the two years immediately following the democratic transition of 1991, when the country was rated as "free," the democracy watchdog organization Freedom House has designated Zambia as "partly free" for every year between 1972, when the organization began ranking countries, and 2001.[5] Zambia's multi-party First and Third Republics were characterized by relatively illiberal forms of democracy, and its lengthy one-party Second Republic was marked by a relatively mild form of authoritarianism. Opposition leaders were detained, independently minded editors and reporters for the government-owned media were fired,[6] and citizens' civil rights were abridged by states

[5] During the one-party Second Republic, Zambia's average "political rights" and "civil liberties" scores were both 5.2, whereas during the multi-party Third Republic they were both 3.8 (lower numbers designate greater freedom on Freedom House's seven-point scale).

[6] In the Third Republic, the government-owned press faced competition for the first time from a group of highly critical independent newspapers. However, the high degree of government intimidation and harassment that these newspapers suffered (Human Rights Watch/Africa 1996) suggests that their presence cannot be

of emergency[7] with almost equal frequency in both one-party and multi-party settings. At the same time, however, authoritarian tendencies such as these were fairly moderate. Detained politicians had recourse in all three periods to a relatively independent judiciary that possessed the autonomy to order and secure their release. The state-owned press, while far from free, nonetheless was more willing to be critical of the government (if perhaps not of the President himself) than in many African countries.[8] And infringements on civil liberties, while slightly more severe toward the end of the Second Republic than in other periods, were never particularly egregious by African standards and did not vary overly much across the three republics. Even during the end of the Second Republic, Lungu (1986: 409) could write that "in terms of basic constitutional rights like freedom of speech, Zambia is closer to a liberal democratic state than to what has now become the 'classic model' of contemporary African dictatorship."

Indeed, when asked what they thought were "the biggest differences between the way things are [in the Third Republic] and the way things were [in the Second Republic]," only 6.7 percent of my survey respondents in 1995 mentioned changes in freedom of speech, assembly, or movement as the most important differences between the one-party and multi-party eras. The most often-mentioned changes, by far, were "pocketbook" issues such as the availability and/or price of consumer goods, the availability of jobs, and the improvement or decline of hospitals, roads, and

taken as evidence of the significantly greater liberalization of the Third Republic regime.

[7] During the First Republic, a state of emergency was declared to combat the threat of armed incursions from Rhodesia. Though justified in its initial period by the threat posed by the white Rhodesian government across Zambia's southern border, the continuation of the state of emergency through the end of the Second Republic – more than a decade after the overthrow of the Rhodesian regime – can be explained only by its usefulness to the government as an opposition-dampening device. As of 2001, two states of emergency had been called during the Third Republic: the first in 1993 following the discovery of a plan by the major opposition party to undermine the government through unlawful means, and the second in 1997 following an aborted coup attempt.

[8] Writing during the Second Republic, Lungu (1986: 406) observed that "with the possible exception of the President, the [Zambian news]papers take issue directly with any leader or any important subject, thereby registering their opinion on public policy... In comparison with the press in some neighboring African countries like Malawi, Zaire and Zimbabwe, and even the so-called capitalist Kenya, Zambian papers have a wider latitude of freedom to express views and report sensational news."

schools. Had the contrast between the degree of political freedom in the two eras been more stark, we would have expected a larger share of respondents to have mentioned such issues first.

Equally important as the relative stability in the level of political freedom across Zambia's three republics is the fact that there is no plausible link between the extent of political liberty enjoyed by citizens and civil society groups and the kinds of ethnic identities that they might choose as bases for political mobilization. While it might be possible to draw a connection between fluctuations in political freedom and the ability of politicians and citizens to build political coalitions, and perhaps even to draw on ethnicity in doing so, there is no obvious theoretical story that links changes in the ability of people to protest or assemble or move freely around the country to changes in the *dimensions of ethnic identity* that they would find it advantageous to mobilize.

### *Opportunities for the Replacement of Incumbents by Challengers*

A second commonly cited difference between one-party and multi-party regimes is the extent to which elections provide meaningful opportunities for replacing parliamentary officeholders. Although this difference across regime types is often overstated, multi-party elections are usually assumed to provide much greater latitude for voters to choose their political representatives than one-party elections, which are usually assumed to be little more than exercises for legitimizing and perpetuating the ruling elite.[9]

While such stereotypical characterizations of one-party and multi-party regime types may apply in other countries, they do not apply in Zambia. If anything, Zambia's four one-party elections were more competitive and resulted in more turnover of incumbents than their multi-party counterparts. Whereas an average of four candidates ran for every seat in the one-party races, an average of just 2.7 candidates ran in the

[9] Multi-party elections are also generally held to provide voters with a greater ability to affect policy making than one-party elections. Since the party that will control the government (and set policy) after the election is definitionally fixed in a one-party state, this is undoubtedly the case. Still, voters in one-party elections have more power to shape the policies that are ultimately adopted by the ruling party than is often assumed. For a discussion of these issues in the African context, see Chazan (1979).

Table 6.1. *Incumbents Defeated in Multi-Party and One-Party Elections*

| | Election type | Number of incumbents running for re-election | Number of incumbents defeated | Percentage of incumbents defeated |
|---|---|---|---|---|
| 1968 | multi-party | 60 | 11 | 18.3 |
| 1973 | one-party | 57 | 15 | 26.3 |
| 1978 | one-party | 82 | 31 | 37.8 |
| 1983 | one-party | 104 | 42 | 40.4 |
| 1988 | one-party | 99 | 36 | 36.4 |
| 1991 | multi-party | 73 | 50 | 68.5 |
| 1996 | multi-party | 74 | 12 | 16.2 |

three multi-party contests analyzed in this study. In addition, as Table 6.1 indicates, incumbents were significantly less likely to be returned to office in the one-party elections of 1973, 1978, 1983, and 1988 than in the multi-party elections of 1968 and 1996. The very high levels of turnover in 1991 are an artifact of that election's transitional nature, which I discuss later.

Another indicator of competitiveness is the number of candidates running unopposed in a given election. By this measure, one-party elections in Zambia again emerge as slightly more competitive than their multi-party counterparts. In the four one-party elections, an average of one constituency in seventeen had an unopposed parliamentary candidate, whereas in the three multi-party contests the average rose to one constituency in twelve.

Zambia's one-party and multi-party elections clearly do not fit the stereotype. But, as with the issue of political freedom, the important question is less whether one-party and multi-party regimes differ than whether the differences that might exist can be linked to a set of expectations about identity choice. If there were a reason to think that the ability or inability of challengers to threaten incumbents in parliamentary elections might account for why political actors choose to construct their political coalitions around linguistic identities rather than tribal identities (or vice versa), then the differences in the competitiveness of Zambia's one-party and multi-party elections might be relevant. But because there is not, the differences in the competitiveness of the two kinds of elections provide no basis for a competing explanation for the cleavage outcome that we observe.

### Government Control over Campaigning Practices and Electoral Appeals

A third way in which one-party and multi-party states tend to differ is in the degree of control exercised by the government over campaigning practices and electoral appeals. In multi-party settings, candidates and parties are usually relatively free to frame their electoral appeals as they wish and to campaign when and where they choose. In one-party settings, by contrast, strict boundaries are frequently put on the issues that can be discussed to solicit votes, and candidates are often forbidden from campaigning outside of official, government-sanctioned channels. In terms of the formal rules that governed electoral campaigning during its one-party and multi-party eras, Zambia closely matches this stereotypical characterization: multi-party campaigns were relatively unregulated, whereas one-party campaigns were (formally, at least) tightly controlled. However, in terms of the nature of the campaigning that actually took place, the differences between institutional settings were actually fairly small.

According to regulations in force during all four one-party general elections, candidates were permitted to campaign only during party-sponsored public meetings and, even then, allowed to talk only about issues sanctioned by the party leadership. A single official campaign poster was produced for each constituency with the pictures and symbols of all the candidates in the race, and candidates were forbidden to produce their own campaign materials or to spend any of their own money in conjunction with the campaign. With respect to the content of the appeals that candidates could make, and to ethnic campaigning in particular, UNIP election rules stipulated that

> the election campaign . . . should focus on those issues which concern you and the nation and not on personalities. It must be based on the desire to bring together all our communities instead of dividing them; it must be used to integrate rather than fragment, to build the nation instead of dividing the people.[10]

As several former candidates described the practice, all the candidates in a given constituency would be called to a public meeting by the district governor. Each would be given ten to fifteen minutes to talk about an assigned subject – President Kaunda's philosophy of Humanism, the

[10] UNIP Rules and Regulations, cited in Chikulo (1979: 206). See also the election regulations reprinted in the *Daily Mail*, 7 September 1983.

government's pensions policy, the threat posed by the white regime in Rhodesia, the meaning of the slogan "One Zambia, One Nation," or some other topic. Only in their concluding remarks or in answering questions from the audience could candidates directly address why voters should support them instead of the other contestants. Even then, candidates were strictly forbidden to make negative remarks about their rivals or to engage in expressly ethnic campaigning.

Although the purpose of these regulations was ostensibly to create an even playing field among the candidates, district governors would sometimes go out of their way to make it clear that the ruling party preferred one candidate over the others. Sometimes this preference would be signaled indirectly through the warmth of an introduction. At other times, the district governor would return to the site of the campaign meeting after the candidates had left and actually tell people which candidate they should support.[11] At the central level, the party could also manipulate the election outcome by vetting contestants that it viewed as troublemakers or as threatening to favored candidates.[12] This prerogative was exercised relatively infrequently, however, and never, evidence suggests, for reasons related to the tribal or linguistic background of the prospective candidate. In the elections of 1973, 1978, and 1983, fewer than 9 percent of the candidates that filed nomination papers or made it through the primary stage were disqualified by the party.[13] In 1988, the share of those vetted rose to just over 13 percent.[14]

Once the Central Committee had decided that a particular candidate presented a threat to the party's interests, that candidate could do little to avoid either disqualification from the race or unequal treatment

[11] Interviews with Hosea Soko, Chipata, 17 October 1995; Leonard Luyanga, Limulunga, 17 November 1995; and Felix Kabika, Lusaka, 30 July 1999.

[12] Party regulations gave the Central Committee the power to exclude any candidate deemed to be "inimical to the interests of the state" (Baylies and Szeftel 1984: 30).

[13] In the elections of 1973 and 1978, aspiring candidates first had to run in primary elections. Unless vetted by the Central Committee, the top three vote winners in the primary would then become candidates in the general election. The primary stage was omitted in the contests of 1983 and 1988. In these elections, any candidate who wanted to run, and who was not vetted, appeared on the ballot. Only 26 candidates were vetted by the Central Committee in 1973, compared with 317 that ultimately took part in the elections. In 1978, the comparable figures were 28 vetted and 344 contested. In 1983, the number of vetted candidates jumped to 46, but the number of those that contested rose even more precipitously to 828.

[14] Ninety-four candidates were vetted, compared with 706 that ultimately appeared on the ballot.

by district-level party officials. Where candidates did have considerable control, however, was in their ability to circumvent the highly regulated formal campaign meetings. Candidates in all four of Zambia's one-party elections actively flouted party regulations by quietly – and sometimes not so quietly – campaigning outside of officially sanctioned channels.[15] Candidates distributed illegal election campaign posters and leaflets, canvassed for support in drinking establishments and residential neighborhoods, and conducted "night campaigns based on tribal lines" (*Times of Zambia*, 23 October 1973). Despite the rule that campaigning could take place only in the presence of party officials, a long-time Zambia Information Services (ZIS) officer with responsibility for organizing official campaign meetings confirmed that most of the real campaigning took place outside of the events he organized: "People who had money would have their election agents go from house to house, or in rural areas from village to village on bicycles. It was illegal but it happened a lot."[16] The *Daily Mail* went so far as to describe candidates' behavior in the 1983 election as being characterized by "a blatant disregard of the rules of the game as far as the Party regulations go" (1 November 1983). On the eve of the 1983 poll, as during the periods leading up to the other Second Republic elections, "most urban centers were aflame with election material which seemed to proliferate during the night. Posters were displayed and leaflets were distributed freely as the drive to woo voters picked up" (*Daily Mail*, 1 November 1983).[17] In the run-up to the 1988 election, the UNIP National Council, "noting with regret that illegal campaigns, use of money and other illegal practices have been reported throughout the country," saw fit to reiterate the official policy that "people concerned should be disqualified from contesting the next parliamentary election."[18]

Former candidates told me that they campaigned privately because that was the only way they could make themselves known to voters. While acknowledging that they risked being punished by the party if they were discovered soliciting votes outside of the organized meetings, former MPs told me that "this was very rare, because you did it under cover. And if

[15] Interviews with Mainza Chona, Lusaka, 31 July 1999; Cosmas Masongo, Kasama, 2 September 1995; and Reuben Motolo Phiri, Chiparamba, 21 October 1995.

[16] Interview with Felix Kabika, Lusaka, 30 July 1999.

[17] For similar reports on the 1988 elections, see *Daily Mail*, 8 September and 22 September 1988. Chikulo (1979) and Gertzel et al. (1984) provide discussions of clandestine campaigning in 1973 and 1978.

[18] Resolutions of the Elections and Publicity Committee of the 22nd UNIP National Council Meeting held in Mulungushi Hall from 17 to 21 December 1987.

people wanted you, they would want to listen to you."[19] The long-time ZIS official put it bluntly: "If you followed the regulations you could not win. You had to campaign privately to win."[20] Summarizing the one-party campaigns, Chikulo (1979: 207) writes:

> The circumspection of issues, coupled with poor attendance at [official campaign] meetings, [explains] the importance of informal campaigns by individual [candidates]. It was the informal campaigns which raised the local issues (or grievances) which the electorate wanted to hear... [including] particularistic appeals based on ethnicity, provincial or family ties. It can thus be concluded that the official campaigns did not at all reflect the essence of the election campaigns.

Chikulo concludes by describing the official campaign meetings as "something of a ritual in which participants discussed abstract notions of development and Humanism, while the real (unofficial) campaigns progressed largely unchecked" (ibid.).

Thus, despite formal rules designed to insure the ruling party's control over the conduct of the one-party elections, electoral campaigns in the Second Republic were not as dissimilar to the comparatively unregulated campaigns of the two multi-party eras as might be assumed. Candidates in the Second Republic did face greater obstacles in directly reaching voters than candidates did in either the First Republic or the Third. But the relative ease with which official channels could be skirted during the one-party period suggests that these obstacles may not have affected candidates' strategic behavior to a significant extent.

Moreover, from the standpoint of testing the expectations of the model, the important factor is that candidates in both multi-party and, once they had circumvented party restrictions, one-party institutional settings were equally free to frame their electoral appeals in terms of tribal or linguistic identities. While the rules governing Second Republic elections may have made it more difficult for candidates to make ethnic appeals per se than in the First or Third Republics, these regulations did nothing to bias the content of those appeals in favor of a particular dimension of ethnic identity. For this reason, and for the reasons outlined earlier, we can discount the possibility that aspects of Zambia's one-party or multi-party systems other than those accommodated in the model might be "doing the work" in explaining the variation we observe over time in the political salience of tribal and linguistic identities.

[19] Interview with Reuben Motolo Phiri, Chiparamba, 21 October 1995.
[20] Interview with Felix Kabika, Lusaka, 30 July 1999.

## *The 1991 Election*

A final issue that bears mention involves a discontinuity not across party system types but within the category of multi-party elections. This is the question of whether the 1991 election was so exceptional and atypical as to justify excluding it from the analyses of coalition-building in multi-party elections that I present in the next two chapters.

Called by President Kaunda in response to a groundswell of public anger that had precipitated strikes, food riots, and "the first [rallies] in Africa on the scale of Leipzig and Prague" (Bratton 1994), the 1991 election was less a regular contest between competing parties than a referendum on change. The election, in fact, took the place of a scheduled referendum on whether Zambia should return to multi-party rule. After two decades of economic decline, the election was viewed by Zambians as an opportunity to overturn the status quo and bring about major political and economic reform. The MMD's landslide victory – it won 125 of the 150 parliamentary seats and more than 75 percent of the popular vote – can be attributed to a combination of voters' thirst for change and the party's success in casting itself as the agent of reform.

The referendum nature of the 1991 election is confirmed by the fact that, when asked who they voted for in 1991, Zambians almost never mention by name the particular candidate or party they supported. Rather, they say "I voted for change" or "I voted for the Hour" – a reference to the MMD's slogan "The Hour Has Come!" As a market seller in Luanshya explained, "when we were voting [in 1991], the MMD was campaigning and we were busy shouting 'The Hour!' 'The Hour!' What we wanted was change. We did not care about [the particular candidate] who stood" (LY-MS-W). Many Zambians also told me that ethnic factors were not a consideration in their decisions in 1991. One focus group respondent noted that in 1991 "whoever stood on an MMD ticket [was elected]. It didn't matter where he came from. Whatever area they stood [in], they all went through" (LIV-M).[21] Another explained that "people were not choosing [based on] which tribe this one is coming from. They only wanted change. And Chiluba being popular . . . nobody looked at his tribe or where he came from" (MON-T). The single-mindedness of voters' motivations was captured well by an MMD politician when he likened

[21] The respondent added that, after the election was over, "it didn't take long before things began to settle down to what people have always been. I don't see a similar thing taking place in the next election."

the campaign to unseat Kaunda to "cutting down a bayobab tree: one with an ax, one with a hoe, one with a pen knife, but all with the goal of cutting it down."[22]

To the extent that Zambians in 1991 were voting for change, the model presented in Chapter 5 will be an inappropriate device for capturing the behavior of Zambian political actors during that election. Voters in 1991 did not decide who to support by weighing the relative advantages of tribal and linguistic identities for securing membership in advantageously sized political coalitions, and candidates did not base their electoral strategies on the expectation that voters would. Both simply decided whether or not they wanted to see a continuation of the status quo and acted accordingly. Although my claim is not that voters are motivated exclusively by ethnic coalition-building concerns in other elections, I do assume that such concerns are at least part of what motivates them to support the candidates that they do. Given that such calculations were clearly trumped by other factors in 1991, it would be inappropriate to treat the 1991 election as a "typical" multi-party contest when I test the predictions of the model. I therefore exclude the 1991 election in the analyses presented in the next two chapters. My practice is to report in a footnote how the results would have differed had I included the data from the 1991 contest. As the results I present make clear, including the 1991 election in the analysis would have made the results even stronger than those I report, not weaker.

[22] Interview with Foxy Hudson Nyundu, Kaoma, 6 August 1993.

# 7

## *Ethnic Campaigning*

### *Testing the Observable Implications of the Argument for Elite Behavior*

In *Identity in Formation*, David Laitin writes that "ethnic entrepreneurs cannot create ethnic solidarities from nothing. They must, if they are to succeed, be attuned to the micro incentives that real people face" (1998: 248). Having identified the micro-incentives that Zambians face in Chapters 4 and 5, this chapter tests whether or not politicians are attuned to them. It investigates whether political elites behave in the way that the model would predict in each institutional setting.

The chapter is divided into three sections. In the first, I present evidence that politicians make different sorts of ethnic appeals in one-party and multi-party political campaigns: tribal in the former and linguistic in the latter. In the second, I show that the shift from multi-party to one-party rule alters parliamentary candidates' choices about the constituencies in which it will be most advantageous for them to run. Whereas running in a constituency where one is a member of the dominant tribe is of paramount importance in one-party elections, it is much less important in multi-party contests, since electoral success in those races is much more a function of a candidate's party affiliation than of his or her ethnic background. Drawing on information about the ethnic demographics of electoral constituencies and the tribal backgrounds of each of the more than 2,200 candidates that ran for Parliament between 1968 and 1999, I present a series of quantitative analyses that show that the different rules for what it will take to win leads candidates to choose to run in different kinds of constituencies in one-party and multi-party elections. In the third section, I present evidence that the one-party or multi-party nature of the political system also affects politicians' behavior during the periods between elections. Specifically, I show that politicians make investments in different sorts of ethnic civic associations in each institutional context.

## THE ELECTORAL APPEALS THAT POLITICIANS MAKE

One of the clearest observable implications of the model developed in Chapter 5 is that politicians will make different sorts of ethnic electoral appeals in one-party and multi-party political campaigns. In multi-party contests, they will make appeals designed to build (or break) political coalitions formed along language group lines. In one-party contests, they will ignore the country's linguistic divisions and instead emphasize constituency-level sources of social cleavage. This will lead them to focus on tribal differences (though in urban constituencies they will continue to emphasize language group distinctions). The demographics of the local political arenas in which politicians are competing for votes do not change, but the altered institutional setting shifts politicians' incentives for emphasizing one of these dimensions of ethnic identity rather than the other. In this section, I present evidence to support this central prediction.

Doing so, however, is complicated by two factors. The first is that it is not always possible to code politicians' ethnic appeals as unambiguously either "tribal" or "linguistic." As I explained in Chapter 4, this difficulty stems from the fact that each of Zambia's four principal language groups carries the same name as the tribe that originally spoke that language. Thus, while appeals for "Tongas" to mobilize to put one of their own in power or for "Lozis" to unite against "Bembas" are clearly ethnic, the fact that the labels "Tonga," "Lozi," and "Bemba" refer to both language groups and tribes makes it difficult to be certain whether the politician making the appeal is seeking to mobilize people along tribal or linguistic lines. I employ several strategies to deal with this problem. One is to look for symbols that the politician invokes that can provide clues about the nature of the coalition he is trying to mobilize. For example, references to Paramount Chief Chitimukulu would suggest that the politician is seeking to build a tribal coalition, since Chitumukulu is the chief of the Bemba tribe but not of the entire Bemba language group – other Bemba-speaking tribes have their own chiefs. But references to the Litunga of Barotseland (the Lozi Paramount Chief) would suggest that the politician is trying to construct a coalition of all Lozi-speakers, since the Litunga is recognized by all Lozi-speaking peoples as their traditional leader.

Another strategy is to make inferences about the implied identity dimension from the nature of the group that the politician identifies as the source of threat. For example, while the call for Lozis to unite against Bembas may be ambiguous with respect to the linguistic or tribal dimension of identity that the politician is trying to invoke, the call for Lozis to unite against the Koma or the Mbunda is clearly a tribal appeal, since the Koma and the Mbunda are unambiguously tribes rather than language groups. Context matters as well. In the Copperbelt town of Ndola, an appeal for Lozis to unite against Bembas would be difficult to code as tribal or linguistic, since Ndola contains both Lozi and Bemba tribespeople and Lozi- and Bemba-speakers who are not members of those tribes. But in Senanga, a homogeneously Lozi-speaking town in Western Province, such an appeal would be easily identifiable as linguistic. The town itself contains no Bembas, so we could safely infer that the politician was trying to mobilize Lozi-speakers by referring to the conflict between Lozi-speakers and Bemba-speakers at the national level.

A second, and more significant, obstacle is that the available evidence on the ethnic appeals that politicians make is scattered and incomplete. Even when not expressly forbidden by party rules, overt ethnic campaigning is frowned upon in Zambian society, and this means that it tends not to be done in public settings. Ethnic campaigning certainly takes place, but politicians prefer to do it away from the scrutiny of researchers or newspaper reporters who might record what they say. Researchers or reporters who do happen to be present at such times are, of course, excellent sources, and I draw on their accounts in what follows. But such accounts are not as plentiful as would be ideal. Thus, while I am able to muster evidence that candidates couch their ethnic appeals in different ways in one-party and multi-party elections, this evidence is not sufficiently complete to provide a comprehensive test of the model's predictions. The discussion that follows is thus meant principally to be illustrative. More systematic tests of the observable implications of the model will come later in the chapter and in Chapter 8.

I begin by providing examples of language group–oriented ethnic campaigning during Zambia's multi-party First and Third Republics. Then I present evidence of tribally oriented ethnic appeals in the one-party Second Republic.

### *Ethnic Electoral Appeals in Multi-Party Contexts*

*The First Republic.* In the First Republic, political conflict revolved around the competition for power between two, and at times among three, major political parties. The largest of the three, the United National Independence Party (UNIP), was the party that led the country to independence. Although its leader, President Kenneth Kaunda, was presumed by many Zambians to be predisposed to favor the interests of the

Bemba-speaking North, the party's role as the principal vehicle of the independence struggle meant that its support was, at least initially, national in scope.[1] Its electoral strategy was to stress its own supra-ethnic credentials – its campaign posters urged Zambians to "Vote National, Vote UNIP" (Molteno and Scott 1974: 186) – while emphasizing the narrow regional/ethnic roots of its competitors. As we saw in Chapter 4, this is an intelligent strategy for an incumbent party in a context where, as in Zambia, no ethnic group constitutes a majority and branding a rival party as "ethnic" can undermine that party's ability to win support outside of its home region.

In the period immediately after independence, the only region of the country where the UNIP's support was challenged was in the Tonga-speaking Southern Province, the home area of the First Republic's second major party, the African National Congress (ANC). Originally named the Zambian African National Congress, the ANC was at one time the umbrella organization for all African opponents of colonial rule. However, disenchantment with the moderate approach taken by the ANC's leader, Harry Mwaanga Nkumbula, led Kaunda and a number of other more militant leaders to break away from the ANC in 1960 to form the UNIP (Mulford 1967). While most of the country rallied behind Kaunda's more radical organization, Southerners remained loyal to the Tonga-speaking Nkumbula and to his party.[2]

In 1966, a third party, the United Party (UP), was formed. Led by Nalumino Mundia and a group of fellow Lozi-speakers from Western (then Barotse) Province, the UP built a strong following in that region and among Lozi-speaking migrants in the Copperbelt. A particular source of grievance exploited by UP organizers was the government's decision in 1966 to prohibit the Witwatersrand Native Labour Association (WENELA) from continuing to recruit men from the Lozi-speaking areas to work in the South African mines. WENELA recruitment had been, since 1940, a critical source of income for the people of western Zambia, and Kaunda's decision to close WENELA to demonstrate his government's

[1] Recall from Chapter 4 that, although Kaunda was born of parents from present-day Malawi, he grew up in the North and was initially viewed as a Northerner. It was not until after his perceived betrayal of Simon Kapwepwe (a Northerner) in 1971 that he came to be identified with Nyanja-speaking Eastern Province, the region that borders and is closely identified with Malawi.

[2] Although portions of the population in several rail-line towns, as well as many people in Eastern Province, also remained loyal to the ANC, the party's principal locus of support lay in the South.

opposition to the South African regime resulted in a sharp drop in incomes for many Lozi-speakers. The UP was short-lived, however. When a violent clash between UP and UNIP cadres in the Copperbelt in August 1968 left six people dead, the UNIP responded by banning the UP. UP organizers reacted to their party's prohibition by joining forces with the ANC and running their candidates in Barotse Province under the ANC label in the general election held later that year.[3]

The final, even more short-lived, First Republic party was the United Progressive Party (UPP). The UPP was formed in 1971 when Simon Kapwepwe and a group of prominent Bemba-speaking politicians broke off from the UNIP to protest President Kaunda's sacking of four senior Bemba-speaking ministers. Kapwepwe was perhaps the most important Bemba-speaking politician of his day, and when he defected from the UNIP many Zambians perceived the party's Bemba core to have defected with him. Thus, unlike the ANC and UP, whose support came almost entirely from non-Bemba-speakers, the UPP directly threatened the UNIP's Bemba-speaking base (Tordoff and Scott 1974: 139). This presented the ruling party with a major problem. Its response was to ban the UPP and detain its leaders, ostensibly because the party's activities threatened the peace and security of the country, but really because its existence threatened the UNIP's hegemony (ibid.: 152).

For reasons discussed in Chapter 4, the ANC, UP, and UPP faced common strategic dilemmas. They could each rely on a strong ethnic support base in their leader's home region. But explicitly courting support from these areas in ethnic terms risked confirming the impression among many voters – promoted by the UNIP – that the candidates that ran on these parties' tickets were little more than vehicles for the interests of particular regionally defined ethnic communities. Accordingly, all three parties sought to play a dual strategy. They sought to maximize their electoral support in their leaders' home regions by playing the ethnic card there, while at the same time playing down their parties' ethnic orientations (or simply electing not to run candidates) in other parts of the country.[4]

[3] Gertzel (1984: 214) notes that UP candidates in Barotse Province, though formally part of the ANC, "campaigned to a large degree independently of the ANC national headquarters, so that their [performance in the election] was essentially that of an alternative Lozi leadership, in place of those Lozi in UNIP who were believed to have let their people down."

[4] Often, the decision not to run candidates was based on a lack of resources rather than a calculation of electoral strategy. Writing about the ANC's efforts in the 1968 election, Molteno and Scott (1974: 179) note that "the scale of the ANC campaign

Given their different support bases, each opposition party directed its ethnic appeal to a different audience: the ANC appealed to the Tonga-speaking south, the UP to the Lozi-speaking west, and the UPP to the Bemba-speaking north and to Bemba-speakers in the Copperbelt. What united the three parties was a strategy of couching those appeals in explicitly linguistic, rather than tribal, terms. Again and again, party leaders and candidates employed symbols and rhetoric that were explicitly designed to frame the country's political conflict in voters' eyes in terms of the struggle for power among the country's four broad language communities. In the campaign for the 1968 general election, for example, ANC candidates in Southern Province sought to win support by depicting their UNIP competitors as members of a Bemba-dominated party that threatened the interests of the province's Tonga-speaking majority (Molteno 1972, 1974). To emphasize the linguistic rather than tribal basis of the Tonga community they claimed to be protecting, ANC candidates "conjured up visions of the Bemba (who generally do not keep cattle) as descending upon the hapless Tonga and stealing all their cattle" (Szeftel 1980: 84). By emphasizing cattle keeping as a marker of Tonga group affiliation, the ANC campaigners were not only drawing a clear distinction between Tongas and Bembas but also reinforcing the unity of the various Tonga-speaking tribes, all of whom keep cattle.

The same tactic was used in 1969 during a national referendum, which the ANC opposed, on whether Parliament could amend the constitution without submitting the proposed revisions to a national vote. Chikulo (1983: 178) cites an official Southern Province government report that alleges that ANC activists went around during the campaign telling peasants that if they voted for the referendum proposition "all their cattle, land, and wives would be for the Bembas due to the fact that the President is a Bemba." Again, the choice of the central mobilizing symbol – the threat to cattle – was employed explicitly to forge a coalition that would be useful in the struggle for power in the national political arena.

was minuscule. It was badly organized, almost without funds [and] lacked adequate transport ... Operating under these restrictions ... the party never really succeeded in contacting large numbers of the electorate outside its areas of strength." When the date for the election was set, the ANC's president, Harry Nkumbula, later recalled, his party "had not even a penny" (183). Nine days before the election, the *Times of Zambia* reported that the ANC "had no funds to print posters and manifestos ... Although the party launched its election campaign weeks ago, not a single poster has been displayed" (10 December 1968). The UP and UPP faced similar financial constraints.

The UP also sought to rally support in its home area by playing on fears of Bemba domination. As the ANC candidates had in Southern Province, UP candidates in Western Province "alleged that, if UNIP won, the Bemba would dominate the government and would discriminate against the Lozi, taking away their land and cattle" (Molteno and Scott 1974: 188). They also emphasized the pro-Bemba favoritism of the UNIP government. An article in the UP's newspaper, *The Mirror*, charged that the government and civil service were almost entirely controlled by Bemba-speakers:

> The President, the Vice President, [and] the Chairm[e]n of the Public Service Commission, Teaching Service Commission, Police Service Commission, University Council of Zambia and Judiciary Service Commission belong to one tribe. The Commissioner of Police and the Secretary to the Cabinet belong to one tribe. These are the people governing the country and all the other ministries and departments are merely branches of some form or other of the above. The same tribe has majority of Permanent and Under Secretaries than any other tribe [*sic*]. It has more people in the foreign service than any other tribe. It has more Directors in Charge of Departments and Semi-Government Organizations such as the Zambia Railways, Zambia Broadcasting Services and the Commissioner of Traffic Departments, etc., etc.... It is also estimated that the same tribe has nearly 150 people in the executive and higher positions of office in the Public Service. The Tongas, the Ngonis and the Lozis range between 30 and 50 people each in similar positions. Can anybody explain why?[5]

Although the article refers to government officials as all belonging to "one tribe," this must be interpreted as a colloquialism rather than an indication that UP publicists sought to frame the competition for government jobs in tribal rather than language group terms. Evidence that the article's authors sought to depict this competition as one among language communities is provided by the fact that the officeholders they mention, though lumped together as "Bemba," are from multiple Bemba-speaking tribes. Moreover, at the end of the quoted passage, they juxtapose the favored Bembas with just three other groups: the comparatively unfavored "Tongas... Ngonis [Nyanjas] and... Lozis." Any Zambian who read the article would understand that the conflict was among the country's four language groups, and, by implication, that the coalition that had to be mobilized to change matters was the one with their fellow language-speakers.

[5] "Tribalism in Zambia: Who Are Encouraging It?" *The Mirror* 1 (March 1968), quoted in Dresang (1974: 1610).

This strategy of language-based political mobilization continued in the 1968 election campaign, as UP candidates (running as ANC members) invoked symbols that would unify Lozi-speakers against the government. One tactic was to accuse the UNIP government of not taking adequate medical measures to prevent the death of the Litunga, which had taken place a short time previously (Molteno and Scott 1974: 188). Another was to blame the ruling party for failing to live up to the provisions of the Barotseland Agreement of 1964, a document signed just prior to independence that committed the government to preserving some of the quasi-independent status that Western Province had enjoyed under colonial rule (Sichone and Simutanyi 1996: 181). Like the exploitation of the cattle symbol by ANC campaigners, both the allegation of the mistreatment of the Litunga and the invocation of the Barotseland Agreement constituted conscious efforts to draw upon symbols that UP strategists knew would resonate deeply with – and unify – the Lozi-speaking residents of the region. "We told [the voters] that this is an opportunity for us," the UP's former publicity chief told me. "We told them President Kaunda was a Bemba who came from Northern Province and now the time has come for us to have a Lozi President from Western Province. Now we have [in the UP] a party that is led by a man from this province. Therefore we should unite together to support him so that he will become the President too."[6]

Of course, politics is always about "uniting together" – about building political coalitions that will help their members capture power. But what made politics in the First Republic distinctive was that the coalitions that were constructed were built to capture power at the national rather than local level. And since tribes were too small to be viable units for that purpose, the cultural glue that was used to cement these coalitions together was language.

*The Third Republic.* Although the UNIP remained a political player during the Third Republic, its resounding defeat in the 1991 election relegated it to a secondary role as an opposition party. In this role, it was closely identified with the Nyanja-speaking Eastern Province, where it won its only concentration of seats. The victor in the election, and the new dominant party, was the Movement for Multiparty Democracy (MMD). Because of the near universality of the desire for change among Zambians in 1991, and because of the MMD's vanguard role in the effort

[6] Interview with Morgan Simwinji, Mongu, 16 November 1995.

to bring about that change, the MMD's support was, like the UNIP's after independence, initially national and multi-ethnic in its scope. Like the UNIP's in the First Republic, the MMD's electoral strategy was to emphasize its own national credentials while branding its rivals as regional parties.

The bandwagoning that led to the MMD's overwhelming electoral victory also produced a situation in which too many prominent politicians had participated in the unseating of Kaunda to be rewarded with senior government appointments in the new administration. Accordingly, a number of well-known politicians who felt insufficiently rewarded in the new government resigned from the MMD in 1993 to form the Third Republic's third major political party, the National Party (NP). Although comprised of senior politicians from every language group, most of the NP's top leaders – including its interim president – were from the Lozi-speaking west, and the party was popularly viewed as a Lozi-dominated organization. It bears underscoring that the NP was formed principally as a vehicle for the advancement of its leaders, not as an instrument for ethnic group advancement. But the non-ethnic rationale for the party's origins did not prevent either its leaders from actively playing upon ethnic identities in their efforts to build their new political organization or the MMD from exploiting assumptions about the NP's ethnic orientation to try to undermine the new party's national viability.

The first opportunity for NP and MMD organizers to "play the ethnic card" in the context of an election campaign came in November 1993, when a series of by-elections were held to fill the seats vacated by six of the MPs that had defected from the MMD to the NP.[7] The most important of these by-elections was in Malole constituency in Northern Province. As I noted in Chapter 4, the importance of the Malole by-election lay in its role as a bellwether of the NP's ability to win support outside of its Western and Southern Province home areas. Political analysts agreed that, if the NP's candidate, former finance minister Emmanuel Kasonde, were to win the seat, not only would it give the NP a strong foothold in Northern Province but, potentially, it would cause the whole of the Bemba-speaking coalition to shift from the ruling party to the opposition (*Weekly Post*, 9 November 1993 and 16 November 1993; *Daily Mail*, 18 November 1993).

[7] As per the provisions of the Constitution (Amendment) Act No. 2 of 1966, an MP that crossed the floor to another party lost the seat and was forced to run in a by-election to win the seat back for the MP's new party.

To prevent this from happening, MMD leaders attempted to depict the NP as a Lozi party and to brand Kasonde as a man who had forfeited his claim to Bemba leadership by "selling out" to the enemy. MMD officials taught their supporters a campaign song, whose refrain was "*Kasonde ale shitisha ulubemba ku ba Lozi*," which translates as "Kasonde has sold the Bembas to the Lozi" (*The Post*, 23 July 1999). A senior MMD minister sought to dramatize Kasonde's "conversion" by branding him "Emmanuel Liswaniso" – "Liswaniso" being a characteristically Lozi name (*Times of Zambia*, 13 February 1998). President Chiluba, who personally led the MMD campaign, brought dozens of senior officials to the constituency, including every single Northern Province politician and a number of other high-ranking Bemba-speakers, in an effort to demonstrate that the entire Bemba-speaking block was united against Kasonde.[8] People in Malole even reported that a rumor circulated during the campaign that, if Kasonde won, Lozis would travel from Western Province (some 1,200 kilometers away!) and actually take possession of Bembas' land.[9] Outlandish as it may seem, the claim that outsiders would come and take people's land was actually believed by many rural villagers, and served as a powerful source of mobilization.[10] The implicit claim in all of this was that a candidate's party affiliation said more about the candidate's ethnic orientation than did his tribal background, which in Kasonde's case was unimpeachably Bemba. Kasonde might have been a Bemba when he was still a member of the MMD – he was, in fact, a relative of the Bemba Paramount Chief – but his defection to the NP marked him as an outsider.

Meanwhile, in the by-elections held in the NP's home turf of Western and Southern Provinces, it was the NP candidates that sought to depict the competition in language group terms by emphasizing the dominance of the MMD's leadership by Bemba-speakers. As an article in the *Times of Zambia* reported, "the electorate was told the elections were about

[8] Interview with Brother John Dunbar, Malole Mission, 4 September 1995.

[9] Later investigation confirmed that the source of the rumor was an MMD campaign official (interviews, Malole and Kasama, 2–8 September 1995).

[10] An identical threat was invoked in a by-election that took place on the same day in Lundazi. This time, however, the tactic was used against the MMD. According to the head of the Eastern Province branch of FODEP, an independent election-monitoring group, "UNIP politicians [during the campaign] claimed that if people voted for MMD the MMD government would relocate people from other regions to Eastern Province and they would take our land and rule us . . . Here in Eastern Province, people believe these things fervently" (interview with Joseph Musukwa, Chipata, 11 January 1994).

breaking the Bemba monopoly on the reigns of power" (18 November 1993). A focus group participant described members of the NP in these areas as "referring to Kaunda as coming from the North, Chiluba again from the North [*sic*], so if they come to power they want somebody from Western or Southern [Provinces] to be president" (LY-T). The NP's Western Province organizing secretary confirmed that the party's strategy in Lozi-speaking areas was to point to Akashambatwa Mbikusita Lewanika, one of the NP's founding members and the son of the late Litunga, or to his sister Inonge, the party's interim president, as Zambia's future head of state.[11]

An additional part of the NP's strategy for winning Lozi-speakers' support was to resurrect the issue of the Barotseland Agreement – a topic that had last been invoked as a campaign theme by the UP more than two decades earlier. In the months immediately before the NP was launched in August 1993, traditional leaders in Western Province issued a series of threats to secede from the country if the Barotseland Agreement was not honored. In the November by-elections (and in those that followed in January 1994 and April and November 1995), the Barotseland Agreement featured prominently in NP campaigning. In public rallies, NP candidates and organizers characterized the abrogation of the Barotseland Agreement by the UNIP government and the refusal by President Chiluba to reinstate the agreement's provisions as "a Bemba ploy to oppress Lozi traditions by humiliating the Litunga" and promised that the NP would negotiate for the agreement's restoration if it were voted into power (*Financial Mail*, 16–23 November 1993; *Daily Mail*, 15 November 1995). As in the First Republic, the prominence of the Barotseland Agreement as a political issue can be explained by its usefulness as a tool for uniting Lozi-speakers and mobilizing them against the ruling party. The implicit claim being made when it was invoked was that whereas NP candidates would work for the interests of Lozi-speakers, MMD candidates would not.

In the 1996 general election, opportunities for ethnic appeal making were limited by both an abbreviated campaign period and a series of constitutional manipulations by the MMD government that caused opposition parties to spend more time arguing in Lusaka over the rules under which the elections would be conducted than engaging in grassroots campaigning in the constituencies (Bratton and Posner 1998). To the extent that political actors did engage in grassroots coalition-building, however,

[11] Interview with Mwitumwa Imbula, Mongu, 15 November 1995.

the ethnic electoral appeals they made were couched in explicitly linguistic terms, just as they had been in the multi-party elections and by-elections that had come earlier.

In the run-up to the 1996 race, for example, the MMD government attempted to win the favor of two key language group coalitions by introducing a bill in the National Assembly to rename the national airport and the University of Zambia after two of the country's late leaders, Simon Kapwepwe and Harry Nkumbula, respectively.[12] The choice of Kapwepwe and Nkumbula was far from accidental: each symbolized the glory days of the Bemba- and Tonga-speaking coalitions, and the attempt to rename the two public institutions after them was widely viewed as "an attempt by the President to bring [back] the old UNIP alliance of the Tonga-speakers and the Bemba-speakers for political points" (*The Post*, 15 August 1995). Although the bill was ultimately withdrawn, the clumsiness of the effort could not obscure the highly strategic coalition-building motivations that lay behind it.

The clearest example of the use of language group appeals in the 1996 election campaign itself again involved the attempt of candidates to win support among Lozi-speakers by raising the issue of the Barotseland Agreement. Six months before the election, an editorial in *The Post* observed that

> suddenly the Barotseland Agreement has become a darling of political parties who are now trying to out-do each other... [Political leaders] who once saw no sense in the Barotse demands are now proponents of the principle. Even Kaunda has the guts to say the Barotseland Agreement that he did not honor for the 27 years of his rule is necessary. (*The Post*, 24 April 1996)

Shortly before the *Post* editorial appeared, the UNIP had announced that it had made a mistake when it failed to adhere to the provisions of the Barotseland Agreement. Addressing a public campaign meeting in the Western Province capital of Mongu, Kaunda went "out of his way... [to] promise the people of Western Province that he [would] restore to them the abrogated... Barotseland Agreement of 1964" (*Zambia Today*, 18 April 1996).[13]

[12] The bill also provided for the renaming of the Zambia Air Services Institute after a third, less well-known, political figure.

[13] Chief Malambeka of Ndola Rural dismissed Kaunda's promise as a cheap political tactic: "Dr. Kaunda had vehemently refused to discuss the Barotse issue when he was in power and therefore his promise to reconsider his stand over the matter is

The UNIP was not the only party to have a change of heart on the wisdom of ignoring the agreement. Following the completion of an internal MMD report that concluded that the party's mishandling of the Barotseland Agreement issue could undermine its electoral prospects in Western Province during the upcoming election, the MMD followed the UNIP's lead and apologized for "mishandling" the discussions it had initiated on the issue with the Barotse Royal Establishment several years earlier (*Daily Mail*, 16 July 1996). "[D]angling like a carrot on a rope," the *Daily Mail* summarized, the agreement became "the darling for political leaders jockeying for [power] in the coming general elections" (1 August 1996). What the "carrot" represented was the prospect of uniting and securing the electoral support of the Lozi-speaking coalition – a strategically important piece of the national electoral pie.

The formation of the United Party for National Development (UPND) in 1998 brought another important political party onto the scene. As the words "united" and "national" in the party's name implied, the UPND did its utmost to avoid having people conclude that because the party's leader, the prominent businessman Anderson Mazoka, was a Tonga, the party was for Tongas only. Indeed, Mazoka was always quick to point out that his party's top leadership was well-balanced with people from all regions of the country. Yet when campaigning in Mazoka's home region of Southern Province, the party took advantage of the widespread assumption that, because it was "Tonga-led," it would put Tonga-speakers' interests first.[14] To signal the party's connection with the Tonga-speaking community, UPND leaders were careful to conduct their Southern Province campaign meetings not in English, as is customary in Zambian campaigns, but in Tonga (*Times of Zambia*, 6 December 1999).

Individual UPND parliamentary candidates also took advantage of the party's presumed language group orientation. In the by-election held in the Southern Province constituency of Mbabala in February 2000, the UPND candidate, a Tonga named Emmanuel Hachipuka, faced two other Tonga candidates. The fact that all three were Tonga, both by tribe and language, did not stop Hachipuka from implying that he was the only "real" Tonga in the race (*Times of Zambia*, 17 February 2000). "Tonganess," he suggested, derived not from a candidate's own background but from

merely an excuse to try and muster Lozi support for the forthcoming polls" (*Daily Mail*, 19 April 1996).

14 This was the way most newspaper reports referred to the party: as the "Tonga-led UPND" (*The Monitor*, 24–30 November 2000).

the condidate's party affiliation: since he was the only candidate running on the ticket of a Tonga party, he was the only true Tonga candidate. Hachipuka did to his rivals precisely what the MMD did to Kasonde in Malole. He undermined their claim to be members of the right ethnic group by asserting that what really mattered was the language group affiliation signaled by the party on whose ticket they were running.

*Non-Linguistic Appeals in Multi-Party Elections.* All of the evidence summarized thus far is in keeping with the expectation that politicians in multi-party elections will emphasize language group differences in their quest for national political power. But while such a strategy may make sense for some parties and candidates, it will not make sense for all of them. Indeed, for some parties and candidates, having the contest revolve around language group differences will be highly disadvantageous. Thus while we would expect to find some politicians in multi-party elections trying to frame the country's political competition in terms of language distinctions, we would also expect to find those politicians who stand to lose from a language-based allocation of support trying to encourage voters to think about political competition in terms of a different dimension of ethnic cleavage. In the language of the model presented in Chapter 5, we can think of such a situation as a case where $w$ chooses its A identity and forms a coalition with $y$, and politicians who are not in the $w + y$ coalition, or who recognize that voters view another politician as the natural $w + y$ leader, try to convince voters that politics is not really about cleavage A but about cleavage B. Such politicians are not likely to win, but these are nonetheless the appeals we would expect to see them make. Two examples illustrate.

The first involves the UNIP's response to the UPP. When Kapwepwe resigned from the UNIP in 1971, his defection triggered a by-election in which he re-contested his seat on the UPP ticket in the Copperbelt constituency of Mufulira West.[15] The UNIP attached special importance to this contest because it knew that a Kapwepwe victory would lend legitimacy to the UPP's claim that it offered a viable alternative to the ruling party. Even more importantly, a UNIP loss had the potential to trigger a wholesale defection of the Bemba-speaking coalition to the opposition

[15] The Mufulira West seat had actually belonged to Justin Chimba, who resigned from the UNIP with Kapwepwe to form the UPP. When Chimba decided not to re-contest the seat, Kapwepwe decided to run there rather than for his old seat in Kitwe.

camp. In this respect, the UNIP faced a situation analogous to the one the MMD would face twenty-two years later in Malole. Unlike the MMD, however, the UNIP was disadvantaged by being viewed as the less obvious "Bemba party" than its upstart rival.

Recognizing that it was not likely to beat the UPP if the election turned on the question of which party would better represent Bemba-speakers' interests, the UNIP tried to undermine Kapwepwe by dividing the Bemba-speaking coalition and turning part of it – the part that came from Luapula Province – against him. Gertzel et al. (1972: 68) explain that several years earlier "Kapwepwe had antagonized many people from Luapula by his alleged reference to them as *batubula* (dumb fishermen)."[16] UNIP sought to exploit the resentment that this comment had caused by handpicking a candidate to run against Kapwepwe who had been born in Mansa, Luapula's provincial capital, and by sending prominent Luapula politicians to the constituency to campaign with him (ibid.: 69). Although the strategy had only limited success – Kapwepwe won his seat despite being in detention at the time and unable to campaign personally – the UNIP's response to the situation illustrates well how political actors that are disadvantaged by the salience of a particular cleavage dimension will try to frame the conflict in terms of another cleavage that is more beneficial.

A second example comes from the Third Republic and involves the MMD's response to the NP. Throughout most of the country, the MMD's strategy for dealing with the NP was to tell voters that the party constituted little more than an "attempt by the Lozi and their Tonga traditional cousins to distance themselves from the Bembas and to enable them to put up a president during the next general elections" (*Financial Mail*, 16–23 November 1993). Within Western Province, however, the MMD knew that this would be not be a useful strategy. Accordingly, its tactic was to try to divide the monolithic Lozi-speaking coalition, just as the UNIP had attempted to break up the Bemba-speaking coalition in Mufulira West. A veteran politician who worked closely with one of the NP candidates in the province explained to me that the

> MMD was trying to use the old methods that Kaunda used. You see, in Western province there is a mixture of tribes. The MMD were appealing to the Luvale tribespeople, of whom there are quite many in the province, by saying that if they

[16] As with the similar slur alleged to have been made by John Mwanakatwe that I describe in Chapter 4, whether Kapwepwe actually referred to Luapulans as *batubula* was less important than the fact that many people believed that he had.

> voted for [the NP] they would be deported to Angola where their forefathers had come from. To a European like yourself, such threats may not seem serious. But to a villager here they are taken literally. Being a Luvale myself I was in a position to refute [these rumors].[17]

Newspaper reports confirm that during the Western Province by-elections "sentiments were being expressed that the Lozis would repatriate the other 24 tribes from the region across the border where they allegedly came from" (*Financial Mail*, 16–23 November 1993).

Note the similarities and differences between this and the Mufulira West example. In both cases, the parties knew that they would lose if voters made their choices based on their language identities, so they sought to encourage them to focus instead on a different dimension of ethnic cleavage. But whereas the UNIP tried to divide the Bemba-speaking vote by "playing province," the MMD tried to divide the Lozi-speaking coalition by "playing tribe." The provincial cleavage was attractive to UNIP campaigners in Mufulira West because the Luapula group was larger than any single tribe and thus would more seriously undermine Kapwepwe's support if it could be turned against him.[18] The UNIP "played province" because the size of the provincial coalition was more useful to it than the size of any of the tribal coalitions that it might have tried to mobilize. MMD strategists, on the other hand, had no choice but to attempt to divide the dominant Lozi-speaking group by mobilizing tribal identities, since tribe was the only other basis of ethnic division that was available to them. Language was shared by all voters in the Province.[19]

These examples illustrate two important aspects of the model: first, that politicians evaluate the ethnic cleavages that are available to them and try to mobilize people in terms of the axis of division that will do the politicians the most good, and second, that their calculations about which cleavage will be most advantageous to them will revolve around the sizes of the groups that each cleavage defines.

17 Interview with William Chipango, Livingstone, 16 December 1995. MMD campaigners were not the only ones to play this strategy against the NP. UNIP campaigners started a similar rumor during the by-election in Kalabo in November 1995.

18 Note that the only reason the provincial cleavage was available to UNIP was because the by-election was taking place in the Copperbelt, which contained not just multiple Bemba-speaking tribes but also Bemba-speaking migrants from both Northern and Luapula provinces.

19 Sub-tribal distinctions along clan lines might have been possible, but these would have been even less useful than tribal distinctions, since they define even smaller groups.

## *Ethnic Electoral Appeals in One-Party Contexts*

In 1973, Zambia became a "one-party participatory democracy." After nearly a decade of multi-party politics, the introduction of one-party rule led, almost overnight, to new patterns of ethnic coalition-building. Whereas politics in the First Republic had revolved around conflicts among broad linguistically defined regional blocs, politics in the Second Republic came very quickly to revolve around competition among local groups, usually defined in tribal terms. The institutions of the one-party state shifted the locus of electoral competition from the national to the local level, and this led to an increase in the salience of more localized ethnic identities. Baylies and Szeftel (1984) explain:

> The sharper focus on local issues and locality tended to parochialize conflict and to intensify lines of cleavage other than those along regional or linguistic lines. In a number of constituencies this resulted in an increased emphasis upon ethnic identity at the local level. (46)

In the new one-party institutional setting, "large regional blocs lost something of their old importance" and "a greater salience [was lent] to far smaller divisions, many hitherto forgotten" (47) during the initial post-independence period.

Summarizing the one-party campaigns of 1973 and 1978, Chikulo echoes these observations about the new salience of localized, "hitherto forgotten" identities. He notes that, with the introduction of intra-party competition, the focus of electoral politics shifted from national-level divisions to those that divide the electoral constituency itself: "cleavage and conflict [become confined] to the local level" (1988: 43). Compared to the patterns of ethnic politics that prevailed during the First Republic, the one-party elections were characterized by a sharp shift in the locus of political conflict "from the national level to disputes based on the organization of smaller, local factions" (Szeftel 1978: 388). This changed the kinds of political coalitions that were formed, as well as the ethnic raw material from which they were constructed. "Within a number of constituencies, individuals who previously might have been members of the same faction now came into conflict as they sought electoral support in competition with each other" (ibid.).

Newspaper reports from 1973 are full of accounts of districts "plagued by tribalism" (*Times of Zambia*, 29 October 1973) and "party leaders engaged in campaigns to insure that people from their tribe get elected to the National Assembly" (*Times of Zambia*, 26 November 1973). When six UNIP officials were suspended "for conducting election campaigns for people from their own tribes," an editorial in the *Daily Mail* felt the need to stress that it was wrong for people to be elected "for what their tribesmen can get for them" (*Daily Mail*, 15 November 1973). After the election results were announced, further charges emerged, largely (and not surprisingly) from the losers, that "tribalism had contributed to their downfall" or that "the whole election campaign [had been] characterized by tribalism and corruption" (*Daily Mail*, 7 December 1973). A branch-level UNIP official summarized the effects of the new electoral institutions on the character of political competition in the country when he lamented that "the one-party system is destroying the party. We are no longer united and are campaigning tribally against each other" (quoted in Gertzel and Szeftel 1984: 144).

Because of a study of the 1973 election conducted by researchers based at the University of Zambia, the record of ethnic coalition-building for that contest is relatively comprehensive.[20] For example, we know that in Zambezi district of Northwestern Province, politicians in the 1973 election sought to win votes by emphasizing the divisions between members of the Lunda and Luvale tribes (Baylies and Szeftel 1984: 47). In Ndola Rural, the central issue in the campaign was whether candidates were Lamba, the dominant tribe in the area, or urban migrants from other tribes (Gertzel and Szeftel 1984: 143). In Western Province, "the greater emphasis upon locality resulted in the articulation of economic grievances in terms of [the region's] smaller ethnic groups" (Gertzel 1984: 225). In all three cases, the emphasis on tribal differences was a marked contrast to the 1968 election, during which national-scale cleavages had served as the basis of political competition and conflict.

A slightly different form of localism emerged in areas that were not only linguistically but also tribally homogeneous. In Sinazongwe constituency in Southern Province, for example, "three candidates were from the same [tribal] and linguistic groups, but nevertheless managed to polarise the constituency in terms of the three chiefs' areas from which they variously came" (Szeftel 1978: 332). Despite the fact that the dimension of identity that became salient was not strictly speaking tribal, the Sinazongwe case still bears out the model's expectation that political competition will revolve around local-constituency-level cleavages in one-party contests. The fact that Sinazongwe was divided by neither tribe nor language simply

[20] Several of the papers that came out of the study became the basis for the chapters in Gertzel et al. (1984).

meant that candidates had to identify themselves at the sub-tribal level in order to construct minimum winning coalitions. The important point is that the emphasis on chiefs' areas was altogether different from what took place in 1968, when campaigning in Sinazongwe, an ANC stronghold, revolved around mobilizing Tonga-speakers as a unified community against the Bembas who controlled the government. The objective distinctions among chiefs' areas that figured prominently in 1973 were, of course, also there in 1968. But they were invisible to the politicians who sought to mobilize voters in that year's multi-party election.

Unfortunately, no comprehensive election studies were conducted during the 1978, 1983, or 1988 one-party elections, so there is little secondary source coverage that might document the appeals made by politicians in these contests.[21] Newspaper reports at the time of these three elections are full of stories about "clandestine tribal campaigning" and warnings against candidates engaging in "tribalism" (*Daily Mail*, 30 November and 4 December 1978; 28 September 1983; 6 October 1988), just as they were in 1973. But absent documentation of the specific appeals that politicians employed in these contests, it is not possible to make strong claims about whether they emphasized tribal rather than language group differences.

Some evidence of the cleavage-shaping effects of the shift from multi-party to one-party rule can nonetheless be gleaned from the appeals that politicians did *not* make. Take the case of the Barotseland Agreement, which, as we have seen, was a key campaign issue in both the First and Third Republics because it helped to mobilize a coalition that was useful for national-scale political competition. Because a coalition that unites all Lozi-speakers is too large for constituency-level political competition – nearly all the rural constituencies that contain Lozi-speakers are homogeneously Lozi-speaking – we would expect politicians to have had little interest in invoking the Barotseland Agreement as a coalition-building device during the Second Republic. Of course, interest groups that would benefit from the restoration of the agreement – such as the Lozi Royal Establishment, which stood to win substantial powers of local government and taxation if the terms of the agreement were ever put into force – should have had strong incentives to put the issue on the agenda irrespective of the institutional setting. Indeed, one of the senior advisors to the Litunga told me that the Lozi Royal Establishment did try to make an issue of the

[21] Chikulo (1988), Baylies (1984), and Gertzel (1984) all deal with the 1978 election but make little mention of the campaign appeals made by candidates.

Barotseland Agreement during the Second Republic.[22] But in the sphere of electoral competition, the agreement's usefulness as a coalition-building tool would be far greater in a multi-party than a one-party setting.

The expectation is borne out. A participant in one of my focus groups in 1995 commented that "in the Second Republic [the issue of the Barotseland Agreement] wasn't there. But immediately [when] multi-partism comes in, they started that issue and it was a burning issue recently" (CPTA-T). An editorial in *The Post* commenting on the resurfacing of the Barotseland Agreement as a political issue after the MMD came to power in 1991 notes that "everyone was silent about the issue under Kaunda's Second Republic" (7 July 1995). A former MP and longtime Western Province politician agreed that the agreement "simply was not an issue until 1991."[23] The agreement seems to have been an issue only when the coalition that it mobilized would be politically useful, and, as the model predicts, this was during multi-party, but not during one-party, elections.

The foregoing examples illustrate how patterns of ethnic coalition-building differed across one-party and multi-party settings. Although they lend plausibility to the arguments developed in Chapter 5, they do not constitute a systematic test of the model's expectations about elite behavior. In the next section, I turn to a series of quantitative tests that do. These tests assess whether candidates run in the kinds of electoral constituencies that the model predicts they will in each institutional setting.

## THE CONSTITUENCIES IN WHICH CANDIDATES RUN

Writing about elections in Kenya, Joel Barkan observes that "because possession of the right ethnic credential is often a prerequisite for being a serious candidate, most serious candidates meet this test" (1984: 92). Given a choice about where to run, Barkan implies, serious candidates will choose (or their parties will choose for them) constituencies where they are a member of the "right" ethnic group. But what if, as in Zambia (and, as I will emphasize in Chapter 9, also Kenya), candidates possess ethnic credentials that allow them to claim membership in more than one ethnic group? Which one will they (or their party strategists) focus on when they try to match their ethnic background with that of the voters?

The argument developed in Chapter 5 suggests that the answer will depend on the institutional context in which the candidate is running.

[22] Interview with Induna Mukulwakushiko, Lealui, 18 November 1995.

[23] Interview with Leonard Luyanga, Limulunga, 17 November 1995.

It suggests that, in Zambia, candidates in one-party elections will seek to place themselves in constituencies where their own tribal background matches that of the voters whose support they are seeking. In multi-party contests, the match between candidates' and voters' tribal identities will be less important than the match between the language group orientations of the parties with which the candidates are affiliated and the predominant language group in the constituency in which they are running. We would still expect to find many candidates in multi-party elections placing themselves (or being placed by their political parties) in constituencies where their tribal backgrounds match those of the voters. After all, being a member of one of the local tribes, while not essential, is not in any way disadvantageous in a multi-party context. But we would expect to find this less often than in one-party settings. In the discussion that follows, I test this expectation in a variety of ways.

## *Where Candidates Run*

The most straightforward test of the expectation that the institutional context will affect the kinds of constituencies in which candidates choose to run is simply to count the percentage of candidates that run in constituencies outside of their home tribal areas in multi-party and in one-party elections. If the model is right, we would expect to find only candidates that are members of the dominant tribe in a given constituency running in one-party races, whereas we should find non-dominant tribe members running in multi-party contests.[24]

Of course, a test of this sort makes sense only if candidates actually have the ability to choose the constituencies in which they run. In multi-party races, where the decision about where a candidate will run is generally made by the party rather than the candidate, we can assume that parties will assign candidates to the constituencies where they will have the greatest chance of winning, and we can make inferences about parties' strategies to achieve this goal from the candidates' locations.[25] But in one-party elections, where by definition a candidate from the ruling party wins, party leaders will have little reason to go out of their way

[24] As we shall see, this formulation is a bit too simple, since the prediction will depend on the number of candidates in the race. I return to this issue in a moment.

[25] On the allocation of candidates to constituencies in the First Republic, see Molteno and Scott (1974: 171–74) and *Times of Zambia*, 24 October 1968. For the Third Republic, see *Weekly Post*, 20–26 September 1991; *Sunday Mail*, 28 July 1996; *Zambia Today*, 12 September 1996; and *Times of Zambia*, 16 September 1996.

Table 7.1. *Where Candidates Run*

| | Number of candidates running for election | | Share of candidates running for election that are members of the dominant tribe in the constituency in which they are running (in %) |
|---|---|---|---|
| | That are members of the dominant tribe in the constituency in which they are running | That are *not* members of the dominant tribe in the constituency in which they are running | |
| 1968 | 34 | 22 | 61 |
| 1973 | 37 | 7 | 84 |
| 1978 | 15 | 3 | 83 |
| 1983 | 28 | 4 | 88 |
| 1988 | 11 | 1 | 92 |
| 1996 | 15 | 5 | 75 |
| one-party total | 72 | 12 | 86 |
| multi-party total | 49 | 27 | 64 |

to match candidates with the "right" (in the sense of ethnically advantageous) constituencies. Of course, candidates themselves will have strong incentives to make sure they are running in the "right" place, but we need to satisfy ourselves that party officials do not prevent candidates from running where they would prefer. The evidence suggests that they do not. Applications to run in a particular constituency were open to all UNIP members in good standing, and it was up to the prospective candidate to decide where he or she would apply (Baylies and Szeftel 1984: 30–31). The former Zambian Vice President and UNIP secretary general, Mainza Chona, confirmed that "there was no restriction at all on people standing where they wanted" during the Second Republic.[26] Chona told me that he could not think of a single example of a person who applied to run in a particular constituency and was told by the party to run somewhere else instead.[27]

Table 7.1 compares the number and share of candidates that ran in constituencies where they were members of the dominant tribe in every competitive election between 1968 and 1996. The analysis includes only rural constituencies, since it is only in rural areas that the model would lead us to predict a difference in candidates' behavior across one-party

[26] Interview with Mainza Chona, Lusaka, 31 July 1999.

[27] Ibid. Although candidates were subject to vetting by the party's Central Committee, this had a much greater effect on whether candidates would be permitted to contest than on *where* they would do so.

and multi-party settings. It also includes only cases where we can be sure that prospective candidates would have no difficulty identifying the dominant tribe, which I define as constituencies where the dominant tribe's population share is at least 20 percentage points greater than that of the next largest tribe. In addition, the analysis excludes candidates that received less than 5 percent of the vote on the grounds that such candidates were not serious and thus cannot be assumed to have made their decisions about where to run based on a careful assessment of what it would take to win.

The analysis also makes one final restriction: it includes only constituencies in which just two candidates were competing. Limiting the analysis in this way is crucial because the incentives for being a member of the dominant tribe will vary depending on the number of candidates in the race. Given plurality rules, the more candidates there are, the greater the likelihood that a non-dominant tribe candidate might win, and thus the greater the incentive for such a candidate to enter. Take the example of Chipangali constituency in Chipata district, which is approximately 60 percent Chewa and 30 percent Ngoni. The constituency's tribal demographics provide a distinct advantage for Chewa candidates, so we would expect Chewa politicians to be the first to enter the race. If only one or two Chewa candidates enter, a Ngoni candidate will have little incentive to join the contest. But as the number of candidates in the race rises (in this case, above two), the possibility of the Chewa candidates dividing the vote among themselves will increase, and the viability of a Ngoni candidacy improves. The number of candidates beyond which entry by a non-dominant tribe member makes sense will vary from constituency to constituency depending on the local tribal demographics. But, generally, the larger the number of candidates in the race, the more viable a non-dominant tribe candidate will be and the more likely it will be for such a candidate to enter. Beyond a certain point, the disincentives for non-dominant tribe candidates to enter are transformed into incentives for entry.[28]

[28] There is, of course, a problem with my Chipangali example. I describe the Ngoni candidate's entry decision as if he is making it as part of a staged process in which he knows who has already entered the race. This may not be an accurate representation of the context in which prospective candidates actually make their choices. The number of candidates that competed in a given race is something I can identify *ex post*, but it is not something that prospective candidates know *ex ante* – at least not reliably. Prospective candidates may have some idea of who has already declared at the time they are considering entering the race. But they may not. And they would have no way of knowing who might enter after they did. This said, controlling for the number of candidates in the race is far better than not doing so.

If the number of candidates running in each constituency were, on average, equal across one-party and multi-party elections, then this "number of candidates effect" would not be a problem. But the average number of candidates in Zambia's elections does vary considerably.[29] This variation makes meaningful comparisons across contests impossible without controlling for the number of candidates. To be absolutely sure that I am getting a "clean" test, I limit the analysis to cases where just two candidates compete.

The trend in Table 7.1 is clear. In the four one-party elections of 1973, 1978, 1983, and 1988, the share of candidates running in constituencies where their own tribal affiliation matches that of the dominant tribe is significantly higher than in the two multi-party contests of 1968 and 1996. Whereas the share for the four one-party races taken together is 86 percent, the share for the multi-party elections is just 64 percent.[30] Note that the multi-party average probably somewhat over-reports the share that the model would predict. Recall that what frees candidates in a multi-party election from the need to run in a constituency in which they are members of the dominant tribe is that the language group label that voters ascribe to them by virtue of their party affiliation trumps their own tribal background. However, this should apply only to candidates that are running on tickets of parties associated with the dominant language group in the constituency. Candidates affiliated with parties that are not viewed this way would actually do best by deliberately trying to locate themselves in constituencies where they *are* members of the dominant group and can at least appeal to voters on tribal grounds.

Furthermore, changes in the direction that the model predicts are evident in these shares on either side of the 1973 and 1991 regime transitions. In the final multi-party election of the First Republic in 1968, only 61 percent of candidates ran in constituencies where they were members of the dominant tribe. Five years later, in the first one-party election of the Second Republic in 1973, fully 84 percent of candidates did so. A similarly

[29] Whereas no constituency in the elections of 1968, 1973, or 1978 had more than three candidates, fully 83 percent of the candidates running in 1983 were running in constituencies with more than four competitors. In 1988 and 1996, the shares were 68 and 43 percent, respectively. In 1973 and 1978, candidates competing in the general election were selected via a primary system in which the top three vote winners advanced to the next stage. The primary stage was eliminated for the 1983 and 1988 elections, and the average number of candidates in each constituency rose precipitously.

[30] A difference-of-means test reveals the differences across one-party and multi-party elections to be significant at greater than the 95 percent confidence interval.

dramatic change took place in the opposite direction between the final Second Republic election of 1988 and the Third Republic multi-party contest of 1996.[31] In the former, 92 percent of candidates ran in constituencies in which they were members of the dominant tribe, whereas in the latter this figure dropped to 75 percent.

Although the results of the test clearly bear out the expectations of the model, it is reasonable to ask why we find *any* candidates in the one-party elections running in constituencies where their tribal affiliation is different from that of the majority of voters – particularly after we have excluded non-serious candidates, constituencies where the dominant tribe is not easily identifiable, and races containing more than two contestants (where entry by non-dominant tribespeople might be a rational strategy). The fact that large numbers of candidates in multi-party elections continue to run in constituencies where they are members of the dominant tribe is not a problem, since nothing in the model suggests that candidates are disadvantaged in multi-party races by matching their tribal background with that of the voters. But the fact that roughly 15 percent of candidates running in one-party contests are from non-dominant tribes raises a legitimate question. The simple answer is that the model does not explain everything. As I have emphasized, the goal of this study is not to demonstrate that ethnic considerations motivate one hundred percent of actors' behavior. Rather, it is to show that the institutional context in which actors are operating will determine the kinds of ethnic identities that matter for politics. In this regard, the relevant finding is the consistent (and statistically significant) difference between the patterns in the one-party and the multi-party races.

The difference between the 1968 and 1996 results also bears mention. If the institutional setting is driving the results, why do we find such significant variation in outcomes within the category of multi-party elections? Two explanations are plausible. First, the 1968 elections took place only four years after independence and in a context where UNIP leaders felt it important to build national unity. Also, the UNIP at the time was sufficiently secure in its hold on power to risk running well-known politicians in constituencies outside of their home areas. As Mainza Chona explains:

> In the First Republic, we tried to put people in areas where they came from, where they were known. But in order to enhance nationalism we also put people in areas

[31] For reasons explained earlier, the results of the 1991 election (in which, employing the same controls, 84 percent of candidates stood in constituencies where their own tribal affiliation matched that of the dominant tribe) are omitted from the analysis. For the purposes of testing the model, the 1996 election is treated as the first multi-party contest of the Third Republic.

> that were not their own but where we thought they would be accepted because they had a national outlook. For example, we put Grey Zulu [a well-known minister and a Chewa] in Kasama [a Bemba constituency]. And, myself [a Tonga], I was put in Western Province [in a constituency dominated by Nkoyas and Lozis]. But we did this sparingly because we knew that there would be a revolt.[32]

The 1968 election probably featured a larger number of candidates running outside of their home tribal areas than would have been the case had the UNIP's leaders been less confident that voters would support well-known freedom fighters irrespective of their ethnic backgrounds. The proximity of the 1968 election to the independence struggle thus probably accounts for part of the difference in the shares of non-dominant tribe candidates in that year and in 1996.

A second factor is learning. The 1996 election took place just five years after the transition from one-party rule, and it is likely that parties and candidates were still used to the idea learned during the long one-party era that candidates should run in constituencies where their tribal background matches that of the majority of the voters. The fact that such a strategy, while not essential in a multi-party setting, was nonetheless not disadvantageous may explain why so many candidates in 1996 were members of the dominant tribes in the constituencies in which they ran. Thus the location of the 1968 election at the beginning of the post-independence era probably biased the share of dominant tribe candidates downward and the location of the 1996 contest shortly after the end of nearly two decades of one-party rule probably biased it upward. The result is greater variation across the two elections than there would have been had they been held closer together. The important point, however, is that, even with learning, the share of candidates that were members of dominant tribes was still significantly lower in 1996 than it had been in any of the one-party elections that preceded it.

In Table 7.1, I restricted the analysis to constituencies where only two candidates competed in the race, so as to provide the cleanest possible test of the model's predictions about candidates' strategic behavior. In Table 7.2, I revisit the analysis, but this time I focus explicitly on how the results change with different numbers of candidates (for space reasons I report only aggregate findings for each party system type). What we find is interesting: as the number of candidates increases, the gap between the

[32] Interview with Mainza Chona, Lusaka, 31 July 1999. Although President Kaunda at one point threatened to bar parliamentary candidates from running in their home regions, the proposal was never implemented (*Times of Zambia*, 15 July 1969).

Table 7.2. *Where Candidates Run, with Different Numbers of Candidates*

| | Number of candidates | Number of candidates running for election: That are members of the dominant tribe in the constituency in which they are running | That are *not* members of the dominant tribe in the constituency in which they are running | Share of candidates running for election that are members of the dominant tribe in the constituency in which they are running (in %) |
|---|---|---|---|---|
| one-party | 2 | 72 | 12 | 86 |
| multi-party | 2 | 49 | 27 | 64 |
| one-party | 3 | 274 | 54 | 84 |
| multi-party | 3 | 43 | 16 | 73 |
| one-party | 4 | 70 | 14 | 83 |
| multi-party | 4 | 79 | 17 | 82 |
| one-party | ≥5 | 330 | 109 | 75 |
| multi-party | ≥5 | 88 | 23 | 79 |

one-party and multi-party outcomes shrinks.[33] This is in keeping with the theoretical expectation that, as the number of candidates rises, the disincentives for non-dominant tribe candidates to enter the race will decrease and, after a point, become incentives for entry. Indeed, when four candidates are in the race, the one-party and multi-party outcome is almost the same. With five or more candidates, we actually find (statistically significantly) more cases of non-dominant tribe candidates entering the race in one-party than in multi-party elections.

### *Candidate Movement*

A second test involves counting, among candidates that ran for Parliament once before and are running again, the share that are running in different constituencies from the last time and, among these candidates, the share whose movement involves a shift either to or from a constituency where they are a member of the dominant tribe. If the nature of the party system shapes politicians' and party strategists' incentives in the way that the model suggests, then the transition from the multi-party to the one-party system in 1973 should have sent a stream of politicians that had previously run in constituencies dominated by tribes other than their own toward constituencies dominated by members of their own tribe. Similarly, the shift from one-party back to multi-party politics in 1991 should have relaxed the necessity for politicians to match their tribal affiliations with that of their constituents and triggered a (more modest) movement of politicians from constituencies where they were members of the dominant tribe toward constituencies where they were not.

Table 7.3 presents the results of the analysis. In each election, I identify every candidate that had previously run for Parliament, even if not in the immediately prior election, and assess whether the candidate is running in the same constituency as the last time.[34] If candidates are running in a

[33] Beyond two candidates, the differences in the one-party and multi-party means cease to be significant at the 95 percent confidence interval.

[34] The re-delimitation of constituencies at the start of the Second and Third Republics makes assessing whether or not candidates have moved more difficult. In the case of the 1991 re-delimitation, the task is made somewhat easier because the re-delimitation involved the division of existing constituencies rather than the wholesale re-drawing of boundaries. In instances where a single constituency was divided into two new ones, I considered the candidate that ran again to be running in a different constituency if the tribal demographics of the two new constituencies were sufficiently different so as to force the candidate to make a choice about which one would be more advantageous.

Table 7.3. *Candidate Movement*

| | Total number of candidates competing | Number (share) that had run previously | Among candidates that had run previously, number (share) running in different constituency | Among candidates that had run previously and were running in a different constituency | | | Ratio of movement *to* to movement *from* |
|---|---|---|---|---|---|---|---|
| | | | | Percentage that moved *to* a "home constituency" | Percentage that moved *from* a "home constituency" | Percentage that moved to an *equally* "home constituency" | |
| 1973 | 245 | 46 (19%) | 23 (50%) | 83 | 4 | 13 | 19 : 1 |
| 1978 | 274 | 122 (45%) | 12 (10%) | 50 | 8 | 42 | 6 : 1 |
| 1983 | 574 | 204 (36%) | 30 (15%) | 63 | 20 | 17 | 3.2 : 1 |
| 1988 | 472 | 245 (52%) | 21 (9%) | 52 | 14 | 33 | 3.7 : 1 |
| 1991 | 259 | 111 (43%) | 32 (29%) | 31 | 28 | 41 | 1.1 : 1 |
| 1996 | 466 | 110 (24%) | 27 (25%) | 44 | 26 | 30 | 1.7 : 1 |

new constituency, I evaluate whether that constituency provides a better match than their old one between their tribal background and that of the dominant tribal group. If it does, I code the case as an instance of movement *to* a "home constituency," where a "home constituency" is simply one where the candidate is a member of the dominant tribe. If it does not, I code it as an instance of movement *from* a "home constituency." If the candidate's new constituency provides an equally good match as the old one between the candidate's tribe and the dominant tribe, I code it as an instance of movement to an *equally* "home constituency." As in the previous analysis, I include only rural constituencies, though this time I do include candidates that won less than 5 percent of the vote (I assume that candidates that go to the trouble to switch their constituencies can be safely assumed to be serious about winning) and constituencies where the dominant tribe's population share is less than 20 percentage points greater than the next largest tribe (I assume that they have made it their business to find out what the tribal demographics of the constituency are before they move to it).

The first thing to note about the results in Table 7.3 is the high percentage of candidates who switched their constituencies following the regime changes of 1973 and 1991. Only 19 percent of the candidates running in 1973 had run in 1968, but, of these, fully 50 percent ran in new constituencies. The 1991 election also brought a significant rise from the previous election in the share of former candidates that were running in new places (from 9 percent in 1988 to 29 percent in 1991). Part of the reason for this trend was undoubtedly the re-delimitation of constituency boundaries, which did away with the constituencies in which many candidates had previously run and forced them to choose new ones. But an equally large part of the explanation was almost certainly the changed institutional environment, which created incentives for many candidates to shift to constituencies that would be more advantageous for them in the new political context. Evidence that this was the case comes from the kinds of constituencies to which candidates were moving.

In 1973, fully 83 percent of the candidates that moved to new constituencies moved from ones where they were not members of the dominant tribe to ones where they would be. In that election, the ratio of candidates moving *to* constituencies where they would be members of the dominant tribe to candidates moving *from* such constituencies was nineteen to one. The trend was so marked as to cause the audience attending a municipal meeting in Kitwe to "demand to know why so many people, particularly Ministers, were rushing to their home areas to stand." One speaker at the meeting volunteered an answer when he suggested that "this clearly shows that the people involved are practicing tribalism and they will be elected on a tribal basis" (*Daily Mail*, 18 October 1973). This is exactly the direction of movement that the argument developed in Chapter 5 would lead us to expect. This trend persisted through the next three Second Republic elections, as candidates continued to relocate themselves to places where their tribal backgrounds would match those of the voters whose support they needed. Across the elections of 1978, 1983, and 1988 taken together, the ratio of movement *to* to movement *from* "home constituencies" was 3.6 to 1. With the return to multi-party politics in 1991, this trend of movement to home areas slowed to a trickle. Many candidates were moving in 1991, but now the share of candidates moving *to* and *from* "home constituencies" was almost equal. The ratio rose slightly in 1996 but still fell well short of even the lowest ratio in the one-party era. These results – particularly the contrast between the directions of movement in the transitional contests of 1973 and 1991 – provide powerful evidence that the one-party or multi-party nature of the political system shaped the ethnic calculations of Zambian political elites.

### *Unopposed Candidates*

A third test of the model's implications for candidates' behavior comes from comparing the kinds of candidates that are able to run unopposed in different kinds of elections. If the model is right, we would expect no unopposed candidate that is not a member of the dominant tribe in the constituency to be able to remain unopposed in a one-party contest. In situations where it looked like a tribal outsider might contest a seat without opposition in a one-party race, it would always make sense for an ambitious tribal insider to challenge the unopposed candidate and turn the election into a referendum on the need for representation by a member of one's own tribal group. In multi-party elections, on the other hand, unopposed tribal outsiders would attract challengers only if both the party for which they were running was not associated with the language group in the region and if an alternative party that *was* associated with the regional language group was in a position to put up a candidate of its own. We would therefore expect unopposed candidates from non-dominant tribes to be extremely rare in one-party elections

Table 7.4. *Unopposed Candidates*

| | Unopposed candidate is a member of | |
|---|---|---|
| | Dominant tribe | Non-dominant tribe |
| 1968 | 10 | 20 |
| 1973 | 12 | 2 |
| 1978 | 6 | 0 |
| 1983 | 0 | 0 |
| 1988 | 10 | 0 |
| 1996 | 3 | 0 |
| 3rd Republic by-elections | 1 | 2 |
| one-party total | 28 | 2 |
| multi-party total | 14 | 22 |

but common in multi-party elections. Table 7.4 confirms that this is the case.[35]

In Zambia's four one-party elections, thirty candidates ran unopposed. Only two of these were not members of the dominant tribe in the constituency in which they were running.[36] In the multi-party elections of 1968 and 1996, and in the Third Republic by-elections that took place through the end of 1999, fully twenty-two of the thirty-six candidates that ran unopposed – slightly less than two-thirds of the total – were members

35 The reported differences across one-party and multi-party elections are statistically significant at greater than 95 percent. As in the previous analyses, I include only rural constituencies. I include the Third Republic by-elections in this analysis because, unlike the two previous analyses, it does not matter here that by-elections do not provide candidates with a full spectrum of constituencies from which to choose.

36 One of these unopposed "outsiders," William Harrington, had a white father and Lozi mother and was running in a Lozi-dominated constituency. I code him as not being a member of the dominant tribe only because a "full" Lozi (i.e., a candidate with two Lozi parents) could have claimed to be a more authentic representative of Lozi interests. This said, Harrington's father was well known and long established in the area, so it is likely that Harrington himself was viewed as a local son. The other non-dominant tribe candidate able to run unopposed was Unia Mwila, a Bemba standing in a constituency where Bembas were the second most numerous tribe, though only 6 percent behind the dominant Mukulus. Mwila was a very well-known figure in Zambia at the time, having served as a minister of state in the Ministries of Finance and Education, and as secretary of state for trade, industry, and mines. At the time of the 1973 election in which he ran unopposed, he was serving as Zambia's ambassador to the United States. So, while these candidates were, strictly speaking, tribal outsiders, they were far from ordinary ones.

Table 7.5. *Unchallenged Constituencies*

| | Total number of constituencies | Number of constituencies without a candidate from the dominant tribe in the race | Percentage of constituencies without a candidate from the dominant tribe in the race |
|---|---|---|---|
| 1968 | 86 | 32 | 37 |
| 1973 | 100 | 10 | 10 |
| 1978 | 100 | 9 | 9 |
| 1983 | 100 | 3 | 3 |
| 1988 | 100 | 5 | 5 |
| 1996 | 122 | 15 | 12 |
| 3rd Republic by-elections | 46 | 1 | 2 |
| one-party total | 400 | 27 | 7 |
| multi-party total | 251 | 48 | 19 |

of tribes other than the dominant tribe.[37] The contrast is striking. It is also exactly in keeping with the model's expectations.

## *Unchallenged Constituencies*

A final test is very similar to the last one. For the same reason that non-dominant tribe candidates that are running unopposed in one-party elections will be likely to be challenged, constituencies in which no dominant tribe candidate has yet entered the race (irrespective of the number of non-dominant tribe candidates that already have) will be very unlikely to remain that way. If it looked like a constituency might wind up with nobody running from the dominant tribe, it would always make sense for a dominant tribe candidate to enter. In a multi-party election, by contrast, there would be no such incentive. On balance, then, we would expect to find a significantly larger number of constituencies with no dominant tribe candidates in multi-party than in one-party elections. As Table 7.5 shows, this is what we find. The share of unchallenged constituencies in one-party races (7 percent) is far lower than in multi-party contests (19 percent).[38]

[37] There were no unopposed candidates in the multi-party elections of 1991.

[38] The differences across one-party and multi-party contests are statistically significant at greater than the 95 percent level. Again, I include only rural constituencies in the analysis.

Taken together, these four quantitative tests provide strong evidence that the shift from one-party to multi-party rule altered the strategic behavior of Zambian politicians in the way the model would predict. Not only do candidates couch their electoral appeals in terms of different dimensions of ethnic identity in each setting, but they attach different importance to matching their own tribal backgrounds with that of the voters when it comes to deciding where, or whether, to run for office. In one-party contests, where a candidate's tribal identity matters, we find that candidates are careful to run in constituencies where they are members of the dominant tribe. In multi-party elections, where the requirement that a candidate be a member of the dominant tribe is secondary to the need to be running on the ticket of a party that is identified with the regional language group, we find that candidates are significantly more willing to run in constituencies outside their tribal home areas.

## INVESTMENTS BY POLITICIANS IN ETHNIC CIVIC ASSOCIATIONS

Thus far, I have focused on the political strategies employed by Zambian politicians either during parliamentary elections or in the period immediately leading up to them. Given that the key variation I seek to explain is the kinds of ethnic identities that become salient for coalition-building in the context of mass-level electoral campaigns, this focus is understandable. But political elites also expend considerable energy during the periods between formal campaigns laying the foundations for the coalitions that they will mobilize at election time. Investments by politicians in traditional ceremonies and ethnic civic associations constitute one of the most important forms of such activity.

Tribal chiefs (who, as we saw in Chapter 2, were created or bolstered during the colonial era for their usefulness as tax collectors) remain influential local actors in many parts of Zambia, and they are recognized by candidates and political parties as useful allies. One of the principal ways in which politicians cultivate chiefs' support is by attending, and sometimes helping to organize and raise money for, their annual traditional ceremonies. These ceremonies are valued by chiefs because they serve as occasions for reinforcing their authority and prestige in the local community. They are valued by politicians because they provide opportunities for them to introduce themselves to the local population and, through their attendance and contributions, demonstrate their commitment to the community's welfare. This mutuality of interest often leads to an unspoken quid pro quo whereby politicians attend and help to underwrite the traditional ceremonies and chiefs, who are by law and custom officially apolitical, reciprocate by quietly indicating their support for the politicians. This is not to say that every politician that attends or contributes to a traditional ceremony will be warmly endorsed by the chief. But, given the potential payoff of a chief's endorsement, politicians have incentives to invest in trying. Sipula Kabanje, the chairman of a Zambian non-governmental organization, puts it well:

> These ceremonies have political flavours ... They are launching pads for someone who wants a rural seat ... You can't afford to miss them if you want to get to political office ... Prospective MPs from the towns will do well to remember that a good impression of generosity to the chief and his *indunas* [advisors] may prove to be a worthwhile investment when election time draws near. (quoted in *Sunday Mail*, 18 October 1998)

It is not surprising, then, that these annual rituals have become important parts of the campaign before the campaign.

Because participation in annual tribal ceremonies provides such a useful means of winning the support of local leaders, politicians tend to participate in them with equal frequency in one-party and multi-party settings. In multi-party contexts, however, we also find politicians trying to build ethnic associations that unite multiple tribes, often along provincial or linguistic lines. The impetus for these more broadly encompassing associations was made explicit in a 1996 letter to the editor of *The Post*. In the letter, the author "challenge[d] and urge[d] the people of Eastern Province to come together and form a strong cultural association that will keep us Easterners together."

> It is my belief that if we the Easterners came together we could do something. Therefore I urge all the Easterners to come together and form a strong association which could deal with the political, cultural and economic development [of our people]. It is my sincere hope that we unite so that we develop our province. (18 July 1996)

Localized tribal associations may be useful in one-party contexts as vehicles for political elites competing at the level of the individual electoral constituency. But, as the author of the letter suggests, associations that bring together and can claim to represent the interests of multiple tribes or even whole language groups or provinces provide their leaders with far greater ability to exert political leverage in a multi-party setting.

An association called Twishibane Mbabanibani, formed in Mkushi district in 2000 by the local constituency chairman of the UPND, provides an illustration. Not only was the organization spearheaded by the representative of a political party, but its purpose was transparently political. Mkushi is an area that, while generally considered Bemba-speaking, is made up primarily of members of the Lala and Swaka tribes that are not core members of the Bemba-language group. People in Mkushi came to be Bemba-speaking largely through the effects of migration from the Bemba-speaking epicenter to the Copperbelt and the rail line, which passed directly through Mkushi, rather than because the area's tribes originally spoke Bemba (see Chapter 3). UPND leaders knew that if they could convince Lalas and Swakas that people from Mkushi were not really Bemba, then they might be able to convince the area's residents to shift their allegiance from the MMD to the UPND. This was precisely the suspicion of Mkushi's MMD district chairman, who charged that the motivation for the establishment of Twishibane Mbabanibani was to "bring together the Swaka/Lalas so that they resigned en masse from their parties to join the UPND and later defeat politically those regarded as the non-indigenous ones" (*Times of Zambia*, 21 February 2000).

An even clearer example of a cultural association constructed explicitly along language group lines and explicitly for political purposes is the Bantu Botatwe Ngoma Yamaanu. Taking its name (which means literally "three peoples") from a linguistic designation referring to the cluster of related language groups in present-day Southern and Central Provinces, the Bantu Botatwe was formed in 1991 for the express purpose of joining members of the Tonga, Ila, Lenje, and associated tribes into a formidable language-based political coalition (Colson 1996). Although the association's constitution defines its purpose in purely cultural terms, its chairman – himself a politician and one of the founders, first of the MMD and later of the NP – admitted that the group's real goals were political from the start. "The Southern and Central Province people desperately needed cohesion because we were so disunited," he explained. "From our common basis of culture we could draw economic and political strength."[39] Two key association organizers in Livingstone – again, both politicians: one was the mayor of, and later MP for, Livingstone, the other a town councilor – echoed their chairman's view when they told me that the Bantu Botatwe was set up "to unify Tongas in the province . . . as

[39] Interview with Aaron Muyovwe, Lusaka, 18 August 1993. Muyovwe is quoted in *The Post* providing the same rationale for the formation of the Bantu Botatwe: "While other provinces were organized and voted people of their tribe to responsible positions, Tongas were ever divided and quarreling among themselves" (9 January 1996).

a response to the perceived domination of the Bembas at the national level."[40] Another Livingstone resident described the group's origins this way: "If all these tribes that fall under the Tonga umbrella can come together, then they can have a President. That was the rationale behind the Bantu Botatwe."[41]

Despite public claims that the association does not engage in open political activities, the group's organizers admitted that the association does support political candidates behind the scenes by advising members on which politicians and parties merit their votes. They explained that "it is just like a church where the pastor tells the people which candidate should be supported."[42] In 1996, the head of the Southern Province Tonga Traditional Association, a related organization, took an explicitly political stand when he urged all Tonga-speakers to participate in the upcoming general elections to make sure that only Tongas were voted into power. He told his supporters:

> The Association has taken inventory of how Tongas have fared in politics and traditional leadership since 1964 and I am afraid to say we have lamentably failed to provide quality leadership . . . We have been too accommodating and this has resulted in authority or top positions slipping through our fingers. *Koona akumane, kuziima kwatujaya. Kubbadama mbulwazi* [We should wake up and start fighting to assume positions in the top]! (*Times of Zambia*, 22 August 1996)

A Bantu Botatwe meeting earlier in the year had resolved that a new party should be formed "that would take care of Tonga interests" (*Zambia Today*, 18 February 1996). Mindful of the group's power as a national political coalition, its leader reminded the government that "our Association covers a very big area from Southern province up to Kapiri with a population of about four million. We will tell our people not to vote for [the MMD]" (*The Post*, 23 September 1996).[43]

Confirmation that it was the multi-party political system that created the impetus for the creation of the Bantu Botatwe Ngoma Yamaanu comes not only from the timing of the group's founding (which was immediately

[40] Interview with Munang'angu Hatembo and S. C. M. Muzyamba, Livingstone, 1 December 1995.

[41] Interview with James Muzumi, Livingstone, 6 December 1995.

[42] Interview with Munang'angu Hatembo and S. C. M. Muzyamba, Livingstone, 1 December 1995.

[43] The chairman's inflated estimate of the size of the Tonga-speaking coalition recalls the similarly exaggerated estimates of Zambia's Bemba-speaking population made by Justin Chimba and Unia Mwila to justify the dominance of Bemba-speakers in the country's top government positions in the First Republic (see Chapter 4).

after the return to multi-party politics in 1991) but also from the fact that Tonga politicians – including some of the same figures that later became active in the Bantu Botatwe – were actively engaged under the one-party state in building cultural associations that were explicitly *tribal* in their scope. Colson (1996: 75) relates that, in the 1970s, Tonga members of the Southern Province branch of the Historical Association of Zambia attempted to create a new annual Tonga traditional ceremony that would "put it on a par" with other major tribes in the country that had, or were then in the process of reinventing, such ceremonies. Although the effort ultimately failed, Colson argues that the attempt demonstrates "that by the 1970s some Tonga intellectuals had decided that they needed to be able to field a range of collective symbols comparable to those that celebrate the unique histories of other peoples in Zambia" (ibid.). She speculates that, in contrast to the founders of the Bantu Botatwe, the organizers of the Tonga traditional ceremony were "not . . . trying to forge a larger ethnic coalition for political purposes since the 1970s and 1980s were the years [of] the one-party state [when] . . . political manoeuvering and strategies used for the advancement of personal interests relied on patronage networks described in terms of kinship and home-ties rather than in ethnic terms" (ibid.: 75–76). Although Colson uses a slightly different vocabulary, her juxtaposition of the local ties that serve as the basis "for the advancement of personal interests" in the one-party state and the broader cultural ties that play this role in the multi-party context is exactly what we would expect to find if the one-party or multi-party nature of the political regime affects elites' calculations in the way the model predicts.

As the evidence presented in this chapter makes clear, the shift from multi-party to one-party and then back to multi-party rule altered the behavior of Zambia's political elites. In Chapter 8, I turn to the effects of these institutional changes on the behavior of Zambian voters.

# 8

## *Ethnic Voting*

### *Testing the Observable Implications of the Argument for Mass Behavior*

In this chapter, I turn to the model's expectations for the behavior of non-elites. The central expectation to be tested is that people will vote for candidates from their own tribes in one-party elections and for parties whose leaders belong to their language groups in multi-party elections. As in Chapter 7, I identify and test a range of observable implications of the model using a variety of data sources and analytical techniques.

The chapter is divided into three sections. In the first, I estimate and compare rates of tribal voting in one-party and multi-party elections. These analyses demonstrate that, while tribal identities are not the only motivation for voters' choices in either type of contest, Zambian voters nonetheless vote along tribal lines at measurably higher rates in one-party elections than in multi-party ones. In the second section, I focus exclusively on voting patterns in multi-party elections. First I present evidence to support the central assumption in the model that voters put more emphasis on candidates' party affiliations than on their individual backgrounds. Then I show that this emphasis on candidates' party affiliations leads voters to allocate their support on language group lines.

In the third section, I test the model's implications in a more fine-grained way through a pair of controlled experiments. The first compares the performance across elections of candidates that ran in the same constituencies in back-to-back contests. If changes in regime type affect the way voters allocate their support, then we should find greater changes in candidates' vote shares when one of the elections is a multi-party contest and the other is a one party contest than when both elections are of the same type. This is, in fact, what I find. I also find that patterns of support vary in ways that the model would predict. When candidates in multi-party contests are running on the tickets of parties associated with the dominant language group in the constituency, they outperform their one-party results. When they are running on the tickets of parties associated with other language groups, they do less well than in the one-party races.

The second controlled experiment compares the performance of two types of candidates whose respective levels of support most clearly capture the model's expectations for voting outcomes in multi-party settings. The first are candidates that are members of the dominant tribe in their constituency but running on the tickets of parties affiliated with language groups from other parts of the country (i.e., candidates who belong to the "right" tribe but the "wrong" party). The second are candidates that are members of non-dominant tribes but affiliated with parties that *are* identified with the local language community (i.e., "right" party, "wrong" tribe). The model would lead us to expect candidates of the latter type to outperform candidates of the former type, and the evidence confirms that they do.

## TRIBAL VOTING IN ONE-PARTY AND MULTI-PARTY ELECTIONS

I begin by examining every electoral constituency in every election held in Zambia between 1968 and 1999 and comparing the share of the dominant tribe in the constituency with the share of the vote won by candidates belonging to that tribe.[1] Notwithstanding a number of caveats to be discussed later, the model predicts that in one-party elections, where voters support members of their own tribal groups, the share of dominant tribe voters in the constituency will mirror the share of votes won by dominant tribe candidates.[2] Of course, focusing only on the behavior of dominant tribe voters addresses only one implication of the model: we would also expect members of the second most numerous tribe to vote for candidates from their group, members of the third most numerous tribe to vote for candidates from their group, and so on. But restricting the analysis to the behavior of members of the dominant tribe in each constituency greatly simplifies the analysis.

In multi-party elections, where voters look past candidates' tribal backgrounds and support people running on the tickets of parties associated with their language groups, the share of dominant tribe voters in the constituency should be a much less good predictor of the share of votes

[1] Some constituencies are excluded, for reasons explained later. For a discussion of how information about the tribal backgrounds of parliamentary candidates and the tribal demographics of constituencies was collected, see Appendices C and D.

[2] This expectation depends on turnout rates being equivalent across groups. I assume that they are.

won by dominant tribe candidates. The expectation is *not* that we will find no evidence of tribal voting in multi-party elections. In multi-party elections, candidates that are supported because of their party affiliations but who happen to be members of the dominant tribe will look, in the data, like they were supported because of their tribal background. But, because candidates affiliated with parties that are identified with the local language group will not always be members of the dominant tribe, we would expect the match between the share of the dominant tribe in the constituency and the share of the vote won by candidates from that tribe to be less good in multi-party contests than in one-party contests. The bias will be toward over-estimating the degree of tribal voting in multi-party elections. Since this will make it more difficult to find a difference between the amount of tribal voting in one-party and multi-party settings, any difference I do find can be interpreted as fairly strong support for the predictions of the model.

Figure 8.1 illustrates the relationship between the share of votes won by dominant tribe candidates and the share of dominant tribe voters in each constituency in multi-party and one-party elections. The former include the general election of 1996 and all by-elections held between 1992 and 1999; the latter include the one-party elections of 1973, 1978, 1983, and 1988. As in Chapter 7, I exclude urban constituencies from the analysis, since it is only in rural areas that tribal voting patterns should differ across one-party and multi-party settings. I also exclude cases in which either all or none of the candidates in the race are from the dominant tribe in the constituency, since such contests provide no opportunity for dominant tribe voters to choose whether or not to vote for a candidate from their tribe, and thus offer no test of the predictions of the model. As in Chapter 7, I exclude the 1991 election from the analysis. I also exclude the 1968 multi-party contest, since the tribal demographic data that I possess for that year are not sufficiently precise to allow me to accurately determine the size of the dominant tribe. I draw the $y = x$ line in the scatterplots for reference.

If the model is right, we would expect the points to be scattered closely about the $y = x$ line in the one-party elections and to be scattered more broadly in the multi-party elections. Yet, the first thing one notices about the two panels in Figure 8.1 is that the points in neither scatterplot lie right along the $y = x$ line. This suggests that factors other than the candidates' tribal backgrounds motivate voters' choices. For our purposes, however, the "tightness of fit" of the scatter around the $y = x$ reference line is less important than the difference in that fit across the two panels. Eyeballing

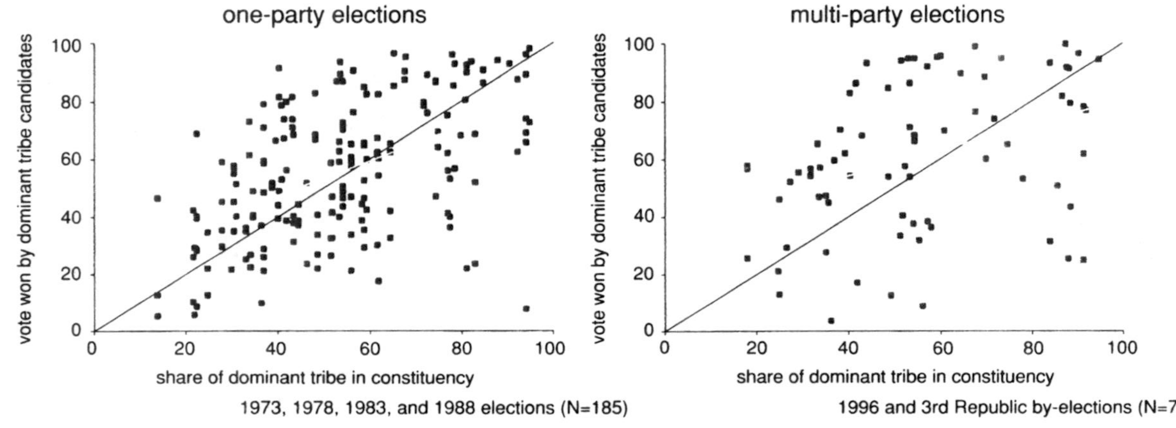


Figure 8.1. Tribal Voting in One-Party and Multi-Party Elections

the data, the fit does seem to be better in the one-party elections than in the multi-party ones.

One way of measuring this difference more systematically is to compare the correlation between the $x$ and $y$ values in each. This correlation is 0.52 for the one-party cases and 0.37 for the multi-party cases.[3] If the outlier case in the lower-right corner of the one-party panel is excluded, the correlation coefficient in the one-party cases rises to 0.55. This outlier case is the 1973 election in Bweengwa constituency, where the independence-era hero and former ANC president, Harry Mwaanga Nkumbula, an Ila by tribe, won overwhelming support against a Tonga opponent in an almost entirely Tonga constituency. This was clearly a special case: Nkumbula, though strictly speaking a tribal outsider, was the symbol of Tonga-speakers' aspirations for national power during the First Republic and was thus still considered an important enough figure to warrant support.

The correlation between the size of the dominant tribe and the share of votes won by its candidates is still far from perfect in the one-party panel, but it is measurably stronger than in the multi-party cases. An even more intuitive way of comparing the degree of tribal voting in each setting is to compare the average distance of each point from the $y = x$ line. If voters were voting purely along tribal lines, the distance would be zero, so values closer to zero reflect greater tribal voting.[4] The average distance in the one-party cases is 17.1 percentage points (16.7 percentage points without the Bweengwa constituency outlier); in the multi-party cases, it is 22.8 percentage points.[5] As with the correlation measure, the results suggest less tribal voting in the one-party elections than the theory would predict, but, nonetheless, measurably more in those elections than in the multi-party ones.

[3] Both correlations are statistically significant at the 0.01 level in a two-tailed test. If the 1991 elections are included, the correlation coefficient in the multi-party sample drops to 0.20.

[4] Note that the comparison across the one-party and multi-party samples is valid only because the distribution of dominant tribe population shares is nearly identical in both settings. Having an identical distribution of dominant tribe population shares is necessary because the maximum deviation from the $y = x$ line depends on the share of the dominant tribe in the constituency (it increases as that share approaches zero or 100 percent). If either the one-party or multi-party samples had a greater share of very homogeneous or very heterogeneous constituencies, it would make the comparison of average distances from the $y = x$ line problematic.

[5] If the 1991 election is included in the multi-party sample, the average distance from the $y = x$ line rises to 25.8 percentage points.

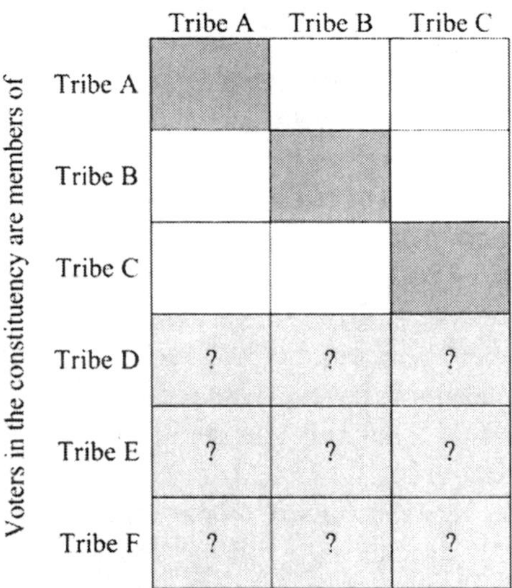


Figure 8.2. Voters Without Candidates from Their Tribes in the Race

While suggestive, this analysis has several important limitations. The first is that for voters to be able to cast their votes for a candidate who comes from their own tribe there must be a candidate from their tribe in the race. This is not always the case. When it is not, voters are left without a decision rule for how to allocate their support. The hypothetical constituency depicted in Figure 8.2 illustrates the problem. The constituency contains six different tribes (Tribes A–F), but only voters from Tribes A, B, and C have candidates from their own tribes in the race. If voters allocate their support strictly along tribal lines, we would expect voters from these three tribes to cast their ballots in the manner suggested by the dark-shaded cells: voters from Tribe A will support candidates from Tribe A, voters from Tribe B will support candidates from Tribe B, and so on. The problem is that the theory generates no predictions about which candidates voters from Tribes D, E, or F will support. When the share of a constituency's population made up of such "free agent" voters is large, it will undermine our ability to make inferences about tribal voting patterns from aggregate data.

Of course, it is possible that, because they do not have a candidate from their own tribe in the race, voters from Tribes D, E, and F will simply abstain from voting. It is also possible that they will divide their support evenly among the candidates from Tribes A, B, and C, or will support them in proportion to these groups' shares of the total population. Any of these responses would make our job much easier, but we cannot assume that voters from Tribes D, E, and F will do any of these things. We are thus left with a problem: the inference we want to make is based on the total vote share won by the candidates from the dominant tribe, but that vote share will necessarily be affected – perhaps quite significantly – by the theoretically unpredictable electoral choices of the "free agent" voters from Tribes D, E, and F.

My solution is to redo the analysis, this time limiting the cases I include to constituencies where at least 85 percent of the population are from tribes that have a candidate in the race. This significantly reduces my sample size, but it also raises my confidence in the results.[6] In the new analysis, the correlation between the share of dominant tribe voters and the share of votes won by dominant tribe candidates is 0.54 in the one-party cases and 0.40 in the multi-party cases.[7] If the Bweengwa outlier case is excluded, the correlation in the one-party cases rises to 0.63. The average distance from the $y = x$ line in the one-party sample is now 17.3 percentage points (16 points without Bweengwa), versus 22.0 percentage points in the multi-party sample.[8] As in the analyses that included all cases, the results suggest that while tribal voting is not the whole story in one-party elections, it is a bigger part of the story in such settings than in multi-party contests. The fact that the correlations and distances from the $y = x$ line are similar in the full and truncated samples does not necessarily imply that excluding cases where most voters did not have a candidate from their tribe in the race was a waste of time (or data). It simply confirms that voters who did not have a candidate from their tribe in the race did, in fact, vote for dominant tribe candidates in rough proportion to the dominant tribe's population share.

There is, however, a second limitation to the analysis: what is known as the "ecological fallacy" (Robinson 1950; Achen and Shivley 1995; King 1997). This problem arises any time a researcher uses aggregate election results to make inferences about individual voting behavior. To

6 Sample sizes are now 53 for the one-party cases and 26 for the multi party cases.

7 The one-party correlation is significant at the 0.01 level; the multi-party correlation is significant at the 0.05 level, both in a two-tailed test. If the 1991 election is included in the multi-party sample, the correlation coefficient falls to 0.01 and ceases to be significant at any level.

8 If the 1991 election is included in the multi-party sample, the average distance for the $y = x$ line rises to 27.3 percentage points.

understand the dilemma it entails, consider a constituency in which the largest tribal group, Tribe X, constitutes 40 percent of the population and 40 percent of all voters cast their ballots for candidates from Tribe X. Given that the percentage of votes received by candidates from that tribe exactly matches the percentage of the population that belongs to it, we might be tempted to conclude that voters had cast their ballots along tribal lines. But however intuitive this inference may seem, it would be equally consistent with the aggregate data for *none* of the voters belonging to Tribe X (and two-thirds of the voters belonging to the other tribes in the constituency) to have supported the Tribe X candidates. Although such a counter-intuitive outcome may not be likely – indeed, we are probably studying this constituency because we have theoretical reasons to expect people there to have voted along tribal lines – it is impossible to rule it out on the basis of ecological (i.e., aggregate) demographic and voting tallies alone.

To deal with this problem, I employ a method developed by King (1997). In its general form, the ecological inference problem that King's method allows us to solve is presented in Figure 8.3. The unknown quantities that we need to estimate for each constituency are the share of voters from the dominant tribe in the constituency that voted for candidates from the dominant tribe ($\beta^d$) and the share of voters from other tribes that "crossed over" and voted for candidates from the dominant tribe ($\beta^n$). Once we have estimated these values we will also know the values for the other two cells, which we can compute by subtracting $\beta^d$ and $\beta^n$ from one. King's method allows us to estimate these quantities at both the national and constituency levels from aggregate information that we know for each constituency: the percentage of dominant and non-dominant tribe voters ($X$ and $1 - X$), the percentage of votes won by candidates from the

| | Vote for Candidates | | |
|---|---|---|---|
| | from Dominant Tribe | from Non-Dominant Tribes | |
| Voters from Dominant Tribe | $\beta^d$ | $1-\beta^d$ | $X$ |
| Voters from Non-Dominant Tribes | $\beta^n$ | $1-\beta^n$ | $1-X$ |
| | $T$ | $1-T$ | $N$ |

Figure 8.3. The Ecological Inference Problem

dominant and non-dominant tribes ($T$ and $1 - T$), and the total number of voters that cast ballots ($N$).

If the model's "pure" expectations about tribal voting in one-party elections are correct, then voters in such contests will support only candidates that are members of their tribes. Thus $\beta^d$ (which captures the frequency of tribal voting among dominant tribe voters) should equal one, and $\beta^n$ (which captures the frequency of cross-tribal voting by non-dominant tribe voters) should equal zero. To the extent that voters weigh factors other than candidates' tribal affiliations in deciding who to support – as the results presented earlier suggest they do – these expectations will not be borne out exactly. But we would still expect $\beta^d$ to be far higher than $\beta^n$ in one-party elections. In multi-party elections, where the model predicts that voters will ignore candidates' tribal backgrounds and support candidates whose party affiliations mark them as representatives of the interests of the voters' own language groups, we would expect to find less evidence of tribal voting (i.e., lower $\beta^d$s) and more evidence of cross-over voting (i.e., higher $\beta^n$s).

Some caution, however, is necessary in interpreting the estimates of $\beta^d$ and $\beta^n$ in the multi-party races. Even if every voter behaved precisely as the model predicts – that is, even if every voter paid no attention to the tribal backgrounds of the candidates in the race – such behavior could easily be hidden in our estimates of $\beta^d$ and $\beta^n$. Consider a voter who is a member of the dominant tribe in her constituency and who casts her vote for a candidate running on the ticket of a party affiliated with her language group, just as the model predicts she will in a multi-party election. If the candidate for whom she has voted also happens to be a member of the dominant tribe, then her vote for that candidate will increase the estimated value of $\beta^d$ in the analysis and it will look, in the results, like she is voting tribally. If the candidate happens to be a member of another tribe, then her vote for the candidate will decrease the estimated value of $\beta^d$ and it will look, in the results, like she is ignoring tribe in making her choice, as, in fact, she is. The problem is that although her behavior is consistent with the model's expectations in both situations, it will have a different effect on our estimate of our quantity of interest depending on the tribal background of the candidate.[9] Given this, I do not use the results of the analysis as a direct test of the model's expectations about voting behavior in multi-party elections. The estimates of $\beta^d$ and $\beta^n$ in multi-party

[9] If the voter is a member of one of the constituency's non-dominant tribes, an analogous scenario can be outlined for the effect of her behavior on $\beta^n$.

Table 8.1. *Estimates of Tribal Voting in One-Party and Multi-Party Elections, Using King's Ecological Inference Method*

| | Estimated percentage of voters from dominant tribes voting for candidates from dominant tribes ($ß^d$) | Estimated percentage of voters from non-dominant tribes voting for candidates from dominant tribes ($ß^n$) |
|---|---|---|
| All one-party elections | 0.72<br>(0.023) | 0.38<br>(0.026) |
| All multi-party elections | 0.68<br>(0.023) | 0.52<br>(0.031) |
| One-party elections where > 85% of voters have a candidate from their tribe in the race | 0.69<br>(0.029) | 0.43<br>(0.074) |
| Multi-party elections where > 85% of voters have a candidate from their tribe in the race | 0.63<br>(0.025) | 0.52<br>(0.091) |

*Ns* = 185, 75, 53, 26. Estimates are weighted averages of the results for all constituencies in the specified elections. Standard errors are in parentheses.

elections can, however, be used as a point of comparison with the estimates of these parameters in one-party contests. Although tribal voting may occur in multi-party elections – or may appear in the data – it should occur with less frequency than in one-party elections. We would therefore expect the estimated values for $ß^d$ to be lower and the estimated values of $ß^n$ to be higher in multi-party elections than in one-party elections.

Estimates of $ß^d$ and $ß^n$ are reported in Table 8.1. I report results both for one-party and multi-party elections generally, and for the smaller set of one-party and multi-party contests in which at least 85 percent of the voters have a candidate from their tribe in the race. As in the analyses presented earlier, I include only rural constituencies in which at least one of the candidates is a member of the dominant tribe and at least one is not. I also exclude the 1991 election from the multi-party estimates.[10]

As the model leads us to expect, $ß^d$ is significantly higher than $ß^n$ in the one-party elections and less different from $ß^n$ in the multi-party

[10] If the 1991 election is included in the multi-party analyses, the estimates for $ß^d$ and $ß^n$ are 0.60 (.014) and 0.53 (.020), respectively, for the full multi-party sample and 0.56 (.018) and 0.56 (.070), respectively, for the limited multi-party sample.

contests. In the one-party cases, dominant tribe voters cast their ballots overwhelmingly (roughly 70 percent of the time in both the full and restricted samples) for candidates from their own tribes, and non-dominant tribe voters "cross over" and support candidates from the dominant tribe fairly infrequently (about 40 percent of the time). In multi-party contests, by contrast, dominant tribe voters are only slightly more likely to support dominant tribe candidates than are non-dominant tribe voters. The former do so approximately 65 percent of the time, while the latter do so 52 percent of the time. Recall, however, that while the estimates of $\beta^d$ and $\beta^n$ in the one-party elections provide a relatively reliable test of the model's implications for voting behavior in that setting, they offer a somewhat weaker test of its implications for voting behavior in the multi-party context. Still, the fact that the pattern of tribal voting (as reflected in the estimated values for $\beta^d$ and $\beta^n$) is more pronounced in the one-party elections than in the multi-party elections confirms that tribal considerations are a more important concern for voters in the former than in the latter.

Thus far, I have focused exclusively on rural constituencies, since it is only in rural areas that the model generates different predictions about voting patterns in each kind of election. But the model does generate a prediction about what we should expect to see in urban constituencies: rates of tribal voting should be quite low, and there should be little difference in the degree of tribal voting in one-party and multi-party contests. Again, the evidence bears out this expectation. If I limit the analysis to urban constituencies (of which, adhering to the same selection rules as in the earlier analyses, there are 56 one-party cases and 28 multi-party cases), I find that the correlation between the share of dominant tribe voters and the share of votes won by dominant tribe candidates is extremely low: 0.16 in the one-party contests and 0.08 in the multi-party contests. This finding is reinforced when I repeat the ecological inference analysis in urban constituencies only. In urban contests, my estimates suggest that the tendency of dominant tribe voters to support members of their own tribes ($\beta^d$) is nearly identical in one-party and multi-party elections: 34 percent in the former, 38 percent in the latter. Meanwhile, the tendency of non-dominant tribe voters to cross over and support candidates from the dominant tribe ($\beta^n$) is also indistinguishable in one-party and multi-party contexts. I estimate that 37 percent of non-dominant tribe voters cross over to support dominant tribe candidates in one-party contests, and 38 percent do so in multi-party contests. These analyses suggest that very little tribal voting takes place in urban constituencies in either one-party or multi-party elections, just as the model predicts.

## LANGUAGE GROUP VOTING IN MULTI-PARTY ELECTIONS

In one-party elections, all the contestants in the race are members of the same party, so party labels offer voters no means of distinguishing one candidate from another. Voters in such a situation have no choice but to focus on the candidates' personal attributes: their experience, their reputation, and, quite centrally, their ethnic backgrounds. But in multi-party contests, where candidates are each running on the ticket of a different political party, voters are forced to choose which cues to weight more heavily: that suggested by the ethnic background of the candidate, or that suggested by the presumed ethnic orientation of the party on whose ticket the candidate is running. A key claim of my argument is that in multi-party elections Zambian voters focus their attention on the latter: on the language group affiliation of the candidate's political party. I therefore begin by presenting evidence to document this assertion. Then I show how the emphasis on party labels generates voting along language group lines.

### *Party Affiliations versus Candidate Backgrounds as a Focus of Voters' Attention in Multi-Party Elections*

In Carey and Shugart's (1995) typology of electoral systems and incentives to cultivate a personal vote, single-member plurality systems with party endorsements, such as is found in Zambia, rank as the most party-oriented system type on the list. Evidence from surveys, interviews, and secondary source accounts bears this out. Summarizing voters' attitudes during the multi-party First Republic, Molteno and Scott (1974: 192) write that Zambians "seem to adhere more strongly to parties than to individuals... [I]ndividual candidates are a relatively minor factor influencing voter behaviour." In a speech to the National Assembly in 1972, Vice President Mainza Chona argued that "under a multi-party system people do not vote according to the merit of the candidate. They are only interested in their party winning the seat" (*Parliamentary Debates*, 6 December 1972, cols. 54–59). Commenting on the strength of party orientations in the Third Republic, a survey respondent observed that in a multi-party system "people will in no way support someone who is not a member of their party" (SR 7). A focus group participant explained that, in weighing candidates' backgrounds, "it was the party they were voting for, not the candidate" (KAS-T). Another focus group participant was explicit in linking the centrality of party labels to the multi-party nature of the political system: "In the [one-party] Second Republic we were voting for people, but now [in the multi-party Third Republic] we are voting for a party not a person" (CPTA-R-M).

Candidates themselves also recognized the importance that voters attach to party labels in multi-party contests. Recalling the 1968 election campaign, in which he had contested (and won) the Nalikwanda constituency seat on the ANC ticket, one former politician told me that his own qualities as an individual simply had not mattered in that election:

> What mattered most was the party: what the party has done for the people, not what [I had done] for the people. This is because it was a multi-party system and in a multi-party system the popularity of the party matters more than the popularity of any individual candidate. If UNIP was more popular, then the candidate for ANC lost and UNIP won. It didn't matter who you were.[11]

This was the situation in 1968. But in 1973, when the same politician ran for re-election under the new one party rules, things had changed. Now, "it was the popularity of the candidate that mattered . . . In the one party state, people had to vote for the man who they thought could do something for them."[12] Horowitz summarizes the phenomenon when he emphasizes that, in a multi-party context, it is not "advantageous to cross party lines to vote for a *candidate* of the same ethnic background as that of the voter if this requires voting for a *party* identified with the opposing ethnic group. Ethnic voting means simply voting for the party identified with the voter's own ethnic group, no matter who the individual candidates happen to be" (1985: 319–20).

Behavioral evidence for the weight that voters attach to candidates' party affiliations can be gleaned from examining the outcomes of parliamentary by-elections. Under Zambian law, parliamentary seats belong to the party rather than to the MP. Thus, when a sitting MP resigns from his or her party to join another political organization, a by-election is automatically triggered in which the defecting MP must re-contest the seat on the ticket of the new party.[13] Such contests provide an ideal opportunity for testing the relative weight that voters attach to a candidate's personal attributes and party affiliation. If voters care more about candidates' personal attributes, then we would expect them to continue supporting the defecting MP in his or her new party. But if voters care more about candidates' party affiliations, then we would expect their support to be conditional on the characteristics of the party to which the MP has defected.

[11] Interview with Morgan Simwinji, Mongu, 16 November 1995.
[12] Ibid.
[13] The relevant provision is the Constitution (Amendment) Act No. 2 of 1966.

If the party to which the MP has defected offers a better match with the voter's language group than the old party, then the voter will follow the candidate to the new party. If it offers a less good match, then the voter will withdraw his or her support from the candidate and remain faithful to the party on whose ticket the candidate originally ran.

The series of by-elections triggered in 1993 by the formation of the NP and the defection to that party of eleven MMD MPs offers an excellent opportunity for testing the importance that voters attach to party labels.[14] All of the defecting MPs were senior politicians who had won their seats in 1991 by wide margins. In that year, Zambians were voting for political and economic reform, and being on the MMD ticket identified a candidate as being an agent of change. By 1993, however, party affiliations had come to take on ethnic overtones, and the MMD had come to be viewed in many parts of the country as a vehicle for the interests of Bemba-speakers from the Northern, Luapula, and Copperbelt Provinces. The NP, meanwhile, drew its top leadership from the Western, Southern, and Northwestern Provinces and was popularly identified with the interests of the non-Bemba-speaking people from these regions. If voters were casting their votes based on party labels, we would expect the defecting MPs from Western, Southern, and Northwestern Province constituencies to fare well when they re-contested their seats on the NP ticket – perhaps not quite as well as they did in the watershed 1991 elections when the sentiment for change was unanimous, but certainly well enough to win their seats by wide margins. In the Bemba-speaking Northern Province, on the other hand, we would expect voters to remain loyal to the (presumed-to-be-Bemba-oriented) MMD and to withdraw their support from the defecting MPs who had, in their eyes, crossed over to a party whose presumed patronage commitments lay with a different language community. As Table 8.2 illustrates, this is exactly what voters in both areas did.

In the Western Province constituencies of Kalabo, Mongu, and Senanga, the Northwestern Province constituency of Solwezi Central, and the Southern Province constituency of Bweengwa, voters followed their defecting MPs en masse from the MMD to the NP. Whereas the defecting MPs from these five constituencies had won an average of 85 percent of the vote when running as MMD candidates in 1991, they won an average

[14] Six of the eleven by-elections were held on 11 November 1993, one on 27 January 1994, and the remaining four on 7 April 1994. In three instances, the defecting MP, having left the MMD, chose not to run for re-election on the NP ticket. I exclude these three cases from the analysis, leaving eight cases.

Table 8.2. *Changes in Candidates' Vote Shares in the 1993–94 By-Elections in Constituencies Where the Incumbent Ran Again on the NP Ticket*

| Province | Constituency (by-election date) | Candidate's vote share in 1991 | Candidate's vote share in by-election | Percentage change in candidate's support |
|---|---|---|---|---|
| Western | Kalabo (11 Nov. 93) | 79.7 | 56.3 | −29.3 |
| Western | Mongu (27 Jan. 94) | 88.2 | 81.7 | −7.4 |
| Western | Senanga (11 Nov. 93) | 88.5 | 72.0 | −18.6 |
| Northwestern | Solwezi Central (11 Nov. 93) | 82.8 | 69.7 | −15.8 |
| Southern | Bweengwa (11 Nov. 93) | 83.9 | 75.0 | −10.6 |
| Southern | Pemba (11 Nov. 93) | 85.6 | 27.4 | −68.0 |
| Northern | Chinsali (7 Apr. 94) | 82.6 | 9.5 | −88.5 |
| Northern | Malole (11 Nov. 93) | 91.4 | 24.1 | −73.6 |

of 71 percent of the vote when they re-contested their seats in the by-elections on the NP ticket. The percentage change in their support across the two contests ranged from −7 to −29 percent. Given the unnaturally high vote shares they won in the 1991 race and the fact that they all faced two opponents in the by-election but only one in the 1991 contest, these results suggest that the shift in their party affiliations was embraced by their constituents. Only in the Southern Province constituency of Pemba did voters maintain their loyalty to the MMD and fail to follow the defecting MP to his new party. Although the MMD did suffer a 38 percent decline in its vote share in that constituency, the defecting MP saw his own vote share decline by 68 percent.

In Northern Province, voters completely deserted the two MPs that re-contested their seats on the NP ticket. One of these MPs saw her vote share tumble by nearly 89 percent; the other suffered a 74 percent decline. This second candidate was former finance minister Emmanuel Kasonde, the powerful Bemba leader whose critical by-election was discussed in Chapter 7. A writer in the *Daily Mail* explained Kasonde's loss as "a rejection of NP by the Bemba-speaking voters [in] reaction to charges that NP was a Lozi-Tonga party trying to use Mr. Kasonde [to establish] a foothold in the area" (18 November 1993). A columnist for another paper argued similarly that it was "not because Kasonde was hated but because he was considered a 'sell-out' to a political party supposedly not associated with the Bembas" that he suffered such a dramatic change in fortune. The writer went on to speculate that if Kasonde and his MMD opponent, the unknown Dismus Kalingeme, had switched parties, "Kalingeme [would] have faced a similar fate" (*Financial Mail*, 16–23 November 1993). The fact that Kalingeme was able to unseat such a powerful and popular rival by a nearly three-to-one margin – Kalingeme won 64 percent of the vote to Kasonde's 24 percent – dramatically illustrates the irrelevance of candidates' personal attributes and the centrality of party affiliations in multi-party settings in Zambia.

Another striking illustration of the power of party labels to affect voters' choices comes from the Copperbelt constituency of Chingola, where political heavyweights Ludwig Sondashi and Enoch Kavindele ran against each other in the 1991 general election and then, again, in a by-election held in April 1995. In the first contest, Sondashi, running on the MMD ticket, easily beat Kavindele, who was then running as a UNIP candidate. By the time of their second meeting in 1995, however, Sondashi had left the MMD for the NP and Kavindele had left the UNIP for the MMD. This time, Kavindele handily defeated Sondashi. While the outcome was reversed for the candidates, it remained the same for the MMD as a political party: the candidate running on the MMD ticket – Sondashi in 1991, Kavindele in 1995 – won almost exactly the same share of vote in both elections. In 1991, Sondashi won 84.3 percent of the vote in a two-way race. In the 1995 by-election, Kavindele won 86.3 percent of the vote in a four-way race (Sondashi managed just 6.3 percent). The candidates may have changed their party affiliations, but both the overwhelmingly Bemba-speaking composition of the constituency and the Bemba orientation of the MMD remained the same. And it was the combination of language group demographics and perceived party orientation rather than the attributes of the candidates that shaped the voting outcome.

### *Evidence of Language Group Voting in Multi-Party Elections*

If voters in multi-party elections focus on candidates' party affiliations, and if parties' ethnic orientations are understood in language group terms, then ethnic voting in multi-party elections should follow language group lines. The examples sketched earlier provide initial suggestive evidence that this is the case. In this section, I present additional empirical support for the link between multi-party politics and language group voting.

To the extent that voters allocate support along language group lines, we would expect the share of votes won in a given constituency by a party identified with a particular language group to be equal to the share of voters in the constituency that are members of that language group. Since most constituencies – and, in fact, most whole regions – are linguistically homogeneous, we would expect entire constituencies (and regions) to focus their support on the party or parties that are identified with that constituency's (or region's) language group.

Initial evidence for the relationship between language group membership and party support is provided in Figures 8.4–8.6, which juxtapose maps of support for each major political party in the 1968, 1991, and 1996 general elections with maps of the distributions of the language groups with which each party was associated. In keeping with the evidence presented in Chapter 4 regarding how Zambians view the ethnic orientations of political parties, each party's language group orientation is determined by the language group affiliation of its president. The shaded areas on the maps of party support (at the top) indicate the districts in which the party in question won more than 60 percent of the vote (except in the maps of the 1996 election, where the threshold for shading districts supporting the NP and the AZ is 20 percent). The shaded areas on the language maps (at the bottom) indicate districts in which more than 80 percent of the population speaks the indicated language as a first or second language of communication (as calculated from 1990 census data). In all three elections, the linguistic basis of party support is evident, particularly for regions that had parties associated with their language group in the race. In regions that did not have parties associated with their language group in the race, voters tended to support the ruling party (or, in 1991, the party viewed as the vanguard of change). This explains the extension of the UNIP's support in 1968 and the MMD's support in 1991 and 1996 beyond their Bemba-speaking "home areas."

More systematic evidence for the relationship between language group membership and patterns of party support during these three general elections is presented in Table 8.3, which records, for each major party in each election, the language group with which the party was identified, the number of constituencies in the country in which that language group was dominant, and a comparison of the average of the party's vote share in constituencies where the party's associated language group was dominant

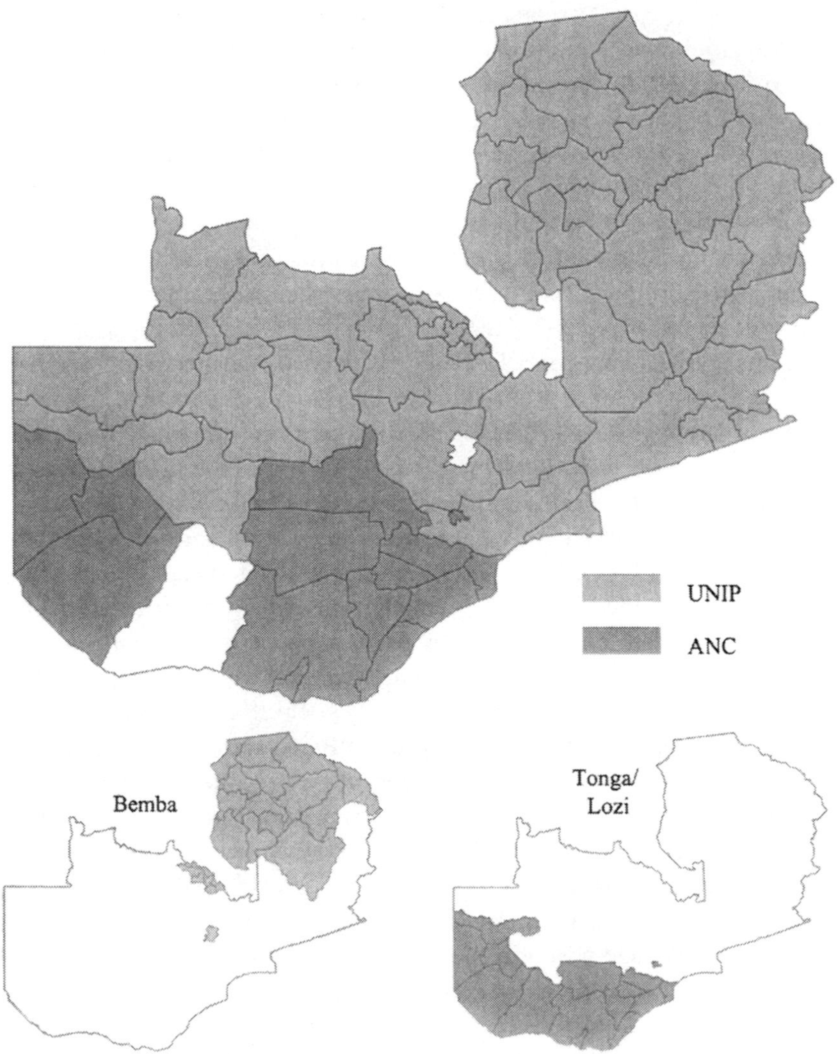


Figure 8.4. Voting in 1968

(which I label "home area" constituencies) and in the rest of the country. Table 8.3 confirms the pattern depicted graphically in Figures 8.4–8.6: in every case (save one), parties received significantly – and, in the case of non-ruling parties, overwhelmingly – more support in "home area" constituencies than elsewhere.

In 1968, for example, ANC candidates won fully 76.2 percent of the vote in constituencies dominated by Tonga-speakers but were able

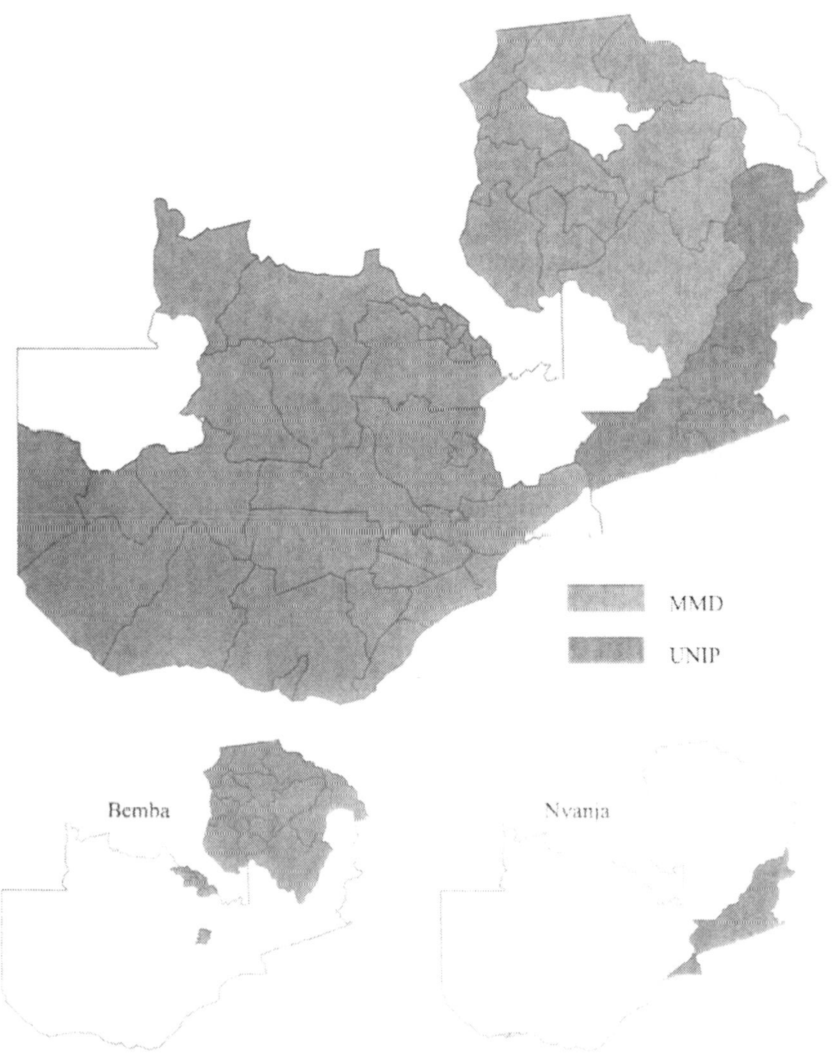


Figure 8.5. Voting in 1991

to capture only 15.9 percent of the vote in constituencies dominated by members of other language groups. Were it not for the fact that Lozi-speakers in 1968 also voted overwhelmingly for ANC candidates (who, in Western Province, were simply former UP candidates running under the ANC banner), the share of ANC votes outside of Tonga-speaking areas would have been lower still. Indeed, if constituencies dominated by Lozi-speaking voters are excluded, the ANC vote

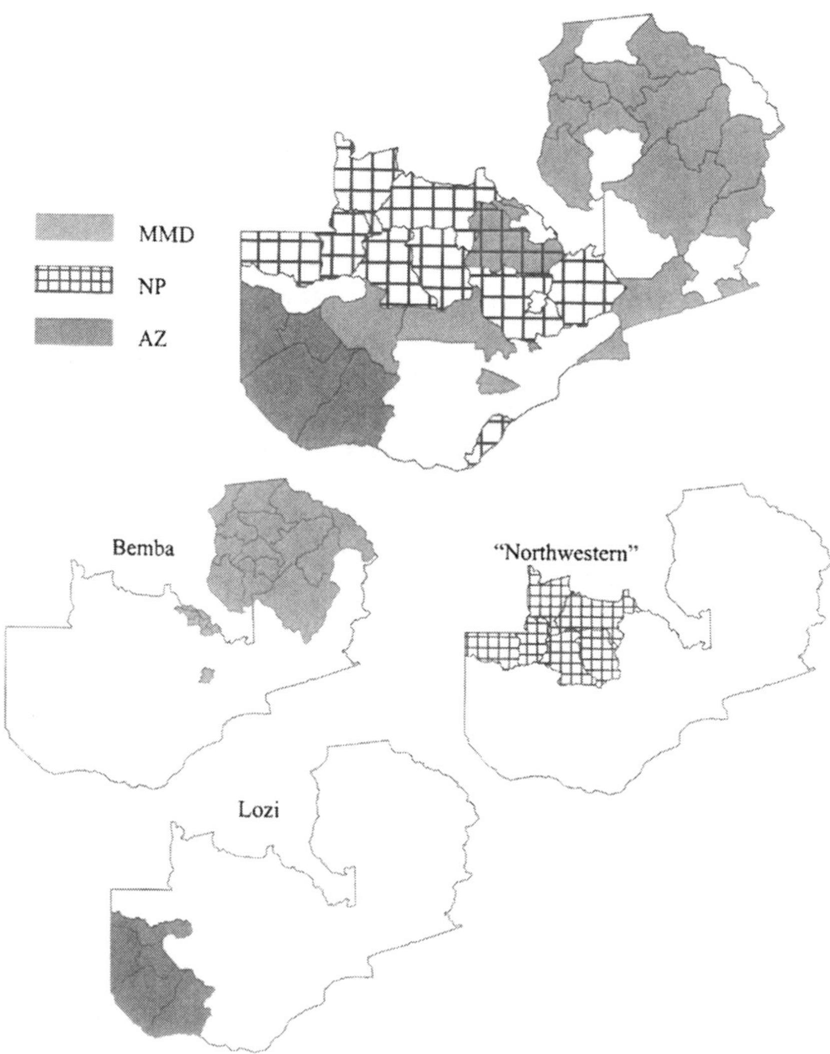


Figure 8.6. Voting in 1996

share in "the rest of the country" drops to just 10.1 percent (in Tonga- and Lozi-speaking constituencies taken together, it was 67.9 percent).[15] As

[15] Support for the ANC by Lozi-speakers, taken separately from Tonga-speakers, was also high. In the eleven constituencies dominated by Lozi-speakers in 1968, 56.7 percent of the vote went to UP candidates running on the ANC ticket, compared with 22.2 percent in the rest of the country (or 10.1 percent if Tonga-speaking areas are also excluded).

Table 8.3. *Party Vote Shares in "Home" Language Group Areas and Elsewhere*

| Party (year) | Language group with which party is identified | No. of constituencies in which party's language group is dominant (of total in which party ran candidates) | Party's average vote share in "home area" constituencies | Party's average vote share in the rest of the country | Ratio of vote share in "home area" to rest of country |
|---|---|---|---|---|---|
| ANC (1968) | Tonga | 16 (of 76) | 76.2 | 15.9 | 4.8: 1 |
| UNIP (1968) | Bemba | 48 (of 76) | 94.1 | 57.1 | 1.6: 1 |
| MMD (1991) | Bemba | 63 (of 150) | 86.6 | 65.0 | 1.3: 1 |
| UNIP (1991) | Nyanja | 21 (of 150) | 73.1 | 17.3 | 4.2: 1 |
| MMD (1996) | Bemba | 63 (of 147) | 66.0 | 55.2 | 1.2: 1 |
| ZDC (1996) | Bemba | 63 (of 142) | 10.6 | 17.5 | 0.6: 1 |
| NP (1996) | "Northwestern" | 10 (of 98) | 39.6 | 6.9 | 5.7: 1 |
| AZ (1996) | Lozi | 7 (of 11) | 33.9 | 6.6 | 5.1: 1 |

*Note:* Uncontested seats are omitted from the analysis. Constituencies in which a particular language group is dominant are defined as those in which a majority of the population, as determined from 1990 census data, belongs to the specified language group. "Tonga" constituencies in 1968 are Mumbwa West, Mumbwa East, and all 14 Southern Province constituencies. "Bemba" constituencies in 1968 are Kabwe, Mkushi North, Mkushi South, Chitambo, Serenje, all 18 Copperbelt Province constituencies, all 10 Luapula Province constituencies, and all 16 Northern Province constituencies except Isoka East. "Bemba" constituencies in 1991 and 1996 are Bwacha, Kabwe, Mkushi North, Mkushi South, Chitambo, Muchinga, Serenje, all 22 Copperbelt Province constituencies, all 14 Luapula Province constituencies, and all 21 Northern Province constituencies except Isoka East. "Nyanja" constituencies in 1991 are all 19 Eastern Province constituencies plus Feira and Isoka East. "Northwestern" constituencies in 1996 are all 12 Northwestern Province constituencies. "Lozi" constituencies in 1996 are Kalabo, Liuwa, Sikongo, Kaoma, Luena, Mongu, Nalikwanda, Nalolo, Senanga, Sinjembela, Mulobezi, Mwandi, and Sesheke.

the final column of the table indicates, the ratio of support for ANC candidates in Tonga-speaking areas and elsewhere was nearly five to one. If Lozi-dominated constituencies are added to the ANC's "home areas" and excluded from its "non-home areas," the ratio rises to nearly seven to one.

Because the UNIP's support in 1968 was strong in several areas that lay outside of its Bemba-speaking base, the pattern of language group voting for the UNIP in that year is somewhat less striking than that reported for the ANC. Still, it is clear that the UNIP's vote share was significantly higher in the 48 constituencies it contested that were dominated by Bemba-speakers than in the 28 constituencies that were not.[16] In the former, fully 94.1 percent of voters supported UNIP candidates, while in the latter UNIP candidates' vote share dropped to 57.1 percent. Although UNIP candidates won more than seven votes out of ten overall in the 1968 election, they were approximately 65 percent more likely to win the votes of people living in constituencies dominated by Bemba-speakers than they were to win the votes of people living in constituencies dominated by members of other language groups.

Similar patterns of in-group linguistic voting were evident in the elections of 1991 and 1996. In 1991, the MMD won 86.6 percent of the vote in Bemba-speaking constituencies and 65 percent of the vote in non-Bemba-speaking constituencies – a relatively modest difference attributable to the referendum nature of the 1991 election. But the UNIP, which by 1991 had come to be identified as a Nyanja-speakers' party, captured fully 73.1 percent of the vote in the 21 Nyanja-speaking constituencies but only 17.3 percent of the vote in the rest of the country. Its ratio of support in Nyanja-speaking and non-Nyanja-speaking constituencies was more than four to one.

In 1996, the MMD again won not only most of the vote in the Bemba-speaking parts of the country but also widespread support among voters in non-Bemba-speaking areas that did not have parties representing their own language groups in the race. Unlike its experience in 1991 (or the

[16] The large number of uncontested seats that were omitted from the analysis bias the results somewhat. However, since the majority of the omitted seats were located in Bemba-speaking areas where we would have expected the UNIP's support to have been strong (the UNIP's presumed strength was almost certainly part of the reason the seats were uncontested), the exclusion of these seats almost certainly results in an under- rather than over-estimation of the extent of language group support.

UNIP's in 1968), however, the MMD was challenged in 1996 by another major party, the ZDC, whose president was also a Bemba-speaker. The 66 percent vote share won by MMD candidates in Bemba-speaking areas in 1996, while greater than the 55.2 percent share won by MMD candidates in non-Bemba-speaking areas, was almost certainly lower than it might have been had the ZDC not been in the race. Similar reasons help to explain why the ZDC's vote share in Bemba-speaking constituencies (10.6 percent) was actually lower than its vote share in non-Bemba-speaking constituencies (17.5 percent).[17]

The two other major parties that competed in the 1996 election, the NP and the AZ, both won a significantly larger share of votes in constituencies located in their presidents' linguistic "home areas" than in other parts of the country.[18] NP candidates won 39.6 percent of the vote in the ten Northwestern Province constituencies that they contested but only managed a 6.9 percent share in the rest of the country.[19] The AZ, which ran candidates in only eleven constituencies (seven of which were in its Lozi-speaking "home" region), captured 33.9 percent of the vote in Lozi-speaking constituencies but only 6.6 percent of the vote outside of

[17] Competition with the MMD for Bemba-speakers' votes probably tells only part of the story, however. When the ZDC was formed, its founders went to great lengths to balance the party's leadership with members of all four major language groups. Thus, in addition to its Bemba-speaking president and secretary general, the party had three vice presidents: one a Lozi-speaker, one a Tonga-speaker, and the third a Nyanja-speaker. In part because of such efforts at language group balancing, and in part because the MMD's status as the ruling party made it the more obvious choice for Bemba-speaking voters seeking to secure patronage resources from the state, the ZDC was only weakly identified as a Bemba party. This helps to account for the low ZDC vote share in its "home area" constituencies. Its balanced leadership also bolstered the ZDC's appeal in areas outside of its alleged linguistic "home," which also helps to account for its higher than expected vote share in the rest of the country.

[18] In addition to the MMD, the ZDC, the NP, and the AZ, a fifth political organization, the National Lima Party (NLP), contested the 1996 election on an agrarian platform and won just over six percent of the total vote. But because its appeal was explicitly to farmers (and also because one of its two leaders was a white Zambian), the NLP had no language group association in voters' minds and is excluded from this analysis. An additional five small parties, none of which managed to capture more than 0.17 percent of the vote, also contested the election. The UNIP boycotted the poll.

[19] Despite the NP's earlier perceived orientation as a Lozi- or Tonga-speakers' party, it had come to be seen as a Northwestern Province–oriented organization in 1995 when Humphrey Mulemba, a Kaonde from Northwestern Province, was selected as its new president.

Table 8.4. *Correlations Between Dominant Language Groups and Party Voting in Multi-party Elections of 1968, 1996, and Third Republic By-elections*

| Dominant language group in constituency | Winning party associated with which language group? | | | | |
|---|---|---|---|---|---|
| | Bemba | Tonga | Nyanja | Lozi | "Northwestern" |
| Bemba | .786* | −.446* | −.306* | −.381* | −.235* |
| Tonga | −.436* | .843* | −.094 | −.117 | −.072 |
| Nyanja | −.360* | −.084 | .951* | −.071 | −.044 |
| Lozi | −.375* | −.116 | −.079 | .854* | −.061 |
| "Northwestern" | −.120 | −.091 | −.063 | −.078 | .667* |

$N = 193$; * correlation is significant at the 0.01 level (2-tailed test). Dominant language groups are identified from constituency-level 1990 census figures. Mambwe- and Namwanga-speakers are included in the Bemba-speaking group; Tumbuka-speakers are included in the Nyanja-speaking group. The ANC in Southern Province in 1968, the NP in 1994–95, and the UPND are coded as "Tonga" parties. The UNIP in the First Republic and the MMD are coded as "Bemba" parties. The ANC in Western Province in 1968, the NP in 1993, and the AZ are coded as "Lozi" parties. The UNIP in the Third Republic is coded as a "Nyanja" party. The NP in 1995–99 is coded as a "Northwestern" party.

them. Language group voting would thus appear to account for a major part of the variation in these two parties' success rates: NP and AZ candidates that were running in constituencies dominated by members of their presidents' language groups were more than five times as likely to win voters' support than were their fellow party members running in other regions of the country.

A final source of evidence for language group voting in multi-party elections in Zambia is provided in Table 8.4, which reports the correlation between the dominant language group and the language group affiliation of the winning political party in each constituency for the multi-party general elections of 1968 and 1996 and for all Third Republic by-elections held between 1992 and the end of 1999. For the purposes of the analysis, I omit cases where there is not a clearly dominant language group (and thus no clear prediction about which party should win), where the dominant language group does not have a party affiliated with it in the race, and where the election was won by an independent candidate. As in the analyses of tribal voting presented earlier in the chapter, I omit the 1991 election (though the results are almost identical when it is included).

If the language group affiliations of parties matter to Zambian voters, then we would expect to find strong positive correlations between each dominant language group and parties affiliated with that group, and weak or negative correlations for all other combinations of language groups and parties.[20] This is exactly what we find. All the correlations along the diagonal (measuring the tendency for parties identified with particular language groups to win seats in constituencies dominated by a voters from that group) are positive and highly significant, while the correlations located off the diagonal (which capture the tendency for voters with the opportunity to elect candidates running on the tickets of parties affiliated with their own language groups to instead elect candidates running on tickets of parties affiliated with different ones) are all negative. The fact that the correlations along the diagonal are not all equal to one confirms – as the analyses presented earlier also make clear – that language group affiliations are not a perfect predictor of electoral behavior in multi-party elections. But the general pattern in the data is still overwhelmingly in keeping with the proposition that linguistic identities drive voting decisions in a multi-party context.[21]

## CONTROLLED EXPERIMENTS

The results presented thus far confirm that tribal voting is more prevalent in one-party than in multi-party elections and that voters in multi-party contests overwhelmingly support candidates running on the tickets of political parties whose language group orientations match their own. These findings are robust across multiple analyses employing different techniques and drawing on varying data sources. In this section, I present the results of a pair of controlled experiments that permit a more finely calibrated test of the model's implications regarding the effects of regime change on tribal and linguistic voting. The first holds the candidates constant and tests, first, whether they fare differently in elections held under different institutional rules and, then, whether the differences in their

[20] Note that the ecological inference problem is not an issue in the language–voting analysis, since the rural constituencies it includes are all almost completely homogeneous with respect to language group membership.

[21] Apart from the general support it provides for the language group voting thesis, an interesting finding that jumps out of the table is the highly significant negative correlations between ethnic dominance by non-Bemba-speakers and support for Bemba parties (the UNIP in 1968; the MMD in the Third Republic). This pattern, which reflects the tendency for non-Bemba-speakers to support parties other than those led by Bemba-speakers, offers empirical confirmation for the claim made in Chapter 4 about the resentment that non-Bemba-speakers feel toward the ruling party.

performance can be accounted for by the match between their party affiliation and the dominant language group in the area in which they are competing. The second experiment looks at how voters behave when they are given an explicit choice between supporting a candidate from their tribe and supporting a candidate whose party affiliation suggests that he or she represents the interests of their language group.

### *Support for Candidates in Back-to-Back Elections*

The intuition behind the first experiment is simple: if the institutional setting is what drives voters' choices, then we should find relative stability within one-party and multi-party contexts in voters' support for candidates running in the same constituencies in different elections, and changes in voters' support levels across elections held under different institutional rules. To test this intuition, I first identified all candidates that had run in back-to-back elections in the same constituency in the elections of 1973, 1978, 1983, 1988, 1991, and 1996. This yielded a total of 780 cases. Then, to insure the comparability of each candidate's performance across election pairs, I excluded all cases in which different numbers of opponents ran against the candidate in each election.[22] This turned out to be a hard standard to meet, and it reduced the total number of cases in the analysis to just 145. Having identified these key test cases, I divided them into two categories: those that constituted pairs of elections *within* an institutional setting (either multi-party or one-party) and those that constituted pairs of elections *across* institutional settings. There were 123 cases in the first category and 22 in the second.

I then calculated the correlation between the candidates' vote shares in the first and second elections for each category, on the logic that higher correlations would indicate less change across elections in candidates' performance. The correlation in the within-regime-type cases was 0.57 (significant at the .01 level in a two-tailed test); the correlation in the across-regime-type cases was 0.30 (below accepted thresholds of statistical significance). I also calculated the average difference in candidate vote shares in each kind of election pair. With this measure, smaller differences imply greater stability. In within-regime-type pairs, candidates' vote shares varied by an average of 14 percentage points; in the across-regime-type pairs, their vote shares varied by an average of 30 percentage points. Both results confirm that regime change matters: support for candidates was

[22] I also excluded all cases where the candidate ran unopposed in either election.

much more stable when the elections were either both one-party or both multi-party than when each election was of a different type.

The more important testable implication of the theory, however, is that a candidate running in a pair of elections across regime types will not only fare differently but fare *predictably better or worse* in the second election depending on whether the party on whose ticket the candidate is running in the multi-party race is affiliated with the dominant language group in the constituency. For example, we would expect that a candidate who ran on the ANC ticket for a Southern Province seat in 1968 (i.e., a candidate that ran on the ticket of the "right" party – the ANC being closely identified with Southern Province Tonga-speakers) and then again as a UNIP candidate (which, under the one-party rules, the candidate would have to be) in 1973, would perform not just differently but far *worse* in the second election, since the candidate would lose the advantage provided in the 1968 contest by the match between the ANC party label and the Tonga-speaking voters that the candidate was courting. Similarly, we would expect a candidate that ran in Northern Province in both 1988 and 1991, but as an MMD candidate in the second of these elections, to win a larger share of the vote in the 1991 contest than in the 1988 race, since, again, the candidate was running on the ticket of the "right" party in the multi-party election – the MMD being closely associated in voters' minds with Northern Province Bemba-speakers. Had the same candidate been running on the ticket of the same party in the same years for a seat in Nyanja-speaking Eastern Province, we would expect the MMD party label to have hurt and to have reduced the candidate's vote share in 1991 relative to what it had been in 1988.

To test this expectation, I first identified, for all candidates that ran in pairs of across-regime-type elections and that met the selection criteria noted earlier, whether or not the party on whose ticket each was running in the multi-party contest was affiliated with the dominant language group in the constituency. I then compared the candidate's performance in that race and in the one-party contest. In *twenty of the twenty-one* cases, the direction of change in the candidate's performance across the two elections could be predicted by whether or not the candidate was running on the ticket of a party associated with the dominant language group in the region.[23] If candidates were, then they won a larger share of the

[23] Twenty-two cases meet the general criteria used, but the candidate in one of the cases ran as an independent in the multi-party contest and had to be dropped from the analysis.

vote in the multi-party contest than in the one-party contest; if they were not, then they received more support in the one-party race. Because this analysis allows us to control for so many of the factors that might have affected the outcome – including a candidate's personal attributes and ethnic background, the ethnic composition of the electorate, and even the number of other candidates in the race – it offers particularly strong support for the expectations of the model. The findings confirm that the one-party or multi-party nature of the election not only affects patterns of electoral support, but does so in exactly the way that the model developed in Chapter 5 would predict.

## *Support for Candidates of Different Types*

One of the weaknesses of the analyses presented earlier in the chapter is that they are unable to distinguish between tribal and language group voting in situations where a candidate is both a member of the dominant tribal group and running on the ticket of a party that is associated with the dominant language community. The problem with such cases is that we cannot be sure whether the candidate's support is coming from her party affiliation or her tribal background. Testing the model's implications more carefully requires that we focus on candidates that are either members of the dominant tribe or running on the ticket of a party associated with the dominant language group, but not both. Figure 8.7 distinguishes among these different types of candidates.

Type A candidates are both members of the dominant tribe in the constituency and running on the ticket of a party that is affiliated with the constituency's dominant language group. We would expect such candidates to perform very well, and they do: of the 82 Type A candidates that ran in the multi-party elections of 1968, 1996, and the Third Republic by-elections

| Is the Party on Whose Ticket the Candidate Is Running Affiliated with the Dominant Language Group in the Constituency? | Is the Candidate from the Dominant Tribe in the Constituency? Yes | No |
|---|---|---|
| Yes | A | B |
| No | C | D |

Figure 8.7. Four Types of Candidates

that were held through the end of 1999, 70 (85 percent) won the seat they were contesting.[24] Type D candidates, by contrast are neither members of the dominant tribe nor running on the ticket of a party that is associated with the dominant language group. To the extent that voters allocate their support along ethnic lines – that is, in terms of *either* their tribal or their linguistic identities – we would expect Type D candidates to fare poorly. Again, the data bear out this expectation: of the 87 such candidates in the analysis, just 32 (37 percent) won the race they were contesting.

One implication of these findings is that ethnicity matters but is not determinative of electoral outcomes. The fact that 85 percent of those candidates whose ethnic backgrounds (both tribally and, through their party affiliations, linguistically) matched those of the plurality of the voters were able to win their election suggests that ethnicity does matter for Zambian voters. But the fact that 37 percent of those candidates whose ethnic background *did not* match that of the dominant group of voters were also able to win the seats they were contesting suggests that factors other than ethnicity also motivate voters' decision making.[25]

From the standpoint of confirming the salience of ethnicity in Zambian voting, comparing the success rates of Type A and D candidates may be illuminating. But from the standpoint of testing the relative salience of tribal and linguistic identities in multi-party elections, the success rates of such candidates are of little use since we have no way of knowing whether their victory or loss was because of their individual tribal affiliation or because of the language group identity ascribed to them by virtue of their party affiliation. The key candidate types to look at for this purpose are B and C.

Type B candidates are running on the ticket of a party that is affiliated with the constituency's dominant language group but do not belong to the

[24] The analysis includes only rural constituencies and constituencies in which the dominant language group is clearly identifiable. It excludes independent candidates, unopposed candidates, and candidates running on the tickets of parties whose language group affiliations are not clear (including all very small parties). The language group affiliations of parties are coded as indicated in the notes to Table 8.4.

[25] It is possible, of course, that these results occur in cases where dominant tribe and language group voters split their support between two or more candidates, thereby making it possible for another candidate, not of the dominant tribe or language group, to emerge victorious. Such an outcome would "look," in the data, like a Type D winner, but would, in fact, be an instance of strict ethnic voting. This possibility does not, however, undermine our ability to test the relative salience of tribal and language group voting, since Type D candidates are members of neither the dominant tribe nor the dominant language community and so provide no leverage on this question.

| | | Is the Candidate from the Dominant Tribe in the Constituency? | |
|---|---|---|---|
| | | Yes | No |
| Is the Party on Whose Ticket the Candidate Is Running Affiliated with the Dominant Language Group in the Constituency? | Yes | 85% | 75% |
| | No | 35% | 37% |

Figure 8.8. Winning Rates for Each Type of Candidate in Multi-Party Elections

dominant tribe. Type C candidates belong to the dominant tribe but are running on the ticket of a party that is not affiliated with the constituency's dominant language group. If voters in multi-party contests were behaving exactly as they did in one-party elections (i.e., if they paid no attention to party affiliations and allocated their support based on the match between their own tribal affiliations and those of the candidates in the race), then we would expect Type C candidates to outperform Type B candidates, and success rates among Type A and C candidates (and among Type B and D candidates) to be roughly the same. In other words, we would expect candidates' column values to be better predictors of their success than their row values. If, on the other hand, as the argument I have advanced in this book suggests, voters in multi-party elections ignore candidates' tribal affiliations and instead cast their votes based on the language group affiliation communicated by the candidates' party labels, then row values will be more important than column values as predictors of candidates' success. We would expect Type B candidates to outperform Type C candidates, and Type A and B (and Type C and D) candidates to perform roughly equally. As Figure 8.8 shows, the latter is exactly what we find. Type B candidates win 75 percent of the time, whereas Type C candidates win just 35 percent of the time. All of the action is in the rows, not the columns.

These results provide strong support for the proposition that voters in multi-party elections put more emphasis on language group ties, as conveyed by the candidates' party affiliations, than on tribal connections.[26] Even more compelling evidence comes from comparing the performance of Type B and C candidates when they are competing directly against one another in head-to-head contests. In the results presented in Figure 8.8,

[26] If the 1991 election is included, the results are even stronger: the shares of winning Type A, B, C, and D candidates become 90, 81, 34, and 37 percent, respectively.

Type B and C candidates are competing against rivals of all types. A superior test is one in which they compete directly against one another with no other candidates in the race. In such a context, voters are given an explicit choice between supporting a member of their tribe who is not running on the ticket of a party affiliated with their language group and supporting a candidate who is affiliated with a party associated with their language group but is not a member of their tribe.

The parliamentary by-election that took place in Mazabuka Central constituency on 30 November 1999 provided voters with just such a choice. Mazabuka is located in the heart of Tongaland and, apart from a Lozi-speaking minority of around 18 percent and a handful of migrants from other parts of the country who work in the nearby sugar estates, the constituency is almost entirely populated by Tonga-speakers who are also Tonga by tribe. Although five candidates contested the 30 November 1999 by-election, the race quickly reduced itself to a contest between the MMD candidate, Gary Nkombo, and the UPND candidate, Griffiths Nang'omba.[27] Nang'omba had the advantage of running on the ticket of the UPND, a party that had a Tonga president and was widely assumed to represent the interests of Tonga-speakers. Nang'omba's own tribal background was a disadvantage, however: he was Lozi running in a constituency that was overwhelmingly Tonga by tribe. Nkombo, on the other hand, was Tonga by tribe but running on the ticket of the MMD – a party identified with Bemba-speakers. The situation offered a perfect test of the predictions of the model. Nkombo was a Type C candidate, and Nang'omba was a Type B candidate. If voters put the candidates' tribal backgrounds before their party affiliations, then Nkombo should have been the winner, since his tribal background matched that of the vast majority of the constituency's population. But if voters put the candidates' party affiliations first, then the seat should have gone to Nang'omba, since he was the one running on the ticket of the party that everyone viewed as the "Tonga party."

In the intense campaign leading up to the by-election, each party did its best to convince voters to focus on the dimension of ethnic identity that would play to its advantage. MMD campaigners "used carefully selected Tonga phrases to tell voters that the Mazabuka Central constituency needed a Tonga MP, and his name was Nkombo" (*The Monitor*, 19–25 November 1999). They "openly campaign[ed] on tribal lines urging voters not to vote for . . . Nang'omba because he is Lozi and not Tonga"

[27] Together, the two candidates ultimately won 94 percent of the vote.

(*The Monitor*, 26 November–2 December 1999). The article goes on to say that "never in the history of this country has a ruling party, or any other party for that matter, so overtly campaigned on a tribal platform to the extent that the MMD has in Mazabuka" (ibid.).

UPND campaigners, meanwhile, emphasized that a vote for Nkombo was a vote for President Chiluba and his Bemba language group, whereas a vote for Nang'omba was a vote for UPND president Anderson Mazoka and the broader Tonga community. Irrespective of Nang'omba's own tribal background, they stressed, a vote for him was a vote for a party committed to advancing the interests of Tonga-speakers. In the end, voters were more persuaded by the UPND's appeals than by the MMD's. Nang'omba won the race with 52 percent of the vote to Nkombo's 42 percent. Although Nang'omba failed to capture *all* the votes, his victory nonetheless provides strong support for the model's expectations – particularly since his opponent was a member of the ruling party and therefore had vastly more resources to draw upon in the campaign.

The Mazabuka Central by-election was not the only head-to-head contests between a Type B and a Type C candidate. Thirteen others took place in the elections of 1968, 1996, and the Third Republic by-elections. In the fourteen such cases, the Type B candidate won ten times.[28]

Another implication of the model is that Type B candidates not only will outperform Type C candidates but also will win a larger share of the vote than their tribe's share of the population would lead us to expect. Even given problems of ecological inference, a finding that a candidate won a larger share of votes than the candidate's own tribe's share of the voting population can be counted as definitive evidence of cross-tribal voting. Analogously, the model also implies that Type C candidates should win smaller shares of the vote than their tribe's population share would lead us to expect.

I was able to test this expectation in the nine head-to-head contests that were held during the Third Republic, where it was possible to draw on census data to identify the exact share of the population that belonged to each candidate's tribe.[29] Eleven Type B and thirteen Type C candidates ran in these nine contests.[30] Of the eleven Type B candidates, nine (or

[28] The total sample rises to nineteen cases, including Mazabuka Central, if the 1991 election is included. The Type B candidate won fifteen times in this larger sample.

[29] Data on the ethnic demographics of electoral constituencies in 1968 was sufficiently good to allow me to identify the dominant tribe in most constituencies, but not precise enough for me to identify that tribe's exact population share.

[30] Two of the races featured one Type B and two Type C candidates.

82 percent) won more votes than their tribe's share of the population would have led us to expect; of the thirteen Type C candidates, eight (or 62 percent) won fewer votes than their tribal share would have led us to expect. Again, the findings are in keeping with the theoretical expectations of the model: tribal voting seems not to take place in multi-party elections in the way that it does in the one-party contests. Ethnicity matters in both contexts, but different dimensions of ethnicity.

PART IV

# Introduction to Part IV

## *Beyond Zambia*

Why, and when, do some social cleavages emerge as politically salient rather than others? In the preceding pages, I have sought to shed light on this question by exploring the case of Zambia – a country that, for the complexity of its ethnic landscape, the richness of its empirical record, and the advantageous pattern of its institutional variation, offers a particularly good laboratory for studying the determinants of identity choice and cleavage change. The specific outcome that I have sought to explain in the Zambian case is why tribal identities served as the basis of electoral mobilization and voting during one-party elections and language group identities played this role during multi-party elections. I began by showing why tribe and language, but not other possible bases of social mobilization, are available to Zambian political actors as potential foundations for political coalitions. Then, to account for why political actors find it advantageous to identify themselves in terms of one of these ethnic identities rather than the other, I developed a simple model to account for why people embrace the ethnic identities they do. Finally, I showed how the incentives that the model illuminates are affected by changes in the rules that specify whether one party or many may legally compete in the political arena.

In its general form, the central argument of the book can be summarized as follows: given a widespread expectation that elected officials will favor members of their own ethnic groups in the distribution of patronage benefits, voters will seek to better their lot by electing members of their own ethnic groups to positions of political power. Politicians, knowing this, will seek to improve their electoral prospects by couching their electoral appeals in ethnic terms. But the simple rule that voters should "support their own" or that politicians should "play the ethnic card" is complicated by the fact that voters and politicians are almost always members of more than one ethnic group. Both sorts of actors possess identity repertoires that provide them with membership in – "admission tickets" to – more than one ethnic community: one defined by their race, another by their religion, a third by their language, a fourth by their tribe, and so forth. This provides voters with access to more than one stream of patronage benefits and politicians with more than one set of potential supporters. The question thus arises as to which group they should claim as their own. When politicians "play the ethnic card," which ethnic card should they play? When voters "support their own," which principle of group membership should they employ to determine which candidates are, and are not, members of their group?

If politicians and voters are interested in political power and the resources it brings, and if political power is allocated via a system in which the plurality group wins, then they should both choose the group membership that puts them in a minimum winning coalition. Being part of a winning coalition is a prerequisite for there to be any resources to distribute, and having that coalition be minimum maximizes the resources that each coalition member will receive. To the extent that this model of political behavior is correct, ethnic identities will not be chosen because of the psychological attachment that actors have toward them or because of the success of some crafty political entrepreneur in convincing voters that a particular identity is more important than others. They will be chosen because the identity gains them entry into a more usefully sized political coalition than the other identities that they might draw upon. The ethnic identity is simply a means to an end.

This simple outcome is complicated by yet another wrinkle. Whether or not a particular group membership will put a person in a minimum winning coalition will depend not just on the size of the group that the identity defines but also on the boundaries of the political arena in which political competition is taking place. A group that might be minimum winning in one setting – say, in a state-level gubernatorial election – might be too small to be winning or too large to be minimum in another setting – say, in the context of a town-level mayoral race or within the nation as a whole. Changes in the boundaries of the relevant arena of political competition will bring about changes in the incentives for actors to choose one identity instead of another. Political institutions are one of the variables that determine these boundaries. Thus when political institutions change, so too can actors' identity choices and, with them, the cleavage outcomes to which these choices give rise.

Applied to Zambia, I show that this argument can account for why tribal identities have served as the basis of political competition and coalition-building during one-party elections and language group identities have played this role during multi-party elections. My claim is not that the shift between multi-party and one-party electoral rules has had any effect on the salience in political life of ethnicity per se. Zambian voters "vote their ethnic groups" and politicians "play the ethnic card" with equal frequency in both institutional settings. What the one-party or multi-party nature of the political system does is determine which ethnic community – their tribe or their language group – Zambian political actors will focus on when they try to mobilize their fellow group members.

Tribal divisions emerge as salient in one-party elections because political competition in such contexts takes place at the level of the electoral constituency and electoral constituencies in Zambia tend to be linguistically homogeneous but tribally heterogeneous.[1] While linguistic identities might generate winning coalitions in such a setting (after all, everyone is a member of the dominant language group), only tribal identities can produce coalitions that are *minimum* winning. This explains why voters in one-party contests focus their attention on the candidates' tribal identities and why political competition and conflict in one-party elections revolves around tribal differences.

In multi-party contests, candidates each run on the ticket of a different party and voters expect candidates, if they are elected, to distribute patronage in ways dictated by their party's leader. In such a context, voters ignore the candidates' own ethnic identities and focus their attention on the presumed ethnic group orientations of the parties with which the candidates are affiliated. Because political parties are competing on the national stage, voters' attention to party labels shifts the effective arena of competition from the local to the national level. National-scale cleavages in Zambia are language cleavages, since tribes are too small to serve as the basis of coalitions that, at that level, are both minimum and winning. This explains why electoral mobilization and counter-mobilization in multi-party settings revolve around language group differences.

[1] As I explain in Chapter 5, ethnic competition in urban constituencies, which are both tribally and linguistically heterogeneous, follows a different logic. But since urban constituencies make up only 20 percent of the total, it is reasonable to make generalizations about the ethnic basis of electoral support in one-party elections based on the outcome in rural constituencies alone.

This simple argument generates a number of observable implications about how the behavior of politicians and citizens will differ across multi-party and one-party elections. In Chapters 7 and 8, I presented a series of analyses that test these implications. In Chapter 7, I showed that Zambian politicians make the kinds of ethnic appeals, invest in the sorts of ethnic association, and choose to run in the kinds of constituencies that the argument would predict. In Chapter 8, I turned to the behavior of non-elites and showed that Zambian voters also behave in accordance with the argument's expectations: they vote for members of their tribes in one-party elections and for parties affiliated with their language groups in multi-party elections. Some of these analyses constitute true tests of the argument's implications, in that they draw on large amounts of randomly selected data (or the entire set of instances in which the phenomenon of interest took place) and employ well-accepted methods of scientific inference. Others are simply anecdotal illustrations of the argument's predictions that do not formally test the theory so much as document its empirical foundations through examples of events, outcomes, or the behavior of key actors. Together, however, the number and variety of these analyses – *all* of which provide support for the theory's expectations – give us great confidence in the argument that the book advances.

Quite apart from these findings, our confidence in the argument's success is reinforced by the fact that two of the key premises on which it is built – that voters expect political leaders to favor members of their own groups when they distribute patronage resources and that, in striving to put members of their own groups in positions of power, voters in multi-party elections pay attention to the ethnic affiliations conveyed by candidates' party affiliations rather than the candidates' own ethnic backgrounds – were substantiated with survey and focus group evidence. By providing empirical evidence to support these two building blocks of the argument (the former in Chapter 4, the latter in Chapter 8) we can have greater confidence that the match between the outcome that the argument predicts and the outcomes that I document in Zambia's one-party and multi-party eras is a product of the causal process that the book describes.

The argument that I advance in the book may account for the variation we observe in ethnic cleavage outcomes in Zambia, but is it portable? Have other African countries that have shifted back and forth between single-party and multi-party rule experienced similar changes in the relative salience of tribal and linguistic (or, more broadly, localized and national-scale) cleavages in their political competition? If so, can the argument be pushed further still? Leaving aside the impact of regime change and moving beyond the specific context of Africa, can ethnic identity matrices such as the ones introduced in Chapter 5 offer more general insights into why particular ethnic cleavages emerge as axes of political competition and coalition-building? The book began with this general question. Does it provide any more general answers? The next two chapters take up these questions. Chapter 9 addresses whether the specific argument developed for Zambia can explain patterns of variation in ethnic cleavage salience across single-party and multi-party elections in other African countries. Chapter 10 applies the argument and the ethnic identity matrix heuristic to still other countries and political arenas to demonstrate the insights the approach offers for thinking about identity choice and ethnic cleavage salience.

# 9

## *Regime Change and Ethnic Politics in Africa*

Do the Zambian findings presented in this book travel to other African nations? Is there any evidence that transitions between one-party and multi-party rule in other African countries have brought changes in the kinds of ethnic cleavages that structure political competition and coalition-building? More than two dozen African nations have held parliamentary elections under both single-party and multi-party political systems, so in principle it should be possible to test whether the Zambian results hold elsewhere in the region. For them to be eligible as comparison cases, the countries would have to have multi-dimensional ethnic cleavage structures (so variation in the cleavage outcome is possible) and to be places where ethnicity is understood by voters to convey information about how politicians distribute patronage. Nearly all African countries meet both of these criteria. Almost all have local cleavages defined by tribal affiliation or clan membership and national-scale divisions based on religion, language, or region. A handful of African countries – Sudan, Zimbabwe, Mauritius, Tanzania, South Africa – have significant racial cleavages as well.

As for the role that ethnicity plays, Africa is a region whose poverty and weak government institutions lead citizens to view the state as a resource to be consumed by the ethnic kin of those who control its offices.[1] Young and Turner summarize the partrimonial basis of African politics well:

> In the richly evocative Nigerian phrase, politics was "cutting the national cake." The output of the state was perceived as divisible into slices of possibly unequal size, sweet to the taste, and intended to be eaten. A "they" category, in control of political institutions, would exploit its power to impose its dominion upon "we," and to reserve for itself the lion's share of state resources. (1985: 147)

[1] I develop this point in Chapter 4.

African politics, Young and Turner suggest, revolves around a struggle for control over patronage resources by coalitions of ethnically defined "we" and "they." Although this represents something of an oversimplification, it captures enough of the essence of African politics to suggest the likely applicability of the Zambian findings to other parts of the region.

However, while these general background conditions hold throughout most of Africa, the specific institutional factors that make the Zambian story work – particularly its single-member plurality (SMP) electoral rules – are absent in all but a relative handful of cases. SMP electoral rules are necessary both to ensure a single salient cleavage outcome and to generate different choice strategies at the national and local levels. Although nearly all former British colonies in Africa began their lives as independent nations with SMP rules, a number of them (Botswana, Gambia, Ghana, Lesotho, and Zimbabwe) never held one-party elections.[2] Others (e.g., Nigeria) adopted federal systems that alter the logic of national political competition by dividing the country into multiple sub-national political arenas. Still others (e.g., Malawi and Uganda) held both one-party and multi-party parliamentary contests, but these elections were insufficiently competitive for meaningful inferences to be made about voting or campaigning behavior.[3] Across all of Africa, only Sierra Leone, Tanzania, and Kenya share both Zambia's SMP electoral system and its record of having held competitive one-party and multi-party elections (even if just a single example of one kind or the other) at some point in their post-independence histories.[4] Sierra Leone held competitive multi-party elections in 1962 and 1967 (Reynolds 1999) and a reasonably

[2] One could argue that all – or nearly all – of the multi-party elections held in Botswana and Zimbabwe have been de facto one-party elections. Yet even if this is the case, this simply means that all of their elections have been one-party contests rather than multi-party contests. Either way, these countries lack the variation in one-party and multi-party competition that is necessary to test whether the Zambian findings hold.

[3] Strictly speaking, Uganda has never held one-party elections, though the "no-party" elections it has held since 1989 are a fairly close approximation (Kasfir 1998). I rule out the Uganda case as a candidate for comparison because its sole multi-party contest, held in 1980, is almost universally viewed to have been rigged (Hansen and Twaddle 1988).

[4] Among former French and Belgian colonies, Burundi, Cameroon, Central African Republic, Seychelles, and Democratic Republic of Congo (then Zaire) all held at least one set of one-party elections under SMP rules. But all five of these countries employed non-SMP electoral systems (PR, multi-member plurality, single-member majority, or mixed systems in which different portions of the legislature were elected under different rules) in their multi-party contests. Ethiopia held one-party elections in 1987 and multi-party elections in 1995, both under SMP rules, but the country's federal system prevents it from being a usable test case.

competitive single-party contest in 1982 (Luke 1985; Hayward and Dumbuya 1985). Tanzania held competitive one-party elections in 1965 (Morgenthau 1965; Cliffe 1967) and competitive multi-party elections in 1995 and 2000 (van Cranenburgh 1996; Hyden 1999).[5] Kenya held competitive multi-party elections in 1963 (just prior to independence), 1966 (the so-called little general election), 1992, and 1997 (Gertzel 1970; Throup and Hornsby 1998; Barkan and Ng'ethe 1998; Hartmann 1999), and imperfect but nonetheless reasonably competitive single-party contests in 1969, 1974, 1979, 1983, and 1988 (Hyden and Leys 1972; Barkan 1987).[6] Comparisons of electoral appeals and voting patterns across these one-party and multi-party contests provide important tests of the portability of the Zambian findings.

Applied to Sierra Leone, the argument would lead us to expect electoral conflict during the country's multi-party elections to have revolved around the struggle between two broad regional coalitions: southern-based Mende-speakers and northern-based Temne-speakers. Abundant evidence suggests that it did (Cartwright 1970; Barrows 1976). During the country's one-party elections, the argument would predict the locus of competition to have shifted and conflicts to have emerged among the twenty or so local tribal groups that nest within the broader Mende and Temne language communities. Internal divisions within these regionally defined ethnic blocs, hidden in the 1962 and 1967 multi-party contests, should have emerged as salient in the campaigns leading up to (and been identifiable in the voting patterns that emerged during) the 1982 one-party election. Kandeh's analysis of this contest suggests that this is exactly what happened. Writing about the changes in Sierra Leone's politics brought by the declaration of a single-party state, Kandeh observes that

> one party rule has engendered the demise of the ethnoregional political unity of northern [Temne] ethnic groups... With... the introduction of a one-party constitution in 1978, northern ethnic groups have become more assertive of their cultural distinctiveness. Time was, especially during decolonization and the first decade of independence [i.e., during the multi-party era], when the political identities of minority northern ethnic groups were generally subsumed by the larger and competitively more significant Temne identity. Although most northern minorities were able to preserve the peculiarities of their respective cultures, the

[5] Tanzania's 2000 elections in Zanzibar were widely viewed as unfair (Commonwealth Observer Group 2001), but the polling on the mainland was competitive.

[6] The 1969, 1974, and 1979 contests were de facto one-party contests, as a one-party state was not formally declared until 1982.

politicization of their cultural identities was...determined largely by...the Mende-Temne rivalry. (1992: 96–97)

With the introduction of one-party competition, the bi-polar Mende–Temne cleavage gave way to political competition revolving around a set of more fine-grained ethnic divisions.

A particularly telling illustration of this shift is provided by the case of Sorie Koroma, Siaka Stevens's long-serving Vice President. Throughout his career, Koroma had publicly identified himself as a Temne – in fact, his identification as such was a critical factor in reinforcing the popular perception that Stevens's All People's Congress was a party for Temnes only. Yet in 1983, shortly after the suspension of multi-party competition and the declaration of a one-party state, Koroma revealed publicly that he was not, in fact, Temne, but a member of the small Mandingo tribe (Kandeh 1992: 97). Although Kandeh writes that "it still remains unclear why Koroma chose to switch ethnic identities," the argument advanced in this book suggests an answer: in the context of a one-party system, in which the effective arena of political competition shrinks to the level of the electoral constituency, local tribal identities (in this case, being Mandingo) are more useful than regional/linguistic ones (in this case, being Temne). Koroma simply chose to redefine himself in terms of the identity that, given the new circumstances, was more politically advantageous for him.[7]

The model seems to have somewhat less explanatory power in Tanzania, largely because of the lesser salience of ethnicity per se in that country than in many others.[8] Yet, even so, there is evidence that national-scale ethnic cleavages involving divisions between Zanzibaris and mainlanders – or, more broadly, between *warabu* (Arabs/Muslims)

[7] Koroma was not the only politician to have had his tribal background overshadowed by his broader regional/linguistic affiliation during the multi-party era – though, in his case, the "mistake" was almost certainly a product of his making a conscious identity choice. Fisher (1969: 623) criticizes a contemporary publication for "call[ing] Sir Henry Lightfoot-Boston a Temne instead of a Creole, and say[ing that] 10 of the 12 paramount chiefs elected to parliament in March 1967 were Mende [when], in fact, only seven chiefs were from the south, and some of these were of other tribes – Sherbro, Vai, or Gallinas." While the publication may have miscoded some of these people, the larger issue was that, in the context of a multi-party system, political actors in Sierra Leone tended to be seen through the lens of the Mende–Temne conflict, even when they were not, strictly speaking (i.e., tribally), members of either group.

[8] One long-time observer of the country goes so far as to state that it is "impossible to make a political career in Tanzania by appealing to tribal values and preferences" (Hyden 1999: 146).

and Christians – as well as divisions among broad regional/linguistic blocs (e.g., among Sukuma-speakers, Nyamwezi-speakers, and Chagga-speakers) have become much more salient since the transition to multi-party elections in 1995 than they were during the long one-party era that preceded it (Campbell 1999; Okema 2000). Unfortunately, the secondary source coverage of Tanzania's one-party elections is too thin to allow for comparisons of the salience of local tribal divisions across one-party and multi-party settings, so it is difficult to be certain whether the escalation of conflicts along national-scale cleavage lines in the 1990s displaced competition among more local tribes. In addition, as in Sierra Leone, the electoral and ethnic demographic data that might allow our theoretical expectations about voting patterns to be tested more systematically are unavailable. The case of Kenya, however, provides sufficiently rich secondary source coverage and data to allow for a comprehensive out-of-sample test of the Zambian findings.

## REGIME CHANGE AND ETHNIC POLITICS IN KENYA

Kenya, like Zambia, is a place where ethnicity matters. It is a place where people view their political representatives as sources of patronage (Barkan 1976, 1979) and where they assume that having a member of their ethnic group in a position of political power will increase their access to state resources (Hyden and Leys 1972; Haugerud 1995).[9] However, Kenya, like Zambia, is also a place where people understand their "ethnic group" in multiple ways. Thus, as in Zambia, the otherwise straightforward rule that a voter should support a member of his or her own ethnic group begs the question: which group?

Kenyans view their country's ethnic landscape through different lenses in different settings. When they think about where they fit within the ethnic landscape of the country as a whole, they identify their "group" in terms of broad ethnic blocs defined by linguistic similarity, region, or even religion. When they think of their "group" in more localized contexts, they do so in terms of their membership in one of the country's forty-two tribes or, in situations where the local context is tribally homogeneous, in terms of their membership in one of numerous sub-tribes or

[9] Haugerud writes that "many Kenyans I talked with in both town and countryside in mid-1993 discussed the nation's political future in explicit ethnic and regional terms, and assumed that the ethnic identity of a new president would define patterns of favoritism" (1995: 42).

clans.[10] As in Zambia, these local ethnic identities nest within the broader national-scale ones. Thus while national-level political competition is often understood in terms of the competition among the Kikuyu, Luo, Kalenjin, Luhya, and Coastal peoples (or Mijikenda), each of these groups subsumes a number of smaller ethnic units that become relevant bases of social identity in more localized settings. For example, the broad Kikuyu bloc subsumes the Embu and Meru (and is thus sometimes referred to collectively as GEMA – the acronym for the Gikuyu [Kikuyu], Embu, and Meru Association).[11] It also contains distinctions between people from the northern and southern Kikuyu-speaking districts and among the several Kikuyu clans (e.g., Kiambu, Gatundu, Muranga, Nyheri). The Kalenjin are a linguistic umbrella category linking members of the Nandi, Kipsigi, Tugen, Pokot, Elgeyo, Keiyo, Marakwet, Seibi, Dorobo, Terik, and Sabaot tribes, and sometimes also the Maasai, Turkana, and Samburu. For this reason, the broader Kalenjin coalition is commonly referred to in the Kenyan press by the acronym KAMATUSA (*Ka*lenjin, *Ma*asai, *Tu*rkana, *Sa*mburu). The Luhya subsume sixteen different smaller tribal groups.[12] The Luo contain dozens of clan divisions. And the Mijikenda contain within their ranks members of the distinct Giriama, Digo, Rabai, Chonyi, Kauma, Ribe, Duruma, and Jibana tribes.

Unlike Zambia, where the relevant axes of ethnic cleavage at the local and national levels are uniform (tribe in the former; language in the latter), the principles of group identification that Kenyans use to categorize themselves at the local and national levels tend to vary from one part of the country to another. For the Mijikenda, whose national-level self-identification is regional or even religious – they are the (predominantly Muslim) people of the coast – local-level distinctions are made in terms of tribal affiliations. For the Luo, the national-level principle of ethnic identification is tribal (which works for them because they are a fairly large tribal group), while local-level distinctions are based on clan affiliations. For the Kalenjin, local-level distinctions are tribal, but the cultural glue that holds the group together when it competes on the national stage

[10] The number forty-two is invoked again and again as the number of tribes in Kenya. Yet this accounting is as arbitrary as the count of seventy-three tribes in Zambia (see Chapter 2).

[11] GEMA was an independence-era cultural and political association that brought together these three peoples and was closely associated with President Kenyatta and his family (Widner 1992).

[12] These are the Bukusu, Maragoli, Tachoni, Kabras, Khayo, Kisa, Marachi, Marama, Nyala, Wanga, Samia, Idahko, Tiriki, Tsotso, Nyore, and Ishukha.

is language (and, to a lesser degree, pastoralism). Yet irrespective of the different principles of group membership that each community employs at each level, the important point is that Kenyans have clearly distinct local and national-scale ethnic identities. This makes it possible to inquire whether, as in Zambia, political actors tend to view their ethnic group in terms of local-level social divisions during one-party elections and in terms of national-level cleavages during multi-party contests. The evidence strongly suggests they do.

### *Kenya's First Multi-Party Era*

After holding multi-party elections just prior to independence in 1963, Kenya's first post-independence multi-party election took place in 1966. Called the "little general election," the contest was actually a series of by-elections triggered by the defection of Oginga Odinga and twenty-nine other MPs from the ruling Kenya African National Union (KANU) to the newly formed Kenya People's Union (KPU). Following the defections, the KANU-dominated Parliament rushed through a constitutional amendment stipulating that any MP who crossed the floor to another party would have to resign his or her parliamentary seat and re-contest it in a by-election. The "little general election" was the series of by-elections triggered by this legislation.

Odinga was the most prominent Luo politician in the country and, although only about a quarter of the MPs that followed him to the KPU were actually Luo, his identification as the Luo leader was so strong that the KPU was immediately assumed to be a vehicle for Luo interests. The fact that Odinga's split with President Jomo Kenyatta had been precipitated principally by ideological differences was irrelevant to most Kenyans. The "little general election" was understood as a clash of big men and their broad ethnic networks, not in ideological or policy terms. Koff argues that "for most Kikuyu, the fact that KPU was headed by a Luo, whose aim was to replace Kenyatta as Kenya's President, probably outweighed any sympathies they may have had for KPU's policies" (1966: 58). Luo voters were similarly motivated by ethnic rather than policy considerations.

Even outside of Luoland and Kikuyuland, the election was viewed as a conflict between the Luo and Kikuyu coalitions for control of the government. As Gertzel emphasizes,

> both Kenyatta and Odinga symbolized an ethnic identity as well as a political stand. Kenyatta embodied not only Kenyan nationalism but the spirit and

identity of Kikuyu nationalism ... Odinga ... symbolized the identity of the Luo ... a position highlighted and reinforced ... by the subsequent attacks upon him and his party as an isolated Luo group separated from the rest of the country. The choice before the others was thus not only between Kenyatta and Odinga, but also in part between Kikuyu and Luo ... While both parties denounced any appeal to tribalism, neither could entirely avoid this ethnic identification. (1970: 90)

The results of the election bear out this interpretation. Whereas the KPU won every seat (and 90 percent of the vote) in Luo-dominated Central Nyanza, it managed to win just two of the remaining twenty-two seats (and less than 42 percent of the vote) in the rest of the country. KANU, as the ruling party, was able to maintain its support across most of the other regions in which the by-elections were held. But its strongest support by far was in its Kikuyu heartland of Central Province and Laikipia and Nakuru districts.

KANU's landslide victory in the Central Province constituency of Kandara offers a particularly illuminating illustration of the logic of ethnic politics in multi-party Kenya (and also clear parallels with what we saw in Zambia). The Kandara contest pitted veteran Kikuyu politician Bildad Kaggia, running on the KPU ticket, against comparatively little-known Tadeo Mwaura, running for KANU. Kaggia was a major figure in Kenyan politics who "probably stood second only to Kenyatta" among Kikuyu political leaders (Gertzel 1970: 90). Mwaura was a much less well-known politician who, a year before, had not even been able to defend his Senate seat. By all accounts, Kaggia should have won the election in a rout. Yet, in an outcome that exactly paralleled the case of Emmanuel Kasonde described in Chapters 7 and 8, Kaggia – the political heavyweight and local favorite son – was overwhelmingly rejected. After handily winning the Kandara seat three years before in the pre-independence election of 1963, he received less than 10 percent of the vote in 1966. When he crossed the floor to the KPU, he ceased to be seen by voters as a representative of Kikuyu interests, and voters withdrew their support. Kaggia's party label, which, in voters' eyes, marked him as an agent for the Luo, overshadowed his own credentials as one of the country's leading Kikuyus.[13] He may

[13] A similar story can be told of the rejection by the Luo community of Tom Mboya who, though Luo himself, was viewed as an enemy by many of his tribespeople for his steadfast defense of KANU during the 1966 election campaign. Gertzel writes that clan elders in Central Nyanza described Mboya's active campaigning against the KPU "in terms of the tribal past when a jealous man within the tribe had joined forces with the enemy against his own people" (1970: 117). As with Kaggia,

have been the "right" candidate, but he was affiliated with the "wrong" party and therefore lost in a landslide. In the vocabulary of the analysis in Chapter 8, Kaggia was a Type C candidate, and, in multi-party contests, Type C candidates lose.

### *One-Party Elections in Kenya*

The emphasis on party labels evaporated with the banning of the KPU and the emergence of a de facto one-party system in 1969.[14] In the new one-party setting, the effective arena of political competition contracted to the level of the electoral constituency and political conflict between broad regional blocs (such as that between the Kikuyu and the Luo) was displaced by competition among locally defined ethnic communities. Rather than mobilize big national-scale coalitions, as they had in 1966, rival candidates in one-party elections

> drew support from different clans or sub-clans . . . and – in ethnically mixed urban constituencies in Nairobi, Mombassa and Nakuru, and in the former White Highlands settlement areas – from particular ethnic groups [e.g., tribes]. In the more ethnically [tribally] homogeneous Central, Nyanza and Western Provinces, candidates appealed to rival sub-clan or clan interests. (Throup and Hornsby 1998: 16)

Hyden and Leys concur that the structure of Kenya's one-party elections "put a premium on clan- and tribe-based politics" (1972: 397). Writing about the 1969 election, they note that

> when we examine the evidence from individual constituencies it is clear that clan and locality cleavages were of fundamental importance. All the constituency reports without exception emphasized the priority accorded by voters to the candidates' tribes (in urban areas) and clans (in rural seats) . . . The candidates' electoral arithmetic . . . began and largely ended with calculations of tribal and clan support. (ibid.: 401)

Mboya's loyalty to the community was assumed to be communicated by his party label rather than by his own lineage. It was only after his assassination in 1969 that he was re-adopted as a Luo son.

14 As in Zambia, Kenya's one-party elections involved multiple parliamentary candidates all running on the ticket of the ruling party, and a President selected by the party leadership rather than by the electorate. Although the contests occasionally involved manipulation by the KANU leadership to make sure that their favored candidate won, they were generally competitive. Hornsby and Throup (1992: 191) note that "candidates for the party nomination [were] vetted by party personnel and some [were] denied KANU endorsement and [were] thus barred. However, apart from the well-publicized barrings of ex-KPU leaders in 1974 and 1979, this was not a major problem."

Take the example of Kisumu Rural, a homogeneously Luo constituency that had voted almost unanimously for the KPU in the "little general election" of 1966. In the 1969 and 1974 one-party elections, this unity disappeared, as political competition came to revolve around the conflict among three major clans: the Seme (with roughly 45 percent of the population), the Nyahera (with roughly 20 percent), and the Kapuonja (with 15 percent). In both elections, the winning candidate came from the largest of these groups, the Seme. In 1969, W. N. Ayah was the only Seme in the race, and he won with 52 percent of the vote. In 1974, a second Seme candidate, Onyango Ayoki, also ran (and won).[15] The two elections were striking not just for how closely voters hewed to clan lines, but for how much the outcomes differed from the results of the multi-party contest held in that constituency in 1966, in which the KPU candidate, Okelo Odongo, won support from the members of all Luo clans and captured fully 97 percent of the vote.

Gem constituency, which neighbors Kisumu Rural to the northwest, exhibited an identical pattern of Luo bloc voting in the late 1960s followed by a shift to clan voting in the one-party elections that followed. Although Gem was not one of the six Central Nyanza constituencies to hold elections in 1966, it did hold a multi-party by-election in 1969 just before the suspension of multi-party competition (Okumu 1969). In that contest, the KPU candidate, Wasonga Sijeyo, depicted his KANU opponent, Wycliffe Rading Omolo, as a Kikuyu agent who had "betrayed his own people." Sijeyo portrayed himself, meanwhile, as "holding the fort against the advancing Kikuyu army in which Rading Omolo was playing a major role" (ibid.: 15). The strategy worked. Sijeyo won the seat with 90 percent of the vote. In the four one-party elections that followed, however, the centrality of the Luo versus Kikuyu cleavage gave way to voting based on membership in the Kojuodhi and Kwenda clans (Alila 1984). In the new one-party context, clan membership trumped tribal affiliation.

In 1979, the centrality of the Kojuodhi/Kwenda cleavage was challenged when a man named Otieno Ambala entered the race. Ambala, though a member of the Kwenda clan, was *ja Alego* (a settler from the neighboring area of Alego), and his opponents sought to undermine his candidacy by asserting that only *jogem asili* ("true sons of Gem") should rightfully represent the constituency in Parliament (ibid.). In the end,

[15] Even dividing the vote between them, the Seme were still sufficiently large to beat their Nyahera and Kapuonja opponents. I thank Timothy Ayieko for his help in identifying the clan backgrounds of the candidates.

Ambala was able to defeat this line of attack and win the election.[16] But the fact that the challenge was even attempted reinforces the point about the importance of local authenticity in one-party elections. In 1966, voters in Gem, as throughout Kenya, understood themselves as members of a homogeneous ethno-regional bloc and voted accordingly, overwhelmingly delivering their seat to a candidate whose party affiliation designated him as a representative of their regional group. In that context, there would have been no question about Ambala's authenticity as a Luo. But in the one-party setting, a candidate's status within the local community was what mattered. The shift to one-party rule transformed the salient cleavage dimension and, with it, the criteria people applied to determine who was and was not a member of their ethnic group. This transformed political allies into political adversaries and fellow group members into ethnic outsiders.

## *The Return of Multi-Party Rule in the 1990s*

With the reintroduction of multi-party competition in the early 1990s, the relevant lines of ethnic cleavage changed once again. In 1992, Kenya held its first multi-party election in more than twenty-five years, and the transition back to multi-party competition brought with it a shift back to the patterns of regional ethnic voting and alliance building that had predominated in the immediate post-independence era. Throup and Hornsby describe the change:

> In previous elections, in the one-party state, the main electoral factors had been clanism and localism ... Many observers and candidates expected that the 1992 general election would be fought on the same basis ... This was not to be ... In the end ... regional and ethnic blocs were to prove the key to the outcome (1998: 339).

Later, they make this point even more clearly:

> If the December 1992 General Election demonstrated anything, it was the importance of party and ethnicity in Kenyan politics ... Every [single-party] General Election in independent Kenya had pointed to the vital role of the individual politician. Now, with the reimposition of a more fundamental set of divisions,

[16] The fact that Ambala was able to win despite the *ja Alego* charges can be explained in terms of the model presented in Chapter 5. In this particular situation, Kwenda *jogem asili* were forced to choose between their insider status as "true sons of Gem" (which would lead them to turn their backs on Ambala) and their membership in the Kwenda clan (which would lead them to embrace Ambala). They chose the latter because, though both coalitions were winning, the Kwenda coalition was *minimum* winning.

> most communities rejected the politics of . . . clanism. Once the single-party state was swept away and ethnically based opposition parties emerged, individual candidates counted for much less than their party and the identity of its presidential candidate . . . *Neo-patrimonialism shifted from the micro- to the macro-level.* (ibid.: 589 [italics added])

The return to multi-party competition did nothing to change Kenyans' assumptions about whether or not patronage distribution would follow ethnic lines: they continued to assume that it would. Nor did it alter their beliefs that they needed to support candidates from their own groups. But it completely changed the criteria they used to determine who were, or were not, fellow group members. Whereas local identities had defined group membership and served as axes of electoral competition in the one-party era, national-level identities and cleavages assumed these roles in the new multi party setting, just as they had in the multi-party elections of the immediate post-independence era.

This shift in the relevant basis of political competition was reflected in the extremely high geographic concentration of the vote in 1992 and 1997. Whereas one-party elections had tended to be fairly close contests, a large number of the 1992 and 1997 races were won in landslides. Indeed, so strongly did parties draw on their regional bases in 1992 and 1997 that Barkan and Ng'ethe (1998) describe the elections as sets of geographically distinct one-party-dominant contests. Roughly 90 percent of voters from the Kikuyu-dominated districts of Central Province and the southeastern part of the Rift Valley supported candidates from the two Kikuyu-led political parties, the Democratic Party (DP) and the Forum for the Restoration of Democracy-Asili (FORD-Asili).[17] KANU candidates won roughly 90 percent of the vote in the Kalenjin home districts.[18] And an equally high share of voters in Luo-dominated constituencies supported Odinga's Forum for the Restoration of Democracy-Kenya (FORD-Kenya) in 1992 and his son's National Development Party (NDP) in 1997.[19]

[17] The DP's leader was Mwai Kabaki; FORD-Asili's leader was Kenneth Matiba. FORD-Asili boycotted the 1997 election, so, in that year, Kikuyu voters focused their support on the DP.

[18] When Kenyatta died in August 1978, he was succeeded as KANU leader by Daniel arap Moi, a Kalenjin, and KANU's principal ethnic support base shifted from the Kikuyu to the Kalenjin.

[19] When Oginga Odinga died in 1994, the mantle of Luo leader passed to his son Raila and FORD-Kenya split into hostile camps. One faction was led by Raila; the other by Kijana Wamalwa, a Luhya. Wamalwa ultimately won the power struggle, and Odinga split off to form his own party, the NDP. FORD-Kenya then came to be identified as the "Luhya party" and the NDP as the "Luo party."

In Kisumu Rural and Gem, the two constituencies discussed earlier, FORD-Kenya's parliamentary candidates won 91 and 95 percent of the vote, respectively, in 1992. This was an almost exact replication of the overwhelming support won by the KPU candidates in 1966 and 1969, and a complete departure from the much more closely fought elections of the one-party era.

This unity-within-regions in 1992 and 1997 did not just happen. It was painstakingly cultivated by the leaders of each party. Throughout the 1992 campaign in the Rift Valley, KANU candidates stressed "the need for Kalenjin unity in the face of the opposition threat" (Oyugi 1997: 53). To foster that unity, they "exacerbated fears among the Maasai, Kalenjin and the other pastoral 'tribes' that a Kikuyu victory would mean that their land would be expropriated by Kikuyu settlers" (Throup and Hornsby 1998: 341). Just as the ANC and the UPND in Zambia had sought to unify Tonga-speakers by invoking the threat to their cattle, KANU campaigners sought to unify their Kalenjin base – and to augment it with their fellow KAMATUSA (i.e., Maasai, Turkana, and Samburu) pastoralists – by conjuring up the threat posed to their grazing lands by the Kikuyu.

Opposition parties also "made open use of tribal solidarity arguments" (ibid.: 349). For example, in Laipika West,

> FORD-Asili's Njenga Mungai campaigned on a strongly ethnic ticket, arguing that the Kikuyu needed to recapture the Presidency and the government for their tribe. He claimed, for example, that if the GEMA people did not vote for [FORD-Asili presidential candidate Kenneth] Matiba, the Presidency would never return to Kikuyuland. (ibid.)

Mungai's strategy, like KANU's in the Rift Valley, was simultaneously to rally his tribal group by presenting the election as a contest between the Kikuyu and other ethnic groups and, through his invocation of GEMA, to extend the boundaries of his natural support coalition to include related peoples (in this case, the Embu and Meru) that grouped themselves under the broader Kikuyu umbrella. Such attempts at ethno-regional coalition-building were nowhere clearer than in the case of Safina Party, whose very name, which means "ark" in Swahili, constituted an explicit call for the Mijikenda peoples to unite under the banner of a single political organization.[20]

[20] One of the party's founders, Richard Leakey, writes that the party's name was part of an explicit effort to unite and win the support of the disgruntled peoples of the coast. "Kiswahili was originally a language of the coastal peoples . . . the government had been hostile to these citizens, and of course, they, in turn, felt as if they weren't

Not surprisingly, these attempts to build ethnically defined regional coalitions were met by efforts to break them up. In some cases, these coalition-breaking efforts involved the instigation of violence. It is well documented that the KANU regime incited ethnic clashes in the run-up to the 1992 election (Throup and Hornsby 1998; Kenya Human Rights Commission 1998). Part of the rationale for doing this was to bear out President Daniel arap Moi's prediction that the return to multi-party politics would send the country into chaos. Yet a second, more insidious, rationale was to solidify the ruling party's support base and to weaken those of the various opposition parties. This is why so much of the violence fomented by KANU in the run-up to both the 1992 and 1997 elections occurred in President Moi's Kalenjin ethnic homeland and in areas adjacent to opposition strongholds. In the former, the violence was part of an attempt to drive non-KAMATUSA – particularly Kikuyu – settlers from the area and thus "cleanse" the voting pool of non-KANU loyalists. The violence was also designed to solidify the party's Kalenjin support coalition by deepening the divisions between Kalenjins and Kikuyus.[21] Elsewhere, the violence was instigated to drive wedges between regionally dominant (and opposition-supporting) groups and their potential allies in neighboring districts. For example, in Southern Nyanza, KANU operatives incited violence between the Luo and the neighboring Kisii and Kuria in an attempt to undermine the ability of the Luo-backed NDP to extend its support base beyond its Central Nyanza core area (Kenya Human Rights Commission 1998: 45–55). KANU also instigated violence in Coast Province in 1997 to sow divisions among the various Mijikenda tribes and thereby prevent them from uniting under the umbrella of the Islamic Party of Kenya (ibid.: 56–80). In this respect, KANU's strategy was akin to the UNIP's attempt to break apart the Bemba-speaking coalition in the Mufulira West by-election in 1971 and to the MMD's attempt to disrupt the Lozi-speaking coalition in 1993 (as described in Chapter 7). The difference, of course, is that KANU's coalition-destroying efforts involved violence, whereas the UNIP's and the MMD's did not.

More systematic evidence for both the ethno-regional basis of Kenya's voting patterns in 1992 and the dramatic change that the transition to multi-party politics brought in the salience of local and national-scale

really a part of the country. Safina would invite them . . . to be part of the change that we hoped to bring to our country" (Leakey 2001: 296).

21 For a more general discussion of how violence is used to polarize voters for electoral purposes, see Wilkinson (2004).

Table 9.1. *Ethno-Regional Voting in Kenya's 1992 Multi-Party Election (number of cases)*

| | Is the party on whose ticket the candidate is running associated with the ethno-regional group dominant in the region?[a] | |
|---|---|---|
| | Yes | No |
| Candidate won seat[b] | 75 | 5 |
| Candidate did not win seat | 15 | 77 |

*Note:* Includes only candidates who also ran in the same constituency in 1988.
[a] DP and FORD-Asili are both coded as Kikuyu parties, despite the fact that DP is more properly seen as representing the northern Kikuyu and FORD-Asili as representing the southern Kikuyu.
[b] Eight winning candidates ran unopposed. All of them were running on the tickets of parties associated with the dominant ethno-regional group in the constituency.

ethnic identities is presented in Tables 9.1 and 9.2. Table 9.1 compares the success rates in the 1992 election of candidates that were and were not running on the tickets of parties that were associated with the dominant ethno-regional group in the constituency. Table 9.2 compares the performance of candidates that ran in the same constituencies in both 1988 and 1992 to test whether, as the argument developed in the book would lead us to expect, candidates running on the tickets of parties associated with the "right" party for their constituency in 1992 out-performed their 1988 results, and candidates running on the tickets of the "wrong" party for their constituency in 1992 under-performed them.

To carry out these tests, I first identified all candidates that had run in the same constituencies in both elections. Selecting candidates in this way was not strictly necessary for the analysis of ethno-regional party voting (summarized in Table 9.1). But, when I compare candidates' performance across institutional settings (in Table 9.2), it allows me to control for the interaction between candidates' personal attributes (including their ethnic background) and the ethnic composition of the electorate they are facing. This provides a much cleaner test of the effects of institutional change. Selecting candidates in this way yielded a total of 172 cases.

My first test was to see whether, as the model would lead us to expect, candidates running on the tickets of parties that were presumed to be affiliated with the dominant ethno-regional group (i.e., KANU with the Kalenjin and their KAMATUSA allies; FORD-Kenya with the Luo;

Table 9.2. *How Did Electoral Performance in Kenya Vary Between 1988 and 1992 Among Candidates Who Ran in Both Elections? (number of cases)*

| | Candidates running on tickets of parties affiliated with the dominant ethno-regional group in the constituency | Candidates running on tickets of parties *not* affiliated with the dominant ethno-regional group in the constituency |
|---|---|---|
| Candidate out-performed his/her 1988 result in 1992 | 45 | 4 |
| Candidate under-performed his/her 1988 result in 1992 | 8 | 58 |

FORD-Asili and DP with the Kikuyu and their GEMA allies) were more likely to win their seats than candidates running on the tickets of parties affiliated with other regions or language groups. Table 9.1 presents the results of this analysis.[22] The results show unambiguously that party labels and the ethno-regional orientations they convey affect voters' choices. Among candidates running on the tickets of parties that were associated in voters' minds with the dominant ethno-regional group in the constituency, 83 percent (75 of 90) were victorious. Among candidates running on the tickets of parties whose ethno-regional commitments were presumed to lie elsewhere, only 6 percent (5 of 82) managed to win their seats.

The more important testable implication of the theory, however, is that candidates running in 1988 and 1992 should have fared predictably better or worse in 1992 depending on whether the parties on whose tickets they were running were associated in voters' minds with the ethno-regional group that predominates in their area. For example, we would expect that a FORD-Asili candidate running in Kiambu district in 1992 would do better than she did when she ran in the same seat in 1988, since Kiambu is a Kikuyu stronghold and her FORD-Asili label would give her an advantage over her competitors that she lacked in the previous election. Similarly, we would expect a candidate competing for the Kiambu seat on a FORD-Kenya or a KANU ticket in 1992 to perform worse than in 1988, since her party label would associate her with the interests of people from

[22] I am indebted to Judy Geist for providing me with the electoral data and for her generous help with coding the ethno-regional orientations of the political parties and the tribal backgrounds of candidates.

other parts of the country and voters who might have supported her five years earlier would think differently this time around. This example is not just hypothetical. In 1997, President Kenyatta's son Uruhu ran for Parliament on the KANU ticket in Gatundu South (in Kiambu district) and was soundly defeated by an opposition neophyte. Like Bildad Kaggia three decades earlier, Uruhu Kenyatta had impeccable credentials as a true Kikuyu. But his party label caused voters to view him as working against the interests of the group, and this undermined his candidacy.

To test this expectation, I compared the performance across elections of all 115 candidates that ran in the same constituencies in both 1988 and 1992.[23] If a candidate won in 1988 but lost in 1992, then I coded him as having under-performed his one-party result in the multi-party election. If the candidate lost in 1988 but won in 1992, then I coded him as having out-performed his one-party result. If the candidate either lost or won in both 1988 and 1992, then I compared the candidate's vote share in each contest with the share he would have received if voters had assigned their votes randomly (i.e., 50 percent in a two-way race; 33 percent in a three-way race, etc.). Thus if a candidate ran against just one opponent in 1988 but against four others in 1992 and received 40 percent of the vote in both elections, he would be coded as having out-performed his 1988 results in the second contest, since winning 40 percent in a five-way race is much harder than winning 40 percent in a two-way contest. Table 9.2 presents the results of the analysis.

In 103 of the 115 cases (90 percent of the time), the increase or decrease in the candidates' vote share across the two elections could have been predicted by whether or not the candidates were running on the ticket of a party associated with the dominant ethno-regional group in their constituency in 1992. If candidates were, then they won a larger share of the vote in the multi-party contest than in the one-party contest; if they were not, then they did better in the one-party race. Again, the findings are exactly in keeping with our theoretical expectations. They also bear strong resemblance to the Zambian findings in the parallel analysis presented in Chapter 8.

This analysis does not reveal precisely what kinds of identities motivated voters in 1988 – and absent reliable information about candidates' sub-tribal and clan backgrounds it would be difficult to know for certain

[23] Fifty-seven of the candidates that ran in both 1988 and 1992 ran unopposed in one or the other of these elections, and were thus dropped from the analysis.

what did. But it does show clearly that these identities were different from the ethno-regional ones that motivated Kenyans' voting decisions in 1992. As in Zambia, the evidence suggests that institutional change brings changes in the kinds of identities that political actors use to define where their interests lie. Taken as a whole, the Kenyan case provides strong support for the generalizability of the Zambian findings.

# 10

## *Beyond Regime Change, Beyond Africa*

Conceived narrowly, this is a book about how transitions between multiparty and one-party rule affect the relative political salience of tribal and language group identities in Zambia. But it is also a book about how political institutions affect social identities more broadly. Its empirical focus may be on an African case, but its implications extend well beyond the African continent. The specific argument the book advances is about how regime change affects people's choices between tribal and linguistic identities, but the general logic it articulates extends well beyond these particular independent and dependent variables. The logic it provides offers a general set of guidelines for thinking about when and why people choose the social identities they do and when and why one social cleavage rather than another becomes salient in political interactions. It also provides a vocabulary and a conceptual framework for thinking about the many different aspects of identity change. Thus while the specific application presented in the preceding chapters may be somewhat narrow, the implications of the analysis and the applications of the argument and framework are potentially far reaching.

### INSTITUTIONS AND BOUNDARY CHANGE

Take the argument about how institutions affect the kinds of identities that become salient. One of the book's central premises is that the identities and cleavages that will emerge as bases of political competition will depend on the boundaries of the arena in which political and social interactions take place. A key corollary is that changes in these boundaries will generate changes in the cleavages that matter for political conflict. In Chapter 5, I provided some illustrations of how changing the boundaries of the political system – by redistricting, partition, state-building, and decolonization – have led to changes in the kinds of identities that actors choose and, through these choices, changes in the salient axes of political and social division. Such examples, and the arguments that account for them, are not new. We have long known that identities are context dependent and that the boundaries of the political system are one of the key determinants of "context" (Horowitz 1975, 1985; Young 1976). Where I go beyond these arguments is by showing that changes in the physical boundaries of the political system are not necessary to generate changes in actors' identity choices. In Zambia, the shift in salient ethnic cleavages was triggered not by changes in the country's internal or external borders but by the changes in the effective arena of political competition caused by the back-and-forth transition between multi-party and one-party rule. Changes in regime type altered the boundaries of the political arena in a way that was analogous to the changes caused by alterations in the physical frontiers of the political system in the cases described earlier. By changing nothing more than a single clause in the national constitution the clause prohibiting or permitting the existence of multiple political parties – Zambia's leaders altered the lens through which political actors viewed their country's ethnic landscape and transformed the kinds of identities they employed as foundations for political coalition-building.

Although the case treated in this book highlights the identity-shaping effects of regime change, shifts from multi-party to one-party rule are not the only source of institutionally driven boundary change. Another way changes in formal rules can alter the boundaries of the effective arena of political competition is when they change the scope of the community that is permitted to participate in politics. Changes in franchise restrictions are a key example. In India, a strict property franchise in the 1920s and early 1930s restricted the electorate to upper caste voters and caused politics to revolve around divisions within the upper caste community (Wilkinson 2004). But with the gradual extension of the franchise to all adults by the 1950s, upper caste voters shrank to between 10 and 15 percent of the electorate in most states and intra–upper caste divisions ceased to be viable bases for political mobilization. In the new context, upper caste parties shifted their appeals to focus on conflicts between Hindus and Muslims (ibid.). By effectively altering the boundaries of the political arena, the expansion of the franchise changed the incentives for political actors to play one identity instead of the other, and this generated a shift in the dimension of social cleavage that came to organize politics.

Another illustration comes from Zaire (now the Democratic Republic of Congo). When the first competitive elections were held in that country in 1957, they were restricted to its seven major cities. Each city served as its own separate electoral arena. In this context, the dominant ethnic cleavages were city-specific: Kongo versus Ngala in Kinshasa, Lulua versus Luba in Kananga, Mongo versus Ngombe in Mbandaka, Kasaian versus "authentic Katangan" in Lubumbashi (Young and Turner 1985: 143). With the introduction of nationwide elections for national and provincial assemblies in May 1960, however, the boundaries of the effective political arena expanded and new ethnic cleavages became politically salient. Whereas tribal distinctions had been central in the politics of the towns, regional cleavages became the axis of political competition in the broader national setting, and political elites began "defining region rather than [tribe] as the political building block" (ibid.: 150). As with the expansion of the franchise in India, the extension of political competition from the towns to the country as a whole altered the kinds of identities that political actors found it advantageous to draw upon.

Whereas most political institutions affect the identities people choose by defining a fixed arena of political competition (and thus generate identity change only when they are altered), federalism provides opportunities for boundary change within the political system itself. By defining multiple levels of political competition, federal institutions give rise to different salient ethnic cleavages and different patterns of ethnic competition at each level.[1] They also provide opportunities for the strategic exploitation of this multi-dimensionality by skillful politicians. Perhaps the most famous example of this is Abraham Lincoln's brilliant question to Stephen Douglas in his 1858 speech at Freeport, Illinois (Riker 1986). At the time, Lincoln was running for the U.S. Senate seat in Illinois against Douglas, the country's foremost Northern Democrat and the likely Democratic nominee for president in 1860. Although Lincoln hoped to win the Senate seat, he also knew that he was probably going to run for

[1] This is the intuition behind the conjecture of Linz and Stepan (1992) that founding democratic elections generate different patterns of ethnic competition when they are held at the "all union" (i.e., federal) level than when they are held at the level of the sub-national units of the political system. Although their argument leads to a different prediction about the kinds of cleavages that will emerge as salient in federal elections from the one presented in this book – they claim that such elections will generate "strong incentives for political activists to create all-union parties, and an all-union agenda" (124–25), whereas my argument suggests that political actors will have incentives to form parties along lines that divide the country into large, nationally viable ethnic units – both approaches emphasize the way that federal systems provide multiple levels of political competition and generate incentives for political actors to play different ethnic cards at each level.

President himself two years later – likely against Douglas. Knowing that what Douglas said during the Senate race would be remembered in the presidential campaign, Lincoln asked Douglas to make public his position on the expansion of slavery to the western territories. The brilliance of the question was that the Illinois electorate and the Democratic Party nationwide had different positions on the issue, and Lincoln knew that by posing the question he was forcing Douglas to take a position that would undermine his viability in one arena or the other. If Douglas indicated that he supported the expansion of slavery, he would hurt his chances in the Senate election in abolitionist Illinois but help himself with the national Democratic Party, whose support he would need to win the presidential nomination in 1860. If he indicated that he was opposed to the expansion of slavery to the territories, he would help himself in the Senate race but hurt his presidential prospects. The trap was ingenious, and the federal system made it possible. Although not an example of ethnic mobilization, Lincoln's ploy nonetheless illustrates how different electoral arenas generate different optimal strategies and how a skillful politician can exploit them.

The issue of Elian Gonzalez, the five-year-old Cuban boy who washed onto a Florida beach in the middle of the 2000 presidential election season, offers a parallel example. National opinion overwhelmingly favored returning the child to Cuba. But the vocal and politically important South Florida Cuban community strongly opposed his repatriation. Candidates George W. Bush and Al Gore were thus forced to choose between positions that would either endear them to voters in the country as a whole but turn the Cuban community against them (and quite possibly lose one of them Florida's Electoral College votes) or make them heroes of South Florida's Cubans (and thus improve their electoral chances in that key state) while alienating a much larger number of more widely dispersed voters. As with the Lincoln example, the dilemma had its origins in the country's federal structure (and, in this case, in the fact that this structure is central to the Electoral College).[2]

An explicitly "ethnic" example of how federalism provides opportunities for political actors to play different strategies in different arenas is offered by the case of the Agila Development Association (ADA) in Nigeria. The ADA was formed in 1964 by Idoma landholders in Agila, in Benue State, northern Nigeria, to resist the encroachment by Igbo

[2] At the time, of course, neither candidate had any idea just how important Florida would turn out to be in the outcome of the election.

migrants from eastern Nigeria on Idoma community land. At the local level, this land conflict was viewed by all parties in tribal terms as a struggle between Igbo outsiders and Idoma sons of the soil. But when the ADA decided to appeal for help in the matter to national politicians, its representatives strategically repackaged the conflict as one between Easterners and Northerners. When they approached the premier of the Northern Region to ask for his intercession in the matter, they did so

> in the name of the Northern Region and not on the basis of Idoma ethnic identity. Agila people were portrayed as loyal northerners at the mercy of a rapacious eastern Nigeria. They were characterized as valiant defenders of northern interests who were expending huge financial resources to ensure northern victory over the Eastern Region. (Agbese 1996: 150)

Agbese observes that "by couching the conflict in regional terms, the ADA was seeking wider sympathies and greater legitimacy than what would be attained by depicting the conflict in [tribal] terms" (ibid.). Shifting the arena in which the appeal was being made from the local to the national level – a tactic made possible by Nigeria's federal structure – led to a strategic shift in the terms in which the conflict was presented.

Like the Zambia case on which this book focuses, all of these examples show how institutional rules define arenas of political competition and how the boundaries of those arenas generate incentives for mobilizing particular dimensions of ethnic identity: caste in restricted-franchise India, religion once the franchise was expanded universally; tribe at the town and village level in Zaire and Nigeria, region at the national level. Although I do not provide them here, one could easily construct ethnic identity matrices like the ones I introduced in Chapter 5 to show how the changes in the boundaries of the political arena produced the changes in the ethnic identities that became axes of competition and conflict in each of these cases.

Ethnic identity matrices are useful for more than just showing how boundary changes affect the kinds of identities that actors choose. They can also help account for why particular social cleavages emerge as salient when the boundaries of the political arena are fixed.

## ETHNIC IDENTITY MATRICES

Ethnic identity matrices are designed to account for outcomes in settings where power-holders are chosen through a process in which group size matters and where the plurality group wins. While this includes settings

| nationality \ language | Moldovan | Russian | Other | |
|---|---|---|---|---|
| Moldovan | 50 | 11 | | 61 |
| Russian | 5 | | | |
| Ukrainian | | | | |
| Other | | | | |
| | 55 | | | |

Figure 10.1. An Ethnic Identity Matrix for Moldova

where the winner is chosen through a set of explicit electoral rules, it need not be limited to such contexts. As long as winning is in some way related to group size, the model should generate at least suggestive predictions about the kinds of ethnic cleavages that will emerge as salient.

To illustrate how ethnic identity matrices can help account for why some social identities become axes of political competition rather than others, take the case of Moldova, where language group differences have been central to the politics of the post-Soviet era (Eyl and Smith 1996). It need not have been this way. Politics could just as easily have come to revolve around competition among members of the country's three principal nationality communities: Moldovans, Russians, and Ukrainians. Indeed, given that the break-up of the Soviet Union proceeded along nationality lines, one would have thought that nationality differences would have been particularly salient to people in post-Soviet Moldova. Yet nationality identities were trumped by language. The ethnic identity matrix for the country depicted in Figure 10.1 suggests a possible explanation.[3] Moldovan-speaking Moldovans are the pivot.[4] They can choose to identify themselves in terms of nationality, in which case they will view fellow Moldovan Russian-speakers as their co-ethnics, or they can choose to identify themselves in terms of language, in which case they will view Moldovan Russian-speakers as ethnic outsiders. Which do they choose? If they want to form a minimum winning coalition, then they will do best by turning their backs on their co-nationals and trying to make politics about the competition between Moldovan-speakers and Russian-speakers. This

[3] I thank Roger Petersen for including this example in an unpublished paper. For further examples of the interplay between linguistic and nationality divisions in the Soviet successor states, see Laitin (1998).

[4] Data on language group and nationality group population shares is from Kolsto and Melberg (2002). Language figures are based on survey data and refer to "the language one thinks in."

religion

| language/tribe | Muslim | Christian | Traditional | |
|---|---|---|---|---|
| Hausa | 29 | 0 | | 29 |
| Yoruba | 21 | | | |
| Igbo | | | | |
| Tiv | | | | |
| Ibibio | | | | |
| Kanuri | | | | |
| Edo | | | | |
| Idoma | | | | |
| Other | | | | |
| | 50 | | | |

Figure 10.2. An Ethnic Identity Matrix for Nigeria

may explain why language differences have been more important than nationality differences in Moldova's post-Soviet politics.

Or, take the case of Nigeria, which is divided at the national level along lines of language/tribe and religion. As we have seen, Nigeria's federal system causes different cleavages to be salient at different levels of the political system. But at the national level, language/tribe has historically trumped religion. Again, an ethnic identity matrix for the country offers an explanation for why. As Figure 10.2 makes clear, the key group is the Hausa Muslims, who must choose whether to emphasize the country's religious differences and identify themselves as Muslims or to focus on tribal/linguistic distinctions and identify themselves as Hausa.[5] They will be in the winning coalition either way. But if they play the Hausa versus Yoruba versus Igbo (i.e, linguistic/tribal) card and successfully divide the country along linguistic/tribal lines, they will have to share the spoils of power with fewer other co-ethnics. These incentives may explain why politics in Nigeria has tended to revolve around differences among language groups and tribes rather than around differences between Christians and Muslims.

It is important to emphasize that the "explanations" that these ethnic identity matrices provide are conditional on a set of rather strong assumptions. For a determinative cleavage outcome to be reached, it must be the case that the only thing that actors care about is maximizing their access to patronage resources and that the only way they can get access to these

[5] Data on religious group and tribal/language group population shares is from the 2001 *World Factbook* (CIA 2001).

resources is by having a member of their own ethnic group win political power. It must also be the case that contests over political power are won by the plurality group rather than through some more complicated rule. Finally, actors must be sufficiently suspicious of the willingness of members of other groups to help them so that cross-group coalitions are not possible. Although these assumptions are probably a reasonable approximation of the conditions in many contexts, they will not hold everywhere. The predictions that ethnic identity matrices generate should therefore be taken as hypotheses to be tested, as baseline starting points for potential explanations rather than as definitive predictions that should be expected to be borne out in every case.

Indeed, when treated in this way, ethnic identity matrices can yield useful insights even when the predictions they generate turn out to be wrong. For example, while the ethnic identity matrix for Nigeria correctly predicts the salience of tribal/linguistic cleavages over religious ones, it *incorrectly* predicts the salience of religion over ancestral city (or sub tribe) in the Nigerian region of Yorubaland. The question of why ancestral city identities are more politically important than religious identities in Yorubaland is the motivating puzzle in David Laitin's *Hegemony and Culture* (1986), one of the handful of studies that explicitly addresses the question of why one axis of social identity emerges as a basis of political conflict rather than another. Unlike most of Nigeria, which is fairly homogeneously Christian or Muslim, Yorubaland is almost equally divided between members of these two religious communities. Laitin's puzzle is why, despite deep socio-cultural divisions between Christians and Muslims in this region, religious identities are so much less important in local political and social affairs than are identities based on peoples' ties to their ancestral cities. Indeed, the ethnic identity matrix for Yorubaland, depicted in Figure 10.3, suggests that the outcome should be the other way around. Oyos are the largest ancestral city/sub-tribal group in Yorubaland, and Muslims are the largest religious community.[6] Thus Oyo Muslims are the pivot. If they want to build a minimum coalition then they should band together with their fellow Oyos and define the region's politics as a struggle among ancestral cities/sub-tribes. However, if they play this strategy, non-Oyo Muslims will still be numerous enough to beat their coalition (in the language of the model, $y > w + x$). This should force the Oyo Muslims to change their tactics and embrace their religious background instead of their ancestral city identity. To guarantee their participation

[6] I thank David Laitin for providing the approximate population shares.

| ancestral city (sub-tribe) | religion: Muslim | Christian | Traditional | |
|---|---|---|---|---|
| Oyo | 12 | 13 | | 25 |
| Ife | 28 | | | |
| Ilorin | | | | |
| Ijebu | | | | |
| Egba | | | | |
| Ondo | | | | |
| | 40 | | | |

Figure 10.3. An Ethnic Identity Matrix for Yorubaland

in the winning coalition, they should embrace their identities as Muslims, and religion should emerge as the salient axis of political division in the region.

As Laitin makes clear, this is not the outcome we observe: politics in Yorubaland revolves around ancestral city/sub-tribal cleavages rather than religious cleavages. One way to interpret the failure of the ethnic identity matrix to predict the observed outcome correctly is to conclude that the model on which it is based is wrong. Another, more constructive, approach is to ask why actors in Yorubaland are not behaving in the way the model would predict. Because the model is based on such a spare and reasonable set of assumptions, its failures can point to puzzles that must be accounted for. By identifying themselves in terms of their ancestral city rather than their world religion, Oyo Muslims are forming a larger coalition than they must and are accepting a smaller payoff than they otherwise might receive. This naturally leads to the question of why, and it forces us to consider – as Laitin does – variables that lie outside the model. It also confirms Laitin's intuition that the salience of ancestral city identities is indeed a puzzle that requires explanation. The larger point is that, like any parsimonious model, the ethnic identity matrix can be a useful a tool for knowledge generation even when its predictions are not borne out by the evidence.

Apart from their predictions about macro-level cleavage outcomes, ethnic identity matrices can also generate useful (and testable) predictions about the behavior of individual actors. In working through the implications of an ethnic identity matrix, our tendency thus far has been to focus principally on the incentives facing members of the pivot group ($w$), since its identity choice determines the ethnic cleavage outcome. But the matrix also generates expectations about the behavior of other players – that is, people in $x$, $y$, and $z$. For example, in Nigeria, we would expect to see

Hausa Muslims (the pivot) define themselves in linguistic/tribal terms. But we would also expect to see non-Hausa Muslims insisting to them that their true interests lie with their fellow Muslims. We might even see this group trying to instigate polarizing conflict along religious lines to force Hausas to mobilize as Muslims, much as Wilkinson (2004) shows Hindu nationalists do in India to prevent Hindu voters from voting along lines other than religion. In Moldova, where Russian-speakers are left out of a winning coalition formed along language lines, we would expect to see Russian-speakers trying to gain admission to the winning coalition by investing in learning Moldovan. We would also expect to see members of the Moldovan-speaking community trying to erect barriers to prevent Russian-speakers from being accepted as full-fledged Moldovan-speakers. We might even expect to see Russian-speakers make a bid to redraw the boundaries of the political arena by seceding en masse and creating their own republic. Indeed, this is exactly what happened in September 1990, when the largely Russophone territory on the left bank of the Dniester River seceded from Moldova and declared itself the Dniester Republic.

In constructing the ethnic identity matrix for a given case, the ethnic cleavage structure of the political system is taken as an exogenous input into the analysis.[7] Of course, this does not mean that explaining a political system's ethnic cleavage structure is not an important part of accounting for why one basis of ethnic division ultimately becomes the cleavage around which political competition and conflict takes place. It just means that the explanation for that cleavage structure must be provided separately from the ethnic identity matrix. Thus, in this book, the task of explaining why Zambians see themselves either in tribal or linguistic terms, and why the landscape of tribal groups contains seventy-odd units whereas the landscape of language groups contains just four units, is accomplished in Part I, before the ethnic identity matrix for Zambia is even introduced. Yet, although I have not emphasized it thus far, part of what makes ethnic identity matrices powerful tools is that they also provide insight into how and why ethnic cleavage structures themselves might change.

Ethnic cleavage structures can change in three different ways: new dimensions of potentially mobilizable ethnic division can emerge, the relative sizes of groups on a particular cleavage dimension can change, and the

[7] Recall from Chapter 1 that a political system's ethnic cleavage structure is defined by the number of cleavage dimensions that the system contains and the number and relative sizes of the groups on each cleavage dimension.

groups on a given cleavage dimension can amalgamate or divide. In the vocabulary of the model, the first kind of ethnic cleavage change involves the introduction of a new cleavage dimension, C. The second and third kinds of change involve changes in the sizes of $a_1$, $a_2$, $a_3$, and so on (or $b_1$, $b_2$, $b_3$, and so on) and their recombinations. Each type of change is driven by a different kind of identity entrepreneurship. One of the strengths of the ethnic identity matrix heuristic is that it generates predictions about the categories of people from which we are most likely to see emerge identity entrepreneurs of each type.

People whose groups are shut out of power by the logic of minimum winning coalition-building – the "outs" in Figures 5.4 and 5.5 – will be the ones most likely to invest in trying to introduce a new cleavage dimension. Since they can never be members of the winning coalition by playing one of their available ethnic cards, they will be the ones who will try to invoke a new axis of ethnic division. Thus we might expect to see minority immigrant groups trying to introduce a new cleavage dimension, "immigrants versus natives," in New York City, or in California, a cleavage dimension "white versus non-white." In both such efforts, the crux of the identity project would be to convince people that "immigrant" or "non-white" is as meaningful a social category as Dominican, Haitian, black, Latino, and the others currently in use.

The new cleavage dimension that is invoked need not be an ethnic one. It could also be a non-ethnic cleavage like class. Indeed, one of the implications of the model is that members of ethnic communities that are not in the $w + x$ or $w + y$ winning coalition will be the initial and/or the most vocal adherents of socialist parties. For similar reasons, this is the segment of the population from whose ranks we would expect demands for secession or the devolution of power to sub-national units to originate. Basque, Eritrean, and Slovenian secessionism, as well as the demands of Kenya's KAMATUSA tribes for *Majimboism* (regional autonomy), offer suggestive illustrations. These are not examples of identity entrepreneurship – members of these groups are trying to redraw the boundaries of the political system, not introduce a new cleavage dimension – but the motivation follows the same logic.

In the example of Moldova, we have already seen an illustration of the second kind of identity entrepreneurship: individuals in the "out" community investing in acquiring the ethnic attributes that will give them entry into the winning coalition. Thus I noted that the logic of the model would lead us to expect at least some Russian-speakers to invest in learning Moldovan. Note that this kind of identity change is different from

| | | religion | | |
|---|---|---|---|---|
| ideology | Catholic | Presbyterian | Episcopalian | |
| Liberal | 40 | 28 | 2 | 70 |
| Tory | 1 | 9 | 20 | 30 |
| | 41 | 37 | 22 | |

Figure 10.4. An Ethnic Identity Matrix for Nineteenth-Century Ireland, after Extension of the Franchise

the within-repertoire change that I have focused on throughout the book. For a Russian-speaking Moldovan, changing one's identity from Russian-speaking to Moldovan involves no identity entrepreneurship, since the person already is both of these things. But for the person to change his or her identity from Russian-speaking to Moldovan-speaking would involve a significant investment in identity acquisition.

Ireland offers an example of the third kind of ethnic demographic change. At the beginning of the nineteenth century, when the Irish franchise was restricted to upper-class voters, Ireland's Episcopalian minority dominated the country's politics. But as the franchise was gradually extended through the 1830s, the numbers of Presbyterian and Catholic voters came to equal, and eventually far surpass, the number of Episcopalians. Wilkinson writes that "this shift in the distribution of voters threatened to confine the Episcopalians and the Tory party they dominated to a permanent electoral minority in many towns, because most of the newly enfranchised voters supported the Liberals" (2003: 15). The situation is summarized in Figure 10.4. To clarify the situation faced by the Episcopalians, I include all the cells of the matrix rather than just $w$, $x$, and $y$.[8]

As Figure 10.4 makes clear, Episcopalians, who were nearly all upper class and Tory supporting (and were therefore almost entirely in $z$), were left out of the ruling coalition. Moreover, they could expect to remain left out of the ruling coalition for the foreseeable future. The Episcopalian elite's strategy for restoring itself to power involved trying to unite Presbyterians and Episcopalians by emphasizing their shared membership in the umbrella category "Protestant." To do this, the Episcopalian leadership invested in Orangeism, the militantly anti-Catholic movement that it had previously shunned (Wilkinson 2003, 2004).

> In Liverpool, Belfast, and Derry, Tory leaders gave financial and organizational support to Orange Lodges and to inflammatory marches that were deliberately

[8] Estimates of the sizes of each group are from Wilkinson (2003).

| | | religion | |
|---|---|---|---|
| ideology | Protestant | Catholic | |
| Liberal | 30 | 40 | 70 |
| Tory | 29 | 1 | 30 |
| | 59 | 41 | |

Figure 10.5. The Ethnic Identity Matrix for Nineteenth-Century Ireland Redrawn

taken through Catholic areas as a way of generating a counter-reaction... [and] mak[ing] their claims of "Protestantism under threat" seem more credible, and therefore raise the salience of the Protestant-Catholic dimension over other categories. (Wilkinson 2003: 17)

By investing in Orangeism, the Episcopalian minority was able to transform the salient religious divisions in Ireland from the tripartite cleavage between Catholics, Presbyterians, and Episcopalians (which kept them in the minority) to the bi-polar one between Protestants and Catholics (which put them in the ruling coalition). As Figure 10.5 illustrates, the transformation of the relevant set of religious categories – achieved through the support for the Orange Lodges – led to a redrawing of the ethnic identity matrix and transformed the Episcopalian Tories from losers into winners.

Both for the macro-level explanations they offer for why politics revolves around one social cleavage rather than another and for the micro-level predictions they generate about the kinds of appeals and identity investments that particular actors will make, ethnic identity matrices constitute powerful analytic tools. They provide a technology for integrating and applying the accumulated findings about both what ethnicity is and how it is used. Forty years of research has documented that individuals possess multiple ethnic identities and that they use these identities instrumentally to improve their status and economic well-being. Ethnic identity matrices provide a simple yet powerful heuristic for applying these insights to the question of why political actors choose the ethnic identities that they do and why, as a consequence, some ethnic cleavages rather than others become axes of political competition and conflict.

## TOWARD ENDOGENOUS ETHNICITY

In 1967, Seymour Martin Lipset and Stein Rokkan called for sociologists and political scientists to focus their attention on the question of why and when some social cleavages rather than others become politically salient. "Conflicts and controversies can arise out of a great variety of relationships in the social structure," they wrote,

> but only a few of these tend to polarize the politics of any given system. There is a *hierarchy of cleavage bases* in each system and these orders of political primacy not only vary among polities, but also tend to undergo changes over time. Such differences and changes in the political weight of sociocultural cleavages set fundamental problems for comparative research: When is region, language or ethnicity most likely to prove polarizing? When will class take the primacy and when will denominational commitments and religious identities prove equally important cleavage bases? ... Questions such as these will be on the agenda of comparative political sociology for years to come. There is no dearth of hypotheses, but so far very little in the way of systematic analysis. (1967: 6)

Nearly four decades after the publication of Lipset and Rokkan's classic essay, there is still "very little in the way of systematic analysis" of these questions. Significant theoretical progress has been made since that time in explaining variation in the occurrence and intensity of inter-group strife.[9] But comparatively little headway has been made in developing theories to explain variation, either across nations or within countries over time, in the social cleavages that define the basis of political competition and conflict.[10] The principal goal of this book has been to redress this imbalance.

Traditionally, and for understandable reasons, analyses of ethnic conflict have limited their focus to the question of why, where, and when ethnic groups come to blows. In these studies, both the ethnic cleavage along whose lines the conflict is being fought and the set of antagonistic groups that are doing the fighting are taken as givens. Conflict or its absence is the outcome to be explained, and the particular basis of social division that defines the conflict's participants is taken as an exogenous social fact – perhaps an independent variable whose effects on the degree of violence or political instability is something to be tested, but not an outcome that requires explanation in its own right. Thus debates rage about whether linguistic conflicts are more intractable than religious ones; whether conflicts among many small groups generate more violence than conflicts among a smaller number of large ones; whether dispersed groups are more or less rebellious than concentrated ones; and whether

[9] Some of the key contributions include those by Cohen (1974), Tilly (1978), Kasfir (1979), Horowitz (1985, 2001), Brass (1991), Fearon (1994), Laitin (1995), Fearon and Laitin (1996, 2003), Kalyvas (2001), Reilly (2001), Sambanis (2001), Varshney (2002), and Wilkinson (2004).

[10] Laitin (1986) is a notable exception.

hegemonic groups tend to provoke or suppress communal strife. These are all important questions. But what the studies that address them almost always ignore is the fact that the central factors at issue – the number of groups in the political system, their relative sizes, their physical locations, and the particular principle of social division that actors use to distinguish in-group members from outsiders – are themselves products of prior historical and political processes. They are as endogenous to politics and history as the outcomes they are used to explain.

Of course, it is convenient to treat the ethnic cleavage that is salient as exogenous, since this makes it possible to treat it unambiguously as a cause. Moreover, in principle, there is nothing wrong with starting one's explanations for why Group A is fighting Group B by assuming that the cleavage structure that includes these groups is the one that is salient – as it probably is if they are fighting. But if we are interested in a more general understanding of the causes of ethnic conflict in a particular community, or even among a specified set of actors, then we need to account not just for why there is (or is not) violence between these groups but why these groups and not others are even potential combatants in the first place. Whether we are interested in the general question of why there is ethnic conflict in India or the more specific question of why Hindus are rioting against Muslims, we first need to entertain the question of why the conflict in India revolves around religious divisions rather than linguistic or caste divisions. Whether we care about ethnic violence in South Africa generally or about the specific problem of violence between Xhosas and Zulus, we first need to explain why the conflict in South Africa revolves around tribal differences rather than race. The question of why these particular ethnic cleavages matter and the others do not is analytically prior to the question of why there is conflict.

Accounting for the ethnic cleavage that matters, I have shown, involves two distinct explanatory projects. The first is to account for the range of social identities that individuals might conceivably choose as bases of mobilization and political identification. The second is to explain why, from this set of available options, people choose the identities that they do. To return to the metaphor of the card game, explaining why one ethnic cleavage is salient instead of another involves accounting first for why actors hold the identity cards they do and then for why they play one card instead of another. Most studies of ethnic conflict begin their analyses after the cards have already been played. This book argues for starting the explanation at the time they are dealt.

# Appendix A

## *Native Authorities and Tribal Identifications*

Tables 2.1 and 2.2 summarize the changes over time in the population shares of tribes that did and did not have their own Native Authorities.[1] Table 2.1 records the changes in these population shares between 1930/33, shortly after Indirect Rule began, and 1962, the year before it ended.[2] Table 2.2 records changes in tribal population shares between 1930/33 and 1990, when, for the first time, data on self-reported tribal identifications became available. Both tables report only aggregate figures for tribes with and without Native Authorities. Tables A.1 and A.2 break down the figures for the individual tribes in each category for the 1930/33–1962 and 1930/33–1990 periods, respectively.

As Tables A.1 and A.2 make clear, individual tribes within each category vary in the changes that took place in their shares of the national population during each period. Although the population share of all tribes that had their own Native Authorities increased by 6.7 percent between 1930/33 and 1962, the degree of change experienced by individual tribes in this category ranged from +140 percent for the Luchazi to −83 percent for the Chikunda (see Table A.1). Similarly, while the population share of tribes that did not have their own Native Authorities fell during the same period by a weighted average of 28.5 percent, individual tribes in this category varied in their population growth or decline from +304 percent for the Kwandi to −95 percent for the Lushange. Similarly large variation is evident in the figures reported for the growth and decline of both tribes

[1] Tribes were coded as having their own Native Authorities if they were included on the list of Native Authorities after the major reorganization of native administration in 1948.

[2] As I explained in Chapter 2, I take the average of the 1930 and 1933 tribal population figures to guard against the unreliability of either tally. The figures are from the Northern Rhodesian *Annual Reports on Native Affairs* for these years.

## Appendix A

Table A.1. *Effects of Native Authority (NA) Designations on Tribal Identities, 1930/33–1962*

| Tribes with NAs after 1948 reorganization | Change in percentage of nat'l population, 1930/33–1962[b] | Tribes without NAs after 1948 reorganization[c] | Change in percentage of nat'l population, 1930/33–1962 |
|---|---|---|---|
| Ambo | 47 | Chokwe | −39 |
| Bemba | 4 | *Fungwe* | −32 |
| Bisa | 14 | Gowa | −46 |
| Bwile | −18 | Imilangu | −83 |
| Chewa[e] | 9 | Iwa | 13 |
| Chikunda[a] | −83 | *Kamanga* | −41 |
| Chishinga | 14 | Koma | −19 |
| Ila | −46 | *Kwandi* | 304 |
| Kabende[a] | 42 | Kwangwa | −8 |
| Kaonde | 31 | *Lambya* | −21 |
| Kunda | −41 | Luba | −47 |
| Lala[a] | 6 | Lukolwe | −94 |
| Lamba | −6 | *Lumbu* | 39 |
| Lenje | 0 | *Lundwe* | −28 |
| Lima | 23 | Lushange | −95 |
| Lozi[d] | −38 | Mashasha | −66 |
| Luchazi | 140 | Mashi | −23 |
| Lunda (Luapula) | 12 | Mbowe | −27 |
| Lunda (NW) | −23 | Mbunda | −16 |
| Lungu | 26 | *Mbwera* | −69 |
| Luvale | −49 | Mwenyi | −26 |
| Mambwe | 16 | Nkoya | −28 |
| Mukulu[a] | 26 | Nyengo | 7 |
| Namwanga[a] | −15 | *Nyika* | 34 |
| Ndembu | 45 | *Sewa* | 79 |
| Ngoni | 5 | Shanjo | −69 |
| Ngumbo[a] | 4 | Simaa | −59 |
| Nsenga | −11 | *Subyia* | 113 |
| Sala | −67 | Swahili | −47 |
| Senga | md[f] | Tabwa | 112 |
| Shila | 41 | Tambo | −6 |
| Soli | −4 | Totela | −29 |
| Swaka[a] | 14 | *Wandya* | −6 |
| Toka-Leya | −21 | *Wenya* | −31 |
| Tonga[g] | 75 | *Yombe* | −7 |
| Tumbuka | 65 | | |
| Unga[a] | −53 | | |
| Ushi | 30 | | |
| Wiwa[a] | −24 | | |

| Tribes with NAs after 1948 reorganization | Change in percentage of nat'l population, 1930/33–1962[b] | Tribes without NAs after 1948 reorganization[c] | Change in percentage of nat'l population, 1930/33–1962 |
|---|---|---|---|
| Weighted avg. of all tribes with NAs | 6.7 | Weighted avg. of all tribes w/o NAs | −28.5 |
| % of tribes with NAs with an increasing share of the nat'l population | 58 | % of tribes w/o NAs with an increasing share of the nat'l population | 23 |

[a] Part of hyphenated Native Authorities (e.g., Mukulu-Unga Native Authority).

[b] Change is calculated as a percentage of the 1930/33 figure, which is an average of the population sizes as listed in the Northern Rhodesian *Annual Reports on Native Affairs* for 1930 and 1933. Data for 1962 are from the *Annual Report on African Affairs* of that year, as reprinted in Brelsford (1965).

[c] Tribes in italics comprised less than 0.25 percent of the population in 1930/33.

[d] The five sub-units of the Barotse Native Authority (Mongu, Libonda, Mwandi, Nalolo, and Naliele) are collapsed into a single category.

[e] The Chewa (Lundazi) and Southern Chewa (Fort Jameson) Native Authorities are collapsed into a single category.

[f] The percent change in the Senga population cannot be calculated because no data were available for the Senga tribe in 1930 or 1933.

[g] The Gwembe Tonga and Plateau Tonga Native Authorities are collapsed into a single category.

with and tribes without Native Authorities between 1930/33 and 1990 (see Table A.2).

The variation within categories does not undermine the larger trend reported in Tables 2.1 and 2.2. Indeed, the aggregate results reported in these tables become even stronger when attention is paid to some of the anomalies that Tables A.1 and A.2 reveal. For example, the results for the 1930/33–1962 period bear out the hypothesis even more clearly when the italicized tribes in Table A.1 (those whose tiny size make them overly sensitive to small fluctuations in their national population shares) are removed from the analysis. When such tribes are excluded, the percentage of tribes without Native Authorities whose population share increased drops from 23 percent to 14 percent.[3]

[3] Given their very small size, the exclusion of these tribes does not have a significant effect on the aggregate percent change in the population share of tribes without Native Authorities.

Table A.2. *Effects of Native Authority (NA) Designations on Tribal Identities, 1930/33–1990*

| Tribes with NAs after 1948 reorganization | Change in percentage of nat'l population, 1930/33–1990[b] | Tribes without NAs after 1948 reorganization[c] | Change in percentage of nat'l population, 1930/33–1990 |
|---|---|---|---|
| Bemba | 103 | Chokwe | −32 |
| Bisa | −27 | Gowa | −59 |
| Bwile | −15 | Imilangu | −97 |
| Chewa[e] | 32 | Koma | −57 |
| Chikunda[a] | −67 | *Kwandi* | 46 |
| Chishinga | −25 | Kwangwa | −68 |
| Ila | −41 | Mashasha | −99 |
| Kabende[a] | −40 | Mashi | 1 |
| Kaonde | 11 | Mbowe | −80 |
| Kunda | −45 | Mbunda | −14 |
| Lala[a] | 6 | Mwenyi | −73 |
| Lamba | 39 | Nkoya | −47 |
| Lenje | −37 | Nyengo | −44 |
| Lima | −77 | Simaa | −86 |
| Lozi[d] | 32 | *Subiya* | −42 |
| Luchazi | 27 | Tabwa | 84 |
| Lunda (Luapula) | −48 | Tambo | −77 |
| Lunda (NW) | −13 | Totela | −88 |
| Lungu | −33 | *Yombe* | −79 |
| Luvale | −68 | | |
| Mambwe | 71 | | |
| Mukulu[a] | −70 | | |
| Namwanga[a] | 277 | | |
| Ndembu | −79 | | |
| Ngoni | 11 | | |
| Ngumbo[a] | −33 | | |
| Nsenga | 24 | | |
| Sala | −78 | | |
| Senga | md[f] | | |
| Shila | −63 | | |
| Soli | 0 | | |
| Swaka[a] | −37 | | |
| Toka-Leya | −40 | | |
| Tonga[g] | 88 | | |
| Tumbuka | 303 | | |
| Unga[a] | −80 | | |
| Ushi | 36 | | |

| Tribes with NAs after 1948 reorganization | Change in percentage of nat'l population, 1930/33–1990[b] | Tribes without NAs after 1948 reorganization[c] | Change in percentage of nat'l population, 1930/33–1990 |
|---|---|---|---|
| Weighted avg. of all tribes with NAs | 10.9 | Weighted avg. of all tribes w/o NAs | −56.9 |
| % of tribes with NAs with an increasing share of the nat'l population | 39 | % of tribes w/o NAs with an increasing share of the nat'l population | 16 |

[a] Part of hyphenated Native Authorities (e.g., Mukulu-Unga Native Authority).

[b] Change is calculated as a percentage of the 1930/33 figure, which is an average of the population sizes as listed in the Northern Rhodesian *Annual Reports on Native Affairs* for 1930 and 1933. Data for 1990 are from the *Republic of Zambia Census of Population and Housing* (1990).

[c] Tribes that were listed in the 1930 and 1933 *Annual Reports on Native Afairs* but were not among the 61 tribes that were enumerated in the 1990 *Census* are omitted. Tribes in italics comprised less than 0.25 percent of the population in 1930/33.

[d] The five sub-units of the Barotse Native Authority (Mongu, Libonda, Mwandi, Nalolo, and Naliele) are collapsed into a single category.

[e] The Chewa (Lundazi) and Southern Chewa (Fort Jameson) Native Authorities are collapsed into a single category.

[f] The percent change in the Senga population cannot be calculated because no data were available for the Senga tribe in 1930 or 1933.

[g] The Gwembe Tonga and Plateau Tonga Native Authorities are collapsed into a single category.

The results reported in Table 2.1 improve further when two other "special case" tribes, the Ila and the Unga, are omitted from the analysis. The Ila had their own Native Authority but, counter to the expectations of the argument advanced in Chapter 2, experienced a 46 percent decline in their share of the national population between 1930/33 and 1962 (see Table A.1). This can be explained by the fact that the Ila suffered an epidemic of venereal disease during the 1940s and 1950s that wiped out large numbers of their population (Brelsford 1965: 150). The decline in the size of the Unga, which, like the Ila, had their own Native Authority, can also be accounted for by special circumstances. Between the 1930/33 and 1962 tribal censuses, the waters of the Bangweulu Swamps rose precipitously, forcing the Unga to flee into Bisa and Kabende areas (ibid.: 151). This explains not only the "unexpected" decline in the population share of the Unga but also part of the rise in the population shares of the Kabende and Bisa during this period (see Table A.1).

# Appendix B

## *Survey and Focus Group Methodologies*

Forty-two individual-level questionnaires and five focus groups were administered in each of six case study districts, yielding a total sample size of 252 for the survey and thirty focus groups. The six case study districts were Lusaka Urban, Luanshya, Livingstone, Mongu, Kasama, and Chipata (see Figure B.1). These districts were chosen because they offered variation in urban/rural location and because they constitute urban/rural pairs with the same dominant language groups, thereby making it possible to assess the effects of urban/rural location while controlling for language. Lusaka Urban, Luanshya, and Livingstone are all urban districts located on Zambia's industrial rail line. Mongu, Kasama, and Chipata are overwhelmingly rural districts, though they all contain the administrative headquarters of their respective provinces.[1] Kasama and Luanshya are both Bemba-speaking. Chipata and Lusaka Urban are both principally Nyanja-speaking. Mongu and Livingstone are both Lozi-speaking.[2]

### *Measuring Ethnic Identities and Attitudes*

Collecting reliable data on respondents' ethnic attachments and attitudes about ethnic politics is fraught with methodological obstacles.[3] The simple-minded solution of simply asking respondents "who they are" or "what they think" about the role that ethnicity plays in political life is undermined by the fact that individuals possess multiple ethnic identities – they "are" many things – and the salience of each identity varies with the

[1] According to 1990 census data, the populations of these three districts were between 73 and 82 percent rural.

[2] Livingstone is a city of mixed Lozi-speakers and Tonga-speakers, but it is historically associated with Lozi settlement.

[3] The discussion in this section draws on Posner (2000).

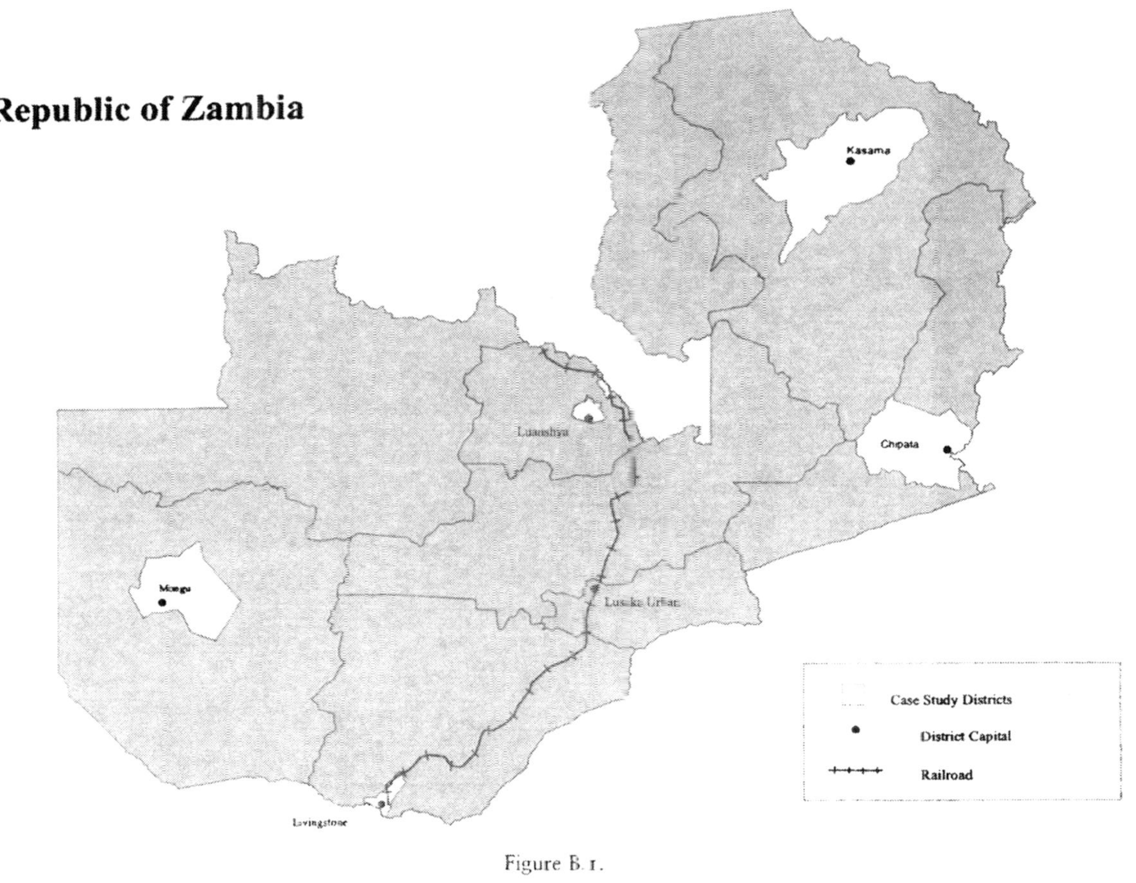
Republic of Zambia
Kasama
Chipata
Luanshya
Lusaka Urban
Mongu
Livingstone
Case Study Districts
District Capital
Railroad

Figure B.1.

context in which the respondents are asked to reflect on who they are and what it means to them. A Zambian friend once told me that he sees himself as a Bemba-speaker when he is in Southern Province, a Northwesterner when he is in the Copperbelt, and a Kaonde when he is in his village. He is, in fact, all of these things. But the place in which he happens to be located at the moment shapes which one of these identities he ranks as most salient – and, importantly, which he would volunteer as his "ethnic identity" to a survey enumerator. Context matters for the answers we get. And "context" is defined not just, as in the example, by the part of the country in which the interview takes place. If this were the case, we could fairly easily control for it. The problem is that "context" is also defined by the particular micro-environment in which the survey is conducted, the events of the moment, and even the other people that happen to be in the room (including the interviewer) at the time the question is asked. A survey administered outside a mosque will prompt different identities from one administered in the marketplace or outside the union hall. An interview undertaken at the height of an ethnically charged election campaign will generate different answers from one administered when the national team is playing in the Africa Cup.

The problem is not simply one of reliability. That is, it is not just that asking the same question in the same way at a different time or in a different place will generate a different response. The real problem stems from the fact that we are probably interested in the respondent's identity because we have some intuition about the behavior it causes, but testing hypotheses about the effects of ethnic identity requires that we be sure that the identity offered in response to the "who are you" question is the same identity that was salient for the respondent at the time of the behavior that we are using the respondent's answer to explain. If it is not, then our measure of ethnic identity will be invalid, in the sense that the identity will be irrelevant for the particular outcome that we are interested in accounting for. The potential mismatch between the identity prompted by the situation in which the interview took place and the identity that motivated the respondent's behavior in the situation we are interested in studying constitutes an enormous impediment to making reliable causal inferences.

A slightly different set of problems plagues attempts to collect information about respondents' attitudes regarding inter-ethnic relations or about their perceptions of the salience of ethnicity in political and social life. Here the difficulty is less the fact that peoples' identities shift across situations as it is the fact that the salience of ethnicity per se, as one of several factors that motivate peoples' behavior, is also context driven. Asking Los Angelenos about their attitudes toward affirmative action in late 1992, immediately after the riots that followed the acquittal of the white police officers in the Rodney King trial, would almost certainly have generated different responses from those that a researcher would have recorded in, say, late 1991, before the King verdict was announced. While these different response patterns might be attributable in part to the reshuffling of the salience of various ethnic identities after the King verdict (with race now trumping all others), they are more likely attributable to the change in the importance of ethnic identity per se.

The distinction I am driving at is akin to that between changing the station on a radio and turning up the volume. "Who are you" questions are plagued by the fact that our radios (research subjects) have many stations (ethnic identities) on their dial, and the particular station they tune to varies from situation to situation. Attitudinal or perceptual questions, by contrast, are plagued by the fact that the situation in which a person finds himself or herself also affects the volume at which his or her radio plays. In some contexts, it provides little more than background music; in others, it drowns out everything else. The problem is that unless we can control the factors that affect the volume level across all respondents (and also make sure that the volume level at the time of the interview matches that at the time of the behavior we are trying to explain) we risk collecting unreliable and invalid information.

Given such potential pitfalls, I attempted to find a way to control the context in which my interviews and focus groups were conducted so as to neutralize, or at least universalize, the situational cues that might affect respondents' identities and attitudes. This entailed trying to do two things: first, eliminate the biases that derived from the fact that respondents would be interviewed at different times, in different places, and, likely, by different interviewers; and, second, frame the context in which respondents considered their answers so as to match the situation in which the behavior that I was using these answers to try to explain took place. To accomplish these ends, I began each of the 252 interviews and thirty focus groups by playing respondents a "prompt dialogue" – a tape-recorded discussion between two friends in which they discuss and debate the role of ethnicity in Zambia's contemporary political life. I then asked the respondents to respond directly to what each of the speakers in the discussion had just

**Prompt Dialogue Script**

FRANK (AGNES): Good morning, Richard (Joyce).

RICHARD (JOYCE): Good morning Frank (Agnes).

FRANK (AGNES): Why do you look so happy?

RICHARD (JOYCE): Haven't you heard the news about the new political party?

FRANK (AGNES): Sure I did. It was on the news last night. But it's just another political party. Nothing to get excited about.

RICHARD (JOYCE): But this one is different. The president of this new party is from our area. Now we will have some of our own people ruling the country.

FRANK (AGNES): I am surprised to hear you say that, Richard (Joyce).

RICHARD (JOYCE): I am just being honest. If a man from our area becomes President, we will benefit. He will appoint ministers from our area and they will make sure that we get development here.

FRANK (AGNES): Richard (Joyce)! I can't believe I am really hearing you say these things! We shouldn't support a political party just because its president is from our group. We should support the president who is capable of delivering goods and services to the people. That is who we should pick, whatever group he comes from. If we take a man from our area who has never been to school before, how can he qualify for that post? How can he do a good job? And the same is true for ministers. Appointments should be based on that person's ability, not on the group he comes from.

RICHARD (JOYCE): I am just telling you what I feel. If a man from our area becomes President or a cabinet minister, people in our area will benefit. He can understand us because he is one of us. Of course we should choose someone who has education. But there are lots of educated people from our area. And in the end, we can only rely on members of our own group.

FRANK (AGNES): Richard (Joyce)! We think so differently that it is hard to believe that we come from the same village! For me, and I think for most people, being a Zambian is much more important than being a member of a particular group.

RICHARD (JOYCE): Frank (Agnes), you have known me since I was a small boy (girl). I am also a Zambian. I served in the army. When the national football team is playing, I cheer for Zambia. But in politics, I support people who come from my area. I am just being honest with you. When it comes to politics, I am a member of our group first and a Zambian second.

FRANK (AGNES): Well, you'll have to do what you think is best. But I disagree. And you are wrong if you think other people from our area will support this party just because its president is from our group. This is 1995, not 1965.

Figure B.2. Prompt Dialogue Script

said. The goal was to provide a uniform context for each respondent that would frame the expressly political situation in which I was interested in understanding the respondents' behavior and attitudes.

To create the script for the prompt dialogue, I spent a week in one of Lusaka's high-density residential compounds conducting open-ended interviews with men and women of different ages about the role that ethnicity plays in their everyday lives and in Zambian politics. At the

RICHARD (JOYCE): I am just telling you the realities of present-day politics. These are not the politics of yesterday when Kaunda was ruling. The days of "One Zambia, One Nation" are over. This is multi-party politics, and the reality today is that if we don't support people from our group, we will be dominated by people from other areas who do.

FRANK (AGNES): Again, I disagree. One thing that President Kaunda did was bring national unity. "One Zambia, One Nation" brought intermarriages and intermarriages brought unity. Zambia still is one nation. Multi-party politics has not changed this.

RICHARD (JOYCE): I am not saying that Zambia will turn into Rwanda. I am just saying that things have changed. Look at all the new parties. Most of them are dominated by people from a particular area. Look at the divisions within the various parties. They are based on differences between people from different groups. Look at the present government. People from one area are dominating the cabinet.

FRANK (AGNES): I think you are overstating things, my friend. These group divisions you have been talking about are not nearly as important these days as you say. And besides, even if you are right, divisions between people from different areas mattered just as much in politics during the Second Republic.

RICHARD (JOYCE): Well, for two people who grew up together, we certainly do find a lot to disagree about. You have your views and I have mine. I suppose that is what freedom of speech is all about.

FRANK (AGNES): Now there's something we can agree about! We can agree to disagree!

Figure B.2 (*continued*)

end of the week, I transcribed these interviews, which I had recorded, and composed a fictitious conversation between two friends, "Frank" and "Richard," that wove together direct quotes from these open-ended discussions. The text of the dialogue is reproduced as Figure B.2. All of the arguments advanced by Frank and Richard and all of the expressions that they use came directly from what interviewees actually said during my week of pilot work. While the issues that I chose to include in the dialogue reflected my own research interests, the words that the actors speak are those of real Zambians.

Since one of the important things that I wanted to learn from the survey was the dimension of ethnic identity (tribal or linguistic) that Zambians have in their heads when they think about political competition, I took great care in composing the dialogue never to specify a particular dimension of ethnic identity. The dialogue is thus filled with neutral phrases like "people from our area" or "members of our group" and never uses the terms "tribe," "province," or "language group." The substitution of the neutral phrases for dimension-specific ones was the only alteration I made in the direct quotes from the open-ended interviews out of which I constructed the prompt dialogue. Having never prompted a particular dimension of ethnic identity, I could then make meaningful inferences about the relative salience of tribal and linguistic identity from the answers I recorded when I asked respondents to identify the "group" – again, specified in neutral terms – to which they belonged.[4]

With the help of colleagues at the Institute for African Studies of the University of Zambia, I translated the dialogue into Bemba, Nyanja, Tonga, and Lozi, the four local languages in which the survey and focus group work were conducted. The parts of Frank and Richard were then acted in each language by the same colleagues and recorded on cassette tapes. Because the "deep Bemba" and "deep Nyanja" spoken in the rural parts of Kasama and Chipata districts appears stilted and awkward to people in Luanshya and Lusaka, where less formal, English-laced versions of these languages are spoken, I also prepared and recorded separate "town Bemba" and "town Nyanja" versions of the dialogues for use in these research sites. In translating the dialogue into the four (six) languages, I took great care to use words that would preserve the neutral (i.e., non-dimension-specific) nature of the references to ethnic affiliations.

I also took steps to eliminate a possible gender bias in the responses I collected. In Zambia, as in many developing countries, one of the great challenges in survey research is to encourage female respondents to be equally at ease as male respondents in expressing their views and opinions, particularly about political affairs. In my own research, the problem was compounded by the fact that the person sometimes asking the questions (me) was a man – and also a foreigner. Part of my strategy for dealing with this issue was to record a separate prompt dialogue in each language in which the parts of Frank and Richard were replaced, and acted on the tape, by women ("Agnes" and "Joyce"). By prompting female survey respondents and focus group participants with the back-and-forth discussion between Agnes and Joyce, I hoped to demonstrate, by their example, that women were capable of holding and expressing opinions about political affairs.

I went into the field with fourteen different taped versions of the prompt dialogue: the Frank/Richard and Agnes/Joyce versions of the dialogue in English, "deep Bemba," "deep Nyanja," "town Bemba," "town Nyanja," Lozi, and Tonga. Each survey respondent and focus group was played the gender- and language-appropriate version of the prompt dialogue. The

[4] The actual survey question asked: "Frank and Richard talked a lot about 'the group' that they belong to. What group do you belong to?"

**INSTITUTE FOR AFRICAN STUDIES, UNZA**

Political Attitudes Questionnaire

date of interview: language of interview:

district: village/compound:

urban ____ rural ____ density: high ____ low ____

------------------------------

In what year were you born? male ____ female ____

Where were you born?

When did you move to your present location?

Where else have you lived? For how long?

What is the highest grade you have finished in your education?

Do you have a job which earns some money?
[If yes] What sort of job?

How much do you earn per month?

Do you support a political party? Which party?

***Now I am going to play a tape recording of a conversation between two friends. Please listen carefully to the conversation. Afterwards, I will ask you for your opinion about some of the views that the two friends expressed.***

Richard and Frank (Joyce and Agnes) talked a lot about "the group" that they belong to. What group do you belong to?

Are you married? [If yes] What group does your spouse belong to?

In their discussion, Richard (Joyce) said that people from his (her) area would benefit if a person from his (her) area was elected President. Do you think this is true? Do the people from the President's region benefit more than people from other areas of the country?

yes _____ no _____ not sure _____

Figure B.3. Political Attitudes Questionnaire

questions on the questionnaire and in the focus group discussion then asked respondents directly about things that Richard and Frank or Joyce and Agnes had said. A reproduction of the survey instrument is provided in Figure B.3.

Do people from this area get their fair share of government services?

yes _____ no _____ not sure _____

Do people from this area get their fair share of government appointments?

yes _____ no _____ not sure _____

Richard (Joyce) said that people can only rely on members of their own group. Do you think that this is true?

yes _____ no _____ not sure _____

Richard (Joyce) said that if people do not support members of their own group then they will be dominated by people from other areas who do. Do you think he (she) is right?

yes _____ no _____ not sure _____

Frank (Agnes) said that Richard (Joyce) was wrong to support a politician just because he was from his (her) own group. He (she) said it was more important to support people because of their ability than because of the particular area that they come from. Which do **you** think is more important, to support a politician from your own group, or to support a politician who has the best abilities, even if he is from a different group?

own group _____ abilities _____ not sure _____

Frank (Agnes) said that being a Zambian was much more important to him (her) than being a member of a particular group. Richard (Joyce) said that, in politics at least, he (she) is a person from a particular area first and a Zambian second. In general, do you think that people in this country think of themselves first a Zambians or first as being from a particular group?

as Zambians _____ as from particular group _____ not sure _____

What about you? When it comes to politics, which do you put first? Being a Zambian or being a member of your group?

being Zambian _____ being from a particular group _____ not sure _____

Figure B.3 (*continued*)

## *The Survey*

Surveys were administered in English or the appropriate local language by either myself or one of five trained research assistants.[5] In selecting

[5] The research assistants were Misheck Banda, Maureen Kashempa, Kris Mwanangombe, Robert Mwanza, and Joseph Tembo.

Richard (Joyce) said that the days of "One Zambia, One Nation" are over and that Zambia is now really many nations. Is he (she) right? These days is Zambia one nations or is it many nations?
one nation _____ many nations _____ not sure _____

Are there more tensions these days between people who come from different areas than there were during the Second Republic?

more tensions now _____ more tensions then _____

no difference between then and now _____ not sure _____

[If there is a difference] Why do you think that is?

[If there is a difference] Can you give me an example of such tensions?

Some people these days are saying that Zambia should introduce a federal system of government in which each province is given greater power to govern its own affairs. Do you think this would be a good idea?

yes _____ no _____ not sure _____

Should chiefs and headmen play a role in governing Zambia today?

yes _____ no _____ not sure _____

[If yes] What role should they play?

Now I want you to think about your three closest friends. How many of them are from groups different from your own? Which groups?

friend #1:

friend #2:

friend #3:

**Thank you very much for participating in our survey.**

Figure B.3 (*continued*)

individual survey respondents, my goal was to produce a sample that would be representative of the voting-age population (i.e., greater than or equal to 18 years old) in each of the six districts in which the survey work was being carried out.[6]

[6] Although the goal was not to generate a nationally representative sample survey, the aggregate results of the survey are probably similar to what the results might have

In the absence of a readily available list of individuals that might have served as a sampling frame for each district, I selected respondents through a stratified quota sampling method. Gender, age, and urban/rural location were employed as the three criteria for the quotas. The quotas for each category were set to reflect the share of the population in each category in each district, as determined from the 1990 census. In each district, six respondents were interviewed each day for seven days, yielding a total of forty-two respondents. Each day was spent in a different site within the district. In the three urban districts (Lusaka Urban, Luanshya, and Livingstone), each site was usually a different urban location or compound.[7] In the three rural districts (Mongu, Kasama, and Chipata), where as much as 20 percent of the population lives within the *boma* (the district capital), two of the seven days were spent in different compounds within the *boma* and the remaining five days were spent in different villages located at least 15 kilometers outside the *boma*. The gender and age quotas were satisfied on a daily basis by choosing one respondent from each gender from each of three age categories: 18–26 years old, 27–44 years old, and 45 years old and over. These age cut-offs were selected because they divide the Zambian voting-age population into three equal-sized groups.

I approached respondents at random until I had filled the age and gender quotas for the day. To avoid snowball sampling, I or my colleague would walk some distance after each interview before approaching the next potential respondent. Once identified, we would introduce ourselves as researchers from the University of Zambia and inquire of those persons we stopped whether we could ask them some questions about their views about the political changes that were presently taking place in the country. We were almost always greeted warmly and willingly. In rare instances where potential respondents expressed reservations about participating in the survey, we thanked them for their time and found another respondent.

been had the sample been selected for that purpose. The close correlation between several of my findings and those reported in Bratton's large-N, nationally representative sample survey (Bratton 1996) bears out this claim.

[7] In Luanshya, roughly half the population lives in the municipal compound, Mikomfwa, and the other half lives in one of the several ZCCM-run mining compounds, which are segregated by employment grade. Three of the days in Luanshya were spent surveying respondents in different areas of Mikomfwa, and the other three days were spent in different mining compounds, each with a different grade of employee.

If the respondent spoke reasonably fluent English, I would administer the survey myself. If their English was not sufficiently fluent to guarantee that they would understand and be able to respond to the questions, my colleague would administer the survey in the respondent's local language. Often, surveys were conducted in a mix of English and the local language. In addition to checking the appropriate boxes and filling in the appropriate blanks on the survey form, I or my colleague recorded in the margins interesting additional comments and elaborations made by the respondent. These comments are referenced in the text by survey respondent number (e.g., "SR 144").

### *The Focus Groups*

Five focus groups of six participants each were conducted in each case study district. The purpose of the focus groups was to "put meat on the bones" of the survey results by providing an opportunity to observe participants discussing and debating at greater length the same issues that were posed in the questionnaire. While the prompt dialogue was useful for defining a uniform context in which the survey questions could be asked, it paid its real dividends in promoting excellent discussion and debate in the focus groups.

One of the five focus groups was always held with a mixed-gender group of primary school teachers. To arrange this group, I would ask the headmaster of one of the primary schools in the district to select six teachers (three men and three women; if possible, some older, some younger) to participate in the group. These focus groups were almost always held in an empty classroom or in the headmaster's office. A pair of focus groups was always held with groups of male and female market sellers from one of the principal markets in the district. To arrange this group, I would usually approach the chairperson of the market (formerly, but no longer, a political position) and ask him or her to help me organize two groups, one comprised of six men and one comprised of six women, to participate in the focus groups. Sometimes, I would circumvent the market chairperson and approach market sellers directly to ask them to participate. To eliminate the inevitable accumulation of observers and unofficial participants that gather when such groups are held in public places, I always held the market seller focus groups away from the market, sometimes in a nearby community hall or sometimes, with the headmaster's permission, in the same school classroom as the teachers' focus group. The groups were segregated by gender to ensure that women, who tend to defer to men in mixed settings, would feel comfortable speaking their minds.[8]

The final pairs of focus groups were different in the urban and rural districts. In the three rural districts, I arranged one focus group with male villagers and one with female villagers, each in a different village located at least 15 kilometers from the district capital. In setting up these groups, I enlisted the help of a variety of different local contacts: a Peace Corps volunteer in one case, a relative of a University of Zambia colleague in another, a relative of my research assistant in a third. The focus group meetings took place in people's huts, in rural school buildings, in agricultural extension offices, under shady trees, and in other quiet settings. In the three urban districts, my practice was to approach the leaders of two different churches in the town and ask them to help me organize a group of men or women to participate in the focus group.[9] These groups were almost always held in a meeting room in the church itself.

Throughout the book, citations of focus group comments are indicated by code. The first part of the code indicates the district in which the focus group meeting took place (LSK = Lusaka; LY = Luanshya; LIV = Livingstone; MON = Mongu; KAS = Kasama; CPTA = Chipata). The second part indicates the type of group (T = teachers; MS = market sellers; R = rural; no code = urban). The third indicates the gender of the focus group participants. Thus, "LSK-T" was a focus group of Lusaka teachers; "MON-MS-W" was a group of market seller women held in Mongu; "LIV-M" was a group of urban men in Livingstone.

With the exception of the market sellers, to whom I gave K1,000 "gifts" (about $2 at the time) as modest compensation for the business they lost while participating in the focus group, I did not pay focus group participants. I did, however, provide soft drinks and cookies. In each district, I would run the teachers' focus group myself in English and my colleague would run the other focus groups in a combination of English and the local language.

8 Generally speaking, educated Zambian women, such as teachers, have no hesitation speaking their minds in mixed-gender settings. Hence my decision to arrange mixed-gender teachers' focus groups but to segregate less well-educated respondents by gender.

9 My decision to enlist the help of ministers or priests came from my experience that people tended to show up for meetings when their pastor asked them to come but tended not to show up when I was the one with whom they had made the appointment. Church leaders were thus approached not for religious reasons but for their organizational capacity.

Before the focus group began, my colleague and I would introduce ourselves, explain the nature of the research project, and encourage all the participants to speak freely during the ensuing discussion.[10] The focus group discussion began with the playing of the prompt dialogue in the appropriate language and gender. Then we went through the same questions that were asked in the survey questionnaire. We did our best to encourage the focus group participants to discuss and debate among themselves the questions that we posed. In the most successful groups, our role was as moderators of an ongoing discussion rather than as questioners. The entire focus group discussion was recorded. Later, verbatim transcripts of the discussion were prepared in English.

If time permitted after the survey questions had been addressed, I sometimes handed out blank maps of Zambia and asked focus group participants to work together to indicate on the maps the locations of "the most important groups in the country" – a deliberately non leading set of instructions. The purpose of this exercise was less to see where people located the "most important groups" than to see which groups people identified, which dimension of identity they employed when they referred to them, and what discussions and disputes arose among the focus group participants in the process of identifying these groups and debating whether or not they should be included. The discussions that took place during this map-drawing exercise were recorded and included in the verbatim focus group transcript.

[10] My ideas for the design and administration of the focus groups were shaped by Knodel, Sittitrai, and Brown (1990).

# Appendix C

## *Tribal Affiliations of Parliamentary Candidates*

Many of the analyses reported in this book involve comparing the tribal backgrounds of parliamentary candidates with the tribal demographics of the constituencies in which they competed. Undertaking these analyses required collecting information about candidates' tribal affiliations. Due to the very large number of candidates whose tribal backgrounds I was interested in ascertaining, it was impossible to contact each candidate or, when they were deceased, their living family members directly. Instead, I took advantage of the fact that a person's tribal affiliation can be discerned from their name with a high degree of accuracy in Zambia, particularly by those who come from the same part of the country.

I began by drawing up a list of every candidate who had run in the elections of 1968, 1973, 1978, 1983, 1988, 1991, and 1996, as well as in all Third Republic by-elections held through the end of 1999. I then sorted this master list by district, generating 57 separate worksheets containing inventories of every candidate that had ever run for Parliament in that district. These worksheets contained a total of 2,231 different candidates.

The data-collection exercise took place during July and August 1999.[1] My strategy was to track down, in Lusaka, people from each district who could serve as informants on the tribal backgrounds of the candidates from their district. I especially sought out older men or women who had spent a major portion of their lives in the district in question. Older men and women were chosen because, as focus group discussions revealed, older Zambians are far more attuned to tribal distinctions than are younger Zambians. I asked each informant to help me fill out the

[1] I am indebted to Richard Banda for his excellent research assistance. My efforts in 1999 replicated and supplemented a similar, preliminary exercise that I undertook during 1995–96. I thank Hilary Mwale and Charlotte Luanga for their help with this earlier work.

worksheet by applying the same tribal codes that were used in the 1990 census, a list of which I provided. I stressed repeatedly that I was interested in the local tribal identities of the candidates, not their language group affiliations. I also asked informants to leave blank any of the candidates' backgrounds about which they were not absolutely sure. In instances where a candidate's name might have suggested membership in more than one tribe – many Zambian names are common to several tribes – I asked the informants to indicate the candidate's background only if they knew the candidate or his or her family personally. Each worksheet was completed by at least two different informants. In cases where informants disagreed on a candidate's background, I sought the advice of at least two other informants. For a number of districts, the candidate codings were checked and double-checked by as many as six or seven different informants.

Although it was fairly easy to find informants for most districts, a number of more remote areas presented difficulties. My solution was to secure permission from the National Pensions Board to interview some of the hundreds of men who gather every day outside its Lusaka offices to await their pension payments. These men – former teachers, civil servants, military officers, and policemen – come to the board's headquarters from every district of the country to secure their terminal pension benefits. Sometimes they wait for months. In the meantime, they sit patiently in the courtyard of the building, and I found them eager to lend their help to my project while they waited. Many were able to identify candidates on the list as personal friends or even distant relatives. One even turned out to be a former candidate himself.

Occasionally, informants told me that a certain candidate had parents belonging to different tribes. Sometimes they were able to tell me this because they knew the candidate (or the candidate's parents) personally; at other times it was because the candidate's name indicated a mixed tribal background. My convention in such cases was to record the candidate's mixed background on the worksheet and, for the purposes of the analyses, code them as members of the non-dominant tribe. My assumption was that a mixed-tribe candidate – even a candidate that had one parent from the dominant local tribe – could be branded as an outsider by a non-mixed-tribe rival and should therefore be coded as such.[2]

[2] Note that doing so is methodologically defensible, since coding the candidate as a member of the non-dominant tribe almost always worked against the hypothesis I was testing.

# Appendix D

## *Tribal Demographics of Electoral Constituencies*

In a context where resources are assumed to be distributed along ethnic lines, and where the fairness of the current pattern of distribution is judged by the correspondence between the share of resources that each group controls and the share of the population it can claim as members, accurate information about the ethnic composition of the country's population can be highly inflammatory (Hirschman 1987; Diamond 1988; Wright 1994; Horowitz 1985). As Horowitz puts it: "Numbers are an indicator of whose country it is" (1985: 194). For this reason, questions about respondents' ethnic backgrounds are simply not asked in the national censuses of most developing nations.[1]

In a striking departure from this norm (and for reasons I do not fully understand), the 1990 *Republic of Zambia Census of Population and Housing* collected data on the tribal backgrounds of census respondents.[2] Although this information was not included in any of the descriptive tables published by the Zambia Central Statistical Office (ZCSO) – "respondent's Zambian tribe" was the only variable omitted from the otherwise comprehensive cross-tabulations – it remained in the raw data, which I was able to obtain from the ZCSO.[3] This data set, which contains the self-reported tribal affiliations of 7,383,097 individuals, provided me with an

[1] African census questionnaires often include broad questions about race, but these are of little use for most analyses of ethnic politics, since the relevant ethnic differences are masked under the umbrella category "African."

[2] Respondents were asked "What is your Zambian tribe?" Enumerators coded the respondent's exact answer according to one of the sixty-one different tribal categories in the census code book. If the respondent's answer did not match any of the available options, the response was coded as "other."

[3] I thank the Julie Blattner Memorial Fund of the Harvard College Library for providing the funds with which to purchase the data. The entire data set has been deposited at the Harvard College Library and is publicly available to researchers.

indispensable (and unparalleled) source of information for the analyses that I undertake in this book.[4]

Using the census data to generate breakdowns of the tribal demographics of electoral constituencies was far from straightforward. A first difficulty stemmed from the fact that the census did not include "electoral constituency" as a variable. Deriving constituency-level tribal demographics therefore required building constituencies out of a different administrative unit that the census data set did contain: the census supervisory area (CSA), of which there are more than 4,400 countrywide. However, mapping the census data onto electoral constituencies required first figuring out which CSAs were located in which electoral constituencies. The problem was that the maps used by the Zambia Electoral Commission to delimit electoral constituencies did not include CSA boundaries. Solving this problem involved borrowing electoral constituency maps from the Electoral Commission, taking them to the ZCSO offices where they could be compared side-by-side with the original colonial-era CSA maps (which were still in use!), and scrutinizing the CSA and electoral maps to find common boundaries such as streams and rivers.[5] The task was complicated further by the fact that the Second and Third Republics each had different numbers of electoral constituencies with different delimitations. Thus the process of mapping CSAs onto constituencies (which I did over the course of several days with the help of a team of staff from the ZCSO) had to be accomplished for 275 different units – 150 constituencies from the Third Republic and 125 constituencies from the Second Republic.[6]

Once the CSAs were mapped onto the electoral constituencies, I aggregated the CSAs into constituencies to produce constituency-level breakdowns by tribe and first and second languages of communication.

4 Since the census questionnaires were enumerated by household, with the household head providing information on the tribal backgrounds of all household members, the tribal affiliations of many individuals were not strictly speaking self-reported. However, this in no way detracts from their accuracy, since the information was reported by a family member who, presumably, knew the person's tribal affiliation.

5 I was helped somewhat by the fact that both CSAs and electoral constituencies are located entirely within districts and that district boundaries were common to both the CSA and constituency maps.

6 I am indebted to Kumbutso Dzekedzeke, the census manager at the ZCSO, for his help in facilitating this process.

# *Bibliography*

Abernethy, David B. 1969. *The Political Dilemma of Popular Education*. Palo Alto, CA: Stanford University Press.

Achen, Christopher H., and W. Phillips Shivley. 1995. *Cross-Level Inference*. Chicago: University of Chicago Press.

Agbese, Pita Ogaba. 1996. "Ethnic Conflicts and Hometown Associations: An Analysis of the Experience of the Agila Development Association." *Africa Today* 43 (2): 139–56.

Alila, Patrick O. 1984. "Luo Ethnic Factor in the 1979 and 1983 Elections in Bondo and Gem, Kenya." Working Paper no. 408, Institute for Development Studies, University of Nairobi.

Apthorpe, Raymond. 1968. "Does Tribalism Really Matter?" *Transition* 7 (October): 18–22.

Ashbaugh, Leslie Ann. 1996. "The Great East Road: Gender, Generation and Urban to Rural Migration in the Eastern Province of Zambia." PhD diss., Department of Anthropology, Northwestern University.

Azarya, Victor, and Nahomi Chazan. 1987. "Disengagement from the State in Africa: Reflections on the Experience of Ghana and Guinea." *Comparative Studies in Society and History* 29: 106–31.

Banton, Michael, and Mohd Noor Mansur. 1992. "The Study of Ethnic Alignment: A New Technique and an Application in Malaysia." *Ethnic and Racial Studies* 15 (October): 599–613.

Barkan, Joel. 1976. "A Reassessment of Conventional Wisdom About the Informed Public: Comment: Further Reassessment of 'Conventional Wisdom': Political Knowledge and Voting Behavior in Rural Kenya." *American Political Science Review* 70 (June): 452–5.

Barkan, Joel. 1979. "Bringing Home the Pork: Legislative Behavior, Rural Development and Political Change in East Africa." In Joel Smith and Lloyd Musolf, eds., *Legislatures in Development*. Durham, NC: Duke University Press, pp. 265–88.

Barkan, Joel. 1984. *Politics and Public Policy in Kenya and Tanzania*. New York: Praeger.

Barkan, Joel. 1987. "The Electoral Process and Peasant-State Relations in Kenya." In Fred Hayward, ed., *Elections in Independent Africa*. Boulder, CO: Westview Press, pp. 213–37.

Barkan, Joel, and Njuguna Ng'ethe. 1998. "Kenya Tries Again." *Journal of Democracy* 9 (April): 32–48.

Barrows, Walter. 1976. *Grassroots Politics in an African State: Integration and Development in Sierra Leone*. New York: African Publishing.

Barth, Frederik. 1969. *Ethnic Groups and Boundaries*. Boston: Little Brown.

Bates, Robert H. 1976. *Rural Responses to Industrialization: A Study of Village Zambia*. New Haven, CT: Yale University Press.

Bates, Robert H. 1981. *Markets and States in Tropical Africa: The Political Basis of Agricultural Policies*. Berkeley and Los Angeles: University of California Press.

Bates, Robert H. 1983. "Modernization, Ethnic Competition and the Rationality of Politics in Contemporary Africa." In Donald Rothchild and Victor A. Olorunsola, eds., *State versus Ethnic Claims: African Policy Dilemmas*. Boulder, Co: Westview Press, pp. 152–71.

Bates, Robert H. 1984. "Some Conventional Orthodoxies in the Study of Agrarian Change." *World Politics* 36 (January): 234–54.

Bates, Robert H. 1988. "Contra Contractarianism: Some Reflections on the New Institutionalism." *Politics and Society* 16: 387–401.

Bates, Robert H. 1989. *Beyond the Miracle of the Market: The Political Economy of Agrarian Development in Kenya*. Cambridge: Cambridge University Press.

Bayart, Jean-François. 1993. *The State in Africa: The Politics of the Belly*. London: Longman Press.

Baylies, Carolyn. 1984. "Luapula Province: Economic Decline and Political Alienation in a Rural UNIP Stronghold." In Cherry Gertzel, Carolyn Baylies, and Morris Szeftel, eds., *The Dynamics of the One-Party State in Zambia*. Manchester: Manchester University Press, pp. 163–205.

Baylies, Carolyn, and Morris Szeftel. 1982. "The Rise of a Zambian Capitalist Class in the 1970s." *Journal of Southern African Studies* 8: 187–213.

Baylies, Carolyn, and Morris Szeftel. 1984. "Elections in the One-Party State." In Cherry Gertzel, Carolyn Baylies, and Morris Szeftel, eds., *The Dynamics of the One-Party State in Zambia*. Manchester: Manchester University Press, pp. 29–57.

Berger, Elena L. 1974. *Labour, Race and Colonial Rule: The Copperbelt from 1924 to Independence*. Oxford: Clarendon Press.

Bettison, David G. 1959. "Numerical Data on African Dwellers in Lusaka, Northern Rhodesia." *Rhodes-Livingstone Communication*, no. 16.

Bostock, Mark, and Charles Harvey, eds. 1972. *Economic Independence and Zambian Copper: A Case Study of Foreign Investment*. New York: Praeger.

Brass, Paul R. 1991. *Ethnicity and Nationalism: Theory and Comparison*. New Delhi: Sage Publications.

Bratton, Michael. 1980. *The Local Politics of Rural Development: Peasant and Party-State in Zambia*. Hanover, NH: University Press of New England.

Bratton, Michael. 1994. "Economic Crisis and Political Realignment in Zambia." In Jennifer A. Widner, ed., *Economic Change and Political Liberalization in Sub-Saharan Africa*. Baltimore: Johns Hopkins University Press, pp. 101–28.

Bratton, Michael. 1996. "Zambia Democratic Governance Project Political Attitudes Survey, 1993 and 1996" [computer file]. ICPSR Study IO2232.

Bratton, Michael, and Daniel N. Posner. 1998. "A First Look at Second Elections in Africa, with Illustrations from Zambia." In Richard Joseph, ed., *State, Conflict and Democracy in Africa*. Boulder, CO: Lynne Rienner, pp. 377–407.

Brelsford, W. V., ed. 1965. *The Tribes of Zambia*. Lusaka: Government Printer.

Bromwich, E. C. 1963. "General History of Roan." Ndola: ZCCM Archives.

Brown, Roger. 1986. *Social Psychology*. 2nd ed. New York: Free Press.

Burawoy, Michael. 1972. *The Colour of Class on the Copper Mines: From African Advancement to Zambianization*. Manchester: Manchester University Press.

Campbell, John. 1999. "Nationalism, Ethnicity and Religion: Fundamental Conflicts and the Politics of Identity in Tanzania." *Nations and Nationalism* 5: 105–25.

Carey, John, and Matthew Shugart. 1995. "Incentives to Cultivate a Personal Vote: A Rank Ordering of Electoral Formulas." *Electoral Studies* 14 (December): 417–39.

Carey Jones, N. S. 1944. "Native Treasuries in Northern Rhodesia." *Human Problems in British Central Africa* 2 (December): 40–48.

Cartwright, John. 1970. *Politics in Sierra Leone, 1947–1967*. Toronto: University of Toronto Press.

Caselli, Francseco, and Wilbur John Coleman. 2001. "On the Theory of Ethnic Conflict." Mimeo. Department of Economics, Harvard University.

Chabal, Patrick, and Jean-Pascal Daloz. 1999. *Africa Works: Disorder as Political Instrument*. Oxford: James Currey.

Chandra, Kanchan. 2004. *Why Ethnic Parties Succeed: Patronage and Ethnic Head Counts in India*. Cambridge: Cambridge University Press.

Chandra, Kanchan, ed. 2001. "Symposium: Cumulative Findings in the Study of Ethnic Politics." *APSA-CP* 12 (Winter): 7–11.

Chandra, Kanchan, and Cilanne Boulet. 2003. "A Model of Change in an Ethnic Demography." Mimeo. Department of Political Science, MIT.

Chanock, Martin. 1985. *Law, Custom and Social Order: The Colonial Experience in Malawi and Zambia*. Cambridge: Cambridge University Press.

Chapman, William. 1909. *A Pathfinder in South Central Africa: A Story of Pioneer Missionary Work and Adventure*. London: W. A. Hammond.

Chazan, Naomi. 1979. "African Voters at the Polls: A Re-examination of the Role of Elections in African Politics." *Journal of Commonwealth and Comparative Politics* 16 (July): 136–56.

Chazan, Naomi. 1982. "Ethnicity and Politics in Ghana." *Political Science Quarterly* 97 (Fall): 461–85.

Chikulo, Bornwell C. 1979. "Elections in a One-Party Participatory Democracy." In Ben Turok, ed., *Development in Zambia*. London: Zed Press, pp. 201–13.

Chikulo, Bornwell C. 1983. "Rural Administration in Zambia: Organization and Performance in a Former Opposition Area." PhD diss., University of Manchester.

Chikulo, Bornwell C. 1988. "The Impact of Elections in Zambia's One-Party Second Republic." *Africa Today* (2nd quarter): 37–49.

Chipungu, Samuel N. 1992a. "African Leadership under Indirect Rule in Colonial Zambia." In Samuel N. Chipungu, ed., *Guardians in Their Time: Experiences of Zambians under Colonial Rule, 1890–1964*. London: Macmillan, pp. 50–73.

Chipungu, Samuel N. 1992b. "Accumulation from Within: The *Boma* Class and the Native Treasury in Colonial Zambia." In Samuel N. Chipungu, ed., *Guardians in Their Time: Experiences of Zambians under Colonial Rule, 1890–1964*. London: Macmillan, pp. 74–96.

Chwe, Michael Suk-Young. 2001. *Rational Ritual: Culture, Coordination, and Common Knowledge*. Princeton, NJ: Princeton University Press.

CIA. 2001. *World Factbook*. http://www.odci.gov/cia/publications/factbook/ [accessed 2 August 2002].

Cliffe, Lionel. 1967. *One Party Democracy*. Nairobi: East African Publishing House.

Cohen, Abner. 1969. *Custom and Politics in Urban Africa: A Study of Hausa Migrants in Yoruba Towns*. Berkeley and Los Angeles: University of California Press.

Cohen, Abner. 1974. *Two-Dimensional Man: An Essay on the Anthropology of Power and Symbolism in Complex Society*. Berkeley and Los Angeles: University of California Press.

Collier, Paul. 2001. "Ethnic Diversity: An Economic Analysis." *Economic Policy* (April): 129–66.

Colson, Elizabeth. 1962. *The Plateau Tonga of Northern Rhodesia*. Manchester: Manchester University Press.

Colson, Elizabeth. 1968. "Contemporary Tribes and the Development of Nationalism." In June Helm, ed., *Essays on the Problem of Tribe*. Seattle: University of Washington Press, pp. 201–206.

Colson, Elizabeth. 1969. "African Society at the Time of the Scramble." In L. H. Gann and Peter Duignan, eds., *Colonialism in Africa, 1870–1960*. Vol. 1. Cambridge: Cambridge University Press, pp. 27–65.

Colson, Elizabeth. 1996. "The Bantu Botatwe: Changing Political Definitions in Southern Zambia." In David Parkin, Lionel Caplan, and Humphrey Fisher, eds., *The Politics of Cultural Performance*. Oxford: Berghahn Books, pp. 61–80.

Commonwealth Observer Group. 2001. "The Elections in Zanzibar, United Republic of Tanzania, 29 October 2000."

Coombe, Trevor. 1968. "The Origins of Secondary Education in Zambia: A Study in Colonial Policy-making." PhD diss., Harvard University.

Crehan, Kate. 1997. "'Tribes' and the People Who Read Books: Managing History in Colonial Zambia." *Journal of Southern African Studies* 23 (June): 203–18.

Crook, Richard C. 1997. "Winning Coalitions and Ethno-Regional Politics: The Failure of the Opposition in the 1990 and 1995 Elections in Côte d'Ivoire." *African Affairs* 96 (April): 215–42.

Dahl, Robert A. 1971. *Polyarchy: Participation and Opposition*. New Haven, CT: Yale University Press.

Davis, J. Merle. 1967. *Modern Industry and the African: An Enquiry into the Effect of the Copper Mines of Central Africa upon Native Society and the Work of the Christian Missions*. 2nd ed. London: Frank Cass. [First edition published in 1933.]

Diamond, Larry. 1988. *Class, Ethnicity, and Democracy in Nigeria : The Failure of the First Republic*. Syracuse, NY: Syracuse University Press.

Doke, C. M. 1945. *Bantu: Modern Grammatical, Phonetical and Lexicographical Studies since 1860*. London: International African Institute.

Dominguez, Virginia. 1986. *White by Definition: Social Classification in Creole Louisiana*. New Brunswick, NJ: Rutgers University Press.

Downs, Anthony. 1957. *An Economic Theory of Democracy*. New York: Harper.

Dresang, Dennis. 1974. "Ethnic Politics, Representative Bureaucracy and Development Administration: The Zambian Case." *American Political Science Review* 68 (December): 1605–17.

Ekeh, Peter. 1975. "Colonialism and the Two Publics in Africa: A Theoretical Statement." *Comparative Studies in Society and History* 17 (January): 91–112.

Epstein, A. L. 1958. *Politics in an Urban African Community*. Manchester: Manchester University Press.

Epstein, A. L. 1978. *Ethos and Identity*. London: Tavistock Publications.

Epstein, A. L. 1981. *Urbanization and Kinship: The Domestic Domain on the Copperbelt of Zambia, 1950–1956*. New York: Academic Press.

Epstein, A. L. 1992. *Scenes from an African Urban Life: Collected Copperbelt Papers*. Edinburgh: Edinburgh University Press.

Eyl, Jonathan, and Graham Smith. 1996. "Moldova and the Moldovans." In Graham Smith, ed., *The Nationalities Question in the Post-Soviet States*. London: Longman Press, pp. 223–44.

Fearon, James D. 1994. "Ethnic War as a Commitment Problem." Paper presented at the annual meeting of the American Political Science Association, New York.

Fearon, James D. 1999. "Why Ethnic Politics and 'Pork' Tend to Go Together." Paper presented at the SSRC-MacArthur-sponsored conference on "Ethnic Politics and Democratic Stability," University of Chicago, May 21–23.

Fearon, James D., and David D. Laitin. 1996. "Explaining Interethnic Cooperation." *American Political Science Review* 90 (December): 715–35.

Fearon, James D., and David D. Laitin. 2003. "Ethnicity, Insurgency, and Civil War." *American Political Science Review* 97 (February): 75–90.

Ferguson, James. 1990. "Mobile Workers, Modernist Narratives: A Critique of the Historiography of Transition on the Zambian Copperbelt [Part I]." *Journal of Southern African Studies* 16 (September): 385–412; and [Part II] 16 (December): 603–21.

Ferguson, James. 1999. *Expectations of Modernity: Myths and Meanings of Urban Life on the Zambian Copperbelt*. Berkeley and Los Angeles: University of California Press.

Ferree, Karen E. 2003. "The Microfoundations of Ethnic Voting: Evidence from South Africa." Paper presented at the annual meeting of the American Political Science Association, Philadelphia.

Fields, Karen E. 1985. *Revival and Rebellion in Colonial Central Africa*. Princeton, NJ: Princeton University Press.

Firmin-Sellers, Kathryn. 1996. *The Transformation of Property Rights in the Gold Coast: An Empirical Analysis Applying Rational Choice Theory*. Cambridge: Cambridge University Press.

Fisher, Humphrey J. 1969. "Elections and Coups in Sierra Leone, 1967." *Journal of Modern African Studies* 7 (December): 611–36.

Franklin, Harry. 1950. *The Saucepan Special*. Lusaka: Government Printer.

Franklin, Harry. 1974. *The Flag-Wagger*. London: Shepheard-Walwyn.

Gadsden, Fay. 1992. "Education and Society in Colonial Zambia." In Samuel N. Chipungu, ed., *Guardians in Their Time: Experiences of Zambians under Colonial Rule, 1890–1964*. London: Macmillan, pp. 97–125.

Gann, L. H. 1958. *The Birth of a Plural Society: The Development of Northern Rhodesia Under the British South Africa Company, 1894–1914*. Manchester: Manchester University Press.

Gann, L. H. 1964. *A History of Northern Rhodesia: Early Days to 1953*. London: Chatto and Windus.

Gertzel, Cherry, 1970, *The Politics of Independent Kenya, 1963–1968*. Nairobi: East African Publishing House.

Gertzel, Cherry. 1975. "Labour and the State: The Case of Zambia's Mineworkers Union – A Review Article." *Journal of Commonwealth and Comparative Politics* 13 (November): 296–303.

Gertzel, Cherry. 1984. "Western Province: Tradition, Economic Deprivation and Political Alienation." In Cherry Gertzel, Carolyn Baylies, and Morris Szeftel, eds., *The Dynamics of the One-Party State in Zambia*. Manchester: Manchester University Press, pp. 206–35.

Gertzel, Cherry, and Morris Szeftel. 1984. "Politics in an African Urban Setting: The Role of the Copperbelt in the Transition to the One-Party State, 1964–73." In Cherry Gertzel, Carolyn Baylies, and Morris Szeftel, eds., *The Dynamics of the One-Party State in Zambia*. Manchester: Manchester University Press, pp. 118–62.

Gertzel, Cherry, Kasuka Mutukwa, Ian Scott, and Malcolm Wallis. 1972. "Zambia's Final Experience of Inter-party Elections: The By-Elections of December 1971." *Kroniek van Afrika* 2: 57–77.

Gertzel, Cherry, Carolyn Baylies, and Morris Szeftel, eds. 1984. *The Dynamics of the One-Party State in Zambia*. Manchester: Manchester University Press.

Gluckman, Max. 1958. Foreward to William Watson, *Tribal Cohesion in a Money Economy: A Study of the Mambwe People of Northern Rhodesia*. Manchester: Manchester University Press, pp. v–xvi.

Gourevitch, Philip. 1998. *We Wish to Inform You That Tomorrow We Will Be Killed with Our Families: Stories from Rwanda*. New York: Farrar Straus and Giroux.

Government of the Republic of Zambia. 1990. *Republic of Zambia Census of Population and Housing*. Lusaka: Government Printer.

Government of the Republic of Zambia. 1998. *Marcoeconomic Indicators*. Lusaka: Ministry of Finance.

Greig, Jack C. E. 1985. *Education in Northern Rhodesia and Nyasaland: Pre-Independence Period*. Oxford Development Records Project Report 13. Oxford: Rhodes House.

Gulliver, P. H. 1969. *Tradition and Transition in East Africa: Studies of the Tribal Element in the Modern Era*. London: Routledge.

Hailey, William Malcolm Baron. 1950. *Native Administration in the British African Territories*. Part II, "Central Africa," and Part IV, "A General Survey of the System of Native Administration." London: HM Stationery Office.

Hall, Peter A., and Rosemary C. R. Taylor. 1996. "Political Science and the Three New Institutionalisms." *Political Studies* 44 (December): 936–57.

Hall, Richard. 1976. *Zambia, 1890–1964: The Colonial Period*. London: Longman.

Hansen, Holger Bernt, and Michael Twaddle. 1988. *Uganda Now: Between Decay and Development*. London: James Currey.

Hardin, Russell. 1995. *One for All: The Logic of Group Conflict*. Princeton, NJ: Princeton University Press.

Harries-Jones, Peter. 1965. "The Tribes in the Towns." In W. V. Brelsford, ed., *The Tribes of Zambia*. Lusaka: Government Printer, pp. 124–46.

Hartmann, Dirk. 1999, "Kenya." In Dieter Nohlen, Michael Krennerich, and Bernhard Thibaut, eds., *Elections in Africa: A Data Handbook*. New York: Oxford University Press, pp. 475–94.

Haugerud, Angelique. 1995. *The Culture of Politics in Modern Kenya*. Cambridge: Cambridge University Press.

Hay, Hope. 1947. *Northern Rhodesia Learns to Read*. London: Livingstone Press.

Hayward, Fred, and Ahmed R. Dumbuya. 1985. "Changing Electoral Patterns in Sierra Leone: The 1982 Single-Party Elections." *African Studies Review* 28 (December): 62–86.

Hechter, Michael. 2001. "From Class to Culture." Paper presented at the fall 2001 meeting of the Laboratory in Comparative Ethnic Processes (LiCEP), Dartmouth College, 28 October.

Hellen, John A. 1968. *Rural Economic Development in Zambia, 1890–1964*. Munich: Weltforum Verlag.

Henkel, Reinhard. 1985. "Mission Stations in Zambia: Their Location and Diffusion Patterns." *Zambian Geographical Journal* 35: 1–18.

Hirschman, Charles. 1987. "The Meaning and Measurement of Ethnicity in Malaysia: An Analysis of Census Classifications." *Journal of Asian Studies* 46 (August): 555–85.

Hobsbawm, Eric. 1996. "Are All Tongues Equal?" In Paul Barker, ed., *Living as Equals*. New York: Oxford University Press, pp. 85–98.

Hornsby, Charles, and David Throup. 1992. "Elections and Political Change in Kenya." *Journal of Commonwealth and Comparative Politics* 30 (July): 172–99.

Horowitz, Donald. 1975. "Ethnic Identity." In Nathan Glazer and Daniel P. Moynihan, eds., *Ethnicity: Theory and Experience*. Cambridge, MA: Harvard University Press, pp. 111–40.

Horowitz, Donald L. 1985. *Ethnic Groups in Conflict*. Berkeley and Los Angeles: University of California Press.

Horowitz, Donald L. 1989. "Incentives and Behaviour in the Ethnic Politics of Sri Lanka and Malaysia." *Third World Quarterly* 10 (October): 18–35.

Horowitz, Donald L. 2001. *The Deadly Ethnic Riot*. Berkeley and Los Angeles: University of California Press.

Human Rights Watch/Africa. 1996. "Zambia: Elections and Human Rights in the Third Republic." 8, no. 4a (December).

Huntington, Samuel P. 1991. *The Third Wave: Democratization in the Late Twentieth Century*. Norman: University of Oklahoma Press.

Huntington, Samuel P. 1996. *The Clash of Civilizations and the Remaking of World Order*. New York: Simon and Schuster.

Hyden, Goran. 1999. "Top-Down Democratization in Tanzania." *Journal of Democracy* 10 (October): 142–55.

Hyden, Goran, and Colin Leys. 1972. "Elections and Politics in Single-Party Systems: The Case of Kenya and Tanzania." *British Journal of Political Science* 2 (October): 389–420.

Jackson, Robert H., and Carl G. Rosberg. 1984. "Personal Rule: Theory and Practice in Africa." *Comparative Politics* 16 (July): 421–42.

Jega, Attahiru. 2000. "The State and Identity Transformation under Structural Adjustment in Nigeria." In Attahiru Jega, ed., *Identity Transformation and Identity Politics under Structural Adjustment in Nigeria*. Uppsala: Nordiska Afrikanstitutet, pp. 24–40.

Johnston, Harry H. 1897. *British Central Africa: An Attempt to Give Some Account of a Portion of the Territories under British Influence North of the Zambezi*. New York: Edward Arnold.

Johnston, Harry H. 1919. *A Comparative Study of the Bantu and Semi-Bantu Languages*. Oxford: Clarendon Press.

Kalyvas, Stathis N. 2001. "Violent Choices in Civil War Contexts." Paper prepared for presentation at the conference "Preferences, Choice and Uncertainty," Davis Program on Economy, Justice and Society, University of California, May 18–19.

Kandeh, Jimmy D. 1992. "Politicization of Ethnic Identities in Sierra Leone," *African Studies Review* 35 (April): 81–100.

Kapur, Devesh, John P. Lewis, and Richard Webb. 1997. *The World Bank: Its First Half Century*. Washington, DC: Brookings Institution Press.

Kasfir, Nelson. 1976. *The Shrinking Political Arena: Participation and Ethnicity in African Politics*. Berkeley and Los Angeles: University of California Press.

Kasfir, Nelson. 1979. "Explaining Ethnic Political Participation." *World Politics* 31 (April): 365–88.

Kasfir, Nelson. 1998. "'No-Party Democracy' in Uganda." *Journal of Democracy* 9 (April): 49–64.

Kashoki, Mubanga E. n.d. "Variety Is the Spice of Life: The Place of Multilingualism in the Concept of One Zambia, One Nation." Unpublished paper.

Kay, George. 1967. *A Social Geography of Zambia*. London: University of London Press.

Kenya Human Rights Commission. 1998. *Killing the Vote: State Sponsored Violence and Flawed Elections in Kenya*. Nairobi: Kenya Human Rights Commission.

Key, V. O. 1949. *Southern Politics in State and Nation*. New York: Vintage.

King, Gary. 1997. *A Solution to the Ecological Inference Problem: Reconstructing Individual Behavior from Aggregate Data*. Princeton, NJ: Princeton University Press.

Knodel, John, Werasit Sittitrai, and Tim Brown. 1990. "Focus Group Discussions for Social Science Research: A Practical Guide with an Emphasis on the Topic of Ageing." Comparative Study of the Elderly in Asia, Research Report no. 90–3. Population Studies Center, University of Michigan.

Koff, David. 1966. "Kenya's Little General Election." *Africa Report* (October): 57–60.

Kolsto, Pal, with Olav Melberg. 2002. "Integration, Alienation, and Conflict in Estonia and Moldova at the Societal Level: A Comparison." In Pal Kolsto, ed., *National Integration and Violent Conflict in Post-Soviet Societies: The Cases of Estonia and Moldova*. Lanham, MD: Rowman and Littlefield, pp. 31–70.

Kuran, Timur. 1995. *Private Truths, Public Lies: The Social Consequences of Preference Falsification*. Cambridge, MA: Harvard Universtiy Press.

Laitin, David D. 1986. *Hegemony and Culture: Politics and Religious Change among the Yoruba*. Chicago: University of Chicago Press.

Laitin, David D. 1992. *Language Repertoires and State Construction in Africa*. Cambridge: Cambridge University Press.

Laitin, David D. 1994. "The Tower of Babel as a Coordination Game: Political Linguistics in Ghana." *American Political Science Review* 88 (September): 622–34.

Laitin, David D. 1995. "National Revivals and Violence." *Archives Européenes de Sociologie* 36: 3–43.

Laitin, David D. 1998. *Identity in Formation: The Russian-Speaking Populations in the Near Abroad*. Ithaca, NY: Cornell University Press.

Leakey, Richard E. 2001. *Wildlife Wars: My Fight to Save Africa's Natural Treasures*. New York: St. Martin's Press.

Lemarchand, Rene. 1970. *Rwanda and Burundi*. New York: Praeger.

Linz, Juan J., and Alfred Stepan. 1992. "Political Identities and Electoral Sequences: Spain, the Soviet Union, and Yugoslavia." *Daedalus* 121 (Spring): 123–40.

Lipset, Seymour M., and Stein Rokkan. 1967. "Cleavage Structures, Party Systems and Voter Alignments: An Introduction." In Seymour M. Lipset and Stein Rokkan, eds., *Party Systems and Voter Alignments: Cross-National Perspectives*. New York: The Free Press, pp. 1–64.

Luchembe, Chipasha. 1992. "Ethnic Stereotypes, Violence and Labour in Early Colonial Zambia, 1890–1924." In Samuel N. Chipungu, ed., *Guardians in Their Time: Experiences of Zambians under Colonial Rule, 1890–1964*. London: Macmillan, pp. 30–49.

Luke, David Fashole. 1985. "Electoral Politics in Sierra Leone: An Appraisal of the 1982 Elections." *Journal of Commonwealth and Comparative Politics* 23 (March): 30–42.

Lungu, Gatian. 1986. "The Church, Labour and the Press in Zambia: The Role of Critical Observers in a One-Party State." *African Affairs* 85 (July): 385–410.

Macmillan, Hugh. 1993. "The Historiography of Transition on the Zambian Copperbelt: Another View." *Journal of Southern African Studies* 19 (December): 681–712.

Mamdani, Mahmood. 1996. *Citizen and Subject: Contemporary Africa and the Legacy of Late Colonialism*. Princeton, NJ: Princeton University Press.

McCulloch, Merran. 1956. "A Social Survey of the African Population of Livingstone." *Rhodes-Livingstone Institute Paper*, no. 26.

Meebelo, Henry S. 1971. *Reaction to Colonialism: A Prelude to the Politics of Independence in Northern Zambia, 1893–1939*. Manchester: Manchester University Press.

Mendelberg, Tali. 2001. *The Race Card: Campaign Strategy, Implicit Messages, and the Norm of Equality*. Princeton, NJ: Princeton University Press.

Mitchell, J. Clyde. 1956. "The Kalela Dance: Aspects of Social Relationships Among Urban Africans in Northern Rhodesia." *Rhodes-Livingstone Institute Paper*, no. 27.

Mitchell, J. Clyde. 1969. *Social Networks in Urban Situations: Analyses of Personal Relationships in Central African Towns*. Manchester: Manchester University Press.

Mitchell, J. Clyde. 1974. "Perceptions of Ethnicity and Ethnic Behaviour: An Empirical Exploration." In Abner Cohen, ed., *Urban Ethnicity*. London: Tavistock, pp. 1–35.

Mitchell, J. Clyde. 1987. *Cities, Society and Social Perception: A Central African Perspective*. Oxford: Clarendon Press.

Moerman, Michael. 1974. "Accomplishing Ethnicity." In Roy Turner, ed., *Ethnomethodology*. New York: Penguin Books, pp. 54–68.

Molteno, Robert. 1972. "Zambia and the One-Party State." *East Africa Journal* (February): 6–18.

Molteno, Robert. 1974. "Cleavage and Conflict in Zambian Politics: A Study in Sectionalism." In William Tordoff, ed., *Politics in Zambia*. Berkeley and Los Angeles: University of California Press, pp. 62–106.

Molteno, Robert, and Ian Scott. 1974. "The 1968 General Election and the Political System." In William Tordoff, ed., *Politics in Zambia*. Berkeley and Los Angeles: University of California Press, pp. 155–96.

Momba, Jotham C. 1985. "Peasant Differentiation and Rural Party Politics in Colonial Zambia." *Journal of Southern African Studies* 11 (April): 281–94.

Moore, Henrietta L., and Megan Vaughan. 1994. *Cutting Down Trees: Gender, Nutrition and Agricultural Change in the Northern Province of Zambia, 1890–1990*. Portsmouth, NH: Heinemann.

Morgenthau, Ruth Schachter. 1965. "African Elections: Tanzania's Contribution," *Africa Report* (December): 12–16.

Moubray, J. M. 1912. *In South Central Africa: Being an Account of Some of the Experiences and Journeys of the Author During a Stay of Six Years in That Country*. London: Constable and Company.

Mulford, David C. 1967. *Zambia: The Politics of Independence, 1957–1964*. Oxford: Oxford University Press.

Mytton, Graham. 1978. "Language and the Media in Zambia." In Sirarpi Ohannessian and Mubanga K. Kashoki, eds., *Language in Zambia*. London: International African Institute.

Nagata, Judith A. 1974. "What Is a Malay? Situational Selection of Ethnic Identity in a Plural Society." *American Ethnologist* 1 (August): 331–50.

North, Douglass C. 1990. *Institutions, Institutional Change and Economic Performance*. Cambridge: Cambridge University Press.

Northern Rhodesia. 1933. *Report of the Northern Rhodesian Government Unemployment Committee*. Lusaka: Government Printer.

Northern Rhodesia. 1938. *Report of the Commission Appointed to Enquire into the Financial and Economic Position of Northern Rhodesia*. Lusaka: Government Printer.

Northern Rhodesia. 1955. Report of the Comptroller and Auditor General of the Public Accounts of Northern Rhodesia. Lusaka: Government Printer.

Northern Rhodesia. Various years. *Annual Report on Native [African] Affairs*. Lusaka: Government Printer.

Ohannessian, Sirarpi, and Mubanga K. Kashoki, eds. 1978. *Language in Zambia*. London: International African Institute.

Okema, Michael. 2000. "Suddenly, This Election Is About Religion." *The East African* 3 November.

Okumu, John Joseph. 1969. "The By-Election in Gem: An Assessment." *East Africa Journal* (June): 9–17.

Ollawa, Patrick E. 1979. *Participatory Democracy in Zambia: The Political Economy of National Development*. Elms Court, UK: Arthur H. Stockwell.

Olzak, Susan. 1992. *The Dynamics of Ethnic Competition and Conflict*. Stanford, CA: Stanford University Press.

Ottaway, Marina. 1999. "Ethnic Politics in Africa: Change and Continuity." In Richard Joseph, ed., *State, Conflict and Democracy in Africa*. Boulder, CO: Lynne Rienner, pp. 299–317.

Oyugi, Walter O. 1997. "Ethnicity in the Electoral Process: The 1992 General Elections in Kenya." *African Journal of Political Science* 2 (1): 41–69.

Palmer, Monte. 1993. *Towards Public Sector Reform: Final Report*. Lusaka: World Bank/Government of Zambia Survey Research Project.

Papstein, Robert. 1989. "From Ethnic Identity to Tribalism: The Upper Zambezi Region of Zambia, 1830–1981." In Leroy Vail, ed., *The Creation of Tribalism in Southern Africa*. Berkeley and Los Angeles: University of California Press, pp. 372–94.

Parpart, Jane. 1983. *Labor and Capital on the African Copperbelt*. Philadelphia: Temple University Press.

Patterson, Orlando. 1975. "Context and Choice in Ethnic Allegiance: A Theoretical Framework and Caribbean Case Study." In Nathan Glazer and Daniel P. Moynihan, eds., *Ethnicity: Theory and Experience*. Cambridge, MA: Harvard University Press, pp. 305–49.

Perrings, Charles. 1979. *Black Mineworkers in Central Africa: Industrial Strategies and the Evolution of an African Proletariat in the Copperbelt, 1911–1941*. New York: Africana Publishing Co.

Petersen, Roger D. 2002. *Understanding Ethnic Violence: Fear, Hatred, and Resentment in Twentieth-Century Eastern Europe*. New York: Cambridge University Press.

Philpott, R. 1945. "The Mulobezi-Mongu Labour Route." *Human Problems in British Central Africa* 3: 50–54.

Popkin, Samuel L. 1979. *The Rational Peasant: The Political Economy of Rural Society in Vietnam*. Berkeley and Los Angeles: University of California Press.

Posen, Barry R. 1993. "The Security Dilemma and Ethnic Conflict." In Michael E. Brown, ed., *Ethnic Conflict and International Security*. Princeton, NJ: Princeton University Press, pp. 103–24.

Posner, Daniel N. 2000. "Measuring Ethnic Identities and Attitudes Regarding Inter-group Relations: Methodological Pitfalls and a New Technique." Paper presented at the fall 2000 meeting of the Laboratory in Comparative Ethnic Processes (LiCEP), University of Pennsylvania, 21 October.

Posner, Daniel N. 2004. "The Political Salience of Cultural Difference: Why Chewas and Tumbukas Are Allies in Zambia and Adversaries in Malawi." *American Political Science Review* 48 (October).

Premdas, Ralph R., and Bishnu Ragoonath. 1998. "Ethnicity, Elections and Democracy in Trinidad and Tobago: Analyzing the 1995 and 1996 Elections." *Journal of Commonwealth and Comparative Politics* 36 (November): 30–53.

Prins, Gwyn. 1980. *The Hidden Hippopotamus: Reappraisal in African History: The Early Colonial Experience in Western Zambia*. Cambridge: Cambridge University Press.

Prunier, Gérard. 1995. *The Rwanda Crisis: History of a Genocide*. New York: Columbia University Press.

Publications Bureau of Northern Rhodesia and Nyasaland. 1950–1959. *Annual Reports*. Lusaka: Government Printer.

Putnam, Robert D. 1993. *Making Democracy Work: Civic Traditions in Modern Italy*. Princeton, NJ: Princeton University Press.

Ragsdale, John P. 1986. *Protestant Mission Education in Zambia: 1880–1954*. Cranbury, NJ: Associated University Presses.

Reilly, Benjamin. 2001. *Democracy in Divided Societies: Electoral Engineering for Conflict Management*. New York: Cambridge University Press.

Reilly, Benjamin, and Andrew Reynolds. 1997. "Electoral Systems and Conflict in Divided Societies." Paper presented at the annual meeting of the American Political Science Association, Washington, DC.

Reynolds, Andrew. 1999. "Sierra Leone." In Dieter Nohlen, Michael Krennerich, and Bernhard Thibaut, eds., *Elections in Africa: A Data Handbook*. New York: Oxford University Press, pp. 789–802.

Richards, Audrey. 1939. *Land, Labour and Diet: An Economic Study of the Bemba Tribe*. London: Oxford University Press.

Riker, William H. 1962. *The Theory of Political Coalitions*. New Haven, CT: Yale University Press.

Riker, William H. 1986. *The Art of Political Manipulation*. New Haven, CT: Yale University Press.

Roberts, Andrew. 1976. *A History of Zambia*. New York: Africana Publishing Co.

Robinson, William S. 1950. "Ecological Correlation and the Behavior of Individuals," *American Sociological Review* 15 (June): 351–57.

Rotberg, Robert. 1965. *The Rise of Nationalism in Central Africa: The Making of Malawi and Zambia, 1873–1964*. Cambridge, MA: Harvard University Press.

Sacks, Harvey. 1992. *Lectures on Conversation.* Oxford: Blackwell.

Sambanis, Nicholas. 2001. "A Review of Recent Advances and Future Directions in the Quantitative Literature on Civil War." Mimeo, Department of Political Science, Yale University.

Scarritt, James R. 1983. "The Analysis of Social Class, Political Participation, and Public Policy in Zambia." *Africa Today* (3rd quarter): 5–22.

Schelling, Thomas. 1978. *Micromotives and Macrobehavior.* New York: W. W. Norton and Company.

Scott, James C. 1998. *Seeing Like a State: How Certain Schemes to Improve the Human Condition Have Failed.* New Haven: Yale University Press.

Shugart, Matthew Soberg. 1995. "The Electoral Cycle and Institutional Sources of Divided Presidential Government." *American Political Science Review* 89 (June): 327–43.

Shugart, Matthew Soberg, and John M. Carey. 1992. *Presidents and Assemblies: Constitutional Design and Electoral Dynamics.* New York: Cambridge University Press.

Sichone, Owen, and Neo R. Simutanyi. 1996. "The Ethnic and Regional Questions, Ethnic Nationalism and the State in Zambia: The Case of Bulozi, 1964–1994." In Owen Sichone and Bornwell Chikulo, eds., *Democracy in Zambia: Challenges for the Third Republic.* Harare: SAPES Books, pp. 173–96.

Sklar, Richard. 1975. *Corporate Power in an African State: The Political Impact of Multinational Mining Companies in Zambia.* Berkeley and Los Angeles: University of California Press.

Sklar, Richard. 1979. "The Nature of Class Domination in Africa." *Journal of Modern African Studies* 17 (December): 531–52.

Snelson, Peter. 1974. *Educational Development in Northern Rhodesia, 1883–1945.* Lusaka: Kenneth Kaunda Foundation.

Spearpoint, F. 1937. "The African Native and the Rhodesian Copper Mines." Supplement to the *Journal of the Royal African Society* 36 (July).

Spilerman, Seymour. 1976. "Structural Characteristics of Cities and the Severity of Racial Disorders." *American Sociological Review* 41 (October): 771–93.

Spitulnik, Debra. 1992. "Radio Time Sharing and the Negotiation of Linguistic Pluralism in Zambia." *Pragmatics* 2: 335–54.

Stone, Jeffrey C. 1979. "A Guide to the Administrative Boundaries of Northern Rhodesia." O'Dell Memorial Monograph no. 7. Department of Geography, University of Aberdeen.

Szeftel, Morris. 1978. "Conflict, Spoils and Class Formation in Zambia." PhD diss., Manchester University.

Szeftel, Morris. 1980. "The Evolving Structure of Zambian Society." Paper presented at the Center of African Studies, University of Edinburgh, 30–31 May.

Szeftel, Morris. 1982. "Political Graft and the Spoils System in Zambia: The State as a Resource in Itself." *Review of African Political Economy* 24 (Summer): 4–21.

Tajfel, Henri, Michael Billig, R. P. Bundy, and Claude Flament. 1971, "Social Categorization and Intergroup Behavior." *European Journal of Social Psychology* 1: 149–78.

Tambiah, Stanley J. 1976. *World Conqueror and World Renouncer: A Study of Buddhism and Polity in Thailand Against a Historical Background*. New York: Cambridge University Press.

Thomson, J. Moffat. 1934. *Memorandum on the Native Tribes and Tribal Areas of Northern Rhodesia*. Livingstone: Government Printer.

Throup, David, and Charles Hornsby. 1998. *Multiparty Politics in Kenya: The Kenyatta and Moi State and the Triumph of the System in the 1992 Elections*. London: James Currey.

Tilly, Charles. 1978. *From Mobilization to Revolution*. Reading, MA: Addison-Wesley.

Tordoff, William, ed. 1974. *Politics in Zambia*. Berkeley and Los Angeles: University of California Press.

Tordoff, William, and Ian Scott. 1974. "Political Parties: Structures and Policies." In William Tordoff, ed., *Politics in Zambia*. Berkeley and Los Angeles: University of California Press, pp. 107–54.

Treisman, Daniel. 1999. *After the Deluge: Regional Crises and Political Consolidation in Russia*. Ann Arbor: University of Michigan Press.

University College of Rhodesia and Nyasaland. 1958. *Gazetteer of Tribes in the Federation of Rhodesia and Nyasaland*.

Vail, Leroy, ed. 1989. *The Creation of Tribalism in Southern Africa*. Berkeley and Los Angeles: University of California Press.

van Binsbergen, Wim. 1982. "The Unit of Study and the Interpretation of Ethnicity: Studying the Nkoya of Western Zambia." *Journal of Southern African Studies* 8 (March): 51–81.

van Cranenburgh, Oda. 1996. "Tanzania's 1995 Multi-Party Elections: The Emerging Party System." *Party Politics* 2 (October): 535–47.

van den Berghe, Pierre. 1971. "Ethnicity: The African Experience." *International Social Science Journal* 23 (4): 507–18.

van Velsen, Jap. 1966. "Labor Migration as a Positive Factor in the Continuity of Tonga Tribal Society." In Immanuel Wallerstein, ed., *Social Change: The Colonial Situation*. New York: John Wiley and Sons, pp. 158–67.

Varshney, Ashutosh. 2002. *Civic Life and Ethnic Conflict: Hindus and Muslims in India*. New Haven, CT: Yale University Press.

Varshney, Ashutosh. 2003. "Nationalism, Ethnic Conflict, and Rationality." *Perspectives on Politics* 1 (March): 85–99.

Waters, Mary C. 1990. *Ethnic Options: Choosing Identities in America*. Berkeley and Los Angeles: University of California Press.

Weiner, Myron, and Mary Fainsod Katzenstein. 1981. *India's Preferential Policies: Migrants, the Middle Classes and Ethnic Equality*. Chicago: University of Chicago Press.

Werbner, Richard, and Terence Ranger. 1996. *Post-colonial Identities in Africa*. Atlantic Highlands, NJ: Zed Books.

Widner, Jennifer A. 1992. *The Rise of a Party-State in Kenya: From "Harambee!" to "Nyayo!"* Berkeley and Los Angeles: University of California Press.

Wilkinson, Steven I. 1999. "Ethnic Mobilization and Ethnic Violence in Post-independence India." Paper presented at the annual meeting of the American Political Science Association, Atlanta.

Wilkinson, Steven I. 2003. "Constructivism and Ethnic Riots." Paper presented at the Constructivist Approaches to Ethnic Groups (CAEG) Project meeting, Philadelphia, 26–28 August.

Wilkinson, Steven I. 2004. *Votes and Violence: Electoral Competition and Ethnic Riots in India.* New York: Cambridge University Press.

Wilson, Godfrey. 1941. "An Essay on the Economics of Detribalization in Northern Rhodesia." Parts 1 and 2. *Rhodes Livingstone Institute Paper*, nos. 5 and 6.

Wina, Sikota. 1985. *The Night Without a President.* Lusaka: Multimedia Publications.

Woodward, Susan. 1999. "Bosnia and Herzegovina: How Not to End a Civil War." In Barbara F. Walter and Jack Snyder, eds., *Civil Wars, Insecurity, and Intervention.* New York: Columbia University Press, pp. 73–115.

World Bank. 2000. *World Bank Africa Database* [CD-ROM].

World Bank. 2002. *World Development Report 2002: Building Institutions for Markets.* New York: Oxford University Press.

Wright, Lawrence. 1994. "One Drop of Blood." *New Yorker*, 25 July, 46–55.

Young, Crawford. 1976. *The Politics of Cultural Pluralism.* Madison: University of Wisconsin Press.

Young, Crawford. 1986. "Nationalism, Ethnicity and Class in Africa: A Retrospective." *Cahiers d'Etudes Africaines* 26: 421–95.

Young, Crawford. 1994. *The African Colonial State in Comparative Perspective.* New Haven, CT: Yale University Press.

Young, Crawford, and Thomas Turner. 1985. *The Rise and Decline of the Zairian State.* Madison: University of Wisconsin Press.

# Index

# Index

**Other Books in the Series** (*continued from page iii*)

Gary W. Cox and Jonathan N. Katz, *Elbridge Gerry's Salamander: The Electoral Consequences of the Reapportionment Revolution*

Jean Ensminger, *Making a Market: The Institutional Transformation of an African Society*

David Epstein and Sharyn O'Halloran, *Delegating Powers: A Transaction Cost Politics Approach to Policy Making under Separate Powers*

Kathryn Firmin-Sellers, *The Transformation of Property Rights in the Gold Coast: An Empirical Study Applying Rational Choice Theory*

Clark C. Gibson, *Politicians and Poachers: The Political Economy of Wildlife Policy in Africa*

Ron Harris, *Industrializing English Law: Entrepreneurship and Business Organization, 1720–1844*

Anna L. Harvey, *Votes without Leverage: Women in American Electoral Politics, 1920–1970*

Murray Horn, *The Political Economy of Public Administration: Institutional Choice in the Public Sector*

John D. Huber, *Rationalizing Parliament: Legislative Institutions and Party Politics in France*

Jack Knight, *Institutions and Social Conflict*

Michael Laver and Kenneth Shepsle, eds., *Cabinet Ministers and Parliamentary Government*

Michael Laver and Kenneth Shepsle, eds., *Making and Breaking Governments: Cabinets and Legislatures in Parliamentary Democracies*

Margaret Levi, *Consent, Dissent, and Patriotism*

Brian Levy and Pablo T. Spiller, eds., *Regulations, Institutions, and Commitment: Comparative Studies of Telecommunications*

Leif Lewin, *Ideology and Strategy: A Century of Swedish Politics* (English Edition)

Gary Libecap, *Contracting for Property Rights*

John Londregan, *Legislative Institutions and Ideology in Chile*

Arthur Lupia and Mathew D. McCubbins, *The Democratic Dilemma: Can Citizens Learn What They Need to Know?*

C. Mantzavinos, *Individuals, Institutions, and Markets*

Mathew D. McCubbins and Terry Sullivan, eds., *Congress: Structure and Policy*

Gary J. Miller, *Managerial Dilemmas: The Political Economy of Hierarchy*

Douglass C. North, *Institutions, Institutional Change, and Economic Performance*

Elinor Ostrom, *Governing the Commons: The Evolution of Institutions for Collective Action*

J. Mark Ramseyer, *Odd Markets in Japanese History: Law and Economic Growth*

J. Mark Ramseyer and Frances Rosenbluth, *The Politics of Oligarchy: Institutional Choice in Imperial Japan*

Jean-Laurent Rosenthal, *The Fruits of Revolution: Property Rights, Litigation, and French Agriculture, 1700–1860*

Michael L. Ross, *Timber Booms and Institutional Breakdown in Southeast Asia*

Alastair Smith, *Election Timing*

David Stasavage, *Public Debt and the Birth of the Democratic State: France and Great Britain, 1688–1789*

Charles Stewart III, *Budget Reform Politics: The Design of the Appropriations Process in the House of Representatives, 1865–1921*

George Tsebelis and Jeannette Money, *Bicameralism*

Nicolas van de Walle, *African Economies and the Politics of Permanent Crisis, 1979–1999*

Georg Vanberg, *The Politics of Constitutional Review in Germany*

John Waterbury, *Exposed to Innumerable Delusions: Public Enterprise and State Power in Egypt, India, Mexico, and Turkey*

David L. Weimer, ed., *The Political Economy of Property Rights: Institutional Change and Credibility in the Reform of Centrally Planned Economies*

CPSIA information can be obtained at www.ICGtesting.com
Printed in the USA
LVOW11s1244280116

472533LV00008B/130/P

9 780521 541794